D1666062

Transglobal Fashion Narratives

Transglobal Fashion Narratives
Clothing Communication, Style Statements and Brand Storytelling

Edited by Anne Peirson-Smith and Joseph H. Hancock II

intellect Bristol, UK / Chicago, USA

First published in the UK in 2018 by
Intellect, The Mill, Parnall Road, Fishponds, Bristol, BS16 3JG, UK

First published in the USA in 2018 by
Intellect, The University of Chicago Press, 1427 E. 60th Street,
Chicago, IL 60637, USA

Copyright © 2018 Intellect Ltd.

All rights reserved. No part of this publication may be reproduced,
stored in a retrieval system, or transmitted, in any form or by
any means, electronic, mechanical, photocopying, recording, or
otherwise, without written permission.

A catalogue record for this book is available from the
British Library.

Cover designer: Aleksandra Szumlas
Copy-editor: MPS Technologies
Production manager: Amy Rollason
Typesetting: Contentra Technologies

Print ISBN: 978-1-78320-844-9
ePDF ISBN: 978-1-78320-846-3
ePUB ISBN: 978-1-78320-845-6

This is a peer-reviewed publication.

Contents

Acknowledgements

We would like to thank Mark Lewis, James Campbell and Amy Rollason at Intellect Books for their steadfast and enthusiastic support for this book project. In addition, we would like to thank the contributors, as the inclusion of their work in this volume has made this book entirely possible.

Anne Peirson-Smith would like to thank her co-editor, Joseph H. Hancock II, for his collegial support and for making this publishing experience a positive and productive one.

Joseph H. Hancock II would also like to thank Anne Peirson-Smith for all her hard work and dedication in organizing the conference that gave rise to this publication, and seeing this volume to completion.

This edited volume represents the interdisciplinary collaborative summation of international scholarship on an emerging and prescient topic, which we hope will stimulate further discussion and dialogue across the field of fashion studies.

Introduction

Communicating Transglobal Fashion Narratives

Anne Peirson-Smith and Joseph H. Hancock II

Numberless are the world's narratives. First of all, in a prodigious variety of genres themselves distributed among different substances […] narrative can be supported by articulated speech, oral or written, by image, fixed or moving, by gesture, and by the organized mixture of all of these substances; it is present in myth, legend, fable tale, tragedy, comic, epic, history, pantomime, painting […] stained glass window, cinema, comic book, news item, conversation. Further, in these almost infinite forms, narrative occurs in all periods, in all places, all societies; narrative begins with the very history of humanity; there is not, there has never been, any people anywhere without narrative, all classes, all human groups have their narratives, and very often these are enjoyed by men of different, even opposing culture: narrative never prefers good to bad literature: international, transhistorical, transcultural, narrative is there, like life.

(Barthes 1977: 20)

Fashion narrates and is narrated about. Fashion communicates and is both the subject and object of communication. Fashion is communicated about and encountered in both visual and verbal, fiction and non-fictional narrative forms. These apparently simple statements are more complex than they may seem, as fashion is represented multimodally with words and images in spoken, written and visual forms highlighting its ubiquitous significance in modern life: '[f]ashion matters. To the economy, to society and to each of us personally. Faster than anything else, what we wear tells the story of who we are – or what we want to be' (Corner 2014: 4). The pervasive presence of fashion as clothing in daily life as 'an unplanned process of recurrent change set against the backdrop of the public realm' (Aspers and Godart 2013: 175) perhaps accounts for its inclusion in many discursive moments and utterances, in creative content driven by the endless quest for novelty and innovation. In this sense, we cannot meaningfully separate fashion from its social and cultural contexts, given that it can be seen as a

social arrangement regarding anything (object or idea) that has currency and is popular […] that will be worn widely […] held in place by the multitude of choices and decisions that momentarily serve the particular appeal and celebrate the new.

(Entwistle 2015)

So much of our social relations appear to depend on fashion's ability to enable imitation and distinction, self-expression and identity creation. In facilitating these social processes, fashion communicates in complex and subtle ways and its agendas and its reach are far from straightforward. This volume focuses on fashion narratives; how fashion communicates and is communicated about in global spaces and places across cultures, in various mediated forms encompassing words and images. This examination of transglobal fashion communication is divided into three distinct thematic sections.

Firstly, it considers how fashion is used to frame, develop or take inspiration from literary and filmic narratives, in addition to cultural texts such as sewing manuals and the garment itself as worn clothing, object, text or artefact. Secondly, it features the application of worn fashion and clothing across a range of mediated genres operating to shape identities and make sense of lived experiences; and thirdly, it examines the commercial discourses of fashion branding and advertising using word and image to promote garments, cities and cultures across a range of imagined communities (Anderson 1991). Organizing the book content in this way emphasizes the nuanced manner in which fashion is used to communicate messages across multiple, mediated platforms throughout various historical, cultural, social, local and global dimensions by a range of players involved in the endless circuit of production and consumption. The main theme emerging from all of the contributions in this volume concerns the fact that the meaning of fashion as subject or object is not fixed or intrinsic, but rather is open to interpretation – which explains its enduring fascination and endless analysis. Each of these three sections incorporate chapters providing a comprehensive set of entry points into the subject matter of fashion and clothing-based discursive narratives.

By way of definition, the term 'fashion' will refer to notions of acceptable appearance that change and become redefined over time, across various cultures and geographic locations. As such, fashion is a cultural practice concerned with navigating both the individual presentation of self and a signalled allegiance to the group, conveying

> a sense of consensus about a desired mode of behaviour or appearance and a sense of successive change, movement and redefinition [...] as identity means creating distinctiveness, fashion always has to balance reflecting the contemporary consensus about fashion with the specific arrangement of signs and symbols that mark out the individual as appearing to be unique.
>
> (Craik 2009: 2).

The term 'clothing', referring to garments and apparel, constitutes the tangible building blocks of fashionable appearance. Fashion, on the other hand, attaches symbolic meanings to those garments in the ways in which it curates certain clothing items in combination to generate social and cultural capital for the wearer, while simultaneously creating economic capital for the maker. Given the transglobal context of this volume, a broader, reworked definition of fashion is advocated following Jennifer Craik's view that fashion is not a purely modern phenomenon fuelled by class, civilization and consumerism (Craik 1993: 3) and also is not an exclusively European-centred phenomenon. There is a deliberate attempt here to move away from the imperialistic, Orientalist 'West/Rest dichotomy' (Niessen 2003: 248), rooted in the Enlightenment's narrative of progress contrasting with notions of non-progressive primitive societies, towards an understanding that fashion, and the clothing that comprises it, are more universally situated and globalized. Accordingly, fashion constitutes clothing behaviour that changes across cultures, societies, time, place and space, rather than being the sole preserve of modern, western, capitalist, consumer culture. For Teri Agins, the commercial fashion system is 'ephemeral, and elusive, a target that keeps moving' (1999: 7), but the same could be said for the ways in which people dress across all cultures and the clothes and adornments that they choose to wear. Equally, the globalized location of textile and garment production, and the porous boundaries that fashion products traverse to reach global markets, highlights the widespread nature of the fashion industry. It also serves to highlight the constructed dichotomy between the conceptual framing of fashion as a western, modern occurrence, in stark contrast to a fashion system that is based on global garment sourcing, production and international trade practices. This suggests that the fashion output emerging from this system is not time or place specific and is multicultural in origin and operation, but are also locatable in specific time periods and should be understood in context.

The complexities and contradictions constituting the western versus non-western stances on fashion and its meanings are fully explored by the chapters in this volume from various interdisciplinary perspectives, highlighting the contested power relations that worn and written fashion espouses in symbolically differentiating class, status, gender, ethnicity, sexuality or social membership. As such, fashion is a communications system 'almost like a language made up of a vocabulary (a collection of items of clothing typical of a culture), syntax (the rules about how clothes can be combined and organized), and grammar (the system of arranging and relating garments) set within the conventions of decoding and interpreting the meanings of a particular look' (Craik 2009: 5). Yet, this communications system based on fashioning the body (Entwistle 2015) is constructed and culturally grounded in the inherent beliefs, ideas and values that constitute a given culture in which the fashion garment and the individual wearer is located. In this sense, the individual wearer of an item of clothing is tapping into a meaning system to produce a particular identity for the garment that they are wearing; yet at the same time, identity is also being constructed for them. So, fashion and clothing as a communication system do not simply convey pre-existing, set messages from sender to receiver as a simple encoding/decoding process of meaning exchange. As Malcolm Barnard suggests, 'There is no meaning until the interaction between cultural values and items of fashion has taken place […] fashion is not a vehicle for conveying messages' (2007: 176). Rather, the wearing of fashion items is a complex interchange of culturally directed, negotiated meanings whereby the statements that they make is 'one of the ways in which cultural structures and individual agency relate and in which they are both constructed and reproduced' (Barnard 2007: 180). Extending this argument further, the shared meanings of fashion as a cultural phenomenon are rooted across cultures, time, space and place so that those meanings are constantly dynamic and evolving.

Fashion Narratives

Communication is based on the production and exchange of meanings for sense-making purposes by both groups and individuals. Narratives and stories are the means of getting those messages across in the process of making sense of our lives through shared experiences that are normally organized into temporal sequence. We are all inveterate storytellers and immerse ourselves in narratives in the pursuit of sense-making, using storytelling through figurative language to maintain and challenge social, cultural, individual and collective identities. In this way, social values, attitudes and beliefs are articulated and negotiated through material objects, behaviours and traditions. Being immersed in the narratives of everyday life,

> [o]ur society has become a recited society, in three senses: it is defined by *stories* (*recits*, the fables constituted by our advertising and informational media), by *citations* of stories, and by the interminable *recitation* of stories. These narratives have the twofold and strange power of transforming seeing into believing, and of fabricating realities out of appearances [...] Fiction defines the field, the status and the objects of vision.
>
> (de Certeau 1984: 186, original emphasis)

Fashion often forms the narrative content for this 'recited society' being firstly defined by stories as a form of vestimentary communication in the realms of journalism and advertising. Here, fashion is defined and promoted by mediated fables that are repeated and replicated across omni-channels and that appear in multiple formats across the systemic process of branding and selling fashion while instructing the consumer to do likewise. Secondly, the visual and material signs of fashion work as objects of vision by referencing other stories and myths from differing cultural and literary sources to create meaningful, intertextual engagement for the viewer, consumer or wearer. Finally, fashion contributes to the recitation of style stories that are dynamic and ever-changing, yet circular, in that they define each season. But these narratives also parody or pastiche former styles in terms of what they are, and what they are not; what is worn and what is not. In this sense, fashion through embodiment and transformation in the design process defines itself and transforms 'seeing into believing' by appearing in other mediated forms as worn clothing, image clothing and written clothing (Barthes 1983). So, fashion communicates by being created and worn, and at the same time is communicated about visually and verbally by being written or talked about, and seen or viewed.

It is maybe no surprise that fashion is the subject and object of so much communication content given its ubiquity in modern life, being found everywhere (Aspers and Godart 2013) and operating across multiple discourse systems and global locations. Equally, the emotion and desire that a fashion item as material object and aesthetic symbol provokes in its 'incessant, cyclical pursuit of the "new"' (Entwistle 2015) finds expression across popular discourse systems of the day as a way of capturing its appeal and cultural currency.

Therefore, the desire to acquire and celebrate the latest new look is articulated in word and image, thereby marking out individual and collective taste.

Fashion Communication

At its most basic level, the wearing of clothing communicates symbolically by differentiating mankind from the animal kingdom (Hegel/Inwood 1983). Thus, worn garments exercise agency, having much to say on behalf of the creator and wearer. As Colin McDowell observes, 'Fashion is potent because it is the outward and visible sign of emotions many of us prefer to keep hidden. Vanity, jealousy and lust are all part of the fashion equation' (McDowell 1989: ix). Beyond this subjective level, whereby fashion is a communicative manifestation of individual taste and identity formation (Bourdieu 1984), it also can perform and 'articulate society in the most direct and revealing of ways' (McDowell 1989: ix). Fashion has the ability to communicate, as

> by passing through written communication, Fashion becomes an autonomous cultural object, with its own original structure and [...] other functions are substituted for or added to the social functions usually acknowledged by vestimentary fashion; these functions are analogous to those found in all literature and can be summarized by saying that, through the language that henceforth takes charge of it, Fashion becomes narrative.
> (Barthes 1990: 277)

Fashion as object, therefore, constitutes a readable text founded on differentiated symbols, referents and rules. We could go as far to say that all textiles are texts that can be meaningfully interpreted. A fashion item is a created and crafted text to be seen and read by the viewer or wearer, as is the written or photographed fashion piece. At the same time, it intertextually utilizes multisensory signs and symbols comprising colour, texture, shape, patterns and logos to convey messages within the design and presentation of garment. As signifier, it calls out to other signifieds, past designs and referents from other texts and contexts (Kristeva 1980) including art, music, poetry, film and literature by featuring fashion as a narrator or character (Bruzzi and Church Gibson 2004) as a way of sense-making through contextualization, and by borrowing interest from known sources. These fashion statements are further decoded and commented upon by fashion writers and re-communicated via print, broadcast or digital media to be further deciphered and disseminated across the blogosphere, for example, extending the discussion in the ongoing, interactive recitation of stories by producer and consumer (de Certeau 1984).

Yet, the nature and significance of fashion 'as' communication, or fashion 'in' communication have been much debated in terms of its linguistic potential or discursive validity as a vestimentary communication system (Davis 1992; Barnard 2002). Arguably, fashion is not a pure language in its own right as some have suggested (Lurie 1981), either visually or verbally, as there are 'no fixed rule-governed formulas, such as exist for speech or writing, for employing and juxtaposing these elements. The correspondence with language is at best metaphoric' (Davis 2002: 6). The signifiers of fashion are not as specific as in speech or writing, and a garment or a collection is a more 'open' text, subject to interpretation.

While fashion critics, editors, novelists, photographers, screenwriters, directors and marketers, for example, may frame fashion in a particular way, emphasizing the desirability of the masculine or feminine aspects of a garment for the wearer, for example, fashion is essentially 'undercoded', or open to interpretation as Umberto Eco would have it (Eco 1979a). Writing featuring the fashion garment and its image is recognized as part of a signifying system connoting rhetorical meaning that naturalizes the vestimentary code (Barthes 1983) and highlights the contested separation between written clothing and image clothing (Barthes [1967] 2006). Yet, both forms are also open to interpretation in fashion's aesthetic code and the aesthetic expressions of its cultural intermediaries, including the critics, writers and creators who try to make sense of the fashion code across various communities of practice (Wenger 1988) with differing interpretations. This enables the reader, viewer, wearer and consumer to draw their own inferences from an outfit or item of clothing in any given context. It also invests the worn garment or object with ideological significance, reflecting the unending hegemonic struggle across extant and non-extant cultural contexts, thereby enabling a fashion outfit or item to challenge prevailing ideologies of the nation or state whether in Revolutionary China or Communist Russia, for example (see both Finnane and Hargassner in this volume). Fashion communicates not in the way of speech, but by conveying social and political identities that frame and reflect contextual cultural values.

Style Writing

The narrative-based representations of fashion across time and culture have included a wide range of fiction and non-fiction, verbal and non-verbal texts disseminated across mobile and static media channels, from print to contemporary digital formats. The way in which fashion narrates, assists narration and is narrated about across these takes various storytelling forms, reflecting fashion's countervailing meanings (Thomson and Hayko 1997). These narratives exhibit an arbitrary nature represented in ambiguous profiles across social, cultural and geographic contexts. In classical commentaries from Plato and Aristotle to Marx, fashion has also been subject to critical analysis and taken as a barometer of civilized society or modern capitalism.

In terms of how it is represented, narratives on fashion oscillate between its elevations to some of the best creative work from catwalk to sidewalk that society can produce and being fashion is vilified as the 'F-Word'; being fluffy, fickle, female and futile. It is accused of having the ability to deceive through manipulating appearance, or as a duplicitous system all out to entrap the hapless consumers into exchanging their hard-earned money for carefully, or hastily, crafted and strategically promoted garments.

In fiction, fashion is often associated with dramatic scenarios or in facilitating the narrative action (Hollander 1978) given that 'literature is not there to give details of cut and construction [...] most authors are not fashion journalists or historians' (Watt 1999: xii). Furthermore, literary works and their authors have often commented critically on the fashionable trends of the day, such as Oscar Wilde's dim view of the sartorial tyranny of ugly, disfiguring bustles (see Cavenish-Jones in this volume), or George Eliot's advocacy of simple female dress (see Mahawatte in this volume). This gives credence to the notion that 'their attitude to clothes coloured the way that they viewed the world, and their dress coloured the way that their world viewed them' (Watt 1999: xii). While fashion as costume in film and television is acknowledged to be a useful device in character creation and plot development through costume and accessory 'fashioning' (see Church Gibson in this volume), the downplaying of the importance of fashion is also reflected in the criticism of fashion in film for being a distracting spectacle that actually gets in the way of the storyline, rather than operating as a useful mediator of meaning (Wollen 1972; Bruzzi 1997). Equally, fashion criticism and journalism – from the first publication with a fashion specialism, *Le Mercure Galant* in the seventeenth century, across Victorian lifestyle publications such as *Blackwood's Lady Magazine* (see Mahawatte this volume), to contemporary, globally based *Vogue* editorials – have consistently been regarded as lacking a critical dimension, being 'informative or celebratory [...] never critical only mildly ironical' (McRobbie 1998: 173). By way of explanation, Barthes suggests that this contradictory stance is also fuelled by mediated fashion writing, which tends to be 'too serious and too frivolous at the same time' (Barthes 1983: 242). Yet, fashion journalism and socially mediated debates on fashion now do appear to go beyond the mere description and pure promotion of fashion, which may have been their traditional brief, becoming more inclined to criticize and evaluate the merits of fashion, albeit in different ways with varied voices and agendas. This multivocal fashion discourse can largely be typified in a binary construction, constituting two main writing genres, given that:

> Among fashion writers today there are almost as many different styles as there are of fashion itself. Two of them, however, predominate: the populist ('hey, let's go and consume together'); and the contextual ('what does this garment say about our particular moment in time?').
>
> (*The Economist* 2000)

In this sense, written fashion, as exemplified in the genre of fashion journalism and editorial, and the dispensing of fashion information and knowledge is perhaps more open and

> less rigid and predictable than has previously been suggested by scholars of the subject, such as Barthes. The language of fashion journalism and writing then might be best regarded as multidimensional, with a range of different qualities and conventions utilized at different times and in different contexts.
>
> (Barnard 2002)

These contested takes on how fashion conveys mediated meaning, represent an ideological desire to dismantle the social differences that fashion reinforces in the search for fixed meanings. While in another way, written, image or worn fashion and appearance can express its role in a more dynamic, open-ended, creative process and as part of a playful pursuit with endless communicative possibilities and levels of agency.

This volume provides a multidisciplinary analysis of the relatively under-researched topic of how fashion is used to communicate identity, ideas and brands, through verbal an non-verbal narratives on behalf of a range of creative producers and consumers for professional, commercial, historical, social, cultural and creative purposes. This is done by examining how fashion is appropriated as a universal, yet differentiated theme for novelists, poets, playwrights, directors, writers, creators, journalists, designers, merchants, advertisers, bloggers, flanêurs and consumers who are all drawn to, and utilize the power of appearance and fashion artefacts to convey key messages about the self and society; the individual and the collective. Here, fashion images and words, by anchoring the clothed subject (Eco 1979b), are encoded in assorted narrative genres by a range of creative communicators. In turn, they are actively interpreted and appropriated by audiences and consumers in the interpretative process of the artistic text becoming aesthetic text (Iser 2000).

As an edited collection, this volume examines multiple fashion-based narrative constructions from a variety of critical and disciplinary perspectives. In doing so, it explores how, why and to what end fashion and clothing appear and are used in various narrative forms as a means of materially and symbolically communicating character, emotion, personality, difference, identity, power and culture. Each chapter utilizes a critical interpretive framework, including literary theory, film theory, visual communication, media theory, fashion theory, communication theory and social interaction theory.

The authors also address common themes, such as why fashion is a common focus for writers, authors and auteurs; how fictional and non-fictional texts utilize fashion as subject and object; whether written fashion is more important than image fashion and vice versa; what the varied narrative roles are that fashion and clothing assume in terms of character, plot, storytelling and identity creation; to what extent fashion delineates and defines culture and ethnicity in its transglobal appropriations; and where and when fashion contributes to social discourses and cultural repertoires, and is in turn influenced by them.

Transglobal Fashion Tales

As a common motif, the chapters in this volume largely take a transglobal approach, covering fashion discourse and narratives from a range of cultures represented by geographic diversity of the authors and their subject focus. This highlights the established and emergent transglobal, multiple flows of fashion discourses embedded in fashion design output and their brand stories.

This volume represents an attempt to broaden the analysis of fashion beyond a purely traditional western or modernist frame of analysis by offering a more representative, international perspective (Rocamora 2009; Craik 1993) given that, historically, fashion systems in China and Asia, for example, have often been overlooked (Finnane 2007) in fashion studies. It extends the notion of fashion and clothing on the basis that fashion is principally a transglobal phenomenon both in terms of how it is produced, created, distributed and consumed, and also in view of its importance across cultures in a transglobal sense, as

> The term 'transglobal' here refers to the flows of goods, ideas and influences across multiple borders given that we live in a visualised world, a world in which we are bombarded everyday and everywhere with images that appear transglobal, capable of crossing geographic and racial divides.
>
> (Thomas 2001: 1)

Such transglobal patterns go beyond a concern with economic structures and the 'workings of capital on a global basis [...] the earlier logics of empire, trade and political domination in many parts of the world' (Appadurai 2001: 3) although these considerations are pertinent to any analysis concerning the fashion system and their underlying complexities and inequities. The focus in this volume will be on the transborder flows of fashion witnessed both at micro (across local and regional community boundaries) and macro levels (across national borders) covering cultures, ethnicities, language, economies, lifestyles and heritage all resulting in cultural hybridity by appropriation. These spatial and temporal transglobal, transnational and translocal flows operate in multiple directions and are no longer typified as purely radiating from west to east. In addition, they no longer automatically suggest outright colonial influence, although this is a valid reading in certain cases, alongside the orientalization of western or non-western fashion collections (Skov 2003) founded on mythic constructions of the 'other' in overworked Chinese signifiers, for example. Where transglobal fashion influences take root locally in the creative process of design and marketing they are often adapted and reworked. In this way, they become unique, communicating a grounded originality, rather than being a faithful replication of the original version. These transglobal flows go beyond the transnational and its concern with nation states and their people to encompass cross-cultural intersections that form and forge the fashion system and its creative outputs.

Increasingly, we are experiencing a world without boundaries representing a more fluid existence where people, commodities, stories, discourses and ideas circulate across the globe in both real and virtual dimensions and across multiple 'scapes' (Appadurai 1996). This is part of the traffic in things and 'the things-in-motion that illuminate their human and social context' (Appadurai 1986: 5) redolent of the ever dynamic and evolving flows of the fashion system (Barthes 1983). It can also be argued that these flows of commodities, cultures and ideas are not a modern phenomenon having existed globally wherever people migrated and traded across the borders of local and regional communities and nations.

Historically, culture in this sense has no territorial boundaries, referring 'as much to commonality as to diversity' (Nederveen Pieterse 2004: 46). Here, there is a blurring of where the global ends and the local begins in the contemporary fashion system in the process of 'glocalization', where universalizing and particularizing tendencies fuse together to form a unique cultural offering (Robertson 1992; Giulianotti and Robertson 2007).

Equally, the resulting global hybridization and cultural hybridity (Huat 2000) of the socio-cultural practices of everyday life and the creative ideas and outputs of fashion practice often result in garments as hybridized cultural objects, from haute couture to high street. In this process, professional fashion brand storytellers tell mythic stories framed within orientalism, colonialism, post-colonialism, postmodernism, heritage, authenticity, soft power, cultural identities, social status and 'copy-cat' cultures. These articulations about fashion map the local against the global. So, while the garment output of the fashion system of production, distribution and consumption, at all levels, appears to be more homogenous, the symbolic values attached to fashionable clothes in a given culture and society will vary depending on:

> the cultural and political history of the country and the characteristics and variety of the ethnic groups of which it is composed. Fashion systems have distinctive characteristics in different countries, depending on the organization of the fashion industry, the nature of the clientele, and the relative influence of marginal subcultures, as well as on the role of the arts and other forms of culture in the country's heritage.
>
> (Crane and Bovone 2006: 324)

Section 1 – Clothing Communication: Fashion as Written/Image

In this first section of the book, the authors consider how fashion is represented and utilized in the context of literature and film, while also acting as the inspiration for factual, textual sources, all intent on their audiences both cognitively and affectively. Fashion is often largely assumed to rely on the visual mode to convey meaning. Yet, writing about fashion also provides a form and structure for its aesthetic, rhetorical and affective regimes. In this sense, fashion produces fiction whereby the:

> men and women of Edith Wharton or Thomas Hardy, George Gissing, Leo Tolstoy, George Moore, Henry James or Marcel Proust carry their stories on their backs, each outfit mapping their social and sexual conquests and their declines.
>
> (McNeil, Karaminas and Cole 2009: 5)

Across history, fashion has been used as a subject for the writers of both fictional and non-fictional genres to disseminate fashion information as content. Literary references to fashion have signalled the status, class and taste of characters from *Gawain and the Green Knight* or

Chaucer to Thomas Hardy and Charles Dickens. The authors of these canonical texts often used fashion to delineate characters based on societal distinction (Veblen 1899) and the tensions that emerge therein (Simmel 1957) in order to facilitate the plot or provide satirical social commentary.

Fashion can also be the source of moral or political debate about the body and how character is presented across time, space and place by institutional structures, vested interests, groups or individuals. As Vinken suggests:

> The discourse on fashion assumes the philosophical form of a critique of mere appea-rances, the cultural-theoretical form of a critique of the market economy or the traditional form of a critique on sexual morality.
>
> (2005: 3)

This usage of fashion in fiction and film as a literary trope, characterization device or rhetorical tool has continued across literary and filmic regimes in mirroring the prevailing social, cultural, political and economic trends of the time, as well as mythically representing them. In this way, fashion is used 'as' fiction, films and non-fiction in the form of subject content, as a social and cultural commentary and as a way of assisting our being and doing. On the other hand, fashion is used 'in' literary, filmic and media texts by supplementing the narrative and thereby enhancing characterization or narrative contextualization through sartorial allusions. In some mediated storylines, fashion also operates as a character in its own right, becoming an indivisible part of the storyline, as the 'fifth character' in the HBO television series *Sex and the City*, for example (Bruzzi and Church Gibson 2004: 115; König 2004), or as the whole context for the plot both in the novel and film versions of *The Devil Wears Prada* (Weisberger 2004; Peirson-Smith 2013).

These mediated representations and adaptations of fashion-oriented and character-based attire can be used as a site of social and economic control to fuel the capitalist logic of late modernity whereby global film and television industries, for example, can create consumer desire for fashion brands through the commodification of celebrity actors and their constructed selves in terms of what they wear both on and off screen. Yet, the adaptation and application of 'the look' or visual attire of book or screen or character (Munich 2011) can also be regarded as a hegemonic response by the viewer or audience who might appropriate this for their own purposes, whether residing in modern urban settings from London to Los Angeles, or in the early twentieth-century political contexts of China or the Soviet Union. Equally, the demonization of commercial fashion writers for penning shameless fashion brand placements as a public relations tactic (McDowell 2010), or the gendered relegation of fashion writing as a womanly concern (Breward 2003) suitably satisfied by 'the women's sections of broadsheet newspapers or celebrity gossip columns' (Barnard 2002: 1) overlooks the active reception by readers and viewers. This consumption community uses fashion-based texts such as 'chick lit' novels or 'fashionista fiction' as active consumers of interpretive interest groups 'to discover truths about their particular lived experience whilst validating their membership of various fashion and lifestyle based consumption communities' (Peirson-Smith 2013: 175).

Opening this section, Pamela Church Gibson's chapter, 'Fashioning Adaptations: *Anna Karenina* on Screen', places a close focus on the filmic adaptations of Anna Karenina and the fashioning of its protagonist in three films spanning an 80-year timeline. In doing so, Church Gibson emphasizes the seminal role that period film costume has played and continues to play in the mutual relationship between feature film, fashion and celebrity in different ways from signifying stardom or informing couturier collections and home-made outfits, to operating as the source of inspiration for advertising storyboards.

Continuing a filmic focus, fashion as represented in selected Soviet films from the mid to late twentieth century, covering the timeline of Stalin's death to the beginning of the Perestroika, is the subject of Julia Hargassner's chapter, 'The Desire for Change and Contrast: Fashion in Soviet Films between 1956 and 1985'. The author employs a semiotic analysis to expose the tensions between Soviet governmental control over the lives and lifestyles of its people in the decade-specific, external fashion influences from the West as showcased in Soviet film costume and fashionable clothes worn by actors of this period both on and off screen.

Turning to the literary domain where fashion meets fiction, Royce Mahawatte, in 'The Sad Fortunes of "Stylish Things": George Eliot and the Languages of Fashion', examines the role played by clothes as narrative trope as worn by the novelist's characters and in wider fashion references within George Eliot's fiction. This literary work aimed at conveying the contestations of emotion, femaleness and social duty, with notable reference to her first published work in 1857, *The Sad Fortunes of Amos Barton*. Mahawatte shows how Eliot, as a realist writer influenced by the Rational Dress Society, 'silver-fork fiction' and the fashion editorial, was often critical of fashion as manifested in its treatment throughout her narratives and character development, while actually serving to mirror the ambiguous content of Victorian fashion journalism.

Extending the literary focus, where fashion meets fiction, Colin Cavendish-Jones' chapter, 'Oscar Wilde and the Philosophy of Fashion', examines Oscar Wilde's often overlooked writing and philosophical pronouncements on fashion, which were also visually grounded in his personal presentation of self. Cavendish-Jones explains that Wilde's essays on male dress and his focus on female clothing in his essay, 'The philosophy of dress' reflected his aesthetic beliefs, close links with the Rational Dress Society, in addition to his socialist and feminist leanings. This is exemplified, he suggests, in Wilde's championing of working dress for its simplicity and noble bearing allied to his visionary prediction that the future of twentieth-century male and female attire would reside in homogeneity that was pragmatically based on employment needs.

In a different geographic location, in Asia, Kathryn A. Hardy Bernal's chapter, 'Lolita through the Looking Glass: Alice, the Japanese Lolita Subculture and the Lolita Complex' investigates the complex intertextual connections between the multilayered styles of the

Japanese Lolita subculture by exploring the possible roots of its aesthetic inspiration in literature and popular culture and its further influence on fashion. Hardy Bernal also finds meaning in the Lolita subculture in terms of what it is not – notably it is not over-sexualized, cosplay or based on Nabokov's novel *Lolita*. By way of contrast, the author prefers to locate expression of meaning in favour of what it actually represents to those who dress up in this way. Hence, the Lolita trend is based on a Japanese love of cuteness and cute characters, as exemplified by the localized recreations of the *Alice in Wonderland* motif, with an expression of assumed playful innocence, noting that this activity cannot be understood on its apparent values and exterior meanings alone.

Using a hermeneutic approach in 'Sewing Manuals in 1950s China: Socialist Narratives and Dress Patterns from New Democracy to Socialist Transformation' Antonia Finnane, after Barthes, uses texts, specifically technical sewing manuals produced in China from 1949 onwards, to provide fascinating insights into what types of clothing people in this historic context were making and wearing. Given the absence of any other form of fashion writing in this period of Chinese history, Finnane reveals how in the short term there may have been instances of heterogeneity in details of dress. Over the long-term of Mao's rule, the technical literature indicates that the guiding principles of dress were governed by militarist homogeneity, albeit with some evidence of individual inventiveness.

Section 2 – Style Statements: Fashioning Identity

In the second section the chapters cover how fashion is appropriated across a range of mediated narrative genres as a way of delineating identity through clothing style. Communication through clothes, as Barthes would have it, can be done in various modes through worn, real or represented garments. Written clothing or image clothing are both forms of vestimentary communication, becoming part of an expressive process adopted by individuals and groups affected by the deeper meanings associated with words and images to naturalize the social order and human activity as a way of life. The ability of fashion and clothing to convey, contest and accommodate individual and group identity through the material and visual expressions of individuality or belonging is a significant part of its communicative power. As Watt observes

> Clothes frame us. They express our individuality and are a means for us to interact with and belong to society. The adoption of what is fashionable at any given time or the rejection thereof may be expressed in the membership of a group or the affirmation of a personal stance.
>
> (Watt 1999: 1)

The chapters in this section all focus on the various ways in which fashion and clothing choices modify appearance and rework the body, by constructing and performing negotiated identities across different cultural sites and geographic locations. Fashion and clothing artefacts are the output of socially constructed signifying practices that generate meaning and forge identity by communicating the emotions, values, beliefs and aspirations of individuals in a given social and cultural milieu. This enables the negotiation and construction of agency, often based on contested power relations, depending on the given cultural habitus, as in the case of performing and fashioning gender.

The first chapter in this section by Efrat Tseëlon frames many of the fashion- and identity-based themes covered in this section. 'The Emperor's New Clothes Revisited: On Critical Fashion, Magical Thinking and Fashion as Fiction' addresses multilevelled notions of fashion as narrative and as an identity marker. Tseëlon explains how the fashion narrative and fashion's many stories including fairy tales, in the broadest sense, encompass all aspects of cultural existence and identity from artefact, concept, performative prop and presentation of self-located in our wardrobe choices. Also, Tseëlon examines various research approaches to uncover how we make sense of, and comprehend differing versions or narratives of truth and authenticity through the clothed self.

The next chapter, 'From Tradition to Fantasy: National Costume for Puerto Rican Miss Universe Contestants' by José Blanco F. and Raúl J. Vázquez-López, features the varied significations of the notion of 'nation' as reflected in the costumes worn by Puerto Rican competitors in the Miss Universe contest. The more recent lack of homogeneity in this presentation of nationhood from traditional national dress to hyper-theatrical costumes, guaranteed to gain media attention, suggests a postmodern engagement driven by market and media influences. Blanco F. and Vázquez-López also contend that this diverse interpretation of nation by country of origin is clear evidence of the move away from the mythic ideas of mono-nationhood, as defined by one singular national dress, to a range of interpretations represented in costume, which include other cultures and social identities that were previously left off the representational agenda.

Our next stop is Australia, where Jennifer Craik, in 'From Iconography to Inspiration: Australian Indigenous References in Contemporary Fashion', focuses attention on the contentious appropriation of Indigenous Australian markers in the current fashion system as a contested form of identity creation and manipulation. Despite awareness-raising by the media or by opinion formers, and attempts at regulation by the legal system to prevent the random 'borrowing' of these symbols of Indigenous artwork in textile design and fashion collections, the situation appears to be unresolved and this Indigenous artwork remains largely unprotected. Ultimately, Craik notes that collaborations between Indigenous people and Indigenous artists and designers, while not yet fully successful in terms of championing cultural authenticity, mean that the fashion industry may hold the potential platform for a future resolution based on a combination of cross-cultural design collaboration and strategic or ethical business management.

Turning their attention to the managed male appearance, Maria Mackinney-Valentin and Trine Brun Petersen's chapter, 'In Your Face: Masculine Style Stories and the

Fashionable Beard', analyses the multiple and changing meanings beneath the management of male facial hair across history and in varied cultural contexts as a way of engaging with masculinity, social status, identity or style trends. Based on ethnographic research and data elicited from focus group analysis with Danish men, Mackinney-Valentin and Brun Petersen test out existing research on representations of the beard. They suggest that the demographic differences of the wearer indicate a range of identities that the beard affords; older males use it to present a self with power-based or masculine values, while younger informants regard it as a way to engage more playfully with identity, style and appearance, often founded on the ambiguous permutations of interpreted meaning.

In 'Becoming Animal, Becoming Free: Re-Reading the Animalistic in Fashion Images', Louise Wallenberg provides a detailed re-interpretation of the philosophy underpinning the representation of animals alongside women in a range of mediated fashion-based images from art, photography, advertising and film. Wallenberg uses Gilles Deleuze and Félix Guattari's notion of 'becoming-animal' to suggest that imagery, which juxtaposes women with animals, can actually be re-read as a celebration of a powerful and liberated female presence, heavily imbued with latent agency to re-establish the notion of female identity.

The contested and complementary discourse between fashion as art and its visual communicative function is the subject of the chapter by Viveka Kjellmer entitled, 'Fragile Fashion: The Paper Dress as Art and Visual Consumption'. Specifically, Kjellmer analyses the work of three Scandinavian designers: Bea Szenfeld from Sweden, Annette Meyer from Denmark and Virpi Vesanen-Laukkanen from Finland who all utilize perishable materials as the basis of their 'visual couture' installations, highlighting questions of the consumptive (real and visual), (im)permanent and evanescent traits of fashion. The role of clothing as cultural artefact and its part in identity construction is further explored, in addition to its ability to communicate a powerful message as a museum exhibit impacting on identifiable sustainable behaviours, as opposed to being merely a wearable, disposable garment.

The final chapter in this section locates its geographic purview in South East Asia in the search for identity via dressing up that is inspired by mediated textual and literary sources. Focusing on a form of dressing up with its origins in Japanese comic book and cartoon texts, Anne Peirson-Smith, in 'O Brave New World that Hath such Costumes in It: An Examination of Cosplay as Fantastical Performance', examines the creative and performative aspects of the practice where young adults make and wear anime and manga-inspired character costumes. Using observational and ethnographic research with informants from Hong Kong, Macau and China, Peirson-Smith suggests that cosplayers are drawing on the combined creative resources of DIY costume making, role-play-based interpretation, collaboration and multimodal expression as a transglobal and transcultural performance of multiple character identities.

Section 3 – Brand Storytelling: Commodified Fashion Tales

The third section of the book examines how narratives are used to position and promote fashion brands and fashion cities in the global marketplace, highlighting fashion's place in the global creative economy by using carefully crafted words and strategically selected images. Here, fashion brand positioning is examined from various geographic perspectives and experiential 'brandscapes', from the creation of a mythic and overworn notion of the fashion city through photography in Hong Kong and Shanghai, to heritage-oriented branding explored through stories of local Shanghai fashion designers trading on vintage fashion trends. Also, the transglobal origins and sustained popularity of the cargo pant is examined as an expression of casual modernity, alongside Japan's attempt to communicate a new world-view through the global promotion of soft power rooted in its unique street fashion.

Fashion branding appears to be a critical driver in the modern fashion system, having become the central pivot of communication between the marketing push of the producer/designer and the pull of the customer. At this point, producer, customer and assorted cultural intermediaries operating across the circuit of production are responsible for creating and curating the fashion brand story (Hancock 2016), while maintaining the fashion brand's existence and longevity (Tungate 2012). Fashion brand managers devise the narrative as they 'attempt to control the overall character of the brand, making it unique from others, bringing it alive, giving it a raison d'etre with a consistently identifiable look and feel' (Peirson-Smith 2014: 68). Essentially, in order to create an iconic global brand, this cultural communication strategy is based on devising, 'a storied product, that is, a product that has distinctive branded features (mark, design, etc.) through which customers experience identity myths' (Holt 2004: 36). The active selection and framing of the fashion brand story engages the consumer in the narrative by skilfully using schemata embedded in keywords, identifiable issues, stylized images and memorable visual and tactile experiences to communicate the brand's position and associated values, 'based on professional considerations of what will capture media attention and connect cognitively and affectively with consumers – especially in pushing their buttons and linking them to the brand more closely' (Peirson-Smith 2014: 69).

Shifting the geographic and mediated focal point to photographic and advertising representations of Shanghai and Hong Kong as incipient fashion capitals in '"Paris of the East"? Collapsing Fashion Capitals through Fashion Photography of Shanghai and Hong Kong', Jess Berry examines the significance of taking a position on the global fashion map. In doing this, Berry suggests that Hong Kong and Shanghai have mimicked and appropriated the visually driven, rhetorical strategies previously employed by more established fashion capitals such as Paris, London and New York to portray their cityscapes as parallel, stylish consumption spaces. At the same time, Berry argues that these rhetorical re-workings of mythic Orientalist representations, while reflecting the similarities between global fashion centres, often serve to replicate a potentially meaningless, overworked discourse. Instead, these two fashion cities, Berry suggests, may be best advised to locate their own distinctive identities as style zones by representing their uniqueness in fashion photography, editorial and advertising.

A situated field trip to Shanghai and a planned stroll through the city's streets provided the inspiration for the chapter by Natascha Radclyffe-Thomas, 'Weaving Fashion Stories in Shanghai: Heritage, Retro and Vintage Fashion in Modern Shanghai'. Radclyffe-Thomas matches up her observations to those of past writers inspired by this modern Chinese city's street life and fashion scene, providing illuminating insights into the construction of Shanghai's heritage-based fashion identity based on a municipal form of brand management.

The notion of 'brandscaping', by which fashion brands create identity and presence across a range of spaces and places is examined by Demetra Kolakis in 'X Marks the Spot: The Phenomena of Visuality and Brandscaping as Material Culture'. The project described in this chapter uses a case study analysis, portraiture and photographic installations/interventions to investigate the use of visual and spatial communication in brandscaping as material culture. The role of aesthetics, form and function in fashion branding are also explored by Kolakis to better understand the role of the fashion environment as a site of spatial communication where X marks the 'it' spot in terms of how the viewer/consumer is encouraged to look into, and engage with the retail space or the store front pre-, during and post-consumption.

In 'Cargo Pants: The Transnational Rise of the Garment that Started a Fashion War' Joseph H. Hancock II shows how a fashion garment is the subject of brand storytelling in blogs, advertising and news stories, while also enabling characterization in popular culture narratives such as films. Hancock tells the evolving story and challenges the origin myths surrounding this ubiquitous male wardrobe staple, the cargo pant, from its contested start as a military garment in Europe and North America, to its continued popularity as a seasonal fixture for many globally based high street brands as a mass casual lifestyle prop. Adapted and adopted across the late twentieth century by a range of subcultures to signify mythic notions of masculinity, reinforced by the multi-brand stories used in advertising the garment for mass consumption, the cargo pant appears to tell a compelling story capturing the popular imagination, despite its detractors.

Taking a more macro-view, Tets Kimura's chapter 'Cool Japan: Fashion as a Vehicle of Soft Power' examines the social, economic and cultural challenges facing Japan across the past decade since the fall out of its bubble economy and this nation's attempts to reposition itself through the lens of soft power manifested in youth and street fashion. Kimura critically assesses the 'Cool Japan' initiative implemented by the government to boost Japan's global and regional economic standing through the dissemination of soft power. In doing so, Kimura also suggests that while manga and anime still appear to be the favoured cultural exports in Asia and beyond, that new street fashion brands may hold the key for future uptake among a fickle global youth demographic.

This edited volume on transglobal fashion originally emerged from an international conference, *Fashion in Fiction: Style Stories and Transglobal Narratives*, which was held at City University of Hong Kong 12–15 June 2014, to examine the narrative and discursive representations of fashion practice across time and culture. The interdisciplinary conference was attended by over one hundred international fashion scholars and practitioners from over twenty countries who came together to share their research and insights on a relatively overlooked, yet increasingly relevant aspect of fashion studies – the transglobal circuit of the fashion system and the fashion narratives that it engenders in the garments produced, created, branded, promoted, bought and blogged about. As a way of sustaining the dialogue beyond the event, this volume was also planned alongside a Special Issue of *Fashion, Style & Popular Culture,* published in the Journal of *Clothing Cultures* (Intellect 2015) also containing selected conference papers.

Concluding Thoughts

In examining how fashion narratives operate and are negotiated, both globally and locally, the chapters move from sweatshop to wardrobe: season to season, page to screen, newspaper to website, camera to blog, catwalk to high street, producer to consumer, writer to reader, artist to audience and across the lifetime of an individual's wardrobe both in fiction and reality. Essentially, the volume addresses the various ways that fashion has been used as a literary and filmic device or trope for character development and authentic scene-setting in novels films, videos, photographs and art and as a mediated form of content for advertising and branding campaigns. In addition, these narratives are addressed as professional expressions of fashion from design to journalistic commentary on the fashion industry in editorials and blogs to the personal expression of individual identity. Taken as a whole, the chapters in this volume represent existing and emerging scholarship focusing on the multiple and myriad ways in which fashion narrates and is narrated about across a range of multimodal channels traversing geographic boundaries in the process of generating and conveying individual and collective meaning.

The all-pervasive nature of fashion and its social significance is communicated transglobally and add to the ability to facilitate expressions of identity, gender, ethnicity and allegiance across style trends and style tribes operating within a fashion system powered by capitalist modernity. This ensures that fashion is woven into the narratives through which we make sense of our existence. Equally, fashion is not part of a fixed linguistic system, but presents itself as an open text in our 'recited society' (de Certeau 1984) to be applied and adapted by a range of producers, taste-makers and consumers appearing across a range of narrative genres and modes.

This edited collection takes the reader on a global journey from Hong Kong and Puerto Rico to Paris and further afield through numberless narratives, inviting them to reflect on the rapidly changing social, cultural, political and economic contexts which fashion is shaped by and also attempts to shape through multimodal storytelling. Fashion impacts on issues and ideologies in the never-ending circuit of change where ultimately it operates as a form of communication exchange across cultures, in terms of the experiences, identities and aesthetics that are shared in the creation and consumption of clothes and their use as the basis of narrative content. In this sense, fashion writing and the narratives that carry the fashion message underscore the notion that fashion is a total social fact (Maus 1966). Fashion as subject and object, appearing both 'as' and 'in' written and visual texts, appears to be of great interest to the readers and viewers of print, broadcast and digital media sources as the growing amount of time and multi-channel content devoted to fashion writing and consumption suggests. The production and consumption habits surrounding the creative expression of fashion involve 'both an active producer and consumer as there appears to be an insatiable demand to discover more about fashion and be immersed in its fictional world' (Peirson-Smith 2013: 176).

We hope that you enjoy this borderless fashion journey across time, space and place, through the messages that these chapters communicate, and the cultures that they encompass. In this way, the reader will take away new insights for future debate and discussion on the evolving topic of transglobal fashion narratives; the multiple stories that are told about fashion, and that only fashion itself can perhaps tell.

References

Agins, T. (1999), *The End of Fashion: How Marketing Changed the Clothes Business Forever*, New York: William Morrow & Co. Inc.

Anderson, B. (1991), *Imagined Communities: Reflections on the Origin and Spread of Nationalism*, London: Verso.

Appadurai, A. (1986), *The Social Life of Things*, Cambridge: Cambridge University Press.

———— (1996), *Modernity at Large: Cultural Dimensions of Globalization*, Minneapolis and London: University of Minnesota Press.

———— (ed.) (2001), *Globalization*, Durham: Duke University Press.

Aspers, P. and Godart, F. (2013), 'The sociology of fashion: Order and change', *Annual Review of Sociology*, 39, pp. 171–92.

Barnard, M. (2002), *Fashion as Communication*, London: Routledge.

———— (2007), 'Fashion statements: Communication and culture', in M. Barnard (ed.), *Fashion Theory: A Reader*, London: Routledge, pp. 170–81.

Barthes, R. ([1967] 2006), *The Language of Fashion* (ed. M. Carter and trans. A. Stafford), London: Bloomsbury Academic.

———— (1977), 'Introduction to the structural analysis of narratives', in *Image-Music-Text* (trans. Stephen Health), London: Fontana, pp. 20–30.

———— (1990), *The Fashion System* (trans. M. Ward and R. Ward), Berkeley: University of California Press.

Bourdieu, P. (1984), *Distinction: A Social Critique of the Judgement of Taste*, Cambridge: Harvard University Press.

Breward, C. (2003), *Fashion*, Oxford: Oxford University Press.

Bruzzi, S. (1997), *Undressing Cinema: Clothing and Identity in the Movies*, London: Routledge.

Bruzzi, S. and Church Gibson, P. (2004), 'Fashion is the fifth character: Fashion, costume and character in *Sex and the City*', in K. Akass and J. McCabe (eds), *Reading Sex and the City*, London: I.B. Tauris, pp. 115–43.

Certeau, M. de (1984), *The Practice of Everyday Life* (trans. Steven Rendall), Berkeley: University of California Press.

Corner, F. (2014), *Why Fashion Matters*, London: Thames & Hudson.

Craik, J. (1993), *The Face of Fashion: Cultural Studies of Fashion*, London: Routledge.

—— (2009), *Fashion: The Key Concepts*, Oxford: Berg.

Davis, F. (1992), *Fashion, Culture, and Identity*, Chicago: University of Chicago.

Diane, C. and Laura, B. (2006), 'Approaches to material culture: The sociology of fashion and clothing', *Poetics*, 34, pp. 319–33.

Eco, U. (1979a), *A Theory of Semiotics*, Bloomington: Indiana University Press.

—— (1979b), *The Role of the Reader: Explorations in the Semiotics of Texts*, Bloomington: Indiana University Press.

—— (1990), *The Limits of Interpretation*, Bloomington: Indiana University Press.

The Economist (2000), 'Fashion writing style', http://www.economist.com/node/279635. Accessed 10 January 2016.

Entwistle, J. (2015), *The Fashioned Body: Fashion, Dress and Modern Social Theory*, Cambridge: Polity Press.

Finnane, A. (2007), *Changing Clothes in China: Fashion, History, Nation*, New York: Columbia University Press.

Gilbert, D. (2006), 'Fashion's world cities: Urban modernity and urban orders', in C. Breward and D. Gilbert (eds), *Fashion's World Cities*, London: Bloomsbury Books.

Giulianotti, R. and Robertson, R. (2007), 'Forms of glocalization: Globalization and the migration strategies of Scottish football fans in North America', *Sociology*, 4:1, pp. 133–52.

Hancock II, J. H. (2016), *Brand/Story: Cases and Explorations in Fashion Branding*, 2nd ed., New York: Fairchild Books.

Hollander, A. (1978), *Seeing through Clothes*, New York: Viking.

Holt, D. B. (2004), *How Brands Become Icons: The Principles of Cultural Branding*, Boston: Harvard Business School Press.

Huat, C. B. (2000), 'Postcolonial sites, global flows and fashion codes: A case study of power *cheongsams* in modern Singapore', *Postcolonial Studies*, 3:3, pp. 279–92.

Hughes, C. (2009), 'The question of costume: Dressing for success in the 19th century novel', in P. McNeil, V. Karaminas and C. Cole (eds), *Fashion in Fiction: Text and Clothing in Literature, Film, and Television*, Oxford: Berg, pp. 11–22.

Inwood, M. J. (1983), *Hegel: The Arguments of the Philosophers*, London: Routledge & Kegan Paul.

Iser, W. (2000), *The Range of Interpretation*, New York: Columbia University Press.

Iwabuchi, K. (2002), *Recentering Globalization: Popular Culture and Japanese Transnationalism*, Durham: Duke University Press.

Kawamura, Y. (2012), *Fashioning Japanese Subcultures*, London: Berg

König, A. (2004), '*Sex and the City*: A fashion editor's dream?', in K. Akass and J. McCabe (eds), *Reading Sex and the City*, London: I.B. Tauris, pp. 130–43.

Kristeva, J. (1980), *Desire in Language: A Semiotic Approach to Literature and Art*, New York: Columbia University Press.

Lefebvre, H. (2003), *The Urban Revolution*, Minneapolis: University of Minnesota Press.

Lurie, A. (1981), *The Language of Clothes*, New York: Random House.

Maus, M. (1966), *The Gift: Form and Function of Exchange in Archaic Societies* (trans. I. Cunnision), London: Cohen and West.

McDowell, C. (1998), *The Pimlico Companion to Fashion: A Literary Anthology*, London: Pimlico.

——— (2010), 'What's wrong with fashion journalism?', Colin McDowell's blog, 3 January, http://colin-mcdowell.blogspot.hk/2010/01/whats-wrong-with-fashion-journalism.html. Accessed November 2014.

McNeil, P., Karaminas, V. and Cole, C. (2009), *Fashion in Fiction: Text and Clothing in Literature, Film, and Television*, Oxford: Berg.

McRobbie, A. (1998), *British Fashion Design: Rag Trade or Image Industry?*, London: Routledge.

Munich, A. (2011), *Fashion in Film*, Bloomington: Indiana University Press.

Nederveen Pieterse, J. (2004), *Globalisation and Culture: Global Melange*, Lanham: Roman & Littlefield Publishers.

Niessen, S. (2003), 'Afterword: Re-orienting fashion theory', in S. Niessen, A. M. Leshkowich and C. Jones (eds), *Re-Orienting Fashion: The Globalization of Asian Dress*, Oxford: Berg, pp. 243–65.

Peirson-Smith, A. (2012), 'Fashioning the fantastical self: An examination of the Cosplay dress-up phenomenon in South East Asia', *Fashion Theory: The Journal of Body, Dress and Culture*, 17:1, pp. 77–112.

——— (2013), 'Redressing the devil's wardrobe: Representing and re-reading the darker side of fashion in chick-lit novels', in J. H. Hancock II, T. Johnson-Woods and V. Karaminas (eds), *Fashion in Popular Culture: Literature, Media and Contemporary Studies*, Bristol: Intellect, pp. 171–89.

——— (2014), 'Comme on down and choos your shoes: A study of consumer response to the use of guest designers by H&M as a co-branded fashion strategy', in J. H. Hancock II, V. Manlow, G. Muratovski and A. Peirson-Smith (eds), *Global Fashion Brands: Style, Luxury & History*, Bristol: Intellect, pp. 57–81.

Pratt, A. C. (2011), 'The cultural contradictions of a creative city', *City, Culture & Society*, 2, pp. 123–30.

Robertson, R. (1992), *Globalization: Social Theory and Global Culture*, London: Sage Publications.

Rocamora, A. (2009), *Fashioning the City: Paris, Fashion and the Media*, London: I.B. Taurus.

Simmel, G. (1957), 'Fashion', *American Journal of Sociology*, 62, pp. 541–58.

Skov, L. (2003), 'Fashion nation: A Japanese globalization experience and a Hong Kong dilemma', in S. Niessen, A. M. Leshkowich and C. Jones (eds), *Re-Orienting Fashion: The Globalization of Asian Dress*, Oxford: Berg, pp. 215–42.

Thomas, J. (ed.) (2001), *Reading Images, Reader in Cultural Criticism Series*, Basingstoke: Palgrave.

Thomson, C. J. and Hayko, D. L. (1997), 'Speaking of fashion: Consumers' uses of fashion discourses and the appropriation of countervailing cultural meanings', *Journal of Consumer Behaviour*, 24:6, pp. 15–42.

Tungate, M. (2012), *Fashion Brands: Branding Style from Armani to Zara*, London: Kogan Page.

Veblen, T. (1899), *The Theory of the Leisure Class: An Economic Study of Institutions*, New York: Dover Thrift.

Vinken, B. (2005), *Fashion Zeitgeist: Trends and Cycles in the Fashion System*, New York: Berg.

Watt, J. (1999), *The Penguin Book of Twentieth-Century Fashion Writing*, London: Viking.

Weisberger, L. (2004), *The Devil Wears Prada*, New York: Broadway Books.

Wenger, E. (1998), *Communities of Practice: Learning, Meaning, and Identity*, Cambridge: Cambridge University Press.

Wollen, P. (1972), *Signs and Meaning in the Cinema*, Bloomington: Indiana University Press.

Section 1

Clothing Communication: Fashion as Written/Image

Introduction

This section features the use of fashion on page and screen to portray fictional characters or to provide social guidelines on how to dress. In this sense, fashion and clothing appear 'in' fiction to supplement characterization or to assist in framing the context of the storyline and plot. At the same time, fashion appears 'as' fiction, or as narrative and informational content, in editorials, documentaries and blogs when it is a topic in its own right for the edification of consumers in terms of the appropriate attire to adopt and how to source desired items of clothing and accessories considered to be fashionable.

Fashion as a text worn by a fictional persona signifies personality and status within an imaginary text, be it short story, comic book, novel, film or film adaptation. This usage of fashion and clothing as a means of enhancing the story by dressing the character to signify their standing (Hughes 2009), class and intention, is interpreted in various iterations depending on the author/auteur and the cultural, geographic or political context in which it appears (see Hargassner in this section). The mythic, hyper-feminine recreation of Lewis Carroll's *Alice in Wonderland* and Nabokov's *Lolita*, for example, is on full public display by the Loli style tribes and its adoption as a fashion outfit (see Hardy Bernal in this volume). The interpretation of the 'look' of a book or film character, while represented in different modes – visual and/or verbal, moving or static, real or virtual – often extends beyond the text and is commoditized by marketers in new fashion lines. Consequently, the sartorial trend is taken up as a form of fetishist mimicry by consumers desirous to copy the fashionable look of a Hollywood film idol or celebrity actress, in film adaptations of Tolstoy's *Anna Karenina*, for example (see Church Gibson in this section).

Fashion writing in its many creative forms also delineates various critical discourses as a way of conveying fashion information in representing it as a marker of social control or liberation. This is in evidence in the functional garments designed and domestically produced during the revolutionary period in China (see Finnane in this section); in the prescriptive dress recommended by the Victorian Rational Dress Society (see Cavendish-Jones in this section); or in fashion trends featured in 'silver-fork fiction' (see Mahawatte in this section).

The authors in this section suggest that literary texts featuring fashion and non-fiction fashion writing are not merely to be read in terms of their surface communicative value but as markers of, or in resistance to social, cultural, political and economic status. This type of fashion writing can also operate as a historic archive providing useful insights into the clothing concerns and styles of the day in a given time period, such as twentieth-century revolutionary China (see Finnane in this section). Fashion used in film characterization can also represent the circuitous flow of mediated influences migrating across geographic borders and operating beyond political constraints, as in mid-century Soviet Union (see Hargassner in this section). Hence, closer attention should be paid to the multi-layered, symbolic meanings attached to written and mediated fashion in terms of why and how it communicates messages and how they are actively consumed, interpreted and appropriated by the reader and viewer in the process of finding multiple pleasures in the text.

Chapter 1

Fashioning Adaptations: *Anna Karenina* on Screen

Pamela Church Gibson

Tolstoy's nineteenth-century novel has been the subject of numerous adaptations, each new version slightly reworked to fit changing mores; this chapter considers three films made across an 80-year period. I am concerned here with 'fashioning' in the widest sense of the word, not merely with the dressing of the heroine, but with her portrayal by leading stars and the different inflections of her character that are created and widely communicated. Each film has at its centre a star popular for her characteristic style as well as for her acting, and each heroine is costumed by designers whose talents reach beyond the screen to influence the fashions of their day. Period films have played a vital part in the complex, changing relationship between fashion and cinema. This chapter looks at each of the three films in this context, using a close textual analysis of each, and considers relevant contemporary material in that process. It closes with a consideration of the genre in the age of viral fashion film and digital platforms.

When we first encounter Tolstoy's heroine, 60 or more pages into the novel named after her, she is presented to the reader through the eyes of Count Vronsky, an officer in the Imperial Guard soon to become her lover, as they meet for the first time. He has gone to the station in Moscow to fetch his mother, and as he approaches the train where she waits for him, Vronsky steps aside to allow a much younger lady to alight. One swift glance tells him that she is someone 'belonging to the very best society' (Tolstoy [1877] 1966: 68). He feels compelled to turn and look at her once more, not only because of her extraordinary good looks, but also to see again the 'attractive expression on her face' (Tolstoy [1877] 1966: 68). This meeting will later lead to an affair with catastrophic consequences for both.

Surely, it is the period setting of this liaison between a lady who moves in the most elegant circles in Russia and a dashing officer, combining as it does beauty, elegance and tragedy with the lavish, cinema-friendly fashions of St. Petersburg in the 1870s, which makes this heroine so very interesting to producers, screenwriters and directors. So far, there have been fifteen cinematic adaptations and several televised versions of *Anna Karenina*. Actors as well as actresses have had the chance for memorable roles – Sean Connery, Sean Bean and Christopher Reeve, for example, have all played the part of Vronsky. Designers too have been pleased to participate, tempted of course by the inherent spectacularity of these particular fashions. In 1935, Greta Garbo was dressed by the leading Hollywood designer Gilbert Adrian, while in 1948, Vivien Leigh was costumed by photographer, designer, illustrator and frequent contributor to *Vogue*, Cecil Beaton. In 2012, Keira Knightley, the favourite cover girl of so many fashion editors, had a vast array of clothes created for her role as Anna by the costume designer, Jacqueline Durran.

We should also mention at the start the emphasis in the novel upon Anna's fashionable attire, as it is mentioned on several significant occasions by those around her. Tolstoy carefully describes an elegant black dress, which Anna wears to the ball that is held soon after her arrival in Moscow, as being in every way more stylish than the dresses of the ladies around her, and marked off from them by its cut, as well as its sombre hue. We might note too that in the nineteenth-century novel, being overly fashionable is not necessarily a good thing. Jane Austen and George Eliot clearly showed their readers the correlation between a too-voracious interest in the latest fashions and an imperfect or weak moral sense (see Mahawatte in this volume).

Those who have set out to film the novel have always been aware of the palpable pleasures that costumes in a period drama provide for an audience, and very generous budgets were provided for the dress and décor of all three films. We might consider the relationships between these three cinematic portrayals, the stars that created them and the real-life women who watched the films, to see how these could perhaps be reflected in the tripartite relationship of star, designer and contemporary fashion.

Greta Garbo and the 'Woman's Picture': Anna in the Depression Era

Garbo was one of MGM's leading stars; she was also an actress who was extraordinarily popular with women at a time when female audiences were seen as dictating, in various ways, the economic success of most cinematic releases (Berry 2000: xiv). Many of the most successful films of the decade were, in fact, examples of what later came to be called the 'woman's picture', a staple feature of the 1930s and 1940s (see Basinger 1994 and Haskell [1974] 1987). The leading roles in such films were given over to female stars, who played strong women seeking to somehow control their own destinies. In these films – which were often melodramas and always had a romantic storyline – the heroines had various problems to contend with and important decisions to make.

The reason for the emergence and the popularity of such films in the 1930s can easily be found in the socio-economic circumstances of the decade. In this period of mass unemployment many women were forced to become family breadwinners in the aftermath of the Depression; most jobs to be found were in the service sector, traditionally a female domain (Berry 2000: xviii). Women's lives became harsher, and there were often repercussions for working women now supporting seemingly redundant men (Berry 2000). The new screen heroines could act on their behalf as figures of fantasy that faced and triumphed over various seemingly impossible difficulties (Haskell [1974] 1987).

Garbo had shown herself to be highly effective as a woman in control. In *Queen Christina* (Rouben Mamoulian, 1933) she faced a clash between her royal duties and her desire for personal happiness with her Spanish lover. The film ends with her abdication; she alone makes this decision. She is seen in the last shot on the prow of a ship, leaving Sweden and sailing towards an uncertain future. Her role as *Anna Karenina* (Clarence Brown, 1935) presented filmmakers with questions around the portrayal of this very distinctive star at this particular historical moment.

Their task was to make an adulterous heroine, who abandons her son and subsequently leaves her second child motherless, into a sympathetic protagonist at a time when family values had been reasserted in a climate of uncertainty (Berry 2000). The second problem was Anna's suicide; in the novel, this is seen as a muddled and impetuous act, not perhaps the choice of a strong heroine. These two problems were swiftly addressed. The narrative here completely omits the child she has with Vronsky, and her husband is rendered cold and reptilian from the outset. Basil Rathbone creates a vengeful Karenin for whom the audience can feel no sympathy. His self-presentation interestingly reinforces this: here, Karenin is as well dressed as his wife. He is dapper throughout, whether at a garden-party in polka-dot cravat and white gloves, or at the races in white dress uniform with a long jacket. The producers cast top child star Freddie Bartholomew as the son; scenes with him are designed to demonstrate Anna's feeling for him. The film is handled so that Garbo is seen as a woman who escapes a punitive husband and is not simply a victim of passion. She also becomes a suitably tragic figure, with a suitable ending, altered so as to make it less unacceptable. Vronsky abandons her, joining a brigade of volunteers – and Anna finds that it is Princess Sorokhin to whom he bids farewell at the station. It is these two blows that prompt her to kill herself. In the novel, of course, he joins the volunteers only in his devastation of grief at her death.

The third problem here might have been how to dress Garbo as her fans wished, to remain in period and to appeal to contemporary taste. Her characteristic style was one of European elegance and sophisticated glamour conveyed in part through make-up, hats and accessories – Berry writes of her 'pale exoticism' (2000: 111). There was, too, the fact that she possessed a quality of androgyny enhancing her appeal, heightened by her penchant for wearing men's trousers off-screen (Berry 2000: 97).

The real-life Paris fashions of the time were now more fluid and more romantic; in 1933 Chanel had heralded 'a return to femininity' and 'a new luxury' (Chanel quoted in Berry 2000: 159). A cover illustration for US *Vogue* in June 1935 shows a woman who might have strayed from the set of *Anna Karenina*, wearing a small straw hat, a corsage and long gloves, in the act of unfurling a parasol, while another illustration by Cecil Beaton in the same issue depicts a heroine dressed as if for the opera in St. Petersburg, her hair piled high and a velvet ribbon around her throat. Designer Adrian would be able to combine period fidelity with fashion – and hopefully to satisfy Garbo's many fans.

Adrian, valued by MGM as the leading designer in Hollywood during the 1930s and early 1940s, worked with Garbo most notably on *Mata Hari* (Curtis Harrington, 1931) and *Grand Hotel* (Edmund Goulding, 1932). In the first, she plays a mysterious spy with a penchant for turbans and skullcaps, who, in one memorable scene, wears head-to-toe gold lamé; in the second, she is a lonely dancer, drifting through the Art Deco hotel in sensual dresses cut on the bias like the Paris designs of Madeleine Vionnet. The highly elaborate, over-decorated dresses of the 1870s might be more problematic, and Adrian was very committed to period authenticity. Three years later, when preparing to dress Norma Shearer as Marie Antoinette, he travelled to France to make hundreds of sketches in order to ensure that the period detail should be as accurate as possible (Lavalley 1987).

Adrian's designs would here be shown off against the lavish sets created by art director Cedric Gibbons, while their overall accuracy might be assessed by a descendant of the author, Andrej Tolstoy, employed on the production as 'Period Advisor'. The film, overall, has the same production values as MGM's lavish musicals of the same period. It opens with a close up of a vast, heavily laden banquet table in a restaurant where the Imperial Guard are conducting a drinking contest; there are gypsy singers and violinists on hand. At first Garbo's clothes are very faithful to the period, and so for some earlier scenes she wears frilled and flounced garments with rather fussy hats. But for two vital scenes – the meeting on the station and the ball where Vronsky and Anna meet again – Adrian was able to create clothes that would be far more appealing to audiences.

Her Cossack-inspired fur-trimmed coat and hat, which she wore in all of the studio publicity shots, became synonymous not only with Anna herself, but with Garbo, Russia and 'romance'. An outfit like this – which could be copied at different market levels – was memorably worn three decades later by Julie Christie as Lara in *Dr. Zhivago* (David Lean 1965). It subsequently became a permanent fixture in the vocabulary of fashion journalism, a referent for both *Anna Karenina* and the iconic Christie persona.

On screen in black and white, Anna's famous black ball gown, with its simplicity of cut and its dark colour, forms a striking contrast to the light frocks around her, just as described in the literary text. Garbo wears a single long strand of pearls, a contemporary touch reinforcing the appeal of this scene. And later, after Anna and Vronsky escape to Venice, she is dressed in simple, less ornate garments, fluid gowns of satin and silk, reflecting the trend described by Chanel. The clean lines embody her characteristic 'look'. For the final visit to the opera she wears a very simple strapless dress of white satin, with an unadorned capelet of white fur; a search through the *Vogue* archives shows the fit of this outfit with contemporary sensibility, and we can also find counterparts of the small black hat with veil and streamers that she wears in the very last scene. 'Parisian' or cinematic hats of the time were reproduced cheaply at mass market level (Eckert [1987] 1990) while the simpler clothes with their subtler edgings and trimmings were exactly the kind of thing to interest a female audience, many of whom made their own clothes if they could not afford a dressmaker (Wilson 1985). Anna here is a dignified victim, a melodramatic heroine, and her carefully created appearance pleased both fans and the film critics; there was no violation of period sensibility in this particular presentation of a 'woman's heroine'.

Figure 1: Another fur hat and cape reinforcing links between Russia and 'romance', 1935.

An *Anna Karenina* for 1948: Scarlett O'Hara, Christian Dior and Post-War Uncertainties

Cecil Beaton, who costumed the 1948 version of the novel directed by Julien Duvivier, is perhaps best known for his long career as a fashion photographer and for the clothes he created for Audrey Hepburn in the film version of *My Fair Lady* (Stanley Donen, 1964). He had discovered Vivien Leigh during the 1930s, when she first appeared on the London stage, and he immediately featured her in British *Vogue* in 1935, wearing a Victor Steibel gown. At this time, of course, the creators of fashion pages relied on socialites, stage actresses and a few select British film stars, for professional models were still anonymous figures who would not achieve recognition until the appearance of such well-connected models as Suzy Parker, Barbara Goalen and Dorian Leigh in the 1950s. Diana Vreeland was apparently also fond of Leigh, who continued to appear in *Vogue* for the next decade or more; she was known to have called her 'a perfect English Rose' (Vickers 2003).

In 1948, both heroine and film were cultural products of a complex period of post-war adjustment in Britain and elsewhere, a climate of uncertainty and continued austerity; everyone, in different ways, was coming to terms with the legacy of the Second World War. Women, once again, had been left on their own while men joined the armed services and, as with the First World War, many of them went out to work, finding a degree of financial independence (Haskell [1974] 1987). Men coming back after the trauma of conflict had their own adjustments to make, for in the turbulence of the war years both men and women often had extra-marital affairs. There was, as a result, a seeming lack of trust, which famously helped to create some rather duplicitous Hollywood heroines, the *femmes fatales* of 1940s 'film noir' (Kaplan 1978). Leigh had already played one unfaithful and tragic wife in the film *Waterloo Bridge* (Mervyn LeRoy, 1942). And she, like Anna, had left her own child behind with her husband after she fell in love with Laurence Olivier.

This background seems to colour her portrayal of Anna – waiting on the station at the end, Anna muses aloud. She seems confused, asking which of the events in her life could actually have happened, which of them might be her imagination. Here, ideas of forgiveness if not reconciliation seem particularly important. Ralph Richardson as Karenin is curiously sympathetic at times, particularly during the period when they share the same roof once more as she recovers after the birth of her second child.

At the start of the war, in 1939, Leigh was famously cast as Scarlett O'Hara in *Gone with the Wind* (Victor Fleming and George Cukor, 1940), one of the most successful films ever made; she delivered a triumphant performance, for which she won an Oscar. She was also featured on the cover of US *Vogue* in the famous green barbecue dress designed by Walter Plunkett. The crinolines, cinched-in waists, sweeping skirts, wide straw hats and parasols of the antebellum South had an extraordinary effect on wartime audiences, designs for a historical war held safely in a vanished era. A contemporary journalist described the film as having 'created a great stir in the pool of fashion', one that would surely 'have an influence on Paris and New York' (Churchill quoted in Maeder 1987: 84). Certainly, there was an immediate 'merchandising blitz unequalled in the history of period film publicity tie-ins' as antebellum accessories were speedily made and marketed (Churchill quoted in Maeder 1987: 84).

I would suggest that Plunkett's clothes and their rapturous reception could perhaps have acted as harbinger of the 'New Look', Dior's radical and romantic collection of 1947. Another wartime film, which could have influenced a post-war revolution in dress, was George Cukor's *The Women*, also released in 1940. Here, in the middle of a black-and-white film, a department store fashion show is shown in vivid Technicolor, while the Adrian clothes in the display become increasingly spectacular and impractical. The models wear tiny hats and wield parasols, while there is even a crinoline-type floor-length skirt. The women who watched these films, dressed in their practical, utilitarian clothes, could do little until the war ended. Scarlett had of course encouraged 'make-do-and-mend' in the famous scene where she fashions herself a dress out of old velvet curtains, but fabric was strictly rationed. The wartime films, however, must have whetted appetites, making these difficult-to-wear outfits seem immensely desirable and creating a favourable climate for the unveiling of the New Look.

The fashion imagery surrounding the New Look reinforced its successful invocation of a selective past. Fashion photographers took their photographs of these clothes in settings that recalled the belle époque, showing models perched on antique sofas, posed beside a marble fireplace, gazing out of vast windows, or leaning on a balustrade. Possibly the most famous photographs of this revolution in dress that Dior inspired were in fact taken by Beaton himself for US *Vogue* in 1948 and show the equally sumptuous evening dresses designed by American couturier Charles James. His endlessly referenced pictures show us models in their opulent gowns, grouped elegantly in a neo-classical drawing room; they are posed so as to emulate women of society who have left a dining room after dinner and wait, sipping their coffee, for the gentlemen to finish their port.

Women might want sweeping skirts, sloping shoulders, tiny waists and decorative hats, perhaps tied under the chin as on the cover of British *Vogue* for March 1948, or with a vast flower-garlanded brim as seen on the cover of US *Vogue* in the following month. There was, however, fierce resistance to overcome; in France, some saw the clothes as re-invoking class privilege (Mitford in Mosley 1993) and in Britain there was anger at the waste of materials (Wilson 1985). Now by a strange irony, the very actress who had seemingly prophesied the New Look and made it so captivating, now, in another role, helped to popularize it. The UK 'campaign book' for *Anna Karenina*

Figure 2: Anna's famous black dress here is different in silhouette and style from the gowns of her peers: its low-cut elegance and unseen train clearly reference the New Look of 1948.

made much of the similarities between Dior's designs and Leigh's onscreen outfits (Smith and Morris 2014). Alexander Korda, the producer, created sets as lavish as those of 1930s Hollywood and ensured that Beaton had a generous budget. His Anna evoked the look of Dior's models; she wore tight peplum jackets, tiny corseted waists, small elegant accessories and evening dresses with massive skirts and very low necklines that mirrored Dior's 'Courolle' line, where neck and shoulders arose from the dress like the stamen of a flower. The designs were nevertheless faithful to the period of the novel and would have pleased the 'etiquette consultant' listed in the film's credits.

For the moments that were perhaps cinematic set pieces, Beaton drew on both past and present, here as throughout. To make her fateful train journey, Anna wears a splendid sable coat and hat – tilted at a becoming angle – with matching muff. Her black ballgown has a very low neckline and in one overhead shot, reminiscent of a fashion photograph, we see the train of this dress curved in a graceful arc. Many of her outfits in their shape and their accessorizing could have moved across and onto the glossy pages of contemporary high-fashion magazines. And if the film itself was unsuccessful, both with the critics and at the box office, this did not diminish its visual impact. Some contemporary reviewers blamed this failure on the casting of the inexperienced young actor Kieron Moore as Vronsky; critic Dilys Powell commented that he reminded her of 'a professional dancing partner'. But the lack of success did not affect Leigh's popularity, and she retained her iconic credentials.

Beaton's costumes in fact spurred imitation in the design houses of Paris themselves – the jewelled collars and the velvet throat ribbons were copied (Maeder 1987: 92) while a velvet and sable outfit at Lanvin the following season was very similar to Anna's travelling clothes. Most interestingly, the House of Dior – whose New Look Leigh maybe helped to inspire, and which she wore, even reinterpreted, in this film – designed an 'Anna Karenina' coat in that same season (Maeder 1987: 92). This coat was of course liberally trimmed with fur and accessorized with both hat and muff. Trimmings including collars, cuffs and jabots were adopted at mass-market level, and paper patterns for 'hooded capes' also appeared.

There is a second fashion coda to this film, given that we are concerned with the costuming of heroines. In 1957, Leigh appeared on the London stage in the play *Duel of Angels*. Her dresses for this were created by Christian Dior himself, working with his young apprentice, Yves St Laurent. One of their designs for this production is now in the possession of the Victoria and Albert Museum. It blends together theatricality, 1950s couture and late-nineteenth-century extravagance, in the very way that Durran deployed in 2012 when costuming an Anna Karenina for a new century.

Post-Millennial or Post-Postmodern? Anna, Chanel and Kiera

Prior to their collaboration on *Anna Karenina* in 2012, director Joe Wright, actress Kiera Knightley and designer Jacqueline Durran had previously worked together on two very successful adaptations, *Pride and Prejudice* (2006) and *Atonement* (2008). All three of them were Oscar nominated on both occasions. Their Anna differs from her precursors, since the

Figure 3: Kiera Knightley in the 'notable necklace' of linked Chanel camellias, 2012.

nineteenth-century heroine is now in a new millennium where divorce is a commonplace, and a settled nuclear family is the exception. More significantly, however, the latest adaptation was created within totally transformed conditions of production and reception, where feature film must take its place within and between new, parallel media discourses. The simple 'product placement' of the twentieth century has been replaced by a complex system of linked images across every manifestation of the media, while the luxury brands, interested as they are in every cultural activity, now wield power in unprecedented ways (Church Gibson 2011). Arguably, their directors now have as much of an influence as the studio moguls of twentieth-century Hollywood, while the star system of that earlier era has been replaced by a complex and distorting 'celebrity system'. Knightley's performance here is not that of a 'star' in the former sense of the word; rather, her on-screen actions are always refracted through her particular 'celebrity' persona.

Knightley's role within the celebrity pantheon is one in which her fashion choices, rather than her private life, are the subject of intensive media scrutiny (Church Gibson 2011). Knightley, with her slender figure and highly photogenic face, is the type of 'celebrity' who – unlike so many others – is welcome within the world of high fashion (Church Gibson 2011). She was taken up by the fashion press after her first major role in *Bend It Like Beckham* (Gurinder Chadha, 2002) and was soon as familiar on the covers of *Vogue* and *Bazaar* as in magazines directly targeting her peers (Church Gibson 2011). In 2007, she was employed by the House of Chanel as the 'face' of Coco Mademoiselle and has featured in the promotional films for the scent – directed, in fact, by Wright himself, also co-opted. She soon became a Chanel 'brand ambassadress', even starring as Coco herself in a film to celebrate the centenary of the House. When she married in 2014, she wore a Chanel couture dress from 2006, accessorizing it with a classic bouclé jacket and – more quirkily – sneakers.

Joe Wright has directed other films for Chanel; one, featuring Brad Pitt, was released shortly before *Anna Karenina*. This short film, cheerfully lampooned on YouTube, was accompanied by a series of still images created by artist Sam Taylor-Wood whose husband, Aaron Taylor-Johnson, plays Vronsky. This accompanying narrative of commercials and cronyism runs along in parallel to the feature film. There was in fact an explicit commercial collaboration, for the multiple ropes of large, luminous pearls, the extravagant diamond necklaces and all the other jewellery worn by Kiera-as-Anna were all from the House of Chanel's 'Haute Joaillerie' line; and they featured in every publicity shot for the film. One notable necklace, in fact, is strung between two large diamond camellias, the flowers so familiar to us as brand signifier. There would also be another form of collaboration at a different market level, between designer Durran and the high-street retailer Banana

Republic, who had previously launched three successful collections created by the designer for the television series *Mad Men,* Janie Bryant.

To reinforce the cultural capital afforded by the adaptation of a high-canonical work, Wright asked respected playwright and theatre director Tom Stoppard to write the screenplay. It was, however, Wright rather than Stoppard who chose the particular and provocative concept of staging, whereby from the very beginning most of the urban scenes are set within an enormous theatre. It is only when the disillusioned suitor returns to the countryside that we see a snow-covered landscape into which he walks, followed by the camera. The film opens on a shot of a theatre curtain, rising to reveal a painted backcloth which proclaims 'Imperial Russia 1874'. A barber crosses the stage with an operatic flourish and approaches his seated customer with exaggerated, balletic steps. We see Anna, reading the letter which will summon her to Moscow, over the head of a maid who circles her and dresses her, slipping a ring on her finger and smoothing the ruffles of her petticoat. The particular sequence of movements here, of raised and lowered arms, makes of this ritual a kind of *pas de deux*. Anna is finally readied, in a dress and peplum jacket of purple shot silk, as partner for Karenin in his grey, braided uniform. The office workers we see in Moscow and the guests at the fateful ball all move as if members of a *corps de ballet,* or the chorus of a grand opera, or – strangely – both. This careful choreography pervades the film, drawing attention to artifice of all kinds, whether of staging or styling.

We might ask what particular inflection of the heroine herself we find in this non-naturalistic version, wearing her near-theatrical costumes and ostentatious jewels, moving through stage sets and the vast auditorium that becomes in turn a frozen lake, a racecourse and grandstand, an opera house, a ballroom. Knightley's high-fashion credentials, her status as 'ambassadress' and icon, create one particular set of expectations; another is dictated by her casting history, her previous roles of strong heroines and active – even wilful – women. She also notably appeared in a film for the charity Women's Aid in 2009, once again under Wright's direction. And unlike her predecessors, she was very much part of a team, consulted as she explained in interviews, about both characterization and costuming. She was also extensively profiled in the run-up to the film's release, interviewed at the Toronto Film Festival, and again at an informal press conference in Beverley Hills, the results of which swiftly infiltrated the Internet and the blogosphere. Her reading of Tolstoy's heroine seemed to focus on Anna's sexual awakening, on her liberation from a stultifying marriage. This Anna is young and even selfish; her genuine love for her child is swiftly displaced by her tumultuous feelings for Vronsky.

Durran also gave a number of interviews to the press, explaining the concept behind the costumes. Here, the notion of 'period authenticity' is both respected and flouted, in order to render the display still more spectacular. Durran explained that Wright wanted her to focus on the silhouette, and she achieved this by referencing 1950s couture, by looking at the collections of Balenciaga and Dior, where the overall shapes were similar to those of the

1870s (interview with Phong Luu 2013). She also stressed the fact that the costumes were the result of teamwork and that she herself was 'adamantly against' symbolism in costume (interview with Phlong Luu 2013).

She did not mention extraneous elements beyond her control that filter into the film from the world of fashion, providing a context for the costumes that could perhaps affect our response to them. We might think of the extraordinary Chanel jewellery, with no narrative function whatsoever, or the casting of top model Cara Delevingne in a cameo role as the Princess Sorokhin. There seems, too, to be a deliberate referencing of Beaton's 1948 *Vogue* photographs of Charles James' ballgowns, in the posed groupings of partygoers at the palace.

There is certainly an extraordinarily strong costume narrative, though it does not operate in traditional Hollywood fashion. Adrian famously claimed that you could line up all the gowns in a film and 'they would tell the story' (Bruzzi 1997; Gaines 1990). Here, it is rather more complicated; dress becomes a spectacle in and of itself. The costumes do indeed tell a story, of Anna's awakened, requited and ultimately desperate passion, through their increasing opulence and extravagance. The dresses work together so perfectly with the spectacular sets and overall staginess that they are occasionally in danger of overwhelming the production. One very beautiful burgundy dress, with medieval sleeves lavishly decorated with pearls, is glimpsed as Anna puts her son to bed. It too seems to have no narrative function, to be yet another display of technical virtuosity, like the sets and the camerawork.

But in the main, the dress does work closely with the narrative, which focuses on the sexual relationship between Anna and Vronsky. This re-imagining of the heroine as a young woman in search of physical pleasure is reflected in the way in which the costumes tend towards a very particular mode of excess. The dresses may indeed have boned corsets, but they also have overly lavish skirts; blouses and nightwear are diaphanous, the opulent furs highly tactile. The continued veiling and unveiling of Anna's face throughout only heightens the erotic potential of period costume. Knightley herself said in interview:

> We wanted sex to be a big part […] a lot of the dresses were based on a kind of lingerie idea, that they're slightly falling off, or there's lace poking out. We actually used bed-linen fabric in one of the dresses to keep that kind of post-coital vibe […].
> (Interview with Tara Aquino for *Complex*, 16 November 2012)

Storytelling through dress also involved what Durran called 'visual markers' (interview with Phlong Luu 2013). The styling of Anna's sunlit picnic with Vronsky, at first romantic and then rather more carnal, shows us Anna's early trust through the pristine white linens in which both are dressed. In the closing shots of the film this is paralleled by a scene in a similar meadow, where Karenin sits reading while Anna's two children play. Anna wears a dramatic black outfit when she ignores the ban against visiting her son on his birthday. Set against this is a spectacular white gown, designed as the double of the ballgown in which she triumphed, which she wears for her humiliation at the opera, swathed with extraordinary white furs and set off with diamonds. We glimpse her alone in her final despair, in a harsh red kimono, smoking an uncharacteristic cigarette. Finally, she gets ready to follow Vronsky to the station, putting on purple figured silk and an extravagant hat that nods to the 1950s; Knightley spoke in interview of finding two paintings of 'the Whore of Babylon' before choosing the colour of this outfit (interview with Aquino 2012).

The clothes for the two 'set-piece' scenes, on the station and at the ball, both work within the traditional costume tradition associated with this heroine while adding notable dramatic – and highly photogenic – touches. Alighting from the train, Anna is dressed in a black coat bordered with thick, sensuous grey fur and embroidered with a dull gold paisley motif; she wears long, noticeable pearl and diamond earrings. At the ball, the other dancers in their pastel-hued dresses seem to withdraw so that Anna in black and Vronsky in white are dancing quite alone. Her black ballgown is notably off-the-shoulder, and her hair dressed with veiling and diamonds.

In the closing scenes of the film, after the central narrative of sexual passion has ended with sterile quarrelling, we now see Anna without her sumptuous overskirt, caged and hampered in the naked wire hoops of her crinoline. Knightley said in interview that she and Durran both saw Anna as 'a bird trapped in a cage'. And for the actress if not for Durran, the furs Anna wears represent death. She is 'suffocating herself in dead skin, trapping herself' (*Guardian* interview 2012). The stuffed birds adorning her hats, the stones around her face and neck – they too have the same connotations (*Guardian* interview 2012). The twinned imagery of sex and death that Knightley finds in her screen wardrobe evokes not only the wilder shores of psychoanalytic theory, but also a high-fashion memory of a specific catwalk moment in the late Alexander McQueen's 'Voss' show of 2001. The imagery here – and the theatricality of all his fashion shows – is something else that has surely fed into the reception of, and response to this film. These performances moved his couture clothes, highly theatrical in themselves, away from the confines of the catwalk into other spaces. And in the year before the film's release, the McQueen retrospective 'Savage Beauty' broke all entrance records at the Metropolitan Museum of Art in New York.

Every film reviewer praised Durran's costumes, as they might; by contrast, the film itself was a financial failure and received very mixed reviews. But fashion magazines ran high-profile features; the Internet was saturated with images from the film and bloggers posted their praises. Durran, who deservedly won an Oscar, had, however, agreed to work in a very different context when she signed up with high street retailer Banana Republic. She was hired to create an 'Anna Karenina' winter range to tie in with the release of the film. Durran and Simon Kneen, Banana Republic's Creative Director, both spoke of a seeming coincidence of inspiration, of what he called a 'kismet moment' (Leah Melby: interview for elle.com 2012). The same coincidence affected those working in high fashion, rather than on the high street. Ralph Lauren actually named his entire Fall/Winter Collection for 2012 the 'Anna Karenina' collection. Elsewhere on the catwalks that season, at Lanvin, Gucci, Valentino, Armani, Alexander McQueen and Rachel Comey among others, there were endless references to the accepted 'look' of the film: sumptuous dark fabrics, beautifully embellished and embroidered blouses, baroque touches and trimmings, fur collars and capes, high boots.

It seems as if what happens to the cinematic heroine of a lavishly costumed film in the new millennium is not that she is stripped of her agency within the narrative; it is rather that the narrative which unfolds on cinema screens simply takes its place within a multiplicity of narratives and images in the age of digital platforms and viral film. High street, couture collections, extravagant advertisements for designer brands, all feed into and extrapolate from the purported on-screen narrative. Magazines, both online and in print, will of course always fasten on something as visually lavish as the fashions of Russia in the 1870s. For just as the novel itself has been reworked for cinema and television, the clothes themselves have gradually become floating signifiers across the ages, detached somehow from the original story. Fashion pages such as 'Russian Winter' (*Glamour* magazine 2012), which combined high street offerings and designer labels, had an easy referent in this heavily mythologized heroine, who has now become wrenched from her original context.

The most successful and certainly the most visually spectacular magazine 'story' to follow the film showed in its very construction how the boundaries between fiction, fact and fashion had been blurred, if not obliterated. Grace Coddington styled a cover shoot and a fashion spread for US *Vogue* in October 2012, photographed by Mario Testino, which featured Knightley wearing a mixture of costumes from the film and current couture outfits, including a striking Valentino ballgown. More bizarre were the Louis Vuitton advertising images in the same season. The catwalk show had been staged in front of a nineteenth-century train. The campaigns showed a group of models inside a similar train, but wearing clothes that were accessorized in such a way as to suggest that the fictional literary world of Anna Karenina had somehow merged with that created for the television series *Downton Abbey*; the clothes, the hats and the holdalls evoked the early years of the twentieth century. The mix of visual and temporal signifiers once seen as typical of postmodernist practice and deemed to have some political potential is here reduced through its very fashionability to a mere exercise in marketing. High fashion seems to have successfully staked its claim to high-canonical literary texts, while the luxury brands have extended their fiefdom still further. Film discourses seemingly overlap with one another, forming a continuous parade of costumed images whose comparative weighting becomes ever more problematic.

The relations between feature film, fashion and forms of stardom are as strong as ever, but operate quite differently today; this chapter charts the process of change across the decades. In 1935, the film acted as a showcase for Garbo, herself almost a synonym for the Hollywood 'star system' at a time when screen actresses had become, for most women, their acknowledged 'fashion leaders'. In 1948, the film showed off the New Look to those outside the world of high fashion. In fact, it fed back into the work of leading couturiers, while providing more modest inspiration for home dressmakers. And in 2012, the production is almost a template for the workings of fashion and film within a changed media landscape. These three adaptations of the same novel also reveal how the dynamics of costuming and fashion influence plot, characterization and *mise-en-scène*, and hence the actual meaning of the adaptations. This practice is something needing further consideration within the developing field of adaptation studies.

References

Aquino, T. (2012), 'Interview with Kiera Knightley and Joe Wright', *Complex*, 16 November.

Basinger, J. (1994), *A Woman's View: How Hollywood Spoke to Women 1930–1960*, London: Chatto and Windus.

Berry, S. (2000), *Screen Style: Fashion and Femininity in 1930s Hollywood*, Minneapolis: University of Minnesota Press.

Bruzzi, S. (1997), *Undressing Cinema: Clothing and Identity in the Movies*, London: Routledge.

Capua, M. (2003), *Vivien Leigh: A Biography*, London: McFarland and Company.

Church Gibson, P. (2011), *Fashion and Celebrity Culture*, London: Berg.

Eckert, C. ([1987] 1990), 'The Carole Lombard in Macy's window', in J. Gaines and C. Herzog (eds), *Fabrications: Costume and the Female Body*, London and New York: Routledge.

Haskell, M. ([1974] 1987), *From Reverence to Rape: The Treatment of Women in the Movies*, London: Penguin Books.

Kaplan, E. A. (1978), *Women in Film Noir*, London: BFI.

Lavalley, S. (1987), 'Hollywood and Seventh Avenue: The impact of period films on fashion', in E. Maeder (ed.), *Hollywood and History: Costume Design in Film*, New York: Thames and Hudson.

Luu, P. (2013), 'Interview with Jacqueline Durran', *Daily Telegraph*, 30 January.

Maeder, E. (1987), 'The celluloid image: Historical dress on film', in E. Maeder (ed.), *Hollywood and History: Costume Design in Film*, New York: Thames and Hudson.

Melby, L. (2012), 'Banana Republic takes on Anna Karenina', elle.com, 13 July, http://www.elle.com/news/fashion-style/banana-republic-anna-karenina-collection-interview. Accessed 12 July 2013.

Mosley, C. (ed.) (1993), *Love from Nancy: The Letters of Nancy Mitford*, London: Sceptre.

Smith, Claire and Morris, Nathalie (2014), 'Anna Karenina: on-screen style icon', BFI, 24 April, http://www.bfi.org.uk/news/anna-karenina-screen-style-icon. Accessed 16 November 2017.

Solomons, J. (2012), 'Interview with Kiera Knightley', *The Guardian*, 2 September.

Tolstoy, L. ([1877] 1966), *Anna Karenina*, London: The Reprint Society.

Vickers, H. (2009), *Vivien Leigh: A Biography*, New York: Little, Brown and Company.

Wilson, E. (1985), *Adorned in Dreams: Fashion and Modernity*, London: Virago.

Zmuda, N. (2013), 'Interview with Catherine Sadler of Banana Republic', *Advertising Age*, 25 March.

Chapter 2

The Desire for Change and Contrast: Fashion in Soviet Films between 1956 and 1985

Julia Hargassner

Fashion in the Soviet Union is a fascinating and controversial subject that has not yet been investigated from potential perspectives. Soviet fashion was influenced by the idea of total control conducted by the Soviet government. Nevertheless, the dichotomy of fashion formulated by Georg Simmel as the wish to belong, and the need for self-differentiation, can be observed in the USSR as well. Proceeding from Emma Widdis' point that clothes carry meaning (see Church Gibson in this volume), I claim that film costumes can be used as a referential point for the analysis of social, economic and inner life of the people in the Soviet Union. Accordingly the chapter explores a variety of relations between the film costumes and everyday life, social history as well as the gender constructions, as they are presented in the following films: *Karnaval'naya noch'* (*Carnival Night*) (Ryazanov, 1956), *Brilliantovaya ruka* (*The Diamond Arm*) (Gaidai, 1968), *Sluzhebnyi roman* (*Office Romance*) (Ryazanov, 1977), and *Samaya obayatel'naya i privlekatel'naya* (*The Most Charming and Attractive*) (Bezhanov, 1985).

Fashion as a Marker of Social Adaptation and Differentiation

At the beginning of the twentieth century, the German sociologist Georg Simmel describes fashion as a cultural factor encompassing different spheres of material, social, psychological and economic life. Simmel states in his fundamental study *Die Philosophie der Mode* (*Fashion*) (Simmel 1971) two vital conditions of fashion. Firstly, 'fashion is the imitation of a given example and satisfies the demand for social adaptation' (Simmel 1971: 296) and secondly, fashion 'satisfies in no less degree the need of differentiation', that is to say 'the desire for change and contrast' (Simmel 1971: 296). Fashion, he argues, is driven on the one hand by the wish of belonging and on the other by the need for self-differentiation (Simmel 1971: 301) and he emphasizes that fashion is 'a product of class distinction' (Simmel 1971: 297) which 'on the one hand signifies union with those in the same class, [...] and, *uno actu*, the exclusion of all other groups' (Simmel 1971: 297, original emphasis). Moreover, 'social forms are constantly transformed by fashion, in such a way, that the latest fashion affects only the upper classes' (Simmel 1971: 299). In this way, Simmel expounds the integral criteria of fashion in western societies, but its existence in Soviet society presages the equality of all its citizens as being more complex and contested.

Fashion and Attire in Soviet Cinema 1956–85

In this chapter, I will investigate four Soviet films, one per a decade, directed between 1956 and 1985, showing the changes in perception and attitude to fashion in the Soviet Union. The choice of films was influenced by their degree of popularity among the Soviet audience.[1] The chapter continues the analytical sequence of the articles treating the question of the relationship between Soviet fashion and Soviet cinema from the 1930s to the end of the 1940s, which has been the focus of former historical, sociological, economic and cultural investigations.[2] Films released in this time span, from Stalin's death up to the beginning of the Perestroika, have not yet been analysed within the context of fashion theory. As I will argue, not only did fashion exist in the Soviet Union, as becomes clear in these films, but also Georg Simmel's dichotomy of fashion (Simmel 1971: 301) can be observed at work here and is also valid for understanding the role of fashion in the Soviet Union. I will take Roland Barthes' analysis of written clothing, *Sisteme de la Mode* (*The Fashion System*) (Barthes 1983) as the basis for the significance of the vestimentary sign in conveying meaning. In what follows, I will first provide a brief overview of the discourse of Soviet fashion from the 1920s to the 1960s; then I will describe and analyse costumes in Soviet films set against the cultural and historical background in order to present how fashion is articulated in these films, and how they communicate the moral values and social tendencies of Soviet society through fashion. Essentially, I would like to spell out what fashion narratives actually impart in Soviet films between 1956 and 1985, the period from Stalin's death, during the 'Thaw', through the 'Stagnation' period, up to the 'Perestroika' to determine what they tell us about the social aspects of fashion in the Soviet Union. This chapter will trace the changes that Soviet fashion has undergone over 30 years in terms of the following research questions: What fashion styles are displayed in these films?; What meaning do film costumes convey?; Is it possible to observe particular social and economic changes in Soviet society of this period through filmic clothing? In this way, the development of Soviet fashion, as it is presented in Soviet films, will be compared with fashion trends of this period in order to observe the influence of film costumes on audience and the impact that fashion has on film costumes. Costume and fashion in these films also enable the tracing of social and economic changes that took place in the Soviet Union during these years.

Vestimentary Signs as Source of Meaning in Film: The Utterance and the Look

The French structuralist, Roland Barthes, in his study, *Sisteme de la Mode* (*The Fashion System*) (1967, 1983) substantiated the idea of conveying meaning through clothing. Essentially, Barthes applied the linguistic structural method in his sociological investigation of clothes and fashion within the scope of the semiotics. Barthes proposed that, 'The vestimentary sign can include several fragments of signifiers [...] and several fragments of signifieds' (Barthes 1983: 213), whereas any particular fragment of the former does not necessarily correspond to any other particular fragment of the latter. Observing the relation between the signifier and the signified, Barthes showcases how the fashion sign 'possesses the point of meaning' (Barthes 1983: 214) and presents a 'complex syntagm, formed by a syntax of elements' (Barthes 1983: 214). 'The garment, which itself is already a system of signification' (Barthes 1983: 9) is the focus of the following investigation. Hence, fashion signs as they are presented in the Soviet films reveal vestimentary and fashion codes in the Soviet Union between 1956 and 1985 giving insights into the social and cultural life of the country.

Adrienne Munich's book *Fashion in Film* explores 'the vital synergy between dress and the cinema, a force as old as film itself' (Munich 2011: 1) in order to illustrate the connections between fashion and film encompassing different layers of meaning, 'aesthetic, commercial, patriotic, political' (Munich 2011: 2). Whereas Barthes uses the term 'fashion utterance' to describe written clothing (Barthes 1983: 226), Munich operates with the term 'the look' which 'refers to an ensemble of visual signs in attire that orients the viewer by its simultaneous strangeness and familiarity and, at a glance, conveys meanings' (Munich 2011: 3).

Proceeding from this thesis that clothes carry meaning (Barthes 1983: 9; Widdis 2008: 49; Munich 2011: 3), I claim that film costumes may be used as a point of reference for an analysis of the social, economic and inner life of people in the Soviet Union. Correspondingly, I intend to explore a whole variety of possible relations between the film costumes and Soviet daily life, social history as well as gender constructions, as presented in these films. To effect this, the analysis specifically focuses on the language of clothes in the following Soviet films: *Karnaval'naya noch'* (*Carnival Night*) (Ryazanov, 1956), *Brilliantovaya ruka* (*The Diamond Arm*) (Gaidai, 1968), *Sluzhebnyi roman* (*Office Romance*) (Ryazanov, 1977) and *Samaya obayatel'naya i privlekatel'naya* (*The Most Charming and Attractive*) (Bezhanov, 1985). Finally, vestimentary signs will be analysed expressing the mechanisms of belonging and differentiation as distinctive features of fashion in film.

All of these films represent the same genre, the (musical) comedy, as the Soviet state was one of the most important transmitters of dominant ideological values (Dashkova 2007: 151). The musical comedy was an appropriate means to depict everyday life in the Soviet Union, because it added softer elements to the social representations (Widdis 2008: 60) by showing socialist reality according to the conventions of the entertainment genre. The comedy was one of the most popular cinematic genres in the Soviet Union, since it was both amusing and easy for the audience to understand and enabled the regime to manipulate viewers' mindsets creating an enhanced vision of Soviet reality.

Fashion in the Soviet Union is a fascinating and controversial subject, which has not yet been investigated in all its complexity and manifold perspectives. Compared with western capitalist fashion, which according to Simmel combines, 'the tendency towards social equalization with the desire for individual differentiation and change' (Simmel 1971: 296), Soviet fashion can hardly be seen as an expression of individuality. In 'Dressing the Part: Clothing Otherness in Soviet Cinema before 1953', British cultural historian Emma

Widdis analyses costume designs in Soviet films from the 1930s up to the death of the Totalitarian leader, Joseph Stalin, in 1953. Widdis provides a brief survey of the ideological imperative of Soviet clothing during this era by analysing four films from the 1930s and 1940s. Widdis states that cinema had a crucial role in the formation of the ideology of Soviet dress (Widdis 2008: 51) which 'was an ideological imperative, a means first distinguishing the Soviet world from the West, and second, within that Soviet world, of distinguishing the good and the bad, the loyal citizen from the saboteur or class enemy' (Widdis 2008: 51). The concept of Soviet fashion was thus constituted by the ideas of practicality, functionality and hygiene (Zakharova 2013: 403) with the opening of the Central House of Fashion in Moscow in 1934, signifying the start of Soviet state run fashion. Prior to this, in the 1920s, one of the most known Soviet designers of the time, such as Nadezhda Lamanova, developed and propagated rules for combining 'the right elements in dress which became the criteria for "good taste"' (Zakharova 2010: 100) and represented a key formation in the concept of Soviet fashion. The attributes of good taste consisted of 'a combination of simplicity and a sense of proportion' (Gurova 2009: 78), as well as softness, modesty and self-control (Gradskova 2014: 127). Soviet designers had to educate the taste of Soviet consumers within the campaign for *kul'turnost'* in the second half of the 1930s (Zakharova 2010: 100). The comprehensive and complex notion of *kul'turnost'* covered a broad scope of knowledge and practices from fashion and hygiene to language and reading, and pursued the aim of self-cultivation and self-development of Soviet people (Papushina 2014: 6). The Russian historian Larissa Zakharova calls Soviet clothing designers civil servants discharging both artistic and industrial tasks, which were 'subordinated to the interests of the garment industry' (Zakharova 2010: 99). Soviet fashion was thus part and parcel of the total control, aimed at by the state: 'In the Soviet context, as a result of the well-known tendency of the party-state apparatus to regiment everyday life, one cannot speak of fashion without reference to policy' (Zakharova 2013: 402). From the 1930s, the Soviet regime was apparently doing its best to create Soviet fashion 'from above' so that it corresponded to the main principle of the socialist way of life, as promulgated by the USSR Constitution of 1936, '[f]rom each according to their abilities, to each according to their needs' (S"ezd Sovetov [The Communist Party Congress] 1937: 287). Zakharova explains this rhetoric being an intention to 'manipulate and regulate material needs' (Zakharova 2013: 403) of Soviet citizens. Hence, Russian sociologist, Olga Gurova sees the phenomenon of Soviet fashion as an oxymoron (Gurova 2009: 73), which she bases on three claims. Firstly, she refers to the work of British historian; Djurdja Bartlett who affirms that Soviet fashion mainly existed in the form of officially approved socialist dress, which largely remained unchanged (Bartlett 2005: 141–42). Gurova further questions the very existence of fashion in the USSR as, '[o]fficial socialist dress was a prisoner of time, as socialism mainly neglected changes in favour of stability, that's why it always looked a bit out of fashion' (Gurova 2009: 73). Secondly, she cites the long production circle of clothing made in the USSR as slowing up the fashion cycle (Gurova 2009: 73). Thirdly, uniformity was considered as the norm and as an integral feature of fashion and where differentiation was rejected in the Soviet official discourse (Gurova 2009: 73). Power and ideology are integral components of fashion discourse, since ideology, according to Barthes, corresponds to meanings that are ascribed to cultural objects like clothes, images, words (Barthes 2000; Gurova 2006: 91). In exploring the ideological context of Soviet consumption history Gurova defines ideology as, 'a system of concepts, ideas, myths and images by means of which people understand, estimate and experience real conditions of their existence' (Gurova 2006: 97). In *Dress and Ideology* Marzel and Stiebel (2015) investigate the relationship between ideology and clothing by differentiating clothing and fashion on the principle of the changeability of dress. Here, clothing innovations are seen as dangerous in challenging 'stability, tradition and their endless repetition' (Marzel and Stiebel 2015: 3). On the contrary, fashion innovations encourage individuality and novelty (Marzel and Stiebel 2015: 2). To support this, they cite the example of the Chinese Communist Party that used clothing to express 'values of simplicity, equality and solidarity according to the communist ethos' (Marzel and Stiebel 2015: 4) echoing Soviet society to the end of Stalin's era. The following section will turn to the analysis of the musical comedies and the application of these notions.

Analysing Fashion and Attire in the Film *Carnival Night*

In 1956 the young director El'dar Ryazanov released his first film, a musical comedy, *Karnaval'naya noch'* (*Carnival Night*) (Ryazanov, 1956), whose narrative featured the organization and the execution of a New Year's Eve carnival party in the House of Culture (*dom kul'tury*), a Soviet recreation centre. The main character in the film and the party hostess is the young, attractive member of the Komsomol committee, Lena Krylova, played by Lyudmila Gurchenko. Lena's antagonist is the manager, comrade Kuznetsov, who rejects the exciting event planned by the young girl. This intrigue and opposition to the party planning is the basis of the storyline. *Carnival Night* is a visually impressive film capturing feelings of joy, celebration and hope, exploiting fashion as an instrument for advertising the Soviet way of life. The film contains a great number of musical and circus acts, some of them displaying unconventional behaviour for the still relatively conservative Soviet Union of the time. Hence, the musicians play jazz, and the dancers tap-dance skilfully representing features more characteristic of an American party than a traditional Soviet celebration. Every Soviet film was heavily censored from the first censor commission at the film studio through the USSR committee of cinematography with the final permission given by the Culture Department of the Central Committee of the Communist Party of the USSR (Kuznetsov 2009). So, why did the Communist party censors allow the distribution of this liberal film?

The shooting of the film *Carnival Night* took place in 1956, 3 years after Stalin's death. In the same year, at the XXth Congress of the Communist Party, Nikita Khrushchev announced changes in foreign and internal policy allowing more contacts with foreign and capitalist countries, such as France and Italy. Gurova noted that Soviet fashion during the whole period of its existence has been strongly influenced by Soviet ideology[3] and defines the 1950s and 1960s in the USSR as 'the period of the ideology of Soviet taste':

> The rise of the idea of Soviet taste can be explained as a reaction to ideological competition with America and other so-called 'bourgeois' countries, to the penetration of patterns of Western culture and fashion, and to the distribution of consumer-type values in the daily life of Soviet people.
>
> (Gurova 2006: 95)

Consumption was thus legitimated and became a potent political force in the competition between the USSR and the West. Bartlett describes the change from a totalitarian to a symbolical mode of control in the 1950s in the USSR (Bartlett 2004), as the Soviet state offered the 'middle class' a better life style in exchange for its support of the Soviet system (Gurova 2009: 77). The concept of Soviet taste implied correct behaviour in choosing consumer goods that corresponded to the accepted Soviet life style as, 'taste formed a common symbolic space for different social groups in Soviet culture' (Gurova 2006: 95) and 'Soviet discourse on fashion and clothes,' was 'built around the opposition of the Soviet lifestyle versus bourgeois or capitalist life style at this time' (Gurova 2006: 95). In this film, Soviet youth enjoy life at their New Years Eve celebration in the House of Culture in parallel with the leisure activities of western youth. This implies that the entertaining genre of the film, in consideration of the Soviet way of life propaganda, gave the director an opportunity to show performances that could be marked out as capitalist or western and to present film costumes that could be identified clearly as Dior's style. In fact, Dior's New Look appeared in Soviet films 10 years after its launch in Paris, young in the spring of 1947. Dior's five-day fashion show came to Moscow in 1959 where he presented his latest collection as the first official fashion show of western designers in the Soviet Union. Only 1,100 people were invited to the show representing the Soviet elite. Larissa Zakharova notes that ballet artists from the Bolshoi Theatre occupied all of the seats at one of the fashion shows (Zakharova 2013: 425). Nevertheless, ordinary Muscovites also had an opportunity to encounter western fashion when Dior's models went out into the streets of Moscow completely styled wearing Dior's dresses. This extraordinary event is documented in unique photographs commissioned in *Life* magazine:

> For the Russians the biggest attraction was a team of 12 shapely Dior models from Paris who flew in to show off a million and a half dollars' worth of shapely fashions. Russian women, who are more used to the baggy babushka look, were enchanted.
>
> (Anon. 1959: 32)

These images show a rare, yet calm confrontation between the two different ideological systems and lifestyles at the time. An ordinary, modest and grey Soviet world encountered a stylish and colourful western world represented by Dior's hyper stylish fashion. The film's costume director, Konstantin Efimov, also used Dior's fashion patterns when creating costumes for the main heroine, Lenochka, such as gorgeous evening dresses with the typical hourglass shape. The seductive charm of the so-called New Look dresses of the party hostess is emphasized pointedly by the actress's tiny waist measurement of only 44 centimetres. Uncharacteristically for a Soviet girl, Lena changes her dresses five times during one evening. On the one hand, all of Lena's hyper-elegance dresses are extraordinarily impressive and do not correspond to the traditional Soviet dress characterized by 'comfort, practicality, functionality and hygiene' (Zakharova 2013: 403). On the other hand, according to the film's narrative, they belong to an ordinary Soviet girl making sense through oppositional meanings 'progressive – conservative, up-to-date – outdated'. The discrepancy of the look and the vestimental utterance can be explained as a reaction to ideological competition with the West, thereby aiming to transmit a feeling of Soviet sufficiency.

The delicate elegance of Lena's dress in the closing scene of *Carnival Night* can be definitely traced back to aesthetic influences from the stylish western world. Wearing a long, black, sparkling dress with white fur muff, Lena embodies complete prosperity. Her outfit is a sign of Soviet affluence and success. Typical of this era, Soviet ideology tried to prove the dominance of Socialism by the means of the use of luxury items in films, such as a fur muff, a fur cape or long gloves (Zakharova 2013: 425). It was difficult to find such pieces in the wardrobe of ordinary Soviet people, but for the elite they were relatable. In her discussion of fashion under Khrushchev, Larissa Zakharova states that in spite of the claim, 'luxury had to become accessible to all members of the society of equals as evidence of the advantages of socialism' (Zakharova 2010: 99), 'luxury models were destined for privileged Soviet social categories and marked a symbolic distinction in Soviet society' (Zakharova 2010: 107). The British cultural historian Church Gibson, treats Dior's New Look in post-war France as a reassertion of 'Parisian supremacy in the world of couture' (Gibson 2012: 199) on the one hand, and 'a reassertion of class supremacy after the seeming democracy of the war years' (Gibson 2012: 199) on the other. In the Soviet Union, these both tendencies can be observed as well, since Parisian fashion conquered the hearts of Soviet women and revealed social differentiation at the same time.

Carnival Night operated, so to speak, as a 'megaphone' of fashion in the USSR. After its first night opening, the New Look style began to spread throughout the Soviet Union, so Larissa Zakharova, who states that Lyudmila Gurchenko, alias Lena, had 'infected' the whole of the USSR with Dior's New Look style (Zakharova 2013: 425). As a consequence, women of all ages endeavoured to make their waists tiny and wore hyper-feminine, taffeta dresses with numerous layers of underskirts. So it became a landmark in the development of Soviet fashion as represented in the film depicting a role model for Soviet women, and – remarkable as it is – one that was sourced from an iconic western fashion designer. The short-lived amity of the Soviet Union towards the West facilitated a moment of fashion transfer and caused a temporary convergence of cultural representation, which can also be found in another film under analysis here.

Analysing Fashion and Attire in the Film *The Diamond Arm*

Brilliantovaya ruka (*The Diamond Arm*) (Gaidai, 1968) by Leonid Gaidai is an innovative text with respect to the gender-specific representation of fashion in Soviet films. The film's storyline deals with a gang of contrabandists, who illegally bring jewellery into the USSR from abroad as the Soviet police struggle to capture them yet eventually win. The ordinary accountant, Semen Gorbunkov, becomes an accidental police assistant in this affair becoming unwittingly embroiled in the gang's work.

The gang consisting of four members, with Gesha Kozodoev played by Andrei Mironov, is of special interest to our fashion discourse. Gesha is a young man who devotes a lot of his time to dressing in a foreign fashion style, often changing his outfits, but always staying true to his core look sporting fashionable, narrow single-breasted suits and turtleneck sweaters, instead of traditional shirts. The latter trend can be dated to Paris, 1967, where the French fashion designer Pierre Cardin introduced turtleneck sweaters as a new male fashion trend (Osipova 2014). In the following year these Cardin-like sweaters appeared in the film with a swift take up of this foreign fashion style that can be explained by the close contact between Soviet and French filmmakers. Some Soviet film stars, like Andrei Mironov, with a reputation as a follower of fashion, had the opportunity to participate in Soviet delegations at this time to Western Europe and observed western fashion with their own eyes.

This period marked a thaw in relations between the USSR and the West seeing an increase in accessibility to foreign consumer goods, including clothing. The uptake of western fashion in the Soviet Union, both legal and illegal, took on different guises, mainly accessed by a select social set of people. Hence, the first trade agreements for elite consumer goods clearly influenced the development of Soviet fashion. In the 1960s, trade exhibitions by foreign companies took place in the Soviet Union where exhibited goods were not intended for mass trade, but were distributed among the Soviet elite (see Adtseeva 2012). Commercial contracts were one of the main official channels for western fashion to enter into the USSR (Zakharova 2013: 62). Nevertheless, it should be mentioned that this trade was based not only on legal contacts, as in 1955 some Soviet artists, notably the parents of Andrei Mironov namely, Alekasndr Menaker and Mariya Mironova, bought American clothes from smugglers in Odessa (Zakharova 2013: 426) suggesting that Soviet celebrities also did not always have an option to buy fashionable western clothes often resorting to illegal ways.

The costume plot in *The Diamond Arm* clearly highlights the theme of identity and belonging, of being Soviet or not. Ordinary Soviet citizens featured in the film wear common, modest clothes; the negatively marked gang members are conspicuous because of their fashionable western clothes where being on trend is a sign of a being dubious character. In this respect, Soviet film costume was used to define character in a traditional sense allowing visible and vestimentary markings only for system breakers such as spies, followers of western fashion style and other negative characters in the plot (Widdis 2008: 59). The 'invisibility' of the characters' costumes is a sign of the simplicity and innocence of their owners and represents a sense of belonging to the Soviet community (Dashkova 2007: 155).

Interestingly, the only female gang member, played by Svetlana Svetlichnaya, embodies elegance and sex appeal. She wears a white trouser suit emphasizing her femininity and is the first Soviet heroine who dares to do a striptease on screen. This fashionable young woman does not fit into the Soviet system with respect to her outfits and her behaviour, breaking with the tradition of puritanical female representation in Soviet films. The 1960s in the USSR are said to be the first decade of 'conscious' Soviet fashion (Adtseeva 2012) when the Soviet population became conscious of the existence and significance of fashion: 'During the Khrushchev period, Soviet fashion remained the subject of debate that centered on its role and place in socialist society' (Zakharova 2013: 428). Young women began to wear miniskirts in Moscow and Leningrad, while the most courageous even dared to put on trouser suits. Yet, newspapers at the time reported cases when women in trouser suits were not allowed to enter offices and restaurants (Adtseeva 2012) as the Soviet public regarded women in trouser suits as an affront to Soviet society. In 1966, the French fashion designer Yves St Laurent introduced his 'City' trouser suit for ladies in Paris and in time the female trouser suit came to compensate for gender inequality by playing 'the same role as a man's suit' (The Metropolitan Museum of Art 2000). The American art and dress historian Anne Hollander expounds the connotation of men's dress:

There is [...] something perpetually more *modern* about male dress itself that has always made it inherently more desirable than female dress. It is not just the sign of power in the world, or of potency in the head, nor has it ever generally been more physically comfortable, but since the late Middle Ages, male dress also has had a certain fundamental aesthetic superiority, a more advanced seriousness of visual form not suggested by the inventors of fashion for women in the past.

(Hollander 1994: 39–40)

The idea of transferring men's superiority to women with the help of the trouser suit for everyday life challenged many in the USSR as it required some openness of mind. The suit, as a mix of feminine and masculine, also encountered resistance in Europe. The Metropolitan Museum of Art provides the following reference:

Although trousers had been acceptable as an element of orientalizing ensembles, for sport, as loungewear, and as an expression of iconoclasm by celebrities like Greta Garbo, Marlene Dietrich, and Katharine Hepburn, they had never been acceptable townwear for a fashionable woman. This radical shift is commensurate with the remarkable ascent of women in society during the 1970s.

(The Metropolitan Museum of Art 2000)

The process of adopting trouser suits in the USSR lasted almost a decade and was accompanied by various misunderstandings, including the confusion over the boundary between male and female representation, which maybe explains an unwillingness to accept this garment. But, in 1970, the All-Soviet Union House of Fashion recommended outfits with trousers for women as a new fashion trend (Gurova 2009: 83). So, the negative reaction of the Soviet population in the 1960s may be less surprising than it might seem at first glance.

The negative female character in this comedy is dressed according to the traditional distinctive principle of visibility from the 1930s and 1940s. Hence, the new fashion trend found a prompt embodiment in Soviet comedy in the traditional depiction of negative characters. The character, Gesha, a male model participating in a fashion show in the film, demonstrates another break from gender role depiction. Besides, Gesha displays non-traditional patterns of behaviour choosing handkerchiefs to correspond with his ties as he powders his nose. This character's behaviour does not correspond with the archetypal image of the Soviet man, who as a rule manifests no interest in fashion or any conscious self-representation. At the same time, it can be seen as an indirect critique of the shortcomings of the Soviet fashion industry unable to produce qualitative and fashionable clothes for the wider population. Hence, the casual trouser suit that Gesha wears on the catwalk could not be transformed into shorts, as originally planned by the designer, so that a fabrication defect makes Gesha look ridiculous. But at the end of the 1960s, this character type is not perceived as one who represents a different gender model, but a comic one. Interestingly, Gesha, an apparently negative figure, became a role model for many young men in the Soviet Union, and after the film's release many people wore turtleneck sweaters with narrow single-breasted suits paying more attention to their appearance.

Taken together, these different characters and their vestimentary signs, continue the traditions of the Soviet film costume in *The Diamond Arm*, where western style costumes are the once again domain of negative characters. However, in this film men enter the domain of fashion, which so far had been marked as a female domain, thereby presenting new role models.

Analysing Fashion and Attire in *Office Romance*

The second of El'dar Ryazanov's films in this analysis is the melodramatic comedy *Sluzhebnyi roman* (*Office Romance*) (Ryazanov, 1977). The film depicts a love story that takes place in a Moscow-based statistical institution in the 1970s. The female director, Lyudmila Kalugina, played by Alisa Freindlich, and her employee, Anatolii Novosel'tsev, played by Andrey Myagkov, fall in love with each other despite some crucial differences in their social positions.

In what follows, I will focus on the visual transformation of the heroine in this film. At the beginning, Lyudmila is a bluestocking, determined to concentrate on her career wearing inexpressive clothes and her coat, suit and shoes are neutral and genderless in every respect in addition to rejecting make-up and hair styling. As the chief of a large state institution, she instinctively emphasizes masculine features and pays little attention to feminine ones. Staff in her institution considers Lyudmila to be a frump. Nevertheless, Lyudmila's career success does not satisfy her wish for love and private happiness and fashion becomes one of the central components of the heroine's wish fulfilment.

The secretary Verochka is Lyudmila's foil – a young woman who pays a lot of attention to fashion. As proof of this, in one main scene, she is seen wearing a blue blouse with embroidered motives, black bell-bottoms and multiple beaded necklaces often sourcing trendy clothes from black market dealers, *fartsovshchiki*. This attire signifies a typical, fashionable Soviet woman from the mid-1970s. Elements of contemporary fashion trends are present in her dress: folk style, blue jeans and a slight hippy style. Hence, it is almost impossible to tell Verochka apart from a European woman of that time. Verochka's job is only a duty for her, as the main focus of her interest is on her appearance, on fashionable clothes and her private life. However, it should be mentioned that privately Verochka is not so successful as her husband left her recently, and so it becomes obvious that fashion cannot secure personal success in life. The contrasting characters of Lyudmila and Verochka are brought together by means of their conversations about fashion and appearance as Lyudmila starts to ask her secretary for style advice. In a comedic scene, when Lyudmila is confused and shows an interest in fashion trends for the first time, Verochka presents the main principles of how to look feminine and how to be fashionable by advising her to buy a trendy, slim-line shirt and blazer, fashionable shoes from the main department store in Moscow, while also placing emphasis on making up her face where the eyes and the eyebrows should be styled perfectly. Fashion, in Verochka's opinion, does not exclusively mean trendy clothes, but is rather the entire image of a contemporary woman. On the verge of the 1980s, fashion was an acknowledged realm of Soviet life and every citizen had the right to follow it as long as new fashion trends did not exceed the limits of official Soviet norms (Gurova 2006: 99). This is why Verochka's modest, yet encouraging advice concerning fashion and femininity fits the ideologically controlled discourse of Soviet fashion. The light content of the film reflected how fashion was treated and sanctioned in the USSR, in line with the current ideological attitude of the Communist Party.

Fashion is often used to indicate one's place in a particular social structure (Barnard 2002: 19). At first sight, it seems to contradict the top-down mechanism on which fashion generally rests, when the upper class heroine adopts the advice of her secretary, representing a definitively lower social stratum. This exception is compensated by the light film genre. Initially Lyudmila does not look like a representative of the Soviet elite and only gains a fashionable appearance to help fulfil this goal. At the end of the film, when a transformed Lyudmila returns to the office, her staff cannot recognize her. The changes are considerable: she is a young, attractive and fashionable woman, who pays a lot of attention to her appearance. This also causes changes in Lyudmila's social behaviour as she becomes more friendly, feminine and sociable. The message of the film is clear: everyone should keep abreast of fashion in order to be up-to-date. The Soviet state needs bright and attractive leaders, who can be successful in both business and private life. In other words, fashion is a significant component leading to the social acceptance of the heroine.

Analysing Fashion and Attire in *The Most Charming and Attractive*

In Gerald Bezhanov's comedy *Samaya obayatel'naya i privlektel'naya* (*The Most Charming and Attractive*) (Bezhanov, 1985) fashion does not effect any social changes, but does reflect the everyday situation in the USSR where both fashion and film production are directly connected with the country's economic situation. *The Most Charming and Attractive* was released at the very end of the Stagnation period in the USSR and the critical economic circumstances became apparent in the film's budget. The film studio Mosfil'm could not supply the staff with film costumes, and the lack of a shooting budget required the film crew to be highly inventive to compensate for this. Hence, the actresses Irina Murav'eva and Larisa Udovichenko had to bring their own clothes onto the film set (Osipova 2011).[4] This comedy film is explicitly concerned with the contradiction of fashion and moral ideals as a means of revealing true moral values of the heroine. A young woman, Nadya Klyueva, played by Irina Murav'eva, is unhappy at being a single, so her experienced psychologist friend, Susanna, suggests a solution for eliminating this shortcoming by embracing a wide range of activities, from autohypnosis to changing her wardrobe. In order to modify Nadya's plain appearance, Nadya and Susanna visit a black market dealer, a *fartsovshchik,* who offers to sell them a collection of clothes from a fur coat up to a Pierre Cardin suit. Nadya's remarks, while choosing and trying on clothes, are worth noting: 'To put it on for the office is not modest, for visiting a theatre – too defiant'. This comment reflects the discourse of Soviet taste, initiated in the 1950s, using modesty as one of its main determiners. The desire to be fashionable forces Nadya to buy cord trousers, French boots and a stylish pullover from the dealer. After almost 30 years, the appearance of the notion of Soviet good taste, the modifiers *modest* and *plain* still determine the vestimentary behaviour of an ordinary young woman.

Hence, in the 1980s the USSR saw clothes as a sign of social status and a reflection of wealth. Clothing produced in capitalist countries provided a better image for their owners and well-dressed people were called '*upakovan v firmu*' ('packed in brand'). The Soviet magazine, *Rabotnitsa* (*Working Woman*), highlighted four fashion styles in the mid-1980s: male, the female, sporty and the vanguard style (Adtseeva 2012). Nadya's clothing choice is interesting as she buys pieces that can hardly be referred to as a defined style, and at most are characteristic of a mixture of styles. Her main criterion for choosing clothes is the origin of production. In order to achieve a higher status in her office Nadya thus purchases foreign branded garments thereby attracting the attention of her office colleagues. The following conversation detects characteristic features of Soviet culture in the mid-1980s on the verge of the 'Perestroika' One of Nadya's male colleagues states, while staring at her, '[e]ven the most retrograde sections of population wear jeans trousers now'. Nadya wants to be accepted by the recognized office fashionista, so she mentions that she possesses unique imported jeans that only a couple of diplomats own. This short conversation shows in a nutshell the eternal Soviet elite access to, and desire for foreign clothing and its distribution. The social elite had access to the most fashionable clothing, while the rest of society tried its best to emulate this. This top-down principle of fashion distribution was always active in the USSR, across all consumer segments.

In the context of belonging and differentiation, Nadya's vestimentary activities are symbolic demonstrating her quest for self-confidence and self-representation. She wants to belong to the same set as her young colleagues, and realizes the necessity of fashionable clothes to achieve that. Yet, once she is accepted on this basis Nadya realizes its emptiness as relationships based on the one and only feature of being fashionable have no content or meaning. To follow fashion does not mean to be a better person; the empty shell of wearing clothing is not sufficient for determining the real moral essence of a person. The inner conflict of an individual within a disintegrating Soviet society can be observed in this melodrama. The conflict can be understood only if we consider the socio-economic situation of the time. The film displays the last attempts to preserve the Socialist idea of the dominance of the intellectual considerations over material goods as the Soviet Union in the 1970s and 1980s are a period of de-materialization: 'The Soviet person was not supposed to be obsessed with or adorating of things, rather, he should look upon them in a functional way' (Gurova 2006: 97). In the 1980s, a new concept of consumption culture replaced this ideology. Also, by the mid-1980s an orientation towards material values took place, which was to become increasingly predominant in post-socialist Russia. On the one hand, Nadya wants to follow the majority, yet on the other hand, she does not want to abandon her moral values in favour of material values. Fashion with its mechanism of belonging and differentiation reveals the inner conflict in the heroine.

The costume narrative of the film tracks Nadya's way to developing her self-confidence. In the beginning, the heroine believes that being a good person is enough for personal success. However, in the middle of the film Nadya defers to her friend Susanna's tastes hoping that being fashionable is the best way to find a partner, and by the end of the film Nadya puts on slightly modified clothes and returns to her initial moral values. The craving for fashion does not satisfy the young woman, as she prefers being judged by her heart, not by her appearance. In this comedy, fashion is set in opposition to morality. In the end, morality wins and fashion and its immoral temptations are defeated.[5]

Conclusion

From the very beginning, the Soviet state claimed to create different spheres of life anew in the Soviet way, and the world of fashion was no exception. Fashion discourse in the period went through various phases, from abandonment to the more conscious use of the concept that there should be a distinctly Soviet form of clothing. Soviet dress, if we may generalize its concept, never corresponded to the basic principles of fashion: it slowly underwent change; 'Being the prisoner of time, Soviet dress lived an eternal life, which is almost impossible for fashionable dress from the West' (Gurova 2009: 74). Although the first All-Union House of Fashion was opened in Moscow in 1934, there was no concept of a famous fashion designer in the Soviet Union, as the dominating principle of the collective did not allow single designers to express their individuality. The only exception to this was Slava Zaitsev, whose designer talent and innovations were appreciated by French fashion designers, such as Pierre Cardin when they accidentally became acquainted in 1965. But, as a consequence, Zaitsev was not allowed to travel abroad. In this way, a clear boundary between the USSR and the rest of the world existed in terms of fashion as well. Second, it was impossible for Soviet designers to realize their creative talent (Turovnikova 2014) because of limited manufacturing resources and a backward industry. These factors caused the absence of any reference to Soviet fashion designers in films, and even if the characters speak about fashion, they never mention actual names or brands.

By way of contrast, French fashions by Christian Dior and Pierre Cardin, for example, are dominant in the films analysed above. In the 1960s Soviet fashion specialists, like designers, engineers, technologists, openly adopted French haute couture creations by Christian Dior, taking over fashion designs, justified by the high quality of designer's work. Besides, Soviet specialists did not imitate western fashion blindly; rather they used a creative and selective approach by adapting only those ideas that were possible to be implemented in Soviet reality (Zakharova 2013: 407) as Soviet designers, 'borrowed only such ideas as could be applied under Soviet conditions' (Zakharova 2013: 407).

Returning to Georg Simmel's twofold criteria for fashion, namely that fashion expresses the tendency towards equalization and individualization (Simmel 1971: 308) as I have argued, these conflicting needs, essential to Simmel's account of fashion, are visible in Soviet film comedies from 1956 to 1985. The heroine of *Carnival Night* stands out in her Dior's evening dresses against the background of her plainly and modestly dressed colleagues. Lenochka gives Soviet women the impetus to adopt new fashion trends to prove the competitive ability of the Soviet way of life. The heroines of *Office Romance* and *The Most Charming and Attractive* follow similar paths: they have to embrace fashion in order to be successful at work and in their social life. But, they still resist being equal to others and distinguish themselves by their individual choice of clothes. The negative male and female characters of *The Diamond Arm* operate as role models by wearing their trendy western outfits often copied by style conscious Soviet youth in order to display their individuality.

It is also important to mention that *Carnival Night* and *The Diamond Arm*, the films of the 1950s and 1960s, explicitly introduced new fashion trends that were not typical of the time. But *Office Romance* and *The Most Charming and Attractive*, from the 1970s and 1980s, reflected everyday clothing styles. This phenomenon can be explained easily. From the 1950s the Soviet state became more conscious about the needs of its population to acquire consumer goods, and allowed more contact with the rest of the world. Thus, fashion was legitimized and became a regular part of Soviet everyday life. While the first comedy depicts a 10-year delay in fashion transfer, the second film presents more up-to-date fashion of the time, while the final two films display no fashion delay at all. Interestingly, the Soviet regime never asked filmmakers to transmit certain fashion trends. Fashion itself, as an integral part of social life, found its way through film to its audience. Consequently, no trendy fashion representations in these films can be identified as being typically Soviet. It is not my task here to distinguish Soviet fashion from western fashion. Yet, one may state that fashion in these films represents borrowed European fashion trends and the significance of this, especially that of French fashion designers, increases notably with every film reaching its peak in the later films. Foreign clothes function as an easily understandable semantic sign indicating the higher social position of its owners. In *Carnival Night* the heroine presents a role model for Soviet women and declares officially the French trend to be fashionable. Her example motivates Soviet women to imitate foreign fashion, without naming the designer. In *The Diamond Arm* the negatively marked characters present the newest fashion trends from abroad. Following the Soviet cinema tradition, fashionable and noticeable clothes are used as a distinctive feature for the representation of everything non-Soviet, but in this film they serve as a role model for the young generation. From this film onwards, foreign clothes are equal to fashionable clothes in filmic discourse as is made clear in *The Most Charming and Attractive*, when foreign clothes cause the heroine to become more socially acceptable to her colleagues. The tendency to appreciate foreign clothes and goods is typical for Soviet consumers who considered them to be a priori and better quality and more stylish than Soviet goods (Lebina 2006: 173). Fashion in the films analysed is directly associated with the desire for change and contrast, be it an opposition to the West at the beginning of the period, or a closer connection to western fashion at the end.

To conclude, these selected Soviet films, covering a period of 30 years, reflect the evolving social and moral situation in the USSR. Concerning the question of whether there is, or was such a thing as Soviet fashion my analysis suggests that in these films it existed, but that there were a variety of factors shaping concepts of fashion and their development. In the 1950s, in the frame of the ideological competition between the USSR and the West, fashion was used as a means for boosting the new post-Stalin Soviet-ness. In the 1960s, an increased interest in western fashion was based on the absence of Soviet fashion that deserved consideration. By the 1970s, the general concept of fashion played an important role in the construction of an up-to-date Soviet person. From the mid-1980s, western fashion seemed to displace Soviet fashion from Soviet fashion discourse. During the time period under analysis, the restricted notion of Soviet fashion was clearly influenced by western fashion. Hence, the desire of Soviet people to be fashionable turns out as a consistent feature as reflected in the fashion narratives used in films throughout the investigated time span.

References

Adtseeva, B. (2012), 'Moda v SSSR retrospektiva' ('Fashion in the USSR, a retrospection'), http://ria.ru/weekend_style/20121130/785652374.html. Accessed 15 April 2014.

Anon. (1959), 'Moscow missions for GUVs and GALs', *Life*, 6 July, pp. 32–34.

Barnard, M. (2002), *Fashion as Communication*, London: Routledge.

Barthes, R. (1983), *The Fashion System*, Berkeley: University of California Press.

—— (2000), *Mythologies*, London: Vintage.

Bartlett, D. (2005), 'Let them wear beige: The petit-bourgeois world of official socialist dress', *Fashion Theory*, 8:2, pp. 127–64.

—— (2011), *FashionEast*, Moskva: Novoe literaturnoe obozrenie.

Bezhanov, G. (1985), *Samaya obayatel'naya i privlekatel'naya* (*The Most Charming and Attractive*), Moscow: Mosfil'm.

Church Gibson, P. (2012), 'To care for her beauty, to dress up, is a kind of work', *Women's Study Quarterly*, 41:1&2, pp. 197–201.

Dashkova, T. (2007), 'Nevidimye miru rjushi. Odezhda v sovetskom predvoennom i voennom kino' ('Invisible rushes. Clothing in Soviet films before and during the war'), *Teoriya mody*, Vesna, pp. 149–62.

Engel, C. (1999), *Geschichte des sowjetischen und russischen Films*, Stuttgart: Metzler.

Gaidai, L. (1968), *Brilliantovaya ruka* (*The Diamond Arm*), Moscow: Mosfil'm.

Gaines, J. (1998), 'Kostüm und filmisches Erzählen: Wie Kleidung die Geschichte der Heldin erz.hlt' ('Costume and filmic narration: How does clothing tell the story of the heroine'), in G. Lehnert (ed.), *Mode, Weiblichkeit und Modernität* (*Fashion, Femininity and Innovation*), Dortmund: Die Werkstatt, pp. 211–65.

Gradskova, Y. (2004), 'Making yourself beautiful? Appearance, body and "girl's dignity" in the life of young women in the 1950s–1960s', in E. Hausbacher, E. Huber, J. Hargassner (eds), *Fashion, Consumption and Everyday Culture in the Soviet Union between 1945 and 1985*, Munich and Washington: Otto Sagner, pp. 125–34.

Gurova, O. (2006), 'Ideology of consumption in the Soviet Union: From asceticism to the legitimation of consumer goods', *Anthropology of East Europe Review*, 24:2, pp. 91–102.

—— (2009), 'The art of dressing: The body, gender and discourse on fashion in the Soviet Russia in the 1950s and 1960s', in E. Paulicelli and H. Clark (eds), *The Fabric of Cultures. Fashion, Identity, Globalization*, London: Routledge, pp. 73–91.

Hollander, A. (1994), *Sex and Suits*, New York: Alfred A. Knopf.

Kuznetsov, A. (2009), 'Podporka dlya polki, chto schitalos' ideologicheski chuzhdym v sovetskom kino' ('Support for the shelf, what counted as ideologically alien in Soviet film'), *Chastnyi korrespondent*, 6 September, http://newsbabr.com/?IDE=80744. Accessed 18 July 2014.

Lebina, N. (2006), *Entsiklopediya banal'nostei: sovetskaja povsednevnost' – kontury, simvoly, znaki* (*The Encyclopaedia of Banality: Soviet Everyday – Contours, Symbols, Signs*), St Petersburg: Bulanin.

Marzel, S.-R., Stiebel, G. D. (eds) (2015), *Dress and Ideology*, London: Bloomsbury.

The Metropolitan Museum of Art (2000), 'Yves Saint Laurent: Pantsuit', *Heilbrunn Timeline of Art History*, New York: The Metropolitan Museum of Art, http://www.metmuseum.org/toah/works-ofart/1984.598.96a-c. Accessed 18 July 2014.

Munich, A. (2011), *Fashion in Film*, Bloomington: Indiana University Press.

Osipova, K. (2011), 'Sovetskij kinematograf i moda' ('Soviet cinema and fashion'), http://depesha.com/arts-culture/culture/soviet-fashion-in-soviet-film. Accessed 15 April 2014.

Papushina, l. (2014), 'Post-soviet mass celebration and kul'turnost': the survey of urban art festival "White nights in Perm – 2012"', *Humanities*, WP BRP 58, pp. 1–17, www.hse.ru/mirror/pubs/lib/data/access/ram/ticket/13/149976990987c34b9f2039f7f4aaf4946b74d58392/58HUM2014.pdf. Accessed 18 July 2014.

Ryazanov, È. (1956), *Karnaval'naya noch'* (*Carnival Night*), Moscow: Mosfil'm.

—— (1977), *Sluzhebnyi roman* (*Office Romance*), Moscow: Mosfil'm.

S"ezd Sovetov (The Communist Party Congress) (1937), Konstitutsiia SSSR (The Constitution of the USSR), Moskva: TsIK SSSR.

Simmel, G. (1971), 'Fashion', in G. Simmel, *On Individuality and Social Forms*, Chicago: The University of Chicago Press, pp. 294–323.

Turovnikova, N. (2014), 'Sovety stareishin: Vyacheslav Zaitsev, model'er' ('Recommendation of elders: Vyacheslav Zaitsev, a fashion designer'), http://vozduh.afisha.ru/art/vyacheslav-zaycev-modeler/. Accessed 18 July 2014.

Widdis, E. (2008), 'Dressing the part: Clothing otherness in cinema before 1953', in S. Norris, Z. M. Torlone (eds), *Insiders and Outsiders in Russian Cinema*, Bloomington: Indiana University Press, pp. 48–67.

Zakharova, L. (2010), 'Dior in Moscow: A taste for luxury in Soviet fashion under Khrushchev', in S. E. Reid and D. Crowley (eds), *Pleasures in Socialism: Leisure and Luxury in the Bloc*, Evanston: Northwestern University Press, pp. 95–120.

—— (2013), 'Soviet fashion in the 1950s–1960s: Regimentation, western influences, and consumption strategies', in E. Gilburd, D. Kozlov (eds), *The Thaw: Soviet Society and Culture during the 1950s and 1960s*, Toronto, Buffalo and London: University of Toronto Press, pp. 402–35.

Notes

1 Difficult as these factors are, they are supported by the statistic data. All of these films are referred to as the most favourite films of soviet audience in the four decades between 1956 and 1985: In 1957, 49 million viewers went to the cinema to watch the film *Carnival Night*, and in 1968 over 76.7 million viewers watched the film *The Diamond Arm*. Equally, in 1977 the film *Office Romance* was seen by 58.5 million people, whilst in 1985 the film *The Most Charming and Attractive* was seen by 44.9 million viewers. Besides, all these films were rewarded in turn with the title 'The film of the year' (Engel 1999: 333ff.).

2 Emma Widdis, for example, explored this topic in her article 'Dressing the part. Clothing otherness in Soviet cinema before 1953' (Widdis 2008) and Tat'yana Dashkova investigated the same subject in her article, 'Nevidimye miru ryushi. Odezhda v sovetskom predvoennom i voennom kino'('Invisible rushes. Clothing in Soviet Films before and during the War') (Dashkova 2007).

3 Olga Gurova defines four phases of the ideology of consumption in the USSR: in the 1920s, the ideology of everyday asceticism; in the 1930s, the ideology of *kul'turnost'* (cultureness); in

the 1950s–1960s, the idea of Soviet taste occurred from the ideological opposition between the Soviet Union and the West; from the 1970s, the idea of dematerialization dominates in the ideology of consumption (Gurova 2006).

4   There is an obvious coincidence between the circumstances of film's shooting. As at the very beginning of Soviet film history in the 1910s–1920s (see Gaines 1998) and in the middle of the 1980s actors and actresses had to supply themselves with their own film costumes.

5   The film partially fulfills an escapist function as during these difficult times of economic shortages it had to cheer up a desperate Soviet audience because of the lack of consumer goods and especially fashionable clothing.

Chapter 3

The Sad Fortunes of 'Stylish Things': George Eliot and the Languages of Fashion

Royce Mahawatte

In the third chapter of *The Sad Fortunes of the Reverend Amos Barton*, the Reverend Amos Barton and his wife Milly both pay a visit to the Countess Czerlaski. Both Amos, and his wife in particular, are enamoured with the Countess:

For the Countess Czerlaski was undeniably beautiful. As she seated herself by Mrs Barton on the sofa, Milly's eyes, indeed, rested – must it be confessed? – chiefly on the details of the tasteful dress, the rich silk of the pinkish lilac hue (the Countess always wore delicate colours in an evening), the black lace pelerine, and the black lace veil falling at the back of the small closely-braided head. For Milly had one weakness – don't love her any the less for it, it was a pretty women's weakness – she was fond of dress; and often when she was making up her own economical millinery, she had romantic visions [*sic*] how nice it would be to put on really handsome stylish things – to have very stiff balloon sleeves, for example, without which a woman's dress was nought in those days.

(Eliot 1988: 27)

This chapter explores the writing of fashion in this first published fiction of George Eliot, serialized in *Blackwood's Edinburgh Magazine* in 1857. It is a work of realism about a couple hopelessly caught up in the Countess' 'fashionable vortex', as the narrator puts it (Eliot 1988: 39). We can see this force at work in this passage, which is worthy of note for scholars interested in the relationship between fashion and Victorian fiction. There is specific fashion language: 'pelerine', 'very stiff balloon sleeves'. We have fashion instruction: 'small closely-braided head', where the reader can visualize the hairstyle. The voice takes on authority: 'without which a woman's dress was nought in those days'. The impulse towards a fashion register ends with the colloquial sounding: 'really handsome stylish things'. We have a direct appeal to the reader's sympathy, because of what follows in the narrative, we need to forgive Milly for her desire to pander to the Countess and for her love of fashionable items. To be beautiful and fashionable are linked, and problematically at that.

I have briefly written about this passage elsewhere in terms of its Gothic adumbrations, but there is much more to say about it in terms of the language of fashion. This short sequence and this story, more generally, I will argue here, can be used to explore the rather complex tone that Eliot uses when she depicts fashion and dress in her writing, which she does much more than you might initially expect (Mahawatte 2009). This narrative highlights the elements of pastiche in Eliot's writing of fashion that challenge some of the existing ideas about the representation of fashion in literature. Anne Hollander writes that in nineteenth-century novels, clothes 'always correctly express character' and Clair Hughes discusses the 'reality effect' where fashion lends tangibility and vividness to fiction (Hollander 1999: 12; McNeil, Karaminas and Cole 2009: 5–6). While being generally applicable, both of these perspectives fail to engage with the mediated nature of fashion's intersection with literature. Here, I want to argue that the writing of fashion in Victorian fiction is more likely to move through different fashion languages and narrative idioms rather than just operate as a form of notation. Eliot's writing of fashion is projected through mid-Victorian fashion genres. We have a Realist story that, in places, engages with forms of fashion writing. This is silver-fork fiction, which I will mention briefly here, and fashion editorial, which I will illustrate via extracts from *Blackwood's Lady's Magazine and Gazette of the Fashionable World*. Eliot was interested in historical accuracy and so it comes as no surprise that the fashions she records were actually a part of the fashion cycles in the leading magazines of the 1830s when the story was set.

George Eliot and Fashion

The definitions and understanding of what fashion is have in recent decades come to form the broader discipline of Fashion Studies. Elizabeth Wilson has described fashion as the repeated circulation of dress styles, a function of modernity, where 'no clothes are outside fashion' (1985: 3–5). The sociological turn of the discipline, in Joanne Entwistle's work, however, sees fashion as very much a part of an embodied experience (Entwistle 2001: 33–59). Prior to these articulations, Roland Barthes in *The Fashion System* (1983) presented fashion as a series of linguistic structures that give temporality and urgency to clothes. To quote Paul Jobling: 'the Fashion System exists to give a great deal of semantic power to "nothing": "nothing" can signify "everything" […] one detail is enough to transform what is outside meaning into meaning' (1999: 76). Applying this idea retroactively, it seems that Eliot is interested in the moral implications of what Barthes came to investigate linguistically. The Victorian period was clearly a time when both the promotion and consumption of fashionable goods and services became, as it were, indices for social and class hierarchies and this will to promote can be found in media and literary forms. In this chapter, I use the word 'fashion' broadly, as a part of a cultural phenomenon. This includes the appreciation of material culture, and particularly dress, but also social aspiration, and the desire for cultural and social capital. As the interest in fashion grew, along came criticism from intellectual circles which, with regards to dress, eventually found force in the Rational Dress Movement towards the end of the nineteenth century.

Mary Anne Evans' painful references to her own 'lack of beauty' and her ambivalent responses to fashion consumption and dress practices in her letters and journals place her very much within the growing critical stance against fashionable dress practices (Haight 1968: 115). Her negative self-image was expressed in her awkward description of her newly dressed hair, done while on holiday in France in 1849:

The people dress and think about dressing here more even than in England. You would not know me if you saw me. The Marquise took on her the office of femme de chambre and drest [sic] my hair one day. She has abolished all my curls and made two things stick out on each side of my head, like those on the head of the Sphinx. All the world says I look infinitely better so I comply, though to myself I seem uglier than ever – if possible.

(Haight 1958: 298)

Evans' disavowal of personal taste ('two things') in the face of the opinion of 'the world' shows modesty or an unhappiness about what she saw as her own separation from structures of discernment and fashion systems. When it came to choosing dress fabrics in the September of 1851, however, Evans had very clear ideas of pattern, composition and quality if not what was the most current (Haight 1958: 361). In Evans' journal of 1854, it is clear that her notes on dress practices in Germany set the stage for George Eliot, the author's, Realist aesthetic:

The women have agreeable fresh-looking faces under the cleanest of caps, generally with long barbs. The barbed caps however are giving way to the less picturesque ribboned, round caps worn by the servants in England.

(Harris and Johnston 1998: 14)

In 1857 the *Westminster Review* published 'Female dress in 1857' article on rationality and fashion, attributed to Harriet Martineau (Houghton 1966: 626) which posited:

There is nothing in the education of women in this country which can secure them from ill-regulated impulse in personal pursuits, on the one hand, or from barbarism in taste on the other. […] The general cultivation of the reason, and the particular education of the taste in early years, would extinguish the follies of female dress and manners; and we have no belief that anything else will.

(Anon. 1857: 315–40)

Although Marian Evans had left the magazine at this time; the opinions of her professional peers place her very much amidst the drive towards rational forms of dress. Nevertheless, across her fiction-writing career, which spanned over 20 years, Eliot's references to clothes, material culture, hairstyles and fashion cycles more generally, are extensive. As a Realist, and as a woman writing about the complexities of female experience, the construction of femininity as an ambivalent social act is a key part of her writing. There is Hetty Sorrell who is warned against wearing earrings in *Adam Bede* (1859); there is Maggie and her unruly hair and plain dresses in *The Mill on the Floss* (1860) (Cheang and Biddle-Perry 2008: 193–205). In *Felix Holt, the Radical* (1864) Mrs Transome describes herself as a 'hag' to her maid and says: 'these fine clothes you put me in are a smart shroud' (Eliot 1980: 313). Of course, Dorothea, in *Middlemarch* (1872) whose beauty is thrown into relief by poor dress is contrasted by Rosamond Lydgate's desire for material goods; Gwendolen Harleth's narrative in *Daniel Deronda* (1877) presents the high-life of diamonds and dresses as an oppressive confinement, which the heroine only becomes truly aware of once she is married and trapped within it. In George Eliot's fiction, clothes play a large role, one that is largely indexical, contradictory and unstable. Fashion, and more importantly, the love of it, is brought into a discourse that conveys tensions between different constructions of femininity, affect and social responsibility. Eliot was in many ways a Puritan writer and it will come as no surprise that she saw fashion broadly as the food of vanity and egotism. At the same time, she strove to extend sympathy for those caught up in the practice, as if they were trapped in a delusion. The depiction of Gwendolen Harleth's fashionable life is the apotheosis of this intention (Mahawatte 2009). A part of Eliot's criticism of fashion lies in the way that she deployed established linguistic registers and literary forms that were already being used for fashion promotion.

Realism versus Silver-Fork School

The Sad Fortunes of Reverend Amos Barton is a work of clerical realism, a tragedy about ecclesiastic professions that in key places uses the writing of fashion as a counterpoint. It tells the story of a headstrong Reverend of a local parish facing competition from Dissenting Christianity, his consumptive wife and six children. Both in the subject matter and in how the narrator relates to the reader, it is a story that advanced the writing of social realism: there is a movement away from 'striking situations, thrilling incident and eloquent writing' (Eliot 1988: 37) and an appeal to understanding mediocrity and the everyday. It sets up a Realist aesthetic about middle-class life, but sectarian Christianity is not the only threat to the stability of the Barton family. The story backs onto the world of European high-life, with the appreciation of material goods, particularly clothes, the desire for social aspiration; gossip and also shame: the abject fear of downward mobility. So, the Reverend Barton has a tepid relationship with a congregation that is slowing turning to Evangelical Christianity, and he finds himself flattered by the widowed Countess Czerlaski, and her brother, Mr Bridman. The Countess is a glamorous figure and the subject of gossip. Why are she and her brother in Shepperton, 'a neighbourhood where they are not known?' (Eliot 1988: 32). And why does Mr Bridman barely resemble his sister? There is also the question of why the Bartons attend to them, why do they hold the Countess in such esteem?

So, while the Bartons allow us to explore clerical realism, the Countess and her brother belong in another genre, to quote Michael Sadleir: 'the writing of fashionable society: "the silver-fork school" that detailed the customs of the European moneyed, social preferment, and the love of materialistic lifestyles' (Sadleir 1931: 124). The term 'silver-fork' comes from William Hazlitt, who deplored the genre's obsession with material culture and cutlery, as he chose to satirize it. The genre started in the 1830s, and by the mid-century was firmly established as a part of the popular cannon. Winifred Hughes, April Nixon Kendra and

Cheryl Wilson have all discussed the genre but they do not make the connection that Eliot was creatively very interested in this stridently popular form (Hughes 1992: 329; Kendra 2004: 25–38; Wilson 2013). Marian Evans, as a journalist for the *Westminster Review*, wittily summed up the form as the 'Mind and millinery' species in 'Silly novels by lady novelists' (1856).

The Sad Fortunes of Reverend Amos Barton, modulates the fashionable characters against clerical life. The narrator is quick to dispel rumours about the Countess, her brother, and the reasons why they are in the Midlands and not in London or Vienna. Mr Bridman is only the half-brother of the Countess, and they reside in Shepperton only because they are down at heel and cannot afford to live in a fashionable watering hole. Perhaps more importantly, the Countess is looking for a new husband and thinks that the provinces will present her with less female competition. This story tries to bring the typical silver-fork novel characters into a nuanced and, arguably more contingent and less idealized narrative idiom.

To this end, the Countess' fortunes take a turn for the worst when her half-brother decides to marry their maid. Now with the maid turned mistress, the Countess refuses to remain in their home for much longer and appeals to the hospitality of the Bartons, where the hierarchy would be clearer and her position within it assured. She stays for over six months and adds to the financial strain on the household and the consumption becomes both metaphorical and also manifested as Milly's tuberculosis. Milly, who is now also pregnant with her seventh child, finds herself as both host and maid to the encroaching airs and graces of the Countess. Meanwhile, the townsfolk gossip about the presence of the Countess in the house and Amos Barton loses the already waning support from the local community. The fashionable novel changes to its Realist counterpart – the narrative of downward mobility. We have a collision of two forms, two economic and political systems, two ideologies and the result is tragedy.

The Languages of Fashion

In this section I want to discuss the other mediated form in Eliot's story: some of the editorial, linguistic and literary features of fashion journalism. Though very much muted, one of Milly's pleasures comes from her dream of being a fashion consumer. *Blackwood's Lady's Magazine* illustrates some elements of the relationship that Eliot's story had with the fashion media. Scholarship on Victorian journalism seems to largely omit the discussion of fashion media, which is rather problematic given that much of the recent contributions to the field look at the role of women, both as writers and as the subject of representation within the journalistic context and marketplace. Hilary Fraser, Stephanie Green and Judith Johnston make some mention of fashion editorial and choose to focus on education, imperial and historical locations of women in Victorian periodicals. This critical survey discusses transgressions of femininity away from fashion norms, such as with the New Women and cycling wear. Although in the conclusion the authors state that they are not presenting a progressivist model of feminist history, where fashion journalism is concerned there is very much a real omission of beauty, consumption, allure and glamour as a significant and telling discourse associated with femininity and female embodied experience. The strictly managed navigation of fashion editorial found in Fraser et al. sidesteps the more conventional writing of fashion excluding it from critical discussion (2003: 190, 199). Eliot was clearly critical of fashion, but she did engage with fashion as a part of the affective and social experience of her characters. It is perhaps time to look at Victorian fashion editorial on its own terms, as a social fact and as a feature of Victorian modernity. How does fashion language function in its contexts and how are we to understand the contradictions connected to the construction of gender within a commercial framework? In a periodical like *Blackwood's Lady's Magazine* there is a range of competing discourses, some features and notices are very much fashion promotion, while others explore the price of aspiration in very personal terms.

The monthly fashion item presents an authority on taste. The 'Fashions for August' from the 1836 issue, spot comes straight 'From our Correspondent' in France. The reader is told on the subject of sleeves:

> Tight sleeves are scarcely worn, except with low dresses; the most general are those with three bouffants. When short sleeves are worn at home, they require to be accompanied with mittens. Therefore, black, grey, white and brown, are numerous, with a little trimming at the top.
>
> (Anon. 1836a: 103)

To the authoritative voice, which is an arbiter of good taste, we can retroactively apply Roland Barthes' idea of the fashion text. By studying the language that accompanied fashion imagery, Barthes created an intricate system that tried to look at the way clothes were transformed by language into a system 'whose justification is no longer utilitarian, but only semantic: it thus constitutes meaning as a true luxury of mind' (1983: 278). This writing of sleeves and the fluctuating rules governing the way they are worn seem to possess 'the sacred halo of divinatory texts' as Barthes says later on in the passage. The language removed utility and economics from the material object and instead renders it to be otherworldly. When taking these ideas to the nineteenth century, the 'mythic dimensions', to use Peter McNeil's phrase, of the 'fashion text' can be seen in all its complexity in the fashion editorial of the period (McNeil, Karaminas and Cole 2009: 1–2). In *The Fashion System*, Barthes goes into the grammatical and 'functional constructions' where he speaks about how the subtleties of fashion editorial create a sense of temporality by giving the reader an awareness of what is both ephemeral and eternal. Here, we have the use of the present tense 'tight sleeves are rarely worn' and also a subjunctive mood: 'When short sleeves are worn at home, they require to be accompanied with mittens' (Barthes 1983). The archaic subjunctive form 'require' creates a sense of atemporality, and yet we have an authority over what is clearly going to be obsolete. The reader is placed in an uncertain position of knowing, yet not being secure in their appreciation of what is fashionable.

Unsurprisingly, by the June 1838 issue, we are told on the subject of sleeves that 'they are worn a trifle larger than last month; ruches both at the shoulder and wrist are thought to be elegant' (Anon. 1838: 46). The language in both of these excerpts has the ability to make the ephemeral seem extremely important and perhaps more importantly to construct a group of idealized consumers for whom good taste and discrimination is naturalized as an aspect of social identity without any reference to how this taste was acquired or how the items of clothing were come by. The only reference to the issue of labour is embedded into the detailed level of description, which would be used to instruct the dressmaker and it hides in plain sight. It is perhaps this language usage that affronted moral and proto-feminist writers of the nineteenth century. The materialistic focus of the writing betrays a *belief* in surface, where self-reproach and reflection come into play.

Other forms of fashion writing accompany this article. The August edition has 'Paris intelligence and court news (from our Paris correspondent)', which talks about marriages and events in society. Editorial instruction, and the presentation of the world of *bon ton*, are not the only voices in the publication though. The August issue opens with a short story 'The Jew of Tolosa', which tells of lovers, whose union is blocked by the young woman's father. The young man chances upon a shadowy Jewish figure, who helps the pair to marry clandestinely. This story plays with representation and the expectations that the reader might have towards the Jewish figure, and at the end it unequivocally presents him as a positive force and a cypher for compassion and understanding rather than as the object of anti-Semitism. The following issue, September 1836, presents the criminal side of high society with the opening story 'The victim', about gambling and fraud in the male world (Anon. 1836: 111). There is a travel piece 'Cork and its Environs' and in the reviews section is a notice for the latest *The Pickwick Club* number and, most interestingly, a notice on a medical work by William Coulson: 'Deformities of the Chest', about the detrimental effects of tight corsetry:

> There is another deformity of the chest well deserving the attention of medical men, produced by too tight lacing of the stays; in which the chest, instead of having the shape of a truncated cone, with its base inferiorly, becomes so utterly changed as to seem inverted, by having its apex inferiorly.
>
> (Anon. 1838: 130)

The September issue of *Blackwood's Lady's Magazine* is subtly circumspect in its broader presentation of fashion consumption and body modification, showing it to be a complex mediation between promotion, debate and reservation. Marjorie Ferguson in her work on magazines pointed out an important feature of Victorian fashion journalism:

> The editors of these specialized publications were intent on improving the minds of their readers, of educating as well as entertaining them. They put into their journals philosophical reflections and snippets of news from home and abroad; they were

concerned with social and political ideas as well as with home management, fashion and fiction. Their tone was one of mental and moral uplift suited to literate, leisured ladies.

(1983: 15)

Interestingly, the broad range of content is actually a source of contradictory tension within fashion magazines of the nineteenth century, a tension that is repeated and crystalized in the silver-fork school of fiction, which showed the problematic and unsustainable elements of fashionable life.

The Sad Fortunes of Stylish Things

So, when we look at passages from *The Sad Fortunes of Reverend Amos Barton* against editorial of the 1830s we can see that Eliot's critical handling of fashion and the fashionable world does not differ that markedly from the sum of the collective threads found in the magazine as a whole. The narrator wants to place the Barton's love of clothes into a clear financial context. Amos earns 35 pounds 10 per annum after the deductions from his stipend have been made. He liked to dress well in a suit of 'flack broadcloth', a 'snowy cravat' and he had to overspend to clothe his wife and children 'with gentility from bonnet-strings to shoe strings' (Eliot 1988: 7). This is a lifestyle that can clearly not be maintained, particularly when the Reverend has scant regard for the number of children he fathers. The narrator is also keen to point out that much of Milly's time, as with the other women of the parish, is taken up repairing and maintaining clothes. Milly is very much involved in the lived experience and the economic reality of clothes and not in their mythic status. She is so skilled that she can repair her husband's clothes and no one would work out that the tailor was a woman (Eliot 1988: 18).

Despite Milly's abilities, by the time the Countess actually leaves the Bartons are in debt. Milly, whose health finally fails, dies shortly after giving birth to their seventh and also short-lived child. Although the community come to help the family, Amos eventually loses the curacy because he has few allies and the family leaves Shepperton. The Countess exploits the Bartons, by her aspirations and her shame. We are given insights into the limits of the Countess' imagination when she can only sit with the sick Milly 'for hours', while not actually attending to her 'probable wants' because: 'ladies of rank and luxurious habits, you know, cannot be expected to surmise the details of poverty' (Eliot 1988: 39).

The passage I highlighted at the beginning of this chapter foreshadows this outcome through the modulations of the narrative voice, which parodies the editorial voice for narrative ends. The technical vocabulary, 'pelerine' instantly takes both Milly's and the reader's awareness to the world of fashion. More specifically, 'balloon sleeves' – the silhouette of the early Victorian period – draws attention to the amount of material that would be required for this particular style. As the excerpts from *Blackwood's Lady's Magazine* show, sleeves and their shape and size were highly contentious (see Cavendish-Jones in this volume). Balloon sleeves consumed large quantities of material and were highly conspicuous, much like the countess herself. They reveal character, but become more poignant when seen through the eyes of Milly, who could not afford this kind of fashion.

With the authoritative fashion voice: 'without which a woman's dress was nought in those days', Eliot's narrator echoes the journalistic voice that makes the important out of the trivial. This element of judgement is striking in its discrimination, when placed against Milly's modest clothing. This voice also aligns with that of the Countess, especially the indirect voice used for her: 'ladies of rank and luxurious habits, you know, cannot be expected to surmise the details of poverty' (Eliot 1988: 39). For Milly, the voice of fashion editorial is that of the Countess, who although fails to ultimately inhabit the high-life, does not stop voicing its values and identifying with its elusive authority.

Then finally, we have the 'really handsome stylish things'. This is non-fashion language – comparatively naïve in Milly's voice when placed against the fashion discourse earlier in the passage, or even the editorial from *Blackwood's Lady's Magazine*. It highlights her inability to really compete within the discourse of fashion. It reveals her level of poverty, and one which the Countess refuses to see, and which Amos Barton can neither alleviate nor stop bringing about by his impulsive behaviour.

George Eliot's handling of literary genre is complex and in this early fiction she checked a popular genre and in places an editorial style, against a moral impulse to explore context and so engender sympathy. The creation of Eliot's literary persona here involved a wide conception of literary languages and how they may be deployed for affective and political ends. As a new author, Eliot was defining her literary identity within a developing literary market place. Mary Poovey, in *Genres of the Credit Economy* (2008) discusses how writers established literary value against other forms of writing: non-fiction, historical and journalistic. She writes '[…] novelists gradually elevated the status of their genre – all the while negotiating the relationship between novels and the other, nonfiction kinds of prose that also mediated value' (2008: 30). She uses the case of *Silas Marner* (1861) to show how notions of literary quality were negotiated in the novel's handing of commercial themes:

> *Silas Marner* provides a particularly clear example of the way that mid-century novelists subjected economic matters – in this case, the monetary value of gold – to the alchemy of a moral lesson by emphasizing the connotative capacity of language – that is, the elevation of figuration and suggestion over denotation and reference […] Eliot's attempt to make reader appreciate the connotative capacities of Literary language by troping terms associated with the market model of value is echoed in numerous Victorian novels.
> (Poovey 2008: 383)

The gold (the lost hoard and the colour of Eppie's hair) aligns the metonymic with the literary and creates a sense of mythos within the story. We are under no illusion as to which gold has the higher value. Poovey's presentation of nineteenth-century literature is highly applicable to *The Sad Fortunes of Reverend Amos Barton*, which places the commercial and utilizing values of fashion within a clear social, economic and provincial context. The theme of consumption (the Countess' behaviour and Milly's medical condition) is handled both literally and metaphorically. The narrative seeks to elide the two: they are equally destructive. This connotative capacity of language feeds into Eliot's allusions to fashion editorial and enables a moral handling of the language of fashion culture.

References

Anon. (1836a), 'Fashions for August', *Blackwood's Lady's Magazine and Gazette of the Fashionable World*, August, p. 103.

——— (1836b), 'Fashions for September', *Blackwood's Lady's Magazine and Gazette of the Fashionable World*, September, p. 143.

——— (1836c), 'The Jew of Tolosa', *Blackwood's Lady's Magazine and Gazette of the Fashionable World*, August, p. 73.

——— (1838), 'Fashions for June', *Blackwood's Lady's Magazine and Gazette of the Fashionable World*, June, p. 46.

——— (1857), 'Female dress in 1857', *Westminster Review*, October, pp. 315–40.

Barthes, R. (1983), *The Fashion System*, trans. Matthew Ward and Richard Howard, New York: Hill and Wang.

Eliot, G. (1980), *Felix Holt*, Oxford: Clarendon Press.

——— (1988), *Scenes of Clerical Life*, Oxford and New York: Oxford University Press.

Entwistle, J. (2001), 'The dressed body', in J. Entwistle, and E. Wilson (eds), *Body Dressing*, London: Bloomsbury Academic, pp. 33–59.

Ferguson, M. (1983), *Forever Feminine, Women's Magazines and the Cult of Femininity*, London and Exeter: Heinemann.

Fraser, H., Green, S. and Johnston, J. (2003), *Gender and the Victorian Periodical*, Cambridge: Cambridge University Press.

Haight, G. (ed.) (1958–78), *The George Eliot Letters*, 9 vols, New Haven: Yale University Press.

——— (1968), *George Eliot: A Biography*, Oxford: Oxford University Press.

Harris, M. and Johnston, J. (eds) (1998), *The Journals of George Eliot*, Cambridge: Cambridge University Press.

Hollander, A. (1999), *Feeding the Eyre*, New York: Farrar, Straus, Giroux.

Houghton, W. (1966), *The Wellesley Index to Victorian Periodicals*, vol. 3, Toronto: University of Toronto Press.

Hughes, W. (1992), 'Silver-fork writers and readers: Social contexts of a best seller', *Novel: A Forum on Fiction*, 25:3, pp. 328–47.

Jobling, P. (1999), *Fashion Spreads*, Oxford: Berg.

Kendra, A. (2004), 'Gendering the silver fork: Catherine Gore and the society novel', *Women's Writing*, 11:1, pp. 25–38.

McNeil, P., Karaminas, V. and Cole, C. (2009), *Fashion, Fiction: Text, Clothing in Literature, Film and Television*, Oxford: Berg.

Mahawatte, R. (2008), 'Hair and fashioned femininity in two nineteenth-century novels', in Sarah Cheang and Geraldine Biddle-Perry (eds), *Hair: Styling, Culture and Fashion*, Oxford: Berg.

——— (2009), '"Life that is not clad in the same coat-tails and flounces": The novel, George Eliot and the fear of the material', in T. Wagner (ed.), *Women's Writing, Special Issue: Silver Fork Novels*, 19:1, pp. 323–44.

Poovey, M. (2008), *Genres of the Credit Economy, Mediating Value in Eighteenth-and Nineteenth-Century Britain*, Chicago and London: University of Chicago Press.

Sadleir, M. (1931), *Bulwer: A Panorama; Edward and Rosina, 1803–1836*, London: Constable.

Wilson, C. (2013), *Fashioning the Silver Fork Novel*, London: Chatto and Pickering.

Wilson, E. (1985), *Adorned in Dreams: Fashion and Modernity*, London: Virago.

Chapter 4

Oscar Wilde and the Philosophy of Fashion

Colin Cavendish-Jones

A fashion is merely a form of ugliness so absolutely unbearable that we have to alter it every six months!

(Wilde 1885: 9)

Oscar Wilde, The Philosophy of Dress

Oscar Wilde was famous for his clothes long before he was famous for his writing. At Oxford and in London in the late 1870s, he became an instantly recognizable figure, dressed in a loose velvet coat, a large flowing necktie, knee-breeches and black silk stockings, topped off with a wide-brimmed hat and black cape. It was just such a costume in which Napoleon Sarony, the celebrated New York photographer, captured Wilde at the beginning of his 1882 lecture tour of North America, and which was parodied by a group of Harvard students at his Boston Music Hall lecture on 31 January that year. According to a report in the *Lowell Daily Courier*:

> The feature of the evening was the entrance of about 60 Harvard college students in single file: all were in evening dress, with knee-breeches and black stockings, and each bore before him, walking in a more or less 'stained-glass attitude', a sunflower.
>
> (2 February 1882: 4)

Wilde, who had been forewarned, arrived wearing conventional evening dress and began by addressing the undergraduates at the front of the house:

> I see about me certain signs of an aesthetic movement. I see certain young men who are, no doubt, sincere; but I can assure them that they are no more than caricatures. As I look around me, I am impelled for the first time to breathe a fervent prayer, 'Save me from my disciples!'
>
> (*Harvard Crimson* 1 February 1882: 5)

A decade later, in 1892, Wilde had given ample evidence of his literary talent in *The Happy Prince, A House of Pomegranates* and *The Picture of Dorian Gray*, and of his mature artistic philosophy in such extended essays as 'The critic as artist' and 'The soul of man'. After the failure of his early plays, he had returned to drama and written *Salome* in French, and *Lady Windermere's Fan*, the first of the social comedies which were to be his most popular and characteristic works. It was the knee-breeches and the oversized neckties, however, that Max Nordau remembered when he attacked Wilde (along with Nietzsche, Ibsen, Tolstoy and many more) in his extended polemic *Degeneration* (*Entartung*), insisting that Wilde's achievements as a writer were subordinate to his dandical persona:

> Wilde has done more by his personal eccentricities than by his works. Like Barbey d'Aurevilly, whose rose-coloured silk hats and gold lace cravats are well-known, and like his disciple Joséphin Péladan, who walks about in lace frills and satin doublet, Wilde dresses in queer costumes which recall partly the fashions of the Middle Ages, partly the rococo modes.
>
> (Nordau 1993: 317)

Nordau's attack is particularly obsessive and sustained. There are several more pages along the same lines, arguing that Wilde's choice of costume is actuated by 'anti-social ego-mania' (1993: 318) and 'a malevolent mania for contradiction' (1993: 319). However, his attitude in writing Wilde off as a *flâneur* because of his sartorial tastes and his interest in fashion as a topic for discussion was common enough among critics during Wilde's lifetime, and for a long time after his death. When, in the 1970s, commentators such as Rodney Shewan and Philip Cohen started to publish reappraisals of Wilde, taking him more seriously as a moral philosopher and social commentator, they showed a reactive tendency to ignore Wilde's interest in fashion as a distraction from the serious purpose of his writing.

In fact, beauty was always the serious purpose of Wilde's writing, and his ideas about fashion are not only consistent with, but also integral to the aesthetic philosophy that was shaped in the lectures he gave to his American audiences in 1882: 'The English Renaissance' and 'The decorative arts'. In both pieces, Wilde is constantly emphasizing the link between beauty and morality, and in particular the moral effect of the decorative arts in everyday life. He says that art will create a new brotherhood by furnishing a universal language, which it may even eradicate war, because one can feel no hatred for a nation if one knows and loves the works of art it has given to the world. He is particularly concerned with the role of art in early education, and argues that to introduce children to beautiful objects is a vital part of their ethical and aesthetic instruction:

> If children grow up among all fair and lovely things, they will grow to love beauty and detest ugliness before they know the reason why. If you go into a house where everything is coarse, you find things chipped and broken and unsightly. Nobody exercises any care. If everything is dainty and delicate, gentleness and refinement of manner are unconsciously acquired.
>
> (Wilde 1913: 171)

In 'The decorative arts' Wilde included several observations on dress, explaining how the general principles of beauty and utility he has outlined apply equally to fine art, applied art, and fashion. Indeed, he comments on the direct connection between modern dress and modern sculpture, remarking:

> At present we have lost all nobility of dress and, in doing so, have almost annihilated the modern sculptor. And, in looking around at the figures which adorn our parks, one could almost wish that we had completely killed the noble art. To see the frock-coat of the drawing-room done in bronze, or the double waistcoat perpetuated in marble, adds a new horror to death.
>
> (Wilde 1913: 162)

This was to become a major theme of Wilde's writing on dress. The late nineteenth century, he argued, was a heroic age in which the world was changing rapidly and great things were being accomplished, but artists could not portray this heroism and dynamism because of the ugly and barbarous nature of modern dress (see Mahawatte in this volume). The gods and heroes of antiquity immediately appeared diminished and ludicrous if one imagined them wearing frock-coats or corsets.

Wilde saw his own aesthetic costume, with wide-brimmed hat and flowing cape, approximated most nearly not by the well-dressed dandies of New York or Boston, but by the silver miners of Colorado, and he used their mode of dress to illustrate the link between the beauty of attire and its practicality.

> In all my journeys through the country, the only well-dressed men that I saw – and in saying this I earnestly deprecate the polished indignation of your Fifth Avenue dandies – were the Western miners. Their wide-brimmed hats, which shaded their faces from the sun and protected them from the rain, and the cloak, which is by far the most beautiful piece of drapery ever invented, may well be dwelt on with admiration. Their high boots, too, were sensible and practical. They wore only what was comfortable, and therefore beautiful. As I looked at them I could not help thinking with regret of the time when these picturesque miners would have made their fortunes and would go East to assume again all the abominations of modern fashionable attire.
>
> (Wilde 1913: 163–64)

When Wilde revised his lectures and added another to his repertoire in March 1882, he further accentuated the importance of clothing, requesting from his American agent a copy of *The Art of Dress* by Eliza Mary Haweis to assist him in his preparations (Wilde 2000: 146). Mrs Haweis, like Wilde's future wife Constance, was a prominent member of the Rational Dress Society and combined artistic and literary scholarship (her first book was on Chaucer) with a Feminist concern for the comfort and practicality of women's clothes.

Whereas 'The English Renaissance', 'The decorative arts' and several shorter lectures and articles on dress, such as 'The relation of dress to art' (Wilde 2000–13: VI.36) have formed part of Wilde's *Collected Works* since Robert Ross's 1908 edition, his most substantial essay on fashion, 'The philosophy of dress', which first appeared in the *New-York Tribune* on 19 April 1885, was not reprinted for 128 years, until it appeared in John Cooper's book, *Oscar Wilde on Dress* in 2013. By 1885, Wilde had altered his own costume, dispensing with knee breeches and silk stockings (which he had never defended in theory, and which he admitted in a letter published in the *Pall Mall Gazette* on 11 November 1884 were 'far too tight' and 'a great mistake'), but retaining the loose, flowing draperies he had advocated in his 1882 lectures. This change did not represent a shift in Wilde's opinions, but rather an attempt to bring his own attire in line with the principles he had expressed in his writing on dress, that clothes should be loose and comfortable and should follow, rather than attempting to amend, the contours of the body.

Wilde had also, in 1884, married a woman with strong views of her own on fashion and dress reform. Constance Wilde was a leading member of the Rational Dress Society, formed in 1881 by Lady Harberton, to oppose such constricting fashions as corsets, high-heeled shoes and heavy, unwieldy skirts. Constance contributed articles to the Society's *Gazette* (which she later edited for a year, from 1888–89), and numerous other periodicals, including *The Woman's World*, which Oscar edited for 2 years from 1887 to 1889, always advocating simplicity and freedom of movement in dress. Her first article for *The Women's World*, 'Children's dress in this century', was a characteristically fierce condemnation of the burdensome costumes Victorian children were forced to wear, and an analysis of the ways in which these clothes restricted their physical and artistic development.

Wilde begins 'The philosophy of dress' by stating the artistic basis of his ideas about fashion. These are more plainly expressed than, but not substantially different from the ideas in his American lectures:

> I hold that the very first canon of art is that Beauty is always organic, and comes from within, and not from without, comes from the perfection of its own being and not from any added prettiness. And that consequently the beauty of a dress depends entirely and absolutely on the loveliness it shields, and on the freedom and motion that it does not impede.
>
> (Cooper 2013: 84)

Wilde argues that the knowledge of the human form which came naturally to the Greeks and Romans 'from the gymnasium and the palaestra, from the dance in the meadow and the race by the stream' (Cooper 2013: 84) must be imparted to the denizens of chillier climes and more conservative cultures by the study of painting or sculpture. Children should learn to draw as early as they are taught to write. Then they will learn that 'a waist is a very beautiful and delicate curve' rather than 'as the milliner fondly imagines, an abrupt right angle suddenly occurring in the middle of the person',[1] and that 'size has nothing to do with beauty' (Cooper 2013: 84). Wilde repeats this observation that 'size is not a quality of Beauty ever' and illustrates his contention with several examples, concluding with the one that most obviously supports his idea that beauty is the inevitable concomitant of freedom and motion:

> A foot is not necessarily beautiful because it is small. The smallest feet in the world are those of the Chinese ladies, and they are the ugliest also.
>
> (Cooper 2013: 84)

Wilde continues to draw parallels with the fine and applied arts when he discusses colour and line. Costume is as dependent on colour scheme as the design of a room, but here too there must be room for the individuality of the person being dressed. A tall person can wear more colours than a short one. Horizontal lines, which diminish the height of the human figure just as a dado rail diminishes the height of a room, are used too often, vertical and oblique lines too seldom. Patterns should accommodate themselves to the human form. Arithmetical patterns are generally unsuccessful, because they impose an unnatural structure upon a natural figure, exaggerating asymmetries and distracting the eye. Many patterns, Wilde complains, are simply too large to be used in clothing:

> I happened lately in London to be looking for some stamped grey plush or velvet, suitable for making a cloak of. Every shop that I went into the man showed me the most enormous patterns, things far too big for an ordinary wallpaper, far too big for ordinary curtains, things, in fact, that would require a large public building to show them off to any advantage. I entreated the shopman to show me a pattern that would be in some rational and relative proportion to the figure of somebody who was not over ten or twelve feet in height. He replied that he was extremely sorry but it was impossible; the smaller patterns were no longer being woven, in fact, the big patterns were in fashion.
>
> (Cooper 2013: 86–87)

This brings Wilde to his second major argument. Thus far, all his observations have tended towards the central point that dress should accommodate itself to the human form, whereas Victorian fashion wrenches that form into unnatural and uncomfortable attitudes. He now makes the related remark that if fashion were based on natural and intelligible laws, rather than on caprice, it would not change so often. Fashion, he says, is 'the great enemy of art':

> Fashion rests upon folly. Art rests upon law. Fashion is ephemeral. Art is eternal. Indeed what is a fashion really? A fashion is merely a form of ugliness so absolutely unbearable that we have to alter it every six months! It is quite clear that were it beautiful and rational we would not alter anything that combined those two rare qualities. And whenever dress has been so, it has remained unchanged in law and principle for many hundred years.
>
> (Cooper 2013: 87)

Wilde has already mentioned the Greek and Roman appreciation of the human form, and he clearly has classical precedents in mind when he talks of dress remaining unchanged for hundreds of years. The toga was retained, largely unaltered, as the formal dress of the Romans for over a thousand years, from the time of Numa Pompilius (715–673 BCE) to the decline of the Western Empire in the fifth century. The characteristic clothing styles of Ancient Greece, the *chiton*, the *chlamys* and the *himation* resembled the toga in being loose draperies, simply formed from a single rectangle of cloth, which also remained largely unchanged for centuries. By the time 'The philosophy of dress' was published, Wilde had already begun to give public lectures on the topic of dress reform. A newspaper report of the first of these lectures, given in Ealing on 1 October 1884, records his admiration for 'the costumes of the Greeks, Assyrians, and Egyptians' and concludes:

> Generally, he expressed himself strongly in favour of such a modification of the Greek costume as would meet the exigencies of our varying climate.
>
> (*Pall Mall Gazette* 2 October 1884: 7)

A lengthy correspondence ensued in the *Pall Mall Gazette*, in which Wilde clarified his position on the adoption of Greek dress in the face of numerous charges of impracticality and antiquarianism. He claimed that the use of wool as the principal material for clothing would answer the practical objections, and said that he wanted to elucidate the principals of dress, which the Greeks had understood, rather than to revive a defunct style:

> I am not proposing any antiquarian revival of an ancient costume, but trying merely to point out the right laws of dress, laws which are dictated by art and not by archaeology, by science and not by fashion.
>
> (*Pall Mall Gazette* 14 October 1884: 6)

A few months later, and a few weeks before publishing 'The philosophy of dress', Wilde returned to the pages of the *Pall Mall Gazette* to expatiate upon his ideas about the relation of dress to art, and the superiority of Ancient Greek to Modern English dress:

> Art is not to be taught in Academies. It is what one looks at, not what one listens to, that makes the artist. The real schools should be the streets. There is not, for instance, a single delicate line, or delightful proportion, in the dress of the Greeks, which is not echoed exquisitely in their architecture. A nation arrayed in stove-pipe hats, and dress improvers, might have built the Pantechnicon, possibly, but the Parthenon, never.
>
> (*Pall Mall Gazette* 28 February 1885: 4)[2]

Wilde adds an economic dimension to his advocacy of a classical form of dress, based on immutable aesthetic principles, by pointing out how expensive it is to acquire new clothes and hats every few months, asserting that 'if I were to state the sum that is spent yearly on bonnets alone, I am sure that one half of the community would be filled with remorse and the other half with despair!' This is not because the latest bonnets from Paris are any finer than last season's fashions. It is rather occasioned by 'that unhealthy necessity for change which Fashion imposes on its beautiful and misguided votaries' (Cooper 2013: 87).

This critique of the wasteful and unsustainable economics of fashion is in line with Wilde's Utopian Socialism, advanced in such works as *The Soul of Man* and his essay on the Chinese philosopher, Zhuangzi, with whom he agrees that, 'The order of nature is rest, repetition, and peace' (Ellmann 1982: 223). Finance-driven fashion, in direct contrast to this idyllic state of repose, demands the 'constant evolution of horror from horror' (Cooper 2013: 88).

Somewhat surprisingly, in view of the elaborate costumes in which he was photographed as an undergraduate, Wilde insists on simplicity as a central principle of dress and condemns the frills, furbelows and flounces of fashionable French milliners as 'execrable to look at, expensive to pay for, and absolutely useless to wear' (Cooper 2013: 91). Although Wilde was a Francophile, fluent in French, a frequent visitor to Paris, and a fervent admirer or French literature, he deplores the influence of Paris fashions on London and New York, not out of insularity, but because he sees the imposition of something alien and pre-fabricated as one of the chief defects of the fashion industry. This accords with his views on the decorative arts, since he often censures rich Americans for importing their furniture and utensils from Europe, rather than encouraging local artisans to create distinctively American styles.

The principal focus of 'The philosophy of dress' is on women's clothing, a shift from that of the 1882 lectures, which were principally concerned with male attire. Throughout the article, Wilde has emphasized the uncomfortable and constricting nature of women's dress, which combined discomfort with ugliness as it forced the female form into unnatural contortions. He even mentions a corset, invented by Catherine de Medici, designed to compress the circumference of a woman's waist to thirteen inches, 'which may be regarded as the climax of a career of crime' (Cooper 2013: 88).[3] For the most part, however, he describes these ungainly fashions as being imposed by male milliners on their female customers, and he ends with an appeal to women to rid themselves of this sartorial tyranny:

> I know that, irrespective of Congress, the women of America can carry any reform they like. And I feel certain that they will not continue much longer to encourage a style of dress which is founded on the idea that the human figure is deformed and requires the devices of the milliner to be made presentable. For have they not the most delicate and dainty hands and feet in the world? Have they not complexions like ivory stained with a rose-leaf? Are they not always in office in their own country, and do they not spread havoc through Europe? *Appello, non ad Caesarem, sed ad Caesaris uxorem.*
>
> (Cooper 2013: 93)

Wilde continued to appeal directly to his female readers to exercise more control over their own attire when he took over the editorship of *The Lady's World* in April 1887. His first act as editor was to change the title of the magazine to *The Woman's World*, an amendment which reflected a more egalitarian social tone. In the first publication Wilde contrasted the ugliness and discomfort of fashionable costume with the simple clothes of factory girls, pit-women and fishwives, all of whom he described as nobly dressed. As John Cooper observes:

> Wilde's paradoxical (and repeated) use of the word *noble* in connection with the working clothes of ordinary people may be deliberate, and if so, is concomitant with the class-based agenda of the dress reform movement.
>
> (2013: 116, original emphasis)

In the same editorial, he predicted that the clothes worn by men and women would gradually become more similar 'as similarity of costume always follows similarity of pursuits' and that twentieth-century attire 'will emphasise distinctions of occupation, not distinctions of sex' (*The Woman's World* November 1887: 1). Wilde's interest in dress is therefore allied not only with his artistic philosophy, but with his Socialist and Feminist political opinions. It is significant that, while he substantially altered the tone and content of *The Lady's World* upon turning it into *The Woman's World*, he did not diminish the portion of the magazine devoted to dress in favour of literature or the fine arts. *The Woman's World* was not solely, or even primarily, a fashion magazine. It concerned itself with numerous aspects of women's lives including literature, art and politics, but Wilde always kept dress and dress reform close to the centre of his remit as editor.

Whereas Wilde's 1882 lectures on decoration and design were widely ridiculed in both England and America, his articles and lectures on dress reform were much more warmly received. Even the *New-York Tribune* in publishing 'The philosophy of dress' remarked that in 1882 Wilde 'was never taken seriously. But he really appears to advantage in his article today' (*New-York Tribune* 19 April 1885: 6). This judgement was widely echoed in the press, even by such unlikely journals as *The American Engineer* and *Railway Conductor's Monthly*, which opined:

> For all we have uttered in derision of Oscar Wilde and his whims, dear friends, forgive us. Here is the most common sense we have seen in many a day on dress and fashion.
>
> (*Railway Conductor's Monthly* 1 July 1885: II.7)

Oscar Wilde's critical fortunes have risen and fallen dramatically since his early notoriety in the 1870s, but perhaps they have never stood higher than they do today. For the last 40 years, his reputation as a major writer and thinker on art, politics, feminism, nationalism, sexuality, critical theory and a host of other subjects has steadily grown. As Harold Bloom observes, 'after more than a hundred years literary opinion has converged in the judgment that Wilde, as Borges asserts, was almost always right. This rightness, which transcends wit, is now seen as central to the importance of being Oscar' (Bloom 1985: 1). This sentiment is echoed in the closing words of Richard Ellmann's landmark biography:

He belongs to our world more than to Victoria's. Now, beyond the reach of scandal, his best writings validated by time, he comes before us still, a towering figure, laughing and weeping, with parables and paradoxes, so generous, so amusing, and so right.

(1988: 589)

Wilde's writing on fashion has been neglected in recent decades because the perceived triviality of the subject accords with the perception of hostile contemporaries such as Nordau, and of scholars for the first 60 or 70 years after his death, that he was little more than a foppishly dressed dilettante who shocked the Victorian public with his cynical wit; rather than with the view of Bloom, Ellmann and a host of other modern critics that Wilde was a considerable and original thinker. Part of the problem lies with the word 'fashion', for which Wilde invariably expressed contempt as an arbitrary notion fundamentally opposed to art, individuality and a timeless conception of beauty. There is also the programmatic approach, typically Victorian whether Wilde would have admitted it or not, of trying to distil all the principles of human attire into a rational system and scientifically establish its relation to the other arts. The elements of Wilde's system, however, from material to colour to pattern to cut and comfort, are always amply justified, and his treatment of the subject raises the question of what we wear from an endless sequence of arbitrary, financial and economically driven adjustments to a profound consideration of the part that beauty can and should play in our lives, as well as its relation to such ethical concepts as freedom, hedonics and sustainability. For these reasons alone, he remains a vital voice in any discussion of the philosophy of fashion.

References

Bloom, H. (ed.) (1985), *Oscar Wilde*, New York: Chelsea House.

Cohen, P. K. (1978), *The Moral Vision of Oscar Wilde*, Rutherford: Fairleigh Dickinson University Press.

Cooper, J. (2013), *Oscar Wilde on Dress*, Philadelphia: CSM Press.

Ellmann, R. (1982), *The Artist as Critic: Critical Writings of Oscar Wilde*, Chicago: Chicago University Press.

———— (1988), *Oscar Wilde*, New York: Knopf.

Haweis, E. M. (1879), *The Art of Dress*, London: Chatto & Windus.

Holland, V. (1999), *Son of Oscar Wilde*, New York: Carroll & Graf.

Moyle, F. (2011), *Constance: The Tragic and Scandalous Life of Mrs. Oscar Wilde*, London: John Murray.

Nordau, M. ([1892] 1993), *Degeneration*, Lincoln: University of Nebraska Press.

Ross, I. (2015), *Oscar Wilde and Ancient Greece*, Cambridge: Cambridge University Press.

Shewan, R. (1977), *Oscar Wilde: Art and Egotism*, London: Macmillan.

Wilde, O. (1885), 'The philosophy of dress', *New-York Tribune*, 19 April, p. 9.

———— ([1908] 1913), *Essays and Lectures* (ed. R. B. Ross), London: Methuen.

—— (2000), *The Complete Letters of Oscar Wilde* (eds V. Holland and H. Davis), New York: Henry Holt.

—— (2000–13), *The Complete Works of Oscar Wilde* (ed. I. Small), vols I–VII, Oxford: Oxford University Press.

Notes

1 Wilde demonstrates elsewhere his understanding that a milliner is a hat-maker, but throughout this article he uses the word to mean 'dress-maker'.
2 The Pantechnicon was a large picture gallery, furniture shop and warehouse, which opened on Motcomb Street in Belgravia in the 1830s. It had a Greek revival façade of Doric columns.
3 Wilde probably learned about Catherine de Medici's corset from a lecture given by Lewis Strange Wingfield at the International Health Exhibition in 1884. Wingfield compared the device to an implement of torture used by the Spanish inquisition. Contemporary newspaper reports mention Wilde's presence at the exhibition, and he cites the work of one of the main contributors, Dr Gustav Jaeger, in 'The philosophy of dress'.

Chapter 5

Lolita through the Looking Glass: Alice, the Japanese Lolita Subculture and the Lolita Complex

Kathryn A. Hardy Bernal

The Japanese subcultural fashion aesthetic known as Lolita is inexorably bound to the archetypical image of the fictional character, Alice, the child heroine of Lewis Carroll's novels, *Alice's Adventures in Wonderland* (1865), better known as *Alice in Wonderland*, and *Through the Looking-Glass, and What Alice Found There* (1871), or *Alice, Through the Looking-Glass*.[1] This is not surprising when one considers that Japan has long been enamoured with Carroll's young female protagonist. It is also fitting that Lolita style resonates with Alice, in that the subcultural movement is represented by adolescent girls and women who dress in doll-like attire reminiscent of Victorian Period clothing for young girls, epitomized and influenced by Alice's silhouette, drawn by the artist Sir John Tenniel for the original *Alice* publications.

However, while the Japanese Lolita style signifies this affiliation with Tenniel's Alice, it is never a direct translation of her image, or a costume, but manifests an embodiment, or an essence, of her persona. Most often, the references are semiotic, and only become more literal if garments are decorated with *Alice* motifs. This Alice-Lolita relationship is further accentuated in other areas of Japanese popular culture related to the subculture, such as *shojo manga* graphic novels, *anime* and fine art.[2] Nori Tomizaki's digital paintings and manipulated photographs are embedded in the more gothic aspects of the Lolita subculture, portraying 'human-doll', Alice-Lolita figures that emphasize the macabre undercurrent of the *Alice* stories. Here, Alice and the Japanese Lolita are juxtaposed to create a sweet-but-scary-little-girl-doll presence. This chapter examines these intertextual relationships between Alice, the Japanese Lolita subculture, popular culture, and the doll-like aspects of the Lolita style. It also explores a common perception that there may be more than a superficial connection between Alice and Lolita, or more than one based merely on surface values and visual observations.

It is thought to be no coincidence that Charles Lutwidge Dodgson (aka Lewis Carroll, 1832–98), is said to have suffered from the same syndrome as the fictional Humbert Humbert, an adult-male character who becomes sexually preoccupied with the female-child subject of Vladimir Nabokov's notorious novel, *Lolita* (1955).[3] This psychological disorder, referred to as the 'Lolita Complex', is designated by an older man's obsession with underage girls; in other words, paedophilia. Furthermore, the author, Nabokov, often spoke of his fascination with Dodgson's infamous reputation, stating that it partially influenced his creation of Humbert's character. Interpretations of the Alice-Lolita style are, therefore, problematized in light of this information, not least because of the branding of the movement as 'Lolita'. This chapter thus leads to an investigation into the validity of the subculture's identification

Figure 1: Alice and the Pirates, Japan. 'Beardsley Rose Alice' baby-doll jumperskirt in rouge (detail), 2009. Photograph by the author.

with the so-called Lolita Complex and argues that there is no *real* evidence to support these circumstantial associations.

The Japanese Lolita as an Identity and Its Relationships with Alice

The Lolita, or 'Gothloli' (*Gosurori, Gosu-loli* or 'Gothic Lolita'),[4] is a member of the Lolita subculture, a phenomenon pertaining to a broader Japanese movement known as Gothic & Lolita (or G&L).[5] While the Gothloli's image references elements of French Rococo, it favours nineteenth-century designs, particularly for the young Victorian child. To add to this little-girl appearance, garments are occasionally adorned with motifs from fairy tales, such as *Rapunzel, Snow White, Cinderella, The Little Mermaid, The Sleeping Beauty* and *Little Red Riding Hood*. However, more often, inspiration comes from Tenniel's illustrations for Carroll's *Alice* stories, and as Masafumi Monden states, '[o]ne of the arenas where the imagery of *Alice* has been a colourful and enduring inspiration is in the world of fashion. Most notably, this is the case for Japanese Lolita' (2015: 86). Monden further claims that 'Lewis Carroll's fictional character Alice has been one of the most famous and beloved literary heroines in contemporary Japanese culture' (2014: 265).

In his book, *Japanese Fashion Cultures*, Monden traces the history of Carroll's literature in Japan, and confirms that the Japanese people have been endeared towards the tales for more than a century:

> [The] two books [...] have had a strong presence in Japan since the first Japanese translation of *Through the Looking-Glass* appeared as a sequential novel of eight episodes published in *Youth's World* (*Shōnen sekai*), a magazine for boys throughout 1899. Maruyama Eikan's *Fantastic Tales of Ai* (*Ai-chan no yume monogatari*), published in 1910 by Naga Shuppan Kyōkai, is said to have been the first complete translation of *Alice*. This [...] book with Tenniel's illustrations, where the heroine is called Ai instead of Alice, indicates the difficulty of fully translating Carroll's word play and puns into Japanese. Nonetheless, the Japanese [...] fascination with *Alice* has continued.
>
> (2015: 86)

Monden believes that the popularity of *Alice* in Japan has been, and is mostly, due to a celebration of Tenniel's drawings. This is evidenced in the embracement of these motifs by the Lolita subculture (Monden 2015: 86). Besides the application of *Alice* characters as decoration, the basic silhouette of the Gothloli's dress harks back to the original fashioning of Carroll's heroine.

Tenniel's nineteenth-century Alice is adorned in a pale-blue, slightly high-waisted, one-piece dress with puffed sleeves and a full skirt, tied with a large bow-sash and supported by a full petticoat. A white pinafore apron, also tied around the middle, covers this frock. Inconsistently, she wears black-and-white-striped tights and a black 'Alice' band, or headband, in some images, and a blue head-bow and white tights, in others. Other variations are a red bow-sash wrapped over her white pinafore; or a yellow dress, with a blue sash and blue tights. On her feet are always black, flat-heeled, 'Mary Jane' court shoes, with one buckled strap. In any and every case, however, the main stylistic elements and shape remain the same. This historical blueprint has been perpetuated via a plethora of film adaptations of the *Alice* narrative since 1903, including *Alice in Wonderland* in 1933 (released in Japan in 1934), and defined by Walt Disney's animated version in 1951 (Japanese distribution in 1952).[6] It was, in fact, Disney's stylization that solidified the typical Alice appearance and helped to secure her image in the minds of popular imagination, as a young girl in a pale-blue, puffed-sleeved, one-piece dress, with a white apron pinafore, white tights, a black headband and black Mary Janes.

While the Japanese Lolita style follows the fundamental aesthetics of this archetypal Alice, the Gothloli's look only begins with the basic design elements. Dressing, literally, as the Alice character is considered to be, alternatively, participating in 'cosplay'. Cosplayers wear replica costumes of fictional figures, from literature, film, television shows, comics and animations, and often 'play' at being those characters. To confuse cosplay with Lolita style is to undermine the meaning of Lolita as a subcultural movement; for many members, Lolita clothing is part of a lifestyle, not fancy-dress costume play (see Peirson-Smith in this volume). As Yuniya Kawamura maintains:

> For the authentic Lolita followers, it is highly offensive for them to be called cosplayers. Lolita is an important part of their life; sometimes, it consumes their entire life.
>
> (2012: 73)

The main danger in confusing the two practices would be in the suggestion that the Gothloli, the 'Lolita', is a character, which would fuel the widespread misunderstanding that the fashion style is related to Nabokov's promiscuous young-girl protagonist, and is thus intended to be sexually provocative. If there is one opinion that rings the loudest throughout worldwide Gothloli communities, it is that they certainly do not wish to be associated with the novel, *Lolita*. Kawamura agrees, stating that 'the Japanese Lolita subculture […] has nothing to do with such references. Many Lolita members know nothing about the Nabokov novel' (2012: 66).

Although there are numerous genres of Lolita style, including the two main categories of Gothic Lolita and Sweet Lolita,[7] the overarching intention of the Gothloli appearance is in sympathy not with Nabokov's Lolita but with the modest and innocent reputation of Alice. There is, therefore, often a high neckline, and usually a no shorter than knee-length hemline. In mimicking an historical young-girls' look, the Gothloli typically chooses from a one-piece dress (OP); a skirt and blouse; or what is termed a 'jumperskirt' (JSK), a pinafore-dress worn over a blouse. All of these garments create a full-circled or bell shape, helped by layers of petticoats, and bloomers. In exaggerating an impression of a child's physique, the bodice may finish at the natural waist, just above it, or even at the baby-doll Empire line, which is frequently tied with a sash. Accessories will be short or long socks, or full tights (sometimes striped liked Tenniel's little girl's); Mary Jane shoes or lace-up boots, platforms or 'rocking-horse ballerinas';[8] and some sort of headwear, such as a Victorian-style headdress or bonnet, beret, mini top hat, mourning/bridal veil, floral wreath, flower or bow hairclips, a bow headband, or an 'Alice' band. While many 'coords' (or coordinates), as they are called in Gothloli circles, evoke an essence of Alice, the addition of a pinafore apron, worn over the OP, is one of the strongest visual elements that succinctly ties the Lolita to the Alice image. The accompaniment of a plush rabbit, as an alternative to a teddy bear, does the same, as these items also enhance the little-girl identity. However, especially in the early days (up until about the mid-2000s), it was a more common practice to carry a doll. Several Lolita garment labels have collaborated with Japanese doll companies to produce sought-after, limited release G&L doll collections, catering to Gothloli tastes. This industry also satisfies the Gothloli's popular love of Alice. Three of the most collected types of dolls, Pullip, Blythe and Dollfie, all manufacture various *Alice* and Lolita ranges, some even replicating adult Lolita designer fashions.

Alice and the Lolita style are even more consciously related through the use of *Alice*-print dress materials. The fashion label most synonymous with Alice in Japan is Baby, the Stars Shine Bright (BTSSB, or Baby). Since at least the turn of the twenty-first century, this Japanese company has produced prolific fashion collections from *Alice* prints, including 'Alice and the Seven Keys' (2006), 'Alice Chess' (2008), 'Alice and the Looking Glass of Time' (2009), 'Disney Alice in Wonderland ~ Episode of the Tea Party' (2012), and yet more variations on the *Alice* theme, some in collaboration with Disney, in 2015. The brand's association with the *Alice* stories was consolidated in 2004, with their creation of a sister label, Alice and the Pirates, which fuses the notion of Wonderland and Neverland in their range titles, for instance, 'Alice's Never Voyage' (2008). Baby's main competitor, Angelic Pretty, has also brought out Disney *Alice* designs, such as 'Disney × Angelic Pretty Alice in Wonderland' (2014). Another main source for acquiring Japanese *Alice*-motif Lolita fashions is Putumayo, while Manifesteange Metamorphose temps de fille,[9] Victorian Maiden, Innocent World, Mary Magdalene, Chocochip Cookie, Juliette et Justine,[10] Millefleurs, Marchenmerry, MAM and Bodyline have also released *Alice*-inspired designs.

The Origins of Lolita Style and the Alice-Lolita Identity

Although the silhouette of the Lolita style has evolved, the basic 'Alice' form has remained the same. It was apparent in trends that would later be recognized as Lolita, emerging in the 1970s, growing as a craze in the 1980s, crystallizing in the 1990s, and establishing what prevailed into the twenty-first century as the authoritative, authentic standard. According to Patrick Macias and Izumi Evers in *Japanese Schoolgirl Inferno*, the Alice-Lolita look came off the Japanese streets, with a forerunner being the *Nagomo-gyaru* style (2007: 121). They claim that these so-called *Nagomo* girls, who apparently followed the music of the Nagomo Records label,[11] 'liked to make their own clothes, constructing strange fashions that toyed with a surreal vision of childhood not too far away from *Alice in Wonderland*' (Macias and Evers 2007: 122). This seventies do-it-yourself, childlike image, which was often combined with vintage clothing to create an eclectic, quaint, old-world appearance, in keeping with other young girls' preoccupations of the times, such as Holly Hobbie dolls, the characters from *Little House on the Prairie* and *Anne of Green Gables*, was marketed in Japan by labels such as Milk, Pink House and Emily Temple Cute, and is now sometimes referred to as Natural *Kei*, or Dolly *Kei*.

Inspired by this movement, it was BTSSB, however, that had one of the greatest influences on formalizing the Lolita style. The original Baby designer, Akinori Isobe, launched his flagship store in Shibuya, Tokyo, with his wife and business partner, Fumiyo, in 1988. Tiffany Godoy states that:

Figure 2: Emily Perkins and Kathryn A. Hardy
Bernal wearing *Alice* border-print Lolita dresses
by Bodyline, Japan, 2013. Photograph courtesy of
James George Stratton Percy.

Isobe started Baby [...] after working at Atsuki Ohnishi's design office. Ohnishi, Baby and the Lolita movement were influenced by designer Isao Kaneko [for Pink House] [...] and his romantic Victorian-meets-*Little-House-on-the-Prairie*-style outfits that were lovely, pink and ruffled. In the early days, Isobe explains, they struggled to find a brand identity [...]. A quick fix was discovered in the addition of lace and ribbons. Lots of them.

(Godoy 2007: 142)

Although Ohnishi is seen as a pioneer of the Lolita subcultural style, there is no doubt that with BTSSB, Akinori Isobe refined and codified what Atsuki Ohnishi, and Isao Kaneko before him, had accomplished, to create the frilly 'Alice' silhouette that Lolita now typifies.

Another important figurehead for the catalyst of the phenomenon, especially the instigation of the gothic aspect of Lolita, even perhaps the term, *Gosu-loli/Gosurori*, was Mana, a musician and now one of the foremost leading designers of G&L. Renowned for taking on the image of the Gothic Lolita, both onstage and off, Mana is still considered by many Gothloli, worldwide, to be their consummate idol. In the company literature for his label, Même-moi-Moitié, he once prescribed the profile of the ideal Lolita:

She should be slender with empty, seductive eyes and five foot four. She should like listening to French Gothic music and reading European children's literature, live in a manor and enjoy going for walks, shopping, visiting galleries and listening to classical concerts.

(Keet 2007: 87–88)

Hence, to be Lolita, Mana declared, is to represent oneself as a cultured little girl. Besides the activities he mentioned, the Lolita subculture also traditionally involves somewhat 'childish' behaviour, such as playing dress-ups, collecting and playing with dolls and attending dolly tea parties. One of the Gothloli's favourite pastimes is to meet up with other doll-like friends to partake in high tea, served from floral porcelain sets. Although the doll, itself, does not correlate to the figure of Alice, nor the *Alice* stories, it is specifically through the Gothloli activity of taking tea, an allusion to the Mad Hatter's tea party in *Alice in Wonderland*, that Alice, the Lolita and dolls are symbolically united.

Japanese Doll Culture and the Alice-Lolita-Doll Identity in Art and Popular Culture

I asked a charming Japanese girl, 'How can a doll live?'; 'Why', she answered, 'if you love it enough, it will live!'

(Davis 1992: 214, citing Hearn 1894)

The Gothloli, even in her image, reflects a strong affinity with dolls (*ningyō*, or 'human shapes'). It is evident that a powerful relationship with dolls is also traditionally Japanese. According to Alan Scott Pate:

Ningyō have played a far more important role in Japanese culture than one might initially imagine. From the dawn of Japanese history right down to the present day, *ningyō* have been woven into the very fabric of Japanese society, serving a multitude of roles from talismanic to onanistic, from high art to child's play and nearly every conceivable shade in between [...]. *Ningyō* represent a category of objects that goes far beyond our limited concept of doll.

(2008: 19)

An indication that, psychologically, the Japanese people have been attached to dolls in more complex ways than are customary in Euro-American societies is the age-old superstition that the *ningyō* possesses a soul. According to Ellen Schattschneider there is:

[A] widely reported sensibility in Japan that *ningyō* (dolls) have a kind of soul (*tamashii*) and that they may carry the identity, motivation or essence of a person who has made, given or owned them.

(2005: 330)

That these beliefs are still relevant in Japan is suggested by the continued existence of ritual practices, or 'rites of separation' (*kuyō*), considered appropriate for the separation of an owner from their doll. Schattschneider also claims that:

> A doll that has been played with by a child is widely held to have taken on certain attributes of that child and cannot be safely discarded until the object's 'spirit' has been separated from it through ritual action.

(2005: 332)

These procedures may even be performed due to a terror that the doll's soul may come back to haunt. According to Angelika Kretschmer, if a doll is just thrown away, its 'spirit might be offended and even curse the human. Therefore, the spirit must be pacified before the object can be discarded' (Kretschmer 2000: 384):

> The chief priest of Awashima Kada Shrine who performs *kuyō* rites for inanimate objects, especially dolls, expresses this sentiment: '[People] come to… dispose of dolls that might bring evil upon them […]. It seems very cruel to treat [the dolls, otherwise] as mere garbage'.

(Kretschmer 2000: 384–85)

The method of disposal is sometimes burial but usually dolls are destroyed by burning as this 'symbolically eliminates impurities and, moreover, mimics human cremation' (Kretschmer 2000: 386).

Schattschneider discusses this phenomenon in regard to yet another purification rite in connection with *nagashi bina* ('floating dolls'), whereby *ningyō*, who are 'understood as capable of absorbing evils or impurities that afflict persons', are floated downstream and out to sea, in boats, from the *Awashima Jinja* Shrine, during the *Hina-nagashi* festival, on Girls' Day, every 3 March, 'carrying away [with them] these forms of pollution' (2005: 332). She highlights the notion that:

> [This] relatively recent practice of *ningyō kuyō* ('doll memorialization'), in which old dolls are burned, floated away, or otherwise disposed of after formal religious memorial services, [exists due to the belief that *ningyō*] […] cannot be safely discarded until the object's 'spirit' has been separated from it through ritual action.

(2005: 332)

The importance of these rituals in Japan can be observed in the prominence of *ningyō* festivals. Another notable event held on Girls' Day, the same day as *Hina-nagashi*, is the centuries-old *Hina-matsuri*. *Hina-matsuri* involves the exhibition of dolls, depicting historical figures from the noble Heian past (794–1185 CE), featuring the imperial couple, or *dairi-bina*, their attendants, ladies-in-waiting, entertainers and ministers, surrounded by an abundance of offerings, such as rice cakes and *sake*, to keep the dolls' 'spirits' satiated. To the Japanese people, these *hina-ningyō* not only have souls but are serious solemn entities, possessing spiritual powers. From the early seventeenth century when this ritual began as an almost exclusive practice for the benefit of the élite, through to the 1800s as it was opened up to people from all walks of life as a seasonal festival, on to the present day, these dolls have been believed to be talismanic spirits with the power to purify the home and protect, especially, girl children. *Hina-matsuri* displays are, therefore, arranged in private households all over Japan, as well as formal, public settings, for the purpose of bringing good health and growth to families raising young girls. Japan's Girls' Day is thus both a celebration of dolls *and* girls. That a special day has been held for over 300 years, specifically for young girls, demonstrates that the idolization of little girls in Japan is not something new.

The affinity between the little Japanese girl and the doll is conspicuous in Japanese popular culture. A notable example, which also connects Alice and Lolita, is the *Rozen Maiden Träumend* series, produced in both *manga* graphic novels and *anime* formats. The storyline revolves around Lolita-styled dolls who 'come to life' and battle with one another in order to win the 'Alice' game, so that they may transcend their existence and become Alice, a perfect, real, little-girl child.

This intertextualization of Alice, Lolita, the little girl and the 'living doll' is exemplified in the art of Nori Tomizaki. Although the little-girl-doll theme is prolific in Japan, Tomizaki is one of the most exalted fine artists of the cute-gothic genre. The value that his imagery holds within Gothic and Lolita communities was highlighted when the company Angelic Pretty commissioned him to design backdrop illustrations for their Autumn Collection catalogue (2006), depicting one of his Alice-Lolita characters and her rabbit friends. Tomizaki's oeuvre is the representation of doll-like Gothloli or lifelike dolls, in which the identity of Alice-Lolita possesses a decidedly gothic edge, portraying a sweet-but-scary-little-girl-doll persona who often inhabits a Wonderland filled with eerie details. These illustrations and digital paintings range from the unsettling to the grisly.

The *Alice* motif is noticeably employed by Tomizaki in *Invitation* (2006), and in two pieces that complement each other to form a diptych, *Tree of Notes* and *Door* (2006). In line with Carroll's narrative, the Alice of these images appears to be too big for the space that she occupies: In *Invitation*, a white rabbit escapes through a tiny door in the wall, as an archetypal Alice, dressed in a pale-blue-and-white dress and black Mary Jane shoes, stares into a 'looking-glass'; she is yet to discover, behind her, the vial of green liquid, tagged with the note, 'Drink Me', which will make her small enough to pursue him; while, in *Tree of Notes*, she is accompanied by rabbits as she emerges from a too-small door.

Perhaps the uncanny aspect of Nori's art is that all of his Alice-Lolita girls are 'ball-jointed' figures. Mimicking dolls, each of their limbs are attached and 'articulated' by ball joints. However, his characters do not appear to be manufactured of plastic materials; their joints look more like sore, reddened, 'human' flesh. This impression is present in all of Nori's paintings but is accentuated in his digitally manipulated, multimedia photographic works, which also carry his signature theme. In an example, *Mayura* (2010), of one of his

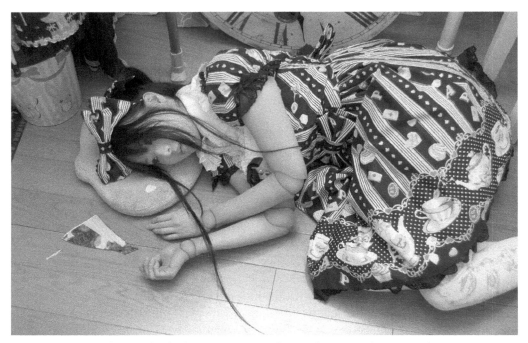

Figure 3: Nori Tomizaki, *Articulated Spheres: Mayura*, 2010. Photograph courtesy of Nori Tomizaki.

Kyuutai Kansetsu Shiki (Ball-Jointed Type) series, entitled *Articulated Spheres*; the Alice-Lolita living-doll (or perhaps 'dead' doll) motif is distinct. Adorned from head to toe in the classic image of the Sweet Lolita, the model wears an all-over patterned dress, with a border design of teapots, jugs and teacups, alluding to the *Alice* tea party; behind her are further *Alice* motifs, a large clock and, near her head, a waste-paper bin decorated with rabbits. She lies on the floor, in a foetal position, inanimate; her head rests on a cushion, which suggests she is asleep and, like Alice, dreaming of a narrative formulated by the imagery around her. However, her eyes are open: she, therefore, could be dead. Perhaps, though, she might be like one of *Rozen Maiden*'s characters, a dormant doll-child, or a doll with a soul, waiting to be 'awakened' or brought to real life. Her flesh-like ball joints strengthen this sensibility. But, this aspect also creates ambiguity: The lines in her wrists and the way she is holding out her hands, combined with her vacantly staring eyes, might equally lead one to read this image as symbolic of suicide.

In *Heart*, another disconcerting image, an Alice-like Lolita holds the key to a barred-window door of what could be perhaps a meat-locker, morgue, laboratory, operating theatre, asylum, gaol cell or dungeon. The wall of the room she stands in is lined with pretty floral paper from which either human or animal hearts hang ominously from meat hooks. A blue-rimmed, white enamel tray, filled with even more hearts, sits on the floor. *Connection* is, again, a grim picture, whereby two 'live' mannequins, or Gothic-Lolita puppet-dolls, add a sinister element to the concept of the tea party. One of the girls is clothed in black; the other is naked, revealing a pubescent body. They sit at a table covered with a blood-soaked, white tablecloth, which seems to have been stained by what may have been the contents of the upset teapot, while the clothed girl cuts the strings from the limbs of the naked girl with a pair of scissors, releasing her from bondage.

Tomizaki's imagery thus idolizes the little girl as it simultaneously fetishizes her, and much of his work may be analysed in context with themes of BDSM.[12] If we take the examples already discussed, there is a subtext of voyeurism, bondage and sexual violence. The 'dungeon', in *Heart*, takes on a new meaning; the cutting of strings and the spilling of blood, in *Connection*, evokes a 'deflowering', or initiation ritual; and the grooves in the girls' wrists and ankles, although also the joins in their ball joints, mimic the marks left after the use of rope restraints, which is an especially unnerving suggestion in the case of 'dead' *Mayura*. An ominous tone is also present in *Invitation*, once one realizes that male figures are standing in the foreground (we can see the backs of their heads) and watching the Alice-Lolita character as she looks at herself in the looking-glass. *Is* the 'invitation' from the white rabbit for her to follow him through the little door? Or is she inviting her voyeurs, and us, to gaze at her, objectify her? This aspect becomes intensely unsettling in another work, *I Dance*, as we view the little girl through the legs of two male onlookers who tower over her. Although we only see the backs of their trousered legs, we sense a deeply menacing atmosphere.

This alternate way of reading Tomizaki's work problematizes the intentions and interpretations of the Lolita style as being sweet and modest, particularly when contemplated in relation to dolls, which carry with them proliferating meanings connected with the sex industry and sex toys. These types of 'little-girl' images in art and popular culture, thus, also bring into question the reputation of Lolita's muse, Alice, as the untainted, perfect child.

The Victorian Cult of the Child, the 'Lolita Complex' and Alice-Lolita as *Shōjo* Icon

One of the paradoxes about Japanese Lolita fashion is that the image is intended to be sweet and innocent, but it is often read in terms of fetish, and thus sexualized. Complicated ambiguities stem from the name, firstly due to the Nabokovian association but, also, in connection with certain imagery widely perceived to be related to the Lolita movement, which objectifies and fetishizes the little girl. The Internet, particularly, is saturated with this material; referred to as *roricon*, or *lolicon*, contracted from 'Lolita' and 'complex', it is comprised of paedophilic, pornographic *manga* and *hentai* (sexually explicit *anime*) depicting young and mostly underage girls, posed provocatively or involved in sexual acts, usually with older boys or men.[13] This exacerbates problems caused by the 'Lolita' terminology. The Gothloli becomes associated with this paradigm because she is often a young girl, and is known as Lolita, which leads to misunderstandings about participation in the Lolita subculture.

To some extent, the same can be said about Nabokov's protagonist, Lolita, as her reputation is dependent on the interpretation of the book. The most common perception is that she is a promiscuous, sexually active child/adolescent. However, that picture is affected by the narrator's perspective; we are influenced by Humbert Humbert's relaying of the story, a paedophile. If we strip away that distortion, we may see that Lolita is a victim of abuse and statutory rape. Similarly, Carroll's Alice is often viewed through a warped lens:

> Perhaps reflecting the 'enigmatic' sexuality of the author, Alice herself has been perceived and interpreted in a dualistic way, namely as an innocent child and a self-assertively sexualized 'Lolita'.
>
> (Monden 2014: 265)

Although Alice and Lolita are more often judged as the antithesis of each other, or in terms of the 'virgin versus whore', there remains a dichotomy in regard to both of their natures. This is the result of connections made between the actual authors of *Lolita* and *Alice*, and perceived associations, of both Vladimir Nabokov and Charles Dodgson (aka Lewis Carroll), with the Lolita Complex. Nabokov, whose novel lends its name to this phenomenon, is said to have been fixated on the reputation of Dodgson as a sufferer of this psychological condition. In 1967, in an interview with Alfred Appel, Jr. for the literary journal, *Wisconsin Studies*, Nabokov, who had translated *Alice's Adventures in Wonderland* into Russian (*Anya v Stranye Chudes*, 1923), spoke of Dodgson's infamy, specifically regarding his practice of photographing nude children:

> Some odd scruple prevented me from alluding in *Lolita* to his wretched perversion and to those ambiguous photographs he took in dim rooms. He got away with it, as so many other Victorians got away with pederasty and nympholepsy. His were sad, scrawny nymphets, bedraggled and half-undressed, or rather semi-undraped, as if participating in some dusty and dreadful charade.
>
> (Nabokov 1967, cited in Vickers 2008: 27)

One of these 'sad and scrawny' models was also the muse for Dodgson's classic children's stories, the very young Alice Pleasance Liddell. Alice, therefore, unlike Lolita, was not just a fictional character, but also the real-life object of the author's illness, if rumours are to be believed. This also implicates and sexualizes the real Alice as subject, particularly as she became the inspiration for *Lolita*, just as Dodgson was the 'real' Humbert Humbert. Reportedly, Nabokov 'always call[ed] him Lewis Carroll Carroll because he was the first Humbert Humbert' (Nabokov, cited in Carroll 1970: 377). This opinion of Dodgson is far from an isolated one. As Will Brooker highlights, he is 'treated like a man you wouldn't want your kids to meet' (Brooker 2005, cited in Woolf 2010).

Dodgson's 'obsession' with Alice should, however, be observed in context with the Victorian 'cult of the child'. The author was certainly not the only contemporary figure to immortalize the child in literature and art. Significantly, a raft of well-known nineteenth-century personalities felt compelled to worship what they saw as the beguiling beauty and innocence of children. According to Jacqueline Banerjee, Associate Editor of the *Victorian Web*, the worship of children and, with it:

> The notion of childhood innocence goes back at least to Greek ideas on human perfectibility [...]. [T]he so-called cult of the child flourished in England when William Blake and the Romantics embodied it in their poetry.
>
> (2007)

Furthermore, Jackie Wullschlager (1995) contends that, in the nineteenth century, prominent writers 'took the Victorian romance with childhood to an extreme but everywhere, in [...] society and art, a fascination with childhood is apparent' (Lebailly 1998). Notable figures included William Wordsworth, Charles Dickens, Edward Burne-Jones, Edward Lear, George Eliot, John Everett Millais, Frances Hodgson Burnett, George Macdonald, Dante Gabriel Rossetti, Julia Margaret Cameron, J. M. Barrie and A. A. Milne, among many others. In painting, Thomas Cooper Gotch memorialized the little girl as icon in two of his most famous works, *My Crown and Sceptre* (1891) and *The Child Enthroned* (1894).

However, the most notorious personality to demonstrate the Victorian preoccupation with the child was Charles Lutwidge Dodgson. Despite praise of his literary accomplishments, the nature of Dodgson's character has come into question, not only because of his 'attachment' to Alice Liddell but, especially, due to suggested motivations behind his alternate occupation as an artist. Those photographs of semi-clothed children that seemed to trouble Nabokov so much have particularly tarnished the memory of Dodgson. Jenny Woolf, in 'Lewis Carroll's shifting reputation', claims that 'of the approximately 3,000 photographs Dodgson made in his life, just over half are of children – 30 of whom are depicted nude or semi-nude' (2010).

Stephanie Lovett Stoffel, in her biography of the author and artist, disagrees with a widely held opinion that Dodgson was, in fact, a paedophile. She defends his position in context with nineteenth-century perceptions about the child:

> The assumption is made that a bachelor's interest in little girls must be sexual and that a photographer of little girls must be a voyeur [...]. But to view him so is to judge him by the standards of our time whilst taking no account of the culture in which he lived [...]. The romanticizing of childhood was part of the Victorian ethos. Dodgson, a devout Christian, saw children [as] [...] freshly arrived from the presence of God, uncontaminated and asexual [...]. As for his photographs, the study of the nude body has been the hallmark of serious artists for centuries and Dodgson truly saw himself as an artist in his medium [...]. The adult nude was to him [...] too sexualized; the female child whose body is not

yet sexual provided a way [...] to celebrate the human form without obliging him to come to terms with [...] sexual beings.

(1997: 40–41, 46)

As Stoffel maintains, to judge Dodgson through modern eyes is to disregard the social framework of his day. Images of juvenile nudes were part of mainstream society and existed not only in art but also in popular culture. As Woolf argues, 'photographs of nude children sometimes appeared on postcards or birthday cards, and nude portraits – skilfully done – were praised in art studies' (2010). Another artist of Dodgson's day, Julia Margaret Cameron, is commended for similar photographs of angelic-looking, often nude or semi-draped children. Should Dodgson be judged differently because he was a man?

More importantly, though, to the artist and his contemporaries, the concept of child pornography was remote. As Woolf states, 'Victorians saw childhood as a state of grace; even nude photographs of children were considered pictures of innocence, itself' (2010). In the Victorian mind-set, the untainted, naked vessel of the child reflected the purity of the soul within, and was thus disconnected from sinful motivation. Contemplation 'dwelt on the holiness of the child', whose image was even seen as 'redemptive' (Banerjee 2007). In line with this construct, Dodgson's interest in the child nude would have been viewed as an artistic endeavour to achieve works of classic perfection; to his peers, this aesthetic preference merely represented the desire to depict the notion of absolute, innocent beauty. As Brooker (2005) argues:

[Dodgson's] image as a man of suspect sexuality 'says more about our society and its hang-ups than it does about Dodgson, himself. We see him through the prism of contemporary culture – one that sexualizes youth, especially female youth, even as it is repulsed by paedophilia'.

(Woolf 2010)

It is important, therefore, before making assumptions about Dodgson, and the real-life Alice, to reconsider their histories in context with the Victorian cult of the child. This framework is also relevant in interpreting the *Alice* stories, although, just as there are 'those who choose to enjoy them merely as a pretty nonsense [...] [there are] those who insist the text has hidden meanings' (Brooker 2005: 90). This dual reading can also be applied to interpretations of the Lolita fashion movement, in which Alice is so entwined. From an outsider's point of view, the Gothloli has connections with the sexualized Lolita, and *lolicon*; from an insider perspective, she represents the popular, innocent version of Alice.

But, why is Alice the subject here? Of course, she is seen as the embodiment of the perfect little girl, the epitome of what many Gothloli aspire to. But, as Monden asks, how is it possible that we can make sense of the attraction to *Alice* when the tales, themselves, are so ensconced in Victorian England and are so removed from contemporary Japanese society? He replies:

I contend that the imagery of Alice as an independent girl with 'infantile' cuteness is a highly appropriate vehicle for women in Japan [...]. Subtly nuanced, sweet aesthetics with no overt hint of female sexual allure is what we notice.

(Monden 2015: 88)

Therefore, Alice complies with Japan's love of all things *kawaii* ('cute') and 'infantile', which is an explanation for why the original *Alice* illustrations are held to be so dear, and also may explain why she is an appropriate muse for the 'cute' and 'infantile' fashions of the Gothloli. Most importantly, though, while Alice once typified the ultimate little-girl icon of the child cult in Victorian society, she continues to emblematize the worship of little girls in Japan, or the Japanese 'cult of the child', represented by occasions such as Girls' Day. Monden's

Figure 4: Nori Tomizaki, *Heart*, 2006. Photograph courtesy of Nori Tomizaki.

argument supports this analogy, claiming that 'what has made Alice popular in Japanese culture', and thus the Lolita subculture, is that she represents the idealization of the *shōjo* and that she can be recognized as a *shōjo* icon (2015: 86):

> In aspects of Japanese popular culture [...] the idea of 'Alice' embodies the idealized image of the *shōjo* (girl), who is situated between child and adult and is largely detached from the heterosexual economy [...]. '*Shōjo*', a term first coined in the late nineteenth century [...] connote[s] the period between young childhood and marriage [...] and characterizes a[n] [...] amalgamation of youth, femininity, innocence, budding sexuality and a sense of autonomy, all traits represented by Carroll's Alice. Moreover, the concept of *shōjo*, like the related concept of '*kawaii*', or 'cute', can be read as having two faces: one being an idealized construction imposed predominantly by men [but] [...] the other being manoeuvred by the girls themselves, thus making it an effective vehicle for women to display agency and creativity.
>
> (Monden 2014: 265–66)

Therefore, Alice is an appropriate symbol for the Japanese Lolita movement, a subculture that not only celebrates girlhood, but also is motivated by members who desire to separate their image from a sexualizing agency.

Conclusion

To analyse the Lolita subculture in terms of a relationship with Alice is, therefore, complex and involves more than just making surface observations about fashion design elements. The multiple complications that arise from the name, 'Lolita', alone, are further problematized when set up against equally controversial connotations associated with Alice. Not least because of the title, which alludes to Nabokov's heroine, also misunderstood as a promiscuous, provocative, sexually active child, or 'nymphet', the ambiguities regarding Alice's sexuality add to the reasons why the Lolita subcultural style is often misinterpreted. Although the Gothloli's appearance is intended to be modest and sweet, it is partially due to these entanglements that it is viewed as a fetish and linked with overt sexuality.

There is no real evidence, though, to suggest that the branding of the subcultural style as 'Lolita' is in any way connected to Nabokov's heroine. To begin with, the origins of the Lolita terminology are elusive, let alone their deeper meaning. As Mariko Suzuki claims, 'it's not clear who came up with this moniker' (2007: 136). Given that Mana introduced his signature range, Elegant Gothic Lolita, quite early in regard to the movement's evolution, he may well have been the first to combine 'Gothic' and 'Lolita'. Macias and Evers believe that to be the case:

as the new millennium was about to roll around, girls who liked to look like antique French dolls or portraits from the rococo period by way of goth fashions still didn't have a name for their scene. It came in the fall of 1999, when Mana, the vampiric-looking leader of the band Malice Mizer, started his own clothing brand, Moi-même-Moitié. He announced the design theme as 'Elegant Gothic Lolita'. Since then, the name has stuck, at least in part.

(2007: 122)

Suzuki identifies the same time for the emergence of the word, 'Gothloli', stating that, 'although this Japanese look is now known as Gothloli, that term did not become popular until around the end of 1999 or 2000' (2007: 136). This *was* concurrent with the founding of Mana's label, but it is still not absolutely certain whether the designation of 'Lolita' preceded him, especially in relation to the Sweet Lolita style that had evolved from Dolly *Kei*. Philomena Keet, who has interviewed the designer, maintains:

Mana recalls there was a Lolita style in Tokyo but he wanted to adapt this to make a new fashion genre. 'I added a dark element to the cuteness of Lolita', in other words a Gothic element, resulting in a mix that combines the frills, lace and puffy skirts of Lolita with the Gothic black and adds lots of Gothic motifs such as crosses, candlestick holders and daggers.

(2007: 86)

This suggests that the label 'Lolita' (albeit separate from the gothic genre) pre-dated Mana's usage. If we are to believe one of Kawamura's informants, then that is possibly the case. She writes:

According to Momo Matsuura, author of *The World, Myself and Lolita Fashion* (2007) and, herself, a Lolita, the term first appeared in the September 1987 issue of a Japanese fashion magazine called *Ryukou Tsushin*; Lolita as a category of fashion appeared in the early 1990s.

(2012: 66–67)

In my mind, though, I would first wish to see this style spread to determine if the clothing, itself, resembled what we know as Japanese Lolita style and, secondly, even if it did, one would need stronger evidence to decide whether the editorial was using terminology that was already around.

From all of the research that I have been able to uncover at this point, the origins of the 'Lolita' tag are sketchy. And, the *reasons* for using this term seem even harder to pin down. In any case, whether or not the Lolita subculture is meant to link it in any way to either Nabokov's sexualized little girl, the Lolita Complex, or *lolicon* imagery, an understanding of the intention/meaning would not serve to completely eliminate a perception of the style as fetish, or undo its links to paedophilic pornography and, most importantly, it would not be able to eradicate the definition of the word, 'Lolita', which has been part of common-language usage, in English at least, since the 1950s, when the novel, *Lolita*, was first published.

However, except for having the same name, the link between the Japanese Lolita and the heroine of Nabokov's novel is perplexing. The Gothloli represents an adult, or young woman, with childish sensibilities; the fictional character, Lolita, is interpreted as a child with adult feelings. Yet, this analysis is also, as previously discussed, dependent on perspective. In a message to me through MySpace, on 16 January 2010, 23-year-old German Gothloli, 'Duplica', had this to say about *Lolita* and any possible connections to the Lolita movement:

> What is a Lolita? 1. A young girl who wants to attract older guys; 2. An adult woman who wants to look like a young girl. What is Dolores [Lolita] in the book? In my honest opinion she was nothing of them! She was a lonely girl without a family. She didn't want to mislead Humbert. She realized that she gets what she wants if she does what Humbert wants of her. [But] especially in the end of the novel it gets clear that she never wanted a romantic relationship with him. Because of that I wonder why people think that Lolita has a negative connotation.
>
> (Personal communication)

In other words, although there is this perception that Lolita 'wants to attract older guys', a deeper understanding of both the novel and the fashion movement reveals that neither Lolita nor her 'namesake' should be seen as intentionally inviting this type of attention, or reputation. As Duplica said, the 'problem is just [in] the interpretation of the book'.

In order to counter-react to the multiple paradoxes and thus (mis)understandings of Lolita style, there is an emphasis to promote the modest little-girl persona in all authorized Lolita fashion texts and periodicals. Expected behaviour, in the forms of dressing up, collecting dolls and attending tea parties, is expounded in, for example, the *Gothic & Lolita Bible*, the definitive guidebook for the Gothloli lifestyle, whereby many references to Alice's own tea party are recurrent. Volume 18, published in 2005, dedicated a major feature to *The World of Alice*, advertising the Alice-Lolita collections of Alice and the Pirates, MAM, Angelic Pretty and Metamorphose temps de Fille, along with ephemera such as *Alice*-character porcelain tea settings, jewellery, key-rings, t-shirts, bags and purses, and even paper patterns with instructions on how to make two *Alice* outfits. This particular issue also incorporated fantastical photo shoots, such as 'Alice in Candy Dreams', in which the motifs of Wonderland and references to the Mad Hatter's tea party were manifested. While this was a most notable homage to the Alice-Lolita theme, it is by no means an isolated occurrence. There is, therefore, no doubt about the esteem that Alice, Lewis Carroll's little-girl heroine, holds in the realm of the Japanese Lolita, and Gothloli worldwide. Moreover, the only *definitive* links that can be made between Alice and the Gothloli are purely aesthetic, and in the innocent natures that they were/are *intended* to embody.

References

Banerjee, J. (2007), 'Ideas of childhood in Victorian children's fiction: The child as innocent', *The Victorian Web: Literature, History, & Culture in the Age of Victoria*, 13 August, http://www.victorianweb.org/genre/childlit/childhood1.html. Accessed 10 April 2011.

Brooker, W. (2005), *Alice's Adventures: Lewis Carroll in Popular Culture*, London and New York: Continuum.

Carroll, L. and Gardner, M. (ed.) (1970), *The Annotated Alice: Alice's Adventures in Wonderland and Through the Looking-Glass*, Harmondsworth: Penguin.

Chuang, B. K. Y. and Hardy Bernal, K. A. (2008), '*Loli-Pop* in Auckland: Engaging Asian communities and audiences through the museum', *Sites: A Journal of Social Anthropology & Cultural Studies* 5:2, pp. 81–110.

Davis, F. H. (1992), *Myths and Legends of Japan*, New York: Dover Publications.

Geczy, A. and McBurnie, J. (2015), 'Adam Geczy's *S/M Wonderland*', http://www.sneakymag.com/art/adam-geczys-sm-wonderland/. Accessed 18 March 2015.

Godoy, T. and Vartanian, I. (eds) (2007), *Style, Deficit, Disorder: Harajuku Street Fashion, Tokyo*, San Francisco: Chronicle Books.

Hardy Bernal, K. A. (2007), 'Lolita in Japan: An innocent Goth', *MQ: The Quarterly Magazine of Auckland War Memorial Museum*, 112, spring, p. 33.

––––––– (2011), 'The Lolita Complex: A Japanese fashion subculture and its paradoxes', M.Phil. thesis, Auckland: Auckland University of Technology.

––––––– (2012), 'Japanese Lolita: Challenging sexualized style and the little-girl look', in S. Tarrant and M. Jolles (eds), *Fashion Talks: Undressing the Power of Style*, New York: State University of New York Press, pp. 117–32.

Hearn, L. P. ([1894] 1976), *Glimpses of Unfamiliar Japan*, Tokyo: Tuttle Publishing.

Kawamura, Y. (2012), *Fashioning Japanese Subcultures*, London: Berg.

Keet, P. (2007), *The Tokyo Look Book: Stylish to Spectacular, Goth to Gyro, Sidewalk to Catwalk*, Tokyo, New York and London: Kodansha International.

Kretschmer, A. (2000), 'Mortuary rites for inanimate objects: The case of *Hair Kuyō*', *Japanese Journal of Religious Studies*, 27, pp. 379–404.

Lebailly, H. (1998), 'Dodgson and the Victorian cult of the child: A reassessment on the hundredth anniversary of "Lewis Carroll's" death', *Contrariwise*, http://contrariwise.wild-reality.net/articles/CharlesDodgsonAndTheVictorianCultOfTheChild.pdf. Accessed 10 April 2011.

Macias, P. and Evers, I. (2007), *Japanese Schoolgirl Inferno: Tokyo Teen Fashion Subculture Handbook*, San Francisco: Chronicle Books.

Monden, M. (2014), 'Being Alice in Japan: Performing a cute, "girlish" revolt', *Japan Forum*, 26:2, pp. 265–85.

———— (2015), *Japanese Fashion Cultures: Dress and Gender in Contemporary Japan*, London and New York: Bloomsbury.

Nabokov, V. and Appel, A. Jr. (ed.) (2000), *The Annotated Lolita*, London: Penguin.

Pate, A. S. (2005), *Ningyō: The Art of the Japanese Doll*, Hong Kong: Tuttle Publishing.

———— (2008), *Japanese Dolls: The Fascinating World of Ningyō*, Tokyo: Tuttle Publishing.

Schattschneider, E. (2005), 'The blood-stained doll: Violence and the gift in wartime Japan', *Journal of Japanese Studies*, 31:2, pp. 329–56.

Stoffel, S. L. (1997), *Lewis Carroll and Alice*, London: Thames and Hudson.

Suzuki, M. (2007), 'Gothic, Lolita, visual-*kei*: First Kansai then the world (via Harajuku)', in T. Godoy and I. Vartanian (eds), *Style Deficit Disorder: Harajuku Street Fashion – Tokyo*, San Francisco: Chronicle Books, pp. 134–37.

Vickers, G. (2008), *Chasing Lolita: How Popular Culture Corrupted Nabokov's Little Girl all Over Again*, Chicago: Chicago Review Press.

Woolf, J. (2010), 'Lewis Carroll's shifting reputation: Why has popular opinion of the author of *Alice's Adventures in Wonderland* undergone such a dramatic reversal?' *Smithsonian*, April, http://www.smithsonianmag.com/arts-culture/Lewis-Carrolls-Shifting-Reputation.html. Accessed 10 December 2012.

Wullschlager, J. (1995), *Inventing Wonderland: The Lives and Fantasies of Lewis Carroll, Edward Lear, J. M. Barrie, Kenneth Grahame and A. A. Milne*, London: Methuen.

Notes

1 Carroll, L. (1865), *Alice's Adventures in Wonderland*, 1st ed., London: Macmillan; and Carroll, L. (1871), *Through the Looking-Glass, and What Alice Found There*, 1st ed., London: Macmillan.

2 *Shōjo* = girl, girls, girls'; *manga* = two-dimensional drawings, or two-dimensional illustration prints; and *anime* = moving-image illustration (animated film).

3 Nabokov, L. (1955), *Lolita*, 1st ed., Paris: Olympia Press.

4 From this point, onwards, I use the term, 'Gothloli', to refer to 'the Lolita', or the generic person, a member of the subculture, to distinguish her from the character, Lolita, from Nabokov's novel (*Lolita*).

5 G&L encompasses Japanese goth fashion/music-based movements as well as its Lolita offshoot.

6 Hepworth, C. M. (1903), *Alice in Wonderland*, Walton-on-Thames, UK: Hepworth Studios; Porter, E. S. (1910), *Alice's Adventures in Wonderland*, New York, NY: Edison Manufacturing Company; Young, W. W. (1915), *Alice in Wonderland*, Chicago, IL: American Film Manufacturing Company; Pollard, B. (1931), *Alice in Wonderland*, Fort Lee, NJ: Metropolitan Studios; McLeod, N. Z. (1933), *Alice in Wonderland*, Hollywood, CA: Paramount Pictures (released in Japan 1934); and Disney, W. (1951), *Alice in Wonderland*, Burbank, CA: Walt Disney Studios (released in Japan 1952) etc.

7 Classic Lolita: The basic 'Alice' form. Garments are constructed from plain fabrics, or patterned with dainty florals, plaids or ginghams, in muted colours.

Gothic Lolita (*Gosu-rori*): Follows the basic 'Alice' form. Grounded in black and contrasted with white or dark jewel colours (sapphire, ruby, emerald, amethyst); or incorporating gothic-themed, printed fabrics (popular motifs are crosses, bats, gravestones, and stained-glass, church-window patterns). Accessories are often the same as those worn by Euro-American goths, such as rosary beads or crucifix pendants. She may also be dressed, head-to-toe, in all black, although this is alternatively deemed to be the Black Lolita (*Kuro-rori*) style.

Sweet Lolita (Ama-rori): Almost the antithesis of the Gothic Lolita. Although she still follows the Classic form, there is a pronounced concentration on the very sweetest aspects of the Lolita style. Her dress, which is often an explosion of frothiness, bows and frills, is generally made up in a combination of pretty pastel colours; fairy-floss or pale pinks, salmon; saxe, duck-egg, powder or baby blues; lemon, butter yellows; mauves and lavenders; mint or soft greens; often grounded by either white or cream. If she is all white or cream, however, she is known as a White Lolita (*Shiro-rori*). If her dress is patterned, the Sweet Lolita's taste is for dollhouse florals, fruit (berries, strawberries or cherries), cakes, lollies, sweets, candy, ice-cream sundaes, tea-sets, teddies, bunnies, ducklings, lambs, kittens, baby deer, rocking horses, carousel ponies, or a combination of these.

Other styles include Princess Lolita (*Hime-rori*), which is often sparkly, and includes the wearing of tiaras and bustled full skirts (more Rococo than Victorian); Punk Lolita, incorporating elements such as tartan, safety pins, tattered fabrics and chains; Guro Lolita (*Guro-rori*), a gory, or wounded, 'broken-doll' look, whereby white dresses are often worn to show contrasting blood stains on clothing and bandages; Wa Lolita (*Wa-rori*), a fusion of the Lolita silhouette with elements of historical Japanese clothing and fabric designs; and Qi Lolita (*Qi-rori*), which combines traditional Chinese dress and motifs, such as dragons, with Lolita.

8   Based on Vivienne Westwood's iconic 'rocking horse ballerinas', as she termed them, these shoes are a fusion of ribboned ballet slippers and the Japanese platformed '*geta*'. They have always been favourites for Gothloli and many girls prefer to buy authentic originals, which are still produced, especially for the Japanese market. They were made synonymous with Lolita style when Kyoko Fukada wore them in her role as the Gothloli, Momoko, in the 2004 film Shimotsuma Monogatari (released in the United States with English subtitles as Kamikaze Girls in 2006).

9   Often shortened to '*Metamorphose temps de fille*' or just *Metamorphose*. Note that designer labels associated with the Japanese Lolita movement are quite often 'French' (usually grammatically incorrect), for affectation. This is to add a romantic connection to the Rococo period.

10   Also see n.12, and its link to notions of fetish and BDSM. Although members of the Lolita fashion subculture profess that the style is meant to be modest and innocent, and are determined to resist the sexualization and fetishization of their style, the naming of Juliette et Justine evokes the writings of the Marquis de Sade (1791 and 1797), and thus sadomasochistic (S/M) perversions (note that the term, 'sadism', is after Sade and refers to his 'sadistic' sexual depravities). This also problematizes the association of the Rococo Period (c.- 1750s–1790s) with the fashion style, as this was the era of the Marquis (b. 1740–d. 1814).

11   This recording label folded in 1987.
12   BDSM = Bondage, Discipline/Domination, Submission/Sadism, Masochism.

   Adam Geczy's recent exhibition, S/M Wonderland, resonates with some of the themes present and underlying in Tomizaki's work. In an interview with Jonathan McBurnie, Geczy makes this statement:

> As a father, and seeing my children evolve, I became more intrigued to see their various inner selves come to the surface. I wanted to address the now obscenely taboo issue of children's sexuality without resorting to what, to my mind, is the rather glib strategy of taking their clothes off, which is guaranteed to shock, any place, any time. As we all know, the Alice story is laced with sublimated and veiled sexuality anyway. I wanted to design sequences in which the audience's 'dirty little secrets' would also be elicited.
>
> (Geczy and McBurnie 2015)

   This line of thought interests me greatly and is absolutely relevant to an investigation of the Lolita subculture. I therefore intend to pursue a study of these relationships in consultation with Geczy.
13   Nori Tomizaki's art is even more multi-layered when examined in relation to this framework. Is his work part of this phenomenon or does it critique/make a statement about it? This is also a question I intend to explore further, in the future.

Chapter 6

Sewing Manuals in 1950s China: Socialist Narratives and Dress Patterns from New Democracy to Socialist Transformation

Antonia Finnane

In the area of fashion research, texts take a variety of forms and are used for different reasons. Obvious examples of texts as research resources are documentary records of textiles and garments, ledger books recording prices and stock, and of course, newspapers and magazines (see Mahawatte in this volume), the latter of critical importance for the creation of the consumer ethos that drives fashion (see Hancock in this volume). Other examples belong to the category of ephemera: free-floating advertisements on posters or flyers, labels and brand names, even samplers and fabrics bearing printed or embroidered texts (see Berry in this volume). All of these examples point to the significance of textual references for understanding a phenomenon that is otherwise imagined via pictures (see Wallenberg in this volume) and directly experienced by visual and tactile means (see Kjellmer in this volume). In *The Fashion System*, Roland Barthes (1983) used fashion as a text, but also showed how text produced fashion.

Among these various forms of text are works of fiction, which often serve as sources of empirical knowledge for fashion historians. In late imperial China, attention to fashionable or at least very elaborate clothing is marked in some significant fictional works. *The Plum in the Golden Vase* (*Jin Ping Mei*) is an outstanding early example (Xiaoxiao Sheng 1993–): the density of detail in descriptions of costume in this famous novel can be considered a response to the commercialization of everyday life in sixteenth-century China (Dauncey 2003). A later work, *Dreams of Seduction* (*Fengliu Meng*), may have been similarly inspired (Hanshang 1988). 'Clothes, jewellery and accessories', writes Patrick Hanan, '[...] are described [in this novel] with a degree of precision that one associates more with a museum catalogue than a novel' (Hanan 1998: 358).

The New Culture Movement of the early twentieth century gave rise to new sorts of fiction in which such passages were stylistically precluded. Republican-era authors often used dress to develop a point about a character. Ding Ling's Wendy is an obvious example: 'her two little feet encased in leather shoes. Her two well-rounded calves were hugged by sheer, flesh-tinted silk stockings [...]' (Ding 1989: 101) in brief, she was a disturbingly modern young woman. In general, however, the brief, suggestive brush-stroke in this self-consciously modern fiction replaced the baroque detail of descriptive passages in earlier works. It was mainly in middlebrow literature, the so-called 'mandarin duck and butterfly genre', that the reader still occasionally found these set pieces on clothing characterizing the fictional text (Link 1981; Finnane 2008: 187–88).

After 1949, fictional writing of all sorts went into decline. Writers fled the country, or were silenced. It remains a poignant fact of Chinese cultural history that the first great historical survey of dress in China was compiled in the People's Republic of China (PRC) by one of the most important fiction writers of the pre-Communist era, Shen Congwen, a writer who resembles Berthold Brecht in that the revolution that he by and large supported marked an end to his creative output (Shen 1981). Such fictional works as were produced in the Mao years, along with stage plays and cinema, did have characters dressed in particular ways, but the clothing they wore is better termed costume than fashion: a sweaty white shirt covering a broad and muscular chest, together with dark blue pants rolled up to knees of sturdy legs would certainly be the costume of an upstanding male member of the revolutionary masses (Yang 1998: 50; cf. Chen 2003). Descriptions of clothing in fiction of this era, especially in the Cultural Revolution, essentially informed readers about the class background and political standpoint of the character concerned, much in the way that face make-up indicated roles in Beijing Opera.

Although the production of novels dropped in the Mao years, there was a great outpouring of other books, mostly produced in the service of creating the socialist state: apart from those aimed at disseminating knowledge of core Party writings (Liu Shaoqi's *How to be a Good Communist*, Mao Zedong's *On the People's Democratic Dictatorship*) these included school textbooks for the rapidly expanding education sector, advice manuals for the management of personal life in New China, translations of Russian works and technical manuals of all sorts. To call these works 'books' may be to overstate the case in many instances. A large volume of publications from the Mao years were pamphlets and booklets – small, closely printed, economically produced works. Examples relevant to the domain of fashion are pattern books, instruction manuals on cutting and sewing and guides to the use and maintenance of sewing machines.

Publications related to the technology of clothing production proliferated in the 1950s. The second-hand market in contemporary China has many works of this genre and from this period. This is consistent with changes in the practices of clothing genre production over the period of regime change, including the decline in the number of professional tailors, the concomitant rise in home-made clothing among urban households and the expansion of the factory-made clothing sector. Sewing schools mushroomed as local authorities in urban centres sought to find ways to absorb women into the workforce. Sewing machines, produced only in very small numbers on the eve of the Communist victory, began to roll out of factories (Finnane 2016). And just as an ephemeral literature was crucial to the growth of literacy among the working poor in nineteenth-century England (Neuberg 1977: 143), so a rudimentary technological literature was necessary for the rapid dissemination of general knowledge about 'scientific' approaches to the production of clothing.

In its post-conflict stage, i.e. after 1949, the revolution in China had an intensely pedagogical character that was evident in the creation of vocational schools (including sewing schools) and the expansion of the education sector at large as well as in the study sessions of the mass campaigns by which Chinese society was mobilized into support for the socialist project. It is easy to imagine technical manuals being read collectively at meetings ranging from the street committee level through to handicraft cooperatives and the factory floor. For individuals seeking to re-make themselves as productive forces in the New China, perhaps after a lifetime of 'parisitism' or 'compradorism' (Kraus 1982: 41), a disciplined acquisition of skills was required.

What did it mean to read one of these books from cover to cover? Briefly, the contents suggest that like other sorts of literature, ranging from fiction to newspaper reports and commentary, they served as primers for learning to be socialist subjects in the communist state. They provided a new story for people to tell about themselves, in the New China, a story in which they, dressed in particular ways, played particular parts. Communist Party members from abroad at this time, brought to Beijing for cadre training, were struck by the extraordinary introspection and spiritual self-renewal demanded of Chinese communism, as opposed to Russian (Aarons 1993: 96–97). Such demands were evident not only in study sessions, which were rather like prayer meetings in style and purpose, but in all walks of daily life. Accordingly, technical texts produced in the Mao years were generally about something more than the technology.

Technical manuals, argues Inger Larssen (2003) are unavoidably caught up in the same linguistic and ideological complex as everything else in the society in which they are produced and disseminated. They experience shifts in convention as surely as do the human actors in the society in which they are destined to circulate. In Mao's China, the shifting conventions of being human, perhaps better phrased as being part of 'the people' (*renmin*), were both described and prescribed in literary texts. The fact that technical manuals, too, should provide guidance as how to observe these conventions confirms Larssen's observations.

Sewing Manuals: The Japanese Heritage

Published guides to cutting and sewing began to appear very early in the twentieth century as features in women's magazines. To the extent that new styles of clothing were being produced and worn in China in the early twentieth century, especially after the 1911 Revolution, this could be explained by the need to guide dressmakers and tailors through the intricacies of making fitted sleeves, ruffles and button holes, among other things. The patterns in the late Qing magazine *Nüzi shijie* (*Women's World*) (1904), however, are for a basic Chinese-style jacket, with its simple lines and few pattern pieces, of a sort that ordinary women had long made in accordance with lessons learned from their mothers. It is probable that women's magazines as a genre were imagined by its creators as including information of this sort, and that educated women were supposed to be hard-working and productive, in line with nationalist thought on the subject of women (Hu 2000: 3). In later magazines, such as *Funü zazhi* (*Women's Magazine*), a wider range of patterns can be found, and a more self-consciously scientific approach to cutting and fitting (Zhao 1925). Dedicated sewing manuals are rather rare for the period before 1949. Knitting and embroidery pattern books were more common. During the Republican era, these handicrafts had greater scope for novelty than did dressmaking, and were techniques by which fashionable effects could be realized on the fairly conservative foundations supplied by the qipao. Embroidery also had considerable commercial value. Although skilled embroiderers were likely to draw their own patterns (Xin 2001: 145), surviving pattern books from the twenties to forties suggest that publishing in this area served a demand for modern patterns.

The compilation and production of sewing guides and pattern books were linked worldwide to the mass production of sewing machines and the rise of sewing schools. Japan was well ahead of China in both these respects (Gordon 2012; Finnane 2016), and it is no surprise that Japanese pattern books abound in China's second-hand book market. An early example is a four-volume set of teaching materials first published in Tokyo in 1925 (Yoshimura 1929). The materials were aimed squarely at the Japanese family, and consisted largely of instructions on how to cut and sew Japanese-style clothes for men and women. But the sections on children's clothing were undoubtedly useful in the Chinese context. While clothing for adults went through phases of westernization and indigenization in both China and Japan, the children of middle-class townspeople very commonly wore western-style clothes, especially in summer: vests, rompers, frocks and sailor suits had wide currency in the region in the 1920s, and indeed across the globe.

Such teaching materials must have been used by Sugino Yoshiko (1892–1978) for classes in her pioneering Dressmaking College for Women in Tokyo, established in 1926. Sugino herself was a successful writer of sewing manuals, of which some ended up in China by one route or another. Her 'teach-yourself manual for cutting western-style clothes' (Sugino 1936), published as a supplement to a popular Japanese women's magazine, *Fujin kurubu*, might have arrived in China in the luggage of Japanese visitors or Chinese returning home, but it is equally likely that it arrived by post. There were Japanese bookshops in China, and the magazine advertised the cost of overseas as well as domestic postage. I have elsewhere noted the importance of Japan in technological transfer in the domain of clothing production and fashion knowledge in East Asia, a topic that deserves more attention than it has as yet received (Finnane 2016). Among the traces of this historical role is a large number of Japanese clothes pattern books in second-hand bookshops in China.

In the 1930s, Chinese technical publications were very inferior to Japanese and they remained so for a long while thereafter. A 1939 manual published in Harbin covers much the same range of clothes as Sugino's 1936 publication, but is mediocre in the quality of its graphics, the details of instruction, the quality of the paper and overall production values (Wang 1939). Handwritten and probably drawn by a dressmaking teacher, Wang Zhizhong, this manual was produced by the director of the school, apparently Russian (transliterated as *Shabuluowa*, perhaps *Shabalov* in the original), and was no doubt used by the school. The patterns are mainly of fashionable women's dress, but include children's clothing, underwear (including brassieres for women and long johns for men) and also standard patterns for qipao and mantle (*doufeng*). Harbin had long hosted a considerable Japanese population with concomitant cultural and industrial institutions, and by 1940 had been under Japanese control for 9 years. This is not evident from the manual: the photo shows four staff (of whom three look to be Russian) and 23 students, some in Chinese dress. Nonetheless,

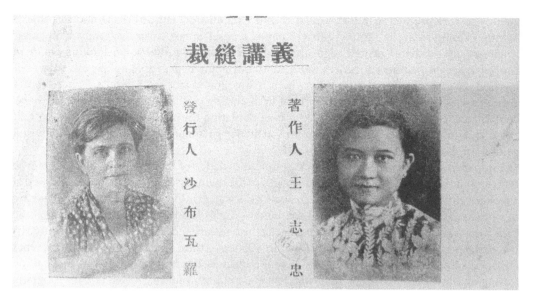

Figure 1: Director Shabalov (?) and instructor Wang Zhizhong, of a sewing school in Japanese-occupied Harbin, 1930s. Source: WANG, ZHIZHONG (1939). *Caifeng jiangyi* (Principles of tailoring). Haerbin: Fulian jieli yinshua suo, frontispiece.

the significance of a broader Japanese context for the school and the clothing regime it supported should not be discounted.

Of interest in this book is a paper pattern piece cut out of newspaper that was left tucked between pages 28 and 29 when it was consigned to the second-hand bookshop. The newspaper is an old *People's Daily*. It does not bear the date of publication, but the text is from an opinion piece on the comparative post-war economies of the Soviet Union and the United States. It would appear, then, that this book continued to be used in the 1950s. Hand-editing shows its travels through space and political time. On the imprint page, someone – perhaps Wang herself – has changed the date of publication from Kangde 6 (the sixth year of the reign of Puyi as emperor of Manchukuo) to 1940. Beneath the title on the same page, a column of characters has been blacked out. After the name of the author, a column of characters has been added, reading 'Current address: Shanghai Hongkou, No 47 Harbin Road'. It can be concluded that Wang Zhizhong moved to Shanghai after the war. She may there have taught dressmaking in one of the many pop-up sewing schools that appeared after 1949.

A Japanese heritage for Wang Zhizhong's undertakings can be inferred, but the evidence is mainly circumstantial. By contrast, Lin Zhengbao, author of a how-to-sew manual published in 1954, was quite upfront about his Japanese connections (Lin 1954). Lin was a 'Red Group' (*Hongbang*) tailor, one of a group with native-place ties in Ningbo, based in Shanghai, and boasting old connections with Japan. In the Republican era he was apparently already at work producing industry-related texts (Ji, Zhu and Feng 2011: 65), and was able to continue doing so in the 1950s. With 118 pages, typeset, smart cover design featuring a set square ruler and the enterprise logo, and multiple fonts, his professional-looking *Guide to Cutting and Sewing* offered readers the 'scientific triangular principle breast-measurement method' of garment construction, by which it was hoped students could advance from a 'more-or-less' approach to scientific precision in cutting clothes to fit the wearer. The book contains tables of sizes, conversion tables for calculating the size of garment based on half chest measurement, amounts of cloth for particular garments, tools of trade and advised colour combinations.

Endpapers provide readers with background knowledge of this scientific tailor. Copies of two diplomas are featured in the opening pages of the manual, showing that he had studied at a western clothes sewing school in Tokyo during the war, gaining qualifications in the making of women's and children's clothes, and gentlemen's high-class wear. An advertisement at the back for another work by the author reveals that he had earlier compiled a manual of patterns for western-style children's dress. This was in 1950, at a time when, with the government's encouragement, many sewing schools were established. Lin had responded to that call by setting up the Meilin School of Tailoring, Sewing and Embroidery, located at 245 Gongping Road in Shanghai's Hongkou district. Admission was limited to women, in accordance with government's preference for feminizing the clothes production sector. Students could take either basic sewing classes or professional tailoring classes. It is probable that the flight of Shanghai tailors to Hong Kong had left a significant gap in the cloth production sector and that Lin's students included numbers of women who now had to sew for their families, whether or not they intended to use these same skills to earn a living (Karnow 1964: 29).

An occasional sewing manual produced around this time already restricted designs to the new standard styles that would come to be seen as representative of the PRC (Fu 1951b), but Lin's portfolio was a cosmopolitan range typical of mid-twentieth century world clothing styles. The introductory drawings show a man wearing shirt and tie, and the woman a petticoat, items of clothing that were soon to disappear from China's national wardrobe. The children are depicted in frocks (the girls), or cap and coat, the small boys looking very like public school students. There are patterns for women's pyjamas, a dressing gown, and a maid's apron and cap. A full-skirted women's overcoat is dubbed 'New Wave' (*nübolang*).

All this was consistent with Japanese trends. In 1950s Japan, women moved from wearing the wartime *monpe* (see Gordon 2012: 144–8) to skirts, blouses and frocks . Pattern books mirror those that were being published in the English-language world of the time, and established North American and European fashions as normative. In 1954, when Soviet models were parading patriotic socialist styles, Japanese models were donning Dior (Anon. 1954). Indigenous Japanese styles retained importance in ritual life but no longer dominated the streetscape. All this is well known and is worth mentioning here mainly because of the obvious contrast with China, where women in the 1950s moved from wearing the qipao to wearing people's fashions: jacket and trousers. Yet this did not happen all at once. Clearly,

Lin Zhengbao was moving along a trajectory determined by his Japanese training, and he thought that the Shanghai's middle class was going to keep him company.

Sewing Manuals and the Socialist Narrative

Lin's main concession to the new realities in China was the inclusion of designs for garments that were coming to characterize the new regime: Zhongshan suit, Lenin suit and People's suit (*renmingzhuang*). In longer historical context, these designs do not seem out of place. The Zhongshan (Sun Yatsen) suit was standard wear for male bureaucrats in the Nationalist Government as well as the Communist, and was worn by both Chiang Kai-shek and Mao Zedong. The Lenin suit was approved wear for women cadres. The People's suit, if destined to supplant both the men's *changpao* and the women's *qipao*, was a plain, workmanlike ensemble and not itself challenging. A comparable mix is found in a Beijing manual published in the same year (Wei 1954): jodhpurs, blouson-style jackets, a duffle coat,; pants in the 'Hong Kong style', fitted blouses with yoke tops, puffed sleeves and various sorts of necklines – square, v-shaped, scooped, and then generic garments of the period: Zhongshan suit, Yanan jacket (*Yananfu*), Lenin suit.

The designs themselves, the pictures and patterns, by no means tell us all that the students would have been absorbing from these teaching materials. It has already been pointed out that Lin Zhengbao's *Guide* was carefully framed, its endpapers attesting on the one hand to the excellence of his training (in Japan) and on the other to his participation on Shanghai society and industry. Especially important in these peripheral texts is the statement of the school's objectives, which were to foster women's independence, boost productivity and serve society through training in tailoring, sewing and embroidery. These objectives gave expression to the ideals used in social mobilization for the creation of the New China: the emancipation of women through their absorption into the labour force, productionism and the eventual realization of socialist society (Song 2007: 49–50). And while this statement was buried in the advertisement at the back of the manual, related principles were brought to the fore at the front, where a chart of lengths of cloth required for a range of garments is framed by the phrases: 'lift production technology; communicate production experience'.

At heart, however, Lin Zhengbao remained 'expert' rather than 'red'. It is difficult to read his *Guide* as other than highly professional, premised on the essential autonomy and self-evident standing and purpose of tailoring in society. If his scientific cutting method identified him clearly with the massification of science in Mao's China (Schmalzer 2014), his incorporation of standard phrases from the political lexicon of the day remained marginal to the text as a whole. These features of his manual are thrown into relief by comparison with some other extant publications of this genre. Wang Guizhang, founder of the King Fair Sewing School, again in Shanghai, was also a 'Red Group' tailor. A graduate in chemistry from the prestigious St John's University, she turned to dressmaking as a business during the war. Her 600-character introduction to *The King Fair Instructions for Sewing and Stitching*, first published in 1949, stamped her enterprise as fully engaged with the productionism that marked New China:

Production in our country at the present time has already became a most important and glorious matter. No matter whether male or female, young or old, knowledgeable or ignorant, rich or poor, the responsibility and duty to produce is the same [...]. With the government encouraging and promoting production, the professions of tailoring and embroidering have an opportunity to develop and truly flourish. At this juncture, the writer has of course exerted to herself to the utmost to respond to the government's call.

(Wang 1950)

Figure 2: Cover illustration of a 1956 pattern book, showing the combination of traditionalism and conservative modernism characteristic of the dress reform campaign of that year. Wang Guizhang, 1956b. *Funü chunzhuang* (spring clothing for women). Shanghai: Shanghai wenhua chubanshe, cover.

This sort of statement was commonplace in technical works in the 1950s, and was a harbinger of textual practices implemented during the Cultural Revolution.

A more striking example of the politicized manual is a two-volume textbook compiled by Fu Yingfei (1954, 5th ed.). Fu was a resident of Beijing, and the director of the Beijing Private Professional Tailoring School, established in late 1949 or 1950. Wang Shuntian's preface to an earlier single-volume version of this textbook tells us that Fu had been engaged in tailoring since 1941. After the fall of Beijing (then Beiping) to the Communists in 1949 he had 'responded to an invitation from Beijing Municipality to teach in the Peace Vocational School' before proceeding to establish his own sewing school. Like Lin and Wang, he had a number of sewing manuals to his name. A large number of extant copies of the various manuals he compiled suggests that he taught many students over the years. Indeed by May 1951, according to Wang Shuntian, between one and two thousand students had come under his instruction (Fu 1951a: Preface).

The two-volume manual published for his sewing school in 1954 rewards browsing because of the great diversity of clothing for which patterns are provided, their obvious fit at various points with world fashion, and the highly local context that is simultaneously evident from the names of garments. Among the items are skirts of many kinds – pleated, cut on the bias, cut in the round – and a corresponding range of shirts, blouses and jackets: the Shanghai shirt, plain or with puffed sleeves; the Lenin jacket; the Michurin shirt (probably inspired by the Soviet film of that name), the peace blouse. The same is true of trousers: patterns for jodhpurs and sailor pants are included. Floral print 'three-cornered pants' (women's underwear) are pictured, and also, astonishingly, a two-piece swimming costume.

Fu Yingfei was well connected in literary circles in Beijing. The title page of his manual features the calligraphy of Zhang Henshui (1897–1967), one of the most popular novelists of Republican Era. The introduction was contributed by well-known teacher and scholar of popular culture, Jin Shoushen (1906–68). Born in the late Qing, educated in the turbulence of the Republic, well-known in Beijing literary circles (Jin was a former student and friend of Lao She, Beijing's most famous novelist), these men were both vulnerable to attack on grounds of class background and ideological leanings evident in their writings. Their collaboration with Fu Yingfei suggests an anxious awareness of this fact.

Jin Shoushen's comments in the introduction to the manual reveal a tortuous effort on his part to embrace the logic of socialist labour. He commences with two questions that point to the novelty of sewing schools and associated teaching materials in China:

Having comfortable clothing is a necessity in daily life: why is it that in the past no on one has studied it? This is a question about people wearing clothes.

When there are people who can make clothes, why is it they don't introduce the method to others? Why not 'use the needle to cure the patient' [as we say of the acupuncturist?] This is a question about making the clothes.

The answers, as he put it, lay in old thinking. In the past:

> [...] if people had money, why should they bother about learning the artisan's skills? They could just buy comfortable clothes. But the situation has changed now. Before, people could only afford new clothes perhaps once in three years; now they can afford three sets of new clothes every year... Now no longer are these all made by workers, families can organise sideline production, and can also learn to sew the clothes they wear themselves [...].

(Jin 1954)

Virtues of egalitarianism and self-reliance are here advocated alongside assertions of the material advantages of life under socialism ('three sets of new clothes every year') and the economic opportunities available to families through initiatives such as sideline occupations. The importance of material life, at the basic level of clothing, is pointed out. Why (he asks) has no one put much effort into studying it in the past? There are shades here of Mao's address at the 1942 Yanan forum on literature and art. The problems of what to write and for whom were, for Mao, 'fundamentally [...] problems of working for the masses and how to work for the masses'. The rhetorical question put by Jin amounts to an affirmation of the significance and worthiness of an undertaking such as Fu Yingfei's sewing school on just these criteria: i.e., it is concerned not with elite knowledge but with a knowledge that is relevant to the masses. A second rhetorical question hints at the old 'feudal' way of transmitting knowledge, which was within the family or broader kinship of the native place group, and was characterized by closely guarded trade secrets. Again the worthiness of the school is implicitly affirmed: the teacher will make the secrets of the trade available to society more broadly. A whole new vision of society can be inferred, one in which 'the people' and 'the nation' take precedence over and indeed supplant the family, the private firm, the small self-interested group. Jin shows a good grasp of the correct view to take of tailoring in the new dispensation. His preface is an exemplary instance of the active collaboration of intellectuals with the CCP in the 1950s. In all probability he was himself unable to make clothes, but from each according to his strengths: he used a pen instead of a needle, and helped craft a new understanding of labour with reference to clothing the broad masses of the people.

All the peripheral texts in the sewing manuals of this period have strong narrative qualities: stories of tailors and sewing schools are told, and situated in the larger story of the establishment of New China. The stories are illustrated: in most cases, the clothes depicted and described in the manuals take the story forward in time because they are distinctively modern. Designs for *changpao* (long gown) and *magua* (Chinese-style jacket) are nowhere to be found and designs for *qipao* (cheongsam) are rare. To the contrary, Fu Yingfei (1954: 47–48) provides directions for how to convert an old-fashioned Chinese-style jacket into a uniform-style jacket. Patterns for pants in the Hong Kong style and shirts in the Shanghai style shirt mean that this story is modern in a *Chinese* way. The Lenin jacket, the Michurin shirt and the peace blouse give it international socialist content, but the rupture with the capitalist world has been only partially effected. Modern western fashions, which were of course worn in the Soviet bloc as well as in NATO countries, have a prominent place in most of these narratives.

Changing Times, Changing Texts

The 1950s began with New Democracy and ended with the Great Leap Forward. In between was 'socialist transformation', a period marked by policy vicissitudes in the domains both of politics and of the economy. The sewing manuals discussed in the preceding section were basically products of the New Democracy era (Dillon 2007: 80–82). Manuals compiled in this period bore the stamp of the individual tailor in association with a privately established sewing school. In the middle and later 1950s, this characteristic is no longer quite so evident: the names of some tailors who were teaching and publishing in the early 1950s begin to fade from view.

A 1956 manual shows the impact on this sector of socialist transformation. In format, this is very similar to some earlier manuals: size, quality of paper, tables showing lengths of cloth for different garments, roughly executed drawings of people wearing the garments and neat but hand-drawn patterns. It is linked to two private sewing schools, named Victorious China (*Shenghua*) and New Masses (*Xinqun*) respectively, but lacks an individual author. It has a collective, organizational author: the Editorial Committee of the Wuhan Municipal Private Part-Time Sewing Schools. The statement of contents is confined to a description of the technical aims and scope of the work. No mission statement is provided, and no information about the schools. But because they are private schools, we can assume that their origins lay in the early 1950s, like the schools referred to above, and that their combination was part of socialist transformation. During socialist transformation, small private businesses were typically combined to form cooperatives, and the larger forced to partner in joint ventures with state-owned enterprises. These two sewing schools appear to have combined with Wuhan Municipality in a joint enterprise. The original owners in these circumstances often lost visibility and even meaningful roles. In any event, the manual is bland except that pattern pieces cut from a 1957 newspaper were left between its pages, and a child has drawn tanks and ships on its back cover (Wuhanshi 1956).

The absence of political framing devices in this manual is unusual for publications of this sort during the Mao years, and most often to be found in those limbo periods when more than one political line was in sight (cf. Cui 1965). This was true in 1956, the year not only of the beginning of the Hundred Flowers' Movement but also of retreat from 'rash advances' in economic policy (Teiwes and Sun 1998: 5). This same year saw the launch of a dress beautification campaign, on foundations laid by committee work conducted in 1955. The Victorious China and New Masses sewing manual from Wuhan was conservative in terms of the dress-styles promoted in this campaign but a waisted frock for a teenaged girl is emblematic of the period (Wuhanshi 1956: 86). Two pattern books compiled by Wang Guizhang (1956a, 1956b) published this same year show a much more adventurous and diversified set of styles, specifically for women, and may have been published as part of this campaign. Of these, one resembles the Wuhan manual in the absence of any sort of justifying statement in its opening pages. That the same cannot be said for the other suggests that Wang may have received advice or faced criticism after the appearance of the earlier publication. The impression is enhanced by the contrast in the cultural values projected by the two manuals.

These two pattern books were both published by Shanghai Culture Press. *Cutting Methods for Women's Clothing* came out in March. Its front cover carries a sketch of a young woman with bobbed hair wearing a belted frock of striped fabric with a Peter Pan collar and puffed sleeves. Indicative sketches of two other western-style dresses appear in the background. The contents consist largely of dresses, skirts and blouses in standard modern style. There is a chapter on underclothing, with patterns provided for underpants, bloomers, bras and singlets, and also one on clothing to be worn in pregnancy, a rare inclusion in any of these early pattern books. The Lenin suit, so popular in earlier years, does not make an appearance here, and neither does the cadre suit (*ganbu zhifu*), which had great prestige at this time and was a favoured form of wedding dress (Finnane 2008: 224). Some attention was paid to Chinese-style clothes, in keeping with advocacy of Chinese heritage in dress design during the dress beautification campaign, but of 130 pages of patterns only twelve are devoted to Chinese styles, for reasons suggested at the beginning of the section:

> Labouring women in rural areas and housewives in cities on the whole like to wear Chinese clothing. Middle-aged and old women are also used to wearing this sort of clothing. In the depths of winter, young students and professional women, too, change into Chinese padded jackets.
>
> (Wang 1956a: 85)

In other words, with the exception of padded jackets in winter, Chinese-style clothing was outmoded, worn mainly by older women, housewives and peasants.

In May, just two months after the appearance of *Cutting Methods*, a second book of patterns by Wang Guizhang was published under the title *Spring Clothing for Women*. A carefully worded introduction to this collection shows close attention to consideration of both the broader national heritage and the Yanan way, or Communist heritage:

> The clothing of people in our country has always been beautiful, generous and rich with national feeling. But in the long revolutionary struggle of the past, women, in accordance with the circumstances of the struggle, wore uniforms. Right now, on the one hand we want to support the fine tradition of frugality and simplicity, but at the same time, with people's material lives steadily improving, we should also be looking – conditions

permitting – to beauty and variety in clothing so as to manifest the happiness, good fortune and healthful lives of the people of our country.

(Wang 1956b: Preface)

The paragraph is consistent with the discourse produced by the dress beautification movement of 1955–56 (Chen 2001; Finnane 2003). It notably endeavours to reconcile the Yanan aesthetic of frugality and simplicity with the imperative to 'dress prettily' (*daban piaoliang*), the result being a sort of socialist joyful fundamentalism in textual form that can be seen in propaganda posters of the era. A jarring assemblage of images on the front cover of this collection of patterns encapsulates the unresolved difficulties of designing for a modern, socialist and patriotic clientele: tailored, modern but not close-fitting clothes for everyday professional life, combined with long, braided hair appropriate to the womanhood of the socialist motherland, and a gorgeously embroidered qipao for formal or evening wear (Figure 2).

Unlike its predecessor, the second of Wang's 1956 collections features Chinese-style clothing front and centre. Even modern fashions are explained in terms of the Chinese heritage. Skirts are a good example. The traditional old skirts that fell to the floor 'are inconvenient for movement, and now no longer appropriate. We do not want to revive the past, but to use and improve on the best elements of our national heritage, making it fit for new styles and new needs' (Wang 1956b: 29). By such rhetorical devices, Chinese-style clothes are removed from the old clothes basket, and are made appropriate for young and progressive women.

Which of these two manuals was the more useful and appropriate to daily life in Shanghai, or at least the more warmly welcomed? An answer can be found in the publication details: in December 1959, the first was reissued for the eighth time. More than 100,000 copies were sold in all. In 1975, it was reprinted. The second went through a third print run in March 1958, reaching at least 31,000 copies. It is possible that there was a reprint in 1959, but that is not evident from extant copies still available, and even if so, the total issue must have fallen well short of that achieved by its competitor. It can be concluded that the humdrum story of everyday life in socialist China, in which women had to make their own underwear and occasionally wear clothes suitable for pregnant bodies, won out over a story of romantic nationalism in which women wore modernized qipao in summer and embroidered, fur-lined Chinese-style jackets with frog fastenings in winter.

1956 is the last date of a known new publication by Wang Guizhang. It is possible that she fell victim to the anti-rightist campaign, or was swallowed up by a state-owned enterprise. During the Great Leap Forward, light industry and handicrafts, including manual work such as tailoring, suffered from neglect. The emphasis in government policy was on heavy industry and mechanization. The artisans and petty bourgeois entrepreneurs who had historically made up the tailoring sector in China's large cities and smaller town ceased to have significant roles in the production of the nation's wardrobe, except insofar as they were employed in garment factories.

Disappearing Tailors and Questions of Homogeneity

Some time in the second half of 1969 the Qingdao Municipal Light Industry Clothing Export Service Group met at its premises on 90 Anti-Revisionist Road to plan the production of a guide on garment measuring and cutting (Qingdaoshi 1969). Qingdao was a leading centre nationally in the textile and apparel industry. This served it poorly in the years of emphasis on heavy industry under Mao but meant that it had a concentration of factories involved in clothing the nation (Chung 1999: 107). The Cultural Revolution, erupting in May 1966, had been particularly fierce here but the convening of the Ninth Party Congress in April 1969 meant the formal end of this so-called revolution: the publication date of this manual, October 1969, shows industry getting back on track (Ding 2009). The quality of the publication shows how far technical drawing had advanced since Fu Yingfei first sat down in 1951 to draw a girl in a dancing skirt. The clothes presented in this publication are simple in the extreme: trousers, different sorts of coat, some plain and rather shapeless shirts, an army greatcoat. Only two patterns for little girls' frocks have any decorative features. But the drawings are clean and crisp, and the patterns have been drawn up with measuring instruments. Even the quality of the paper shows a marked improvement over that used in the 1950s.

A bizarre feature of this publication is the near absence of women (one image out of sixteen) in the figures or part-figures drawn to illustrate measuring techniques. The reason may be the political sensitivities attendant on graphic representations of female bodies in this period. In 1954, it will be recalled, it was possible to publish a drawing of a woman in a two-piece swimsuit (Fu) or a woman in a petticoat (Lin). Fifteen years later, it was not possible even (or perhaps especially) to demonstrate a chest measurement for women. The illustration shows the tape around a man's chest, with accompanying text including advice of how to adjust for a woman. Reticence is apparent also in the drawings of the garments, which in the case of clothing for men show shaping to the body while the few women's garments show hardly a curving line between them.

Publications of this period, not surprisingly, showed peak intensity of political content with a high incidence of direct reference to Mao and quotations from his works. In this manual, the front page is fully given over to 'the highest directive', a term reserved for extracts from Mao's works and given canonical status during the Cultural Revolution. Here quotations from Mao are displayed, beginning with '[i]t is the Communist Party of China that is the *core strength* leading us in our endeavour' (1954) and ending with '[y]ou must interest yourselves in national affairs, and implement the Great Proletarian Cultural Revolution to the end', a statement originally made by Mao in audience with the masses on 10 August 1966.

On the obverse of the title page, a short prologue or 'explanatory note' relates Maoist directives more specifically to the group's undertaking:

In accordance with the teaching of our great leader Chairman Mao that we should 'serve the people with our whole hearts and whole minds', and to satisfy the great masses of

Figure 3: Front cover of a Cultural Revolution-era pattern
book, showing hammer and sickle in place of sewing
machine and scissors. Source: Qingdaoshi Qinggongye
Xitong Fuzhuang Chukou Fuwuzu (ed.), 1969. *Fuzhuang
liangcai* (garment measuring and cutting).

the workers, soldiers and peasants who urgently seek to study the techniques of garment
measuring and cutting, we have tidied up and supplemented the former edition of
Garment Measuring and Cutting, publishing a new edition to serve as reference materials
for the broad masses to study techniques of garment measuring and cutting.

(Qingdaoshi 1969)

Here notice is given of an idealized readership for the manual: the workers, soldiers and
peasants who were the vanguard classes of the Cultural Revolutionary period. The logo on
the front cover, showing a gun standing erect between a crossed hammer and sickle,
appropriately refers to this grouping. That the actual end users were more probably garment
makers in Qingdao factories is suggested by a professionally drawn-up pattern piece for a
collar, left within the pages of the manual. There were in fact cheaper and cruder publications
available for the broad masses of the people.

A second paragraph in the explanatory prologue makes it clear how and why the Cultural Revolution is regarded as having continued long after it was officially deemed to have concluded:

> Due to our insufficient study of Chairman Mao and our low levels of political ideology, combined with the limitations of our technological skills, it has been difficult for us to avoid shortcomings and errors. We earnestly hope that comrades will offer criticisms and corrections, so that we can make further additions and improvements when the time comes for another edition.
>
> (Qingdaoshi 1969)

The statement is simultaneously formulaic and expressive. Like a prayer to ward off evil, it has been positioned at or near to the beginning of the publication, helping – like the page of Mao's sayings – to insulate it against possible charges of deviationism, cleaving to the 'four olds', or showing foreign influences. To the extent that it is typical of the times, it shows how utterly cowed Chinese society had become, after 20 years of government by the Chinese Communist Party.

The Qingdao pattern book, with its conservative range of clothing designs, careful layout and effectively anonymous group authorship, is a minor but illustrative example of the narrowing in scope of what could be written in the People's Republic of China since its founding. The severe diminution in the range of narrative possibilities in literature and the performing arts is a well-recognized characteristic of the Cultural Revolution. The technical literature connected with the textile and apparel industries shows these effects. Looking back at the 1950s, when individual tailors and sewing instructors were the major producers of this literature, we can see that despite the fact that these petty entrepreneurs were careful to identify their various undertakings with the political and cultural position of the new government, they continued to be visible as individual actors in the commerce and industry sector. It is not surprising, then, that a variety of stories about them and by them should have emerged from the how-to-sew advice literature of that decade, especially its early years. After the formation of cooperatives and joint ventures in the period of socialist transformation fewer tailors were able to leave their mark on the documentary record, and during the Cultural Revolution, they are hardly to be found.

The range of clothing designed, depicted and worn became correspondingly narrower over this period. The great variety of garments to be found in pattern books by Fu Yingfei and Wang Guizhang gave way to a few generic pieces in the manual produced by the Qingdao Export Group, which was not untypical of publications in this sector through the 10 years of the Cultural Revolution. In a large format, full-colour display magazine produced by a Tianjin clothing export company (Tianjinshi 1973), the range of designs produced in Qingdao four years earlier is reduplicated with just a few additions. Many scholars, including the present writer, have been at pains to point out the ways in which the oft-mentioned homogeneity and androgeneity of dress in the Cultural Revolution is belied by evidence of inventiveness and fads during these years (Evans 2006; Finnane 2008; Sun 2013). Yet from the technical literature in this sector, the long-term trend of clothing styles towards homogenization seems unmistakable. Much as the prescriptive literature might have differed from daily practice, it is questionable whether too much weight should be given to the many small instances of departure from norms.

Despite the contrasts between the early fifties and the late sixties, the trend towards homogenization can be traced back to the 1950s, when the plain, militarist fashions associated with the new government and the Yanan heritage made their appearance in pattern books and how-to-sew manuals. It is helpful to think about these materials in terms of the sometimes contradictory narratives embedded in them: on the one hand, a narrative about modern womanhood told by simply sketched female figures in skirts and blouses with permed hair and pinched-in waists; on the other, a narrative of socialist revolution grounded in Yanan. As the successive reprints of Wang Guizhang's *Cutting Methods* showed, the latent appeal of the former was very strong. In the short term, however, the Yanan story won out. Technical education in garment production was bound up with learning about the productive roles to be played by women in the New China. The costume for such roles was undoubtedly better imagined as the Lenin jacket than as a two-piece swim suit.

It is not possible now to recover the reading strategies employed by students in the sewing schools where these materials were used, but reading aloud was standard practice in Chinese pedagogy and we can well imagine was employed in the classroom. If the teacher was attentive enough to the political climate to include an introduction that explained the teaching materials in the context of contemporary social circumstances, we may be sure that the students would be made aware of this context. The strategy of setting up a manual in the early fifties through references to China, socialism and the tailor's own undertaking proved in the end not too different from that used during the Cultural Revolution, when the Chairman's 'highest directives' were used as a framing device. In a given workshop, the machinists very probably chanted these directives in unison.

The biggest difference between publications of the earlier and later periods lay finally in the attribution of authorship, which was to individual authors in the earlier works and to committees in the later. Working backward from Larssen's observations, mentioned above, we might conclude that the absence of individually authored works in this sector between 1965 and 1975 onwards meant in effect the absence of individuals (so construed) from the sector. The private sewing schools had long since disappeared, and so too, with very few exceptions, the individual tailor shops. What happened to the tailors themselves – Lin Baozheng, Fu Yingfei, Wang Guizhang – is impossible to say. It is almost as Carlo Ginzburg wrote of a sixteenth-century heretic named Marcato: 'he and so many others like him lived and died without leaving a trace' (Ginzburg 1980: 128) – almost, but not quite, for in the sewing manuals that have survived from the 1950s, we do find fragments of their stories.

Acknowledgements

Research for this chapter was supported by a Discovery Project grant from the Australian Research Council. The author thanks Dr Anne Peirson-Smith for the opportunity to develop the theme in a keynote address at the *Fashion in Fiction* conference, City University of Hong Kong, 12–14 June 2014.

References

Aarons, E. (1993), *What's Left?*, Ringwood: Penguin.

Anon. (1954), 'Top mannequins in Moscow and Tokyo', *Sun-Herald*, 17 January, p. 27.

—— (2009), *Courtesans and Opium* (trans. P. Hanan). New York: Columbia University Press.

Barthes, R. (1983), *The Fashion System*. New York: Hill and Wang.

Chen, T. M. (2001), 'Dressing for the party: Clothing, citizenship, and gender-formation in Mao's China', *Fashion Theory: The Journal of Dress, Body & Culture*, 5:2, June, pp. 143–71.

—— (2003), 'Proletarian white and working bodies in Mao's China', *Positions: East Asia Cultures Critique*, 11:2, fall, pp. 361–94.

Chung, J. H. (1999), 'Preferential policies, municipal leadership, and development strategies: A comparative analysis of Qingdao and Dalian', in J. H. Chung (ed.), *Cities in Post-Mao China: Recipes for Economic Development in the Reform Era*, London: Routledge, pp. 103–37.

Cui, X. (1965), *Shiyong caifengfa (Practical Methods of Tailoring)*, Harbin: Heilongjiang renminchubanshe.

Dauncey, S. (2003), 'Illusions of grandeur: Perceptions of status and wealth in late-ming female clothing and ornamentations', *East Asian History*, 5:26, pp. 43–68.

Dillon, N. (2007), 'New democracy and the demise of China's private charities', in C. A. Connolly, J. Brown and P. G. Pickowicz (eds), *Dilemmas of Victory: The Early Years of the People's Republic of China*, Cambridge: Harvard University Press, pp. 254–56.

Ding, L., Barlow, T. E. and Bjorge, G. J. (1989), *I Myself Am a Woman: Selected Writings of Ding Ling*, Boston: Beacon Press.

Evans, H. (2006), 'Fashion and feminine consumption', in K. Latham, S. Thompson and J. A. Klein (eds), *Consuming China: Approaches to Cultural Change in Contemporary China*, London: Routledge, pp. 313–45.

Finnane, A. (2003), 'Yu Feng and the 1950s dress reform campaign: Global hegemony and local agency in the art of fashion', in C. M. Yu (ed.), *Wu sheng zhi sheng: jindai Zhongguo funü yu wenhua, 1650–1950 (Silent Voices: Women and Modern Chinese Culture, 1650–1950)*, vol. 2, Taipei: Academia Sinica.

—— (2008), *Changing Clothes in China: Fashion, History, Nation*, New York: Columbia University Press.

—— (2016), 'Cold War sewing machines: Production and consumption in 1950s China and Japan', *Journal of Asian Studies*, 75:3, pp. 755–83.

Fu, Y. (1951a), *Xinfa jiancai: fengren jiaoben (New Method Tailoring: A Sewing Textbook)*, Beijing: Fu Yingfei.

—— (1951b), *Yangcai jiaoben* ('Cutting for Western garments: A textbook'), Beijing: Xinsheng yangcai zhiye xuexiao.

—— (1954), *Xinfa jiancai: fengren jiaoben* (*New Method Tailoring: A Sewing Textbook*), 2 vols, Beijing: Fu Yingfei.

Ginzburg, C. (1980), *The Cheese and the Worms: The Cosmos of a Sixteenth-Century Miller* (trans. J. Tedeschi and A. Tedeschi), Baltimore: The Johns Hopkins University Press.

Gordon, A. (2012), *Fabricating Consumers: The Sewing Machine in Modern Japan*, Berkeley: University of California Press.

Hanan, P. (1998), 'Fengyue Meng and the courtesan novel', *Harvard Journal of Asiatic Studies*, 58:2, December 1998, pp. 345–72.

Hanshang, M. ([1848] 1988), *Fengyue meng* (*Illusions of Romance*), Beijing: Beijing daxue chubanshe.

Hu, Y. (2000), *Tales of Translation: Composing the New Woman in China, 1899–1918*, Stanford: Stanford University Press.

Ji, X., Zhu, X. and Feng Y.-Z. (eds) (2011), *Hongbang caifeng pingzhuan* (*Lives of Hongbang Tailors*), Hangzhou: Zhejiang daxue chubanshe.

Jin, S. (1954), *Xinfa jiancai: fengren jiaoben* (*New Method Tailoring: A Sewing Textbook*), 2 vols, Beijing: Fu Yingfei.

Karnow, S. (1964), 'Fashion: Asia enters the rage race', *Saturday Evening Post*, 237:3, 25 January, pp. 24–31.

Kraus, W. (1982), *Economic Development and Social Change in the People's Republic of China*, New York: Springer-Verlag.

Larssen, I. (2003), *Accessibility and Acceptability in Technical Manuals: A Survey of Style and Grammatical Metaphor*, Amsterdam: John Benjamins Publishing Co.

Lin, Z. (1954), *Caijian zhinan* (*Guide to Cutting and Sewing*), Shanghai: Meilin caijian fengxiu chuanxisuo zongjingxiao.

Link, E. (1981), *Mandarin Ducks and Butterflies: Popular Fiction in Early Twentieth-Century Chinese Cities*, Berkeley: University of California Press.

Neuberg, V. E. (1977), *Popular Literature: A History and Guide*, London: The Woburn Press.

Nüzi shijie (*Women's World*) (1904), 5 April, pp. 29–34.

Qingdaoshi qinggongye xitong fuzhuang chukou fuwuzu (Export services group for the Qingdao municipal light industry system (ed.) (1969), *Fuzhuang liangcai* ('Garment measuring and cutting'), n.p.: Qingdao.

Schmalzer, S. (2014), 'Self-reliant science: The impact of the Cold War on science in socialist China', in N. Oreskes and J. Krige (eds), *Science and Technology in the Global Cold War*, Cambridge: The MIT Press, pp. 75–106.

Shen, C. (1981), *Zhongguo gudai fushi yanjiu* (*Clothing in Pre-Modern China*), Hong Kong: Shangwu yinshuguan.

Song, S. (2007), 'The state discourse on housewives and housework in the 1950s in China', in M. Leutner (ed.), *Rethinking China in the 1950s*, Berlin: Dr. W. Hopf, pp. 49–63.

Sun, P. (2013), *Shishang yu zhengzhi: Guangdong minzhong richang zhuozhuang shishang (1966–1976)* (*Fashion and Politics: Fashion in the Daily Wear in Guangdong, 1966–1976*), Beijing: Renmin Chubanshe.

Sugini, Y. (1936), *Yōsai fujinfuku* ('Women's clothing in the Western cut'), Tokyo: Kōbunsha.

Teiwes, F. C. and Warren, S. (1999), *China's Road to Disaster: Mao, Central Politicians, and Provincial Leaders in the Unfolding of the Great Leap Forward, 1955–1959*, Armonk, New York: M.E. Sharpe.

Tianjinshi Hepingqu disi fengrenshe hongfeng (Tianjin municipality Heping district No.4 sewing team, Red Wind) (ed.) (1973), *Fuzhuang yangpin (Patterns for Clothing)*, Tianjin: Tianjinshi renmin yinshuachang.

Wang, G. (1950), *Jinghua fengcaixiu zhinan (The King Fair Instructions for Sewing and Stitching)*, Shanghai: Jinghua.

—— (1956a), *Funü fuzhuang caizhifa (Cutting Methods for Women's Dress)*, Shanghai: Shanghai Wenhua Chubanshe.

—— (1956b), *Funü chunzhuang (Spring Clothing for Women)*, Shanghai: Shanghai Wenhua Chubanshe.

Wang, Z. (1939), *Caifeng jiangyi (Principles of Tailoring)*, Haerbin: Fulian jieli yinshua suo.

Wei, Q. (1954), *Xinshi fengren jiancai fa (New Style Cutting and Sewing Methods)*, Beijing: Beijing wenhua chubanshe.

Xiaoxiaosheng (1993–), *The Plum in the Golden Vase* (trans. D. T. Roy), Princeton: Princeton University Press.

Xin, F. (2001), *The Memoirs of Xin Fengxia* (trans. J. Chinnery), Oxford: Oxford University Press.

Yang, L. (1998), *Chinese Fiction of the Cultural Revolution*, Hong Kong: Hong Kong University Press.

Yoshimura, C. (1929), *Gendai saihō kyōkasho (Teaching Materials for Modern Dressmaking)*, Tokyo: Tokyo Kaiseikan.

Zhao, J. (1925), 'Yifu caifa ji cailiao jisuan fa' ('Method of cutting and measuring cloth'), *Funü zazhi*, 1 September, pp. 1450–61.

Section 2

Style Statements: Fashioning Identity

Introduction

The range of chapters in this second section of the book interrogates notions and expressions of fashion as a type of dress or style and the roles and performances that it affords in various discourses across time, space and place in terms of its critical role in negotiating and articulating identity through display.

In focussing on the ways that fashion is used to express individual or collective identity in relation to difference and belonging, the content of this section ranges from analysing fashion as cultural artefact representing design ideologies and ethnic identity, to its role in defining ethnicity in televised beauty competitions, and the coded meanings underlying the beard or feminized animal tropes across a range of mediated fashion images. It also includes an exploration of the fantastical manga and anime inspired cosplay costumes as way of communicating and performing individual identity and insider allegiance to a group style tribe. In this way, multi-mediated fashion statements are enabled by their producers and users to sense-make and present a sense of self in terms of the aesthetics, identities and lived experiences gained from, yet differentiated by the various geographic centres in which they are located.

Fashion and clothing can perform identity by celebrating individuality through everyday attire across the range of prescribed roles that are played throughout life (see Tseëlon in this section). As a communicative phenomenon, fashion and clothing through the techniques of fashioning and adornment enable the expression of individuality, group identity, status and differentiation from others, as in the case of male beards signifying masculine traits among an older male demographic versus the more nuanced style statements of the younger hirsute brethren in Denmark (see Mackinney-Valentin and Brun Petersen in this section).

Ideologically, fashion and clothing are also credited with the ability to reinforce or challenge and change the dominant notions of class, gender and ethnicity through the reinterpretation and celebration of Puerto Rican national dress and nationhood in beauty competitions (see Blanco F. and Vázquez-López in this section). Equally, Australian designers have used motifs on fashion garments as markers of belonging and place identity. By appropriating Indigenous signs and symbols such as boomerangs, often out of context, in contemporary fashion, the resulting contested issues of copyright, ownership and cultural authenticity emerge from this negotiated inter-cultural discourse (see Craik in this section). Female animalistic representation in fashion images can also be considered as an expression of feminist empowerment. This gendered portrayal operates beyond the traditional binary notions of gender identity and the objectified female form, thereby highlighting the dynamic nature of meaning. In addition to challenging gender and identity politics, the use of animal images in fashion advertising can also be interpreted as being anti-anthropomorphic by redefining human-animal relations from a more ethical standpoint (see Wallenberg in this section).

The imparting of fashion information and knowledge and its encoding and decoding in visual and verbal form in the context of the art gallery or exhibition space to showcase the work of Scandinavian fashion designers can also perform a didactic function and highlight critical issues in the transglobal fashion system associated with environmental impact, for example. This underlines the role of designer as auteur and storyteller and the active role of the audience in decoding the message and identifying with it in their own lives. The design stories on show in a public context, such as a gallery or museum, provoke the art as fashion debate. These material narratives also enable fashion to communicate ideologically in the interface between the material artefact such as paper clothing and its symbolic commentary on our disposable society and wasteful lifestyles, and ultimately address how the fashion consumer identifies with this (see Kjellmer in this section).

Dressing into a unique style tribe, and dressing out of other presentations of self, signals a strong statement about the wearer's belief and value system as a form of individually performed identity creation. At the same time, it highlights the expressive capacity of fashion and clothing to convey inclusivity and exclusivity. The cosplay re-presentation in the South East Asian context, for example, of a crinolined Marie Antoinette character motif from the Rose of Versailles anime, illustrates how individual costume constitutes the spectacular presentation of self within a segmented collective (see Peirson-Smith in this section) as the ultimate performance of fashioned identity.

Chapter 7

The Emperor's New Clothes Revisited: On Critical Fashion, Magical Thinking and Fashion as Fiction

Efrat Tseëlon

This chapter is an opportunity to reflect on the relationship between fiction and fashion, as this is at the core of the *Critical Fashion* perspective that I have been developing since the late 1980s. *Critical Fashion* hinges on identifying the 'story construction' elements in the taken-for-granted accounts of our world. This chapter outlines some aspects of the history and methodologies of fashion scholarship and sketches out a map of fashion research and its relation to fictions and narratives. My starting point here is that we are all storytelling creatures. My use of the concept of 'stories' applies to different types and levels of narratives: from works of fiction (fairy tales, myths and all manner of creative writing), to popular culture discourses about fashion and at the meta-level to reasoning about our lived experiences, including our very 'storytelling' activities.

The Emperor's New Clothes

My chapter is framed within a story, which I am using as a root metaphor. This follows a tradition – the most eloquent proponent of which is the sociologist Erving Goffman – of using metaphors to guide inquiry and analysis. Goffman coined some of the most well-known metaphors and terminologies, which we habitually use to describe social life, including *stigma* (1968), *facework* (1955) and the *theatre* (1959). I will refer to his dramaturgical metaphor later. At this point, it is enough to note that metaphors are a very effective way of structuring thinking and research. This is because metaphors are used as heuristic tools, rather than as absolute equivalents of the phenomena they describe as they bridge art and science, which is where the study of fashion lies.

Hans Christian Andersen's tale, *The Emperor's New Clothes*, has been appropriated in many ways for different purposes. Here, it is used to analyse some relationships between fashion and fiction, which are salient, for the critical practice of fashion studies. The story is about a king known for his love of sumptuous finery: he is something of the order of a royal dandy, or a fashion victim. Andersen's own critical voice is evident in the irony with which he introduces this character.

Many years ago there was an Emperor so exceedingly fond of new clothes that he spent all his money on being well dressed. He cared nothing about reviewing his soldiers, going to the theatre, or going for a ride in his carriage, except to show off his new clothes.

He had a coat for every hour of the day, and instead of saying, as one might, about any other ruler, 'The King's in council', here they always said 'the Emperor's in his dressing room'.

(Andersen [1837] 1949)

The king falls prey to fraudster tailors who come to his court. They boast of their ability to weave extraordinary fabric with a magic capacity, so that the clothes made from it are invisible to anyone who is stupid or unfit to hold office. The king pays them large sums of money and grants their demands forever more silk and gold. After some days he sends his most trusted advisers to see how the work is progressing. Of course, there is nothing on the looms, although the tailors look to be working very hard. None of the advisers dares admit that they cannot see the magic cloth, for fear that each might be a fool, unfit for office. On the day before the procession when the new clothes are to be unveiled, the king arrives with his courtiers and is handed empty clothes by the 'tailors' who are no more than mime artists. Having failed to see any clothes, he too fears to admit that he may be unfit to rule, so he praises the clothes instead. He takes off his own garments, so he can be dressed with the new suit, and gazes into the mirror, while his courtiers admire the colours, design and fit of the imaginary clothes. The courtiers leave the atelier carrying the train of the pretend mantle. The people who gather to view the king in his new splendid outfit similarly endorse the common conspiracy of admiration. Nobody dares to challenge the con men, for fear of making fools of themselves. It is left to a small child, to call the bluff of this storytelling act that so many people have colluded in, out of fear of standing out, fear of being embarrassed or fear of losing position and face. In his innocent and direct way, the child simply declares what his eyes see, and tears into the web of fictions. He declares that the king is, in fact, naked.

This story can be interpreted in several ways, on multiple levels. It is a story that shows how our perceptions are conditioned by a culture that teaches us what to see, what to expect, to assume, to take for granted, to doubt or to ignore. It is a story about a little boy representing untainted naked truth, with nothing to lose or gain, puncturing the pretensions of courtly hypocrisy and political spin. According to one Buddhist psychologist, it also illustrates the power of the Buddha's gaze to 'really seeing' things as they are, unobstructed by distractions such as delusion or suffering (Ovadia 2013). It is also a story that registers an old and somewhat persistent belief in the authenticity of depth over surface behaviours. In popular culture the metaphor of the Emperor's naked ambitions is used to refer to a situation where an obvious truth is officially denied through political expediency, or through political correctness, in contrast with the evidence of people's own eyes or experience. Finally, the story often refers to situations where the overwhelming majority of observers willingly share in a collective ignorance, or disavowal of an obvious fact despite individually recognizing the absurdity.

The story has probably been applied more to politics than to fashion, but metaphorically it also has specific fashion relevance. It can be read as a moral story about the value of *essence* and the vanity of *appearances*. It is a story that deconstructs the futility of personal vanity, and of adherence to the dictates of fashion or personal appearance in general, or to brand worship in particular. It can also be seen as a story about the dishonesty of fashion consultancy masquerading as honest opinion, or about how distorted a self-image can become, when it is divorced from how others see us. The 'invisible' clothes can be seen as exposing the fiction of 'magical clothes': a recurrent motif in fairy tales, but also ubiquitous in contemporary culture. Examples range from the mantra, 'if you look good you feel good', to the cultural belief that lucky clothes can win us friends and jobs, or give us confidence, or even the magical belief in the transformative power of school uniforms (Tseëlon 2006).

It is also a story that reveals – as Goffman so richly and powerfully identified – the fundamental motivation underlying what makes the social order possible. It is fear of embarrassment and the anxiety of losing face, expressed in the desire to fit in, to comply, not to commit a faux pas, and also, if need be, to engage in damage limitation. The reason why nobody dared to tell the king the truth about his pretend clothing was a desire to avoid standing out and being shown up as foolish or incompetent. So, they all complied, against the evidence of their own eyes.

By voicing the very thing that was taboo, the child removed the threat, and opened the way for people to laugh at the king. Ironically, what happens then is that by appearing naked in public, the king, who is the one who symbolizes the social order, casts himself in a position that in contemporary legislation is regarded as violating civil and moral order. In his analogy between law and fashion, Watt (2013) makes reference to a case of a naked rambler who was jailed in Scotland for doing what he thought was his right: walking without clothes along a public path. Watt notes that the sentence revealed that nakedness is considered indecent, and that dress is invested with authority to police moral boundaries. So, it is illegal to be naked in public, unless you are a Rihanna, a Kardashian or some other high-profile celebrity, and unless nudity is stylized as fashion.

Stories are seductive. Stories have features that channel us to certain ways of seeing and thinking. They tend to dramatize, to simplify and to follow one or more of a stock of narratives (Propp [1928] 1968). By operating within the paradigmatic universe they create for us, we move away from a position of a critical distance, which asks for an examination of the story from the outside. An 'outside view' investigates the story's underlying assumptions, and problematizes its taken-for-granted meanings and the way they structure and influence our thought and conduct.

Therefore, as researchers we need to be in the space that Goffman defined in *Role Distance* (1961), which is the capacity to be both inside and outside, to reflect upon, as well as to be part of. An enduring metaphor he provides is that of an adult (maybe as a guardian of a child) who rides the funfair carousel and feels a bit embarrassed about indulging in a child-like pleasure. To counteract this feeling the adult engages in some activity that disavows the extent and the seriousness of their involvement.

Critical Fashion

The seductive power of stories leads me to the point I want to make about the paradigm change in thinking about and researching fashion that I call *Critical Fashion*. I came to define the field of *Critical Fashion* as a result of a critique I conducted of the existing ontologies, epistemologies and methodologies as part of my doctoral work in Social Psychology at Oxford in the late 1980s. At that time, the field of fashion studies hardly existed. What did exist was what I broadly call the *stereotype approach*, and I contrast it with my own take on this, the *wardrobe approach* (see Table 1).

Table 1: The stereotype and the wardrobe approaches to fashion.

Stereotype approach	Wardrobe approach
Categorical approach	Process approach
Meaning is stable	Meaning is fluid
Outside view	Inside view
Style (focus on garments)	Experience (focus on wearers)
Garment-focused method	Wearer-focused method
Object-based	Conceptual
Extreme or iconic fashion	Everyday clothes

The Stereotype and the Wardrobe Approaches to Fashion

The underlying assumptions of the *stereotype approach* to fashion (from costume history and anthropology, to psychology) was object-based and focused on *type* and *style* of garments as carrying fixed meanings (of class, gender, personality, emotions or morality). Its methodologies, contrasting opposite extremes of styles (e.g. jeans vs ball gowns, casual vs formal), favoured and reproduced stereotypes (Tseëlon 1989, 1992, 2012). In popular culture it gained currency in self-help books, style guides and advice columns. Alison Lurie's (1981) *The Language of Clothes* and a host of contemporary style guides (e.g. Woodall and Constantine, 2005, *What Your Clothes Say about You*), as well as self-styled and very topical 'fashion psychologists' belong to this category.

All of these approaches shared huge generalizations and an assumption that the meaning of clothes is stable and inherent. The examples that were used in research referred to extreme styles and atypical contexts, or occasion-dress. They featured clothes for the most visible or dramatic occasions, but left out the more mundane behaviour of most people most of the time. By their very nature they superimposed a visible minority phenomenon, which follows ritual or distinct group norms, on a broader and more diffuse class of behaviours which are typically not as heavily laden with signifying meaning as the theory would have us believe.

Underlying the research, which seeks fixed meanings attributed to clothes or their wearers, is ontology of a fixed identity. In contrast, my *wardrobe approach* did not assume either that clothes have invariable meanings, or that they refer unproblematically to rigid personal or group characteristics. Instead, I examined clothes in context, combining the 'inside view' of the wearers' accounts of the meanings of their clothes, together with the 'outside view' of observers' interpretations.

The research that I carried out in the late 1980s for my doctoral thesis challenged the stereotype paradigm, thereby paving the way for a variety of alternative methods and ontologies. In this, my approach moved from the dramatic to the ordinary, and from iconic dresses to everyday clothes (or from fashion to clothing). It shifted the dominant focus from the 'outside view' (the garments) by complementing it with the 'inside view' (the wearers), and it extended the exclusive emphasis on a wholly visual approach to also include the experiential approach, and the discursive approach. These approaches are not just concerned with how the object looks. The experiential approach examines how people interact with objects, how they use them and how they feel about them in different situations and with different people. The discursive approach looks at how fashion is talked about and represented in different venues, from conversations to media messages and ads. Finally, my research demonstrated that meaning is not an independent fixed entity, but is negotiated in interaction.

The Fiction of Fashion as Communication Comes Undone

If we are challenging the notion that meaning is inherent in a particular garment, if we are challenging the notion that individuals or groups have a certain essence (identity) that is transmitted through appearance, how do clothes signify, or what is the meaning of signification at all? The semiotic approach also comes under scrutiny. To address this question I developed the masking paradigm for capturing the journey that clothes have travelled throughout the history of fashion. Also, I applied to fashion Baudrilliard's division between different orders of signification (Tseëlon 2015). The first order, founded on *imitation*, characterized the pre-modern period where appearances *reflect* reality in direct signifier-signified links. The second order, founded on *production*, characterized the modern period where appearances *conceal* reality through indirect signifier-signified links. The third order, founded on *simulation*, characterized the postmodern period where appearances *deconstruct* reality in a play of signifiers without a signified, which means that there is no depth to meaning. Thus, nothing is more real than anything else, and you can take things like religious symbols and use them for jewellery, or you can advertise a shoe brand, or underwear line with a motif of the national flag, for example.

My research empirically demonstrated the problematics of privileging the type of story involved in categorical thinking (which is central to the *stereotype approach*), which relies on the fiction of a fixed identity and objects with identifiable and well-defined properties in order to be communicated. While historically, certainties, stabilities and visible signs served as boundary markers (of classes, of genders, of national cultures, of professions), as the twentieth century rolled on, they were being challenged. Traditional groups were diffused into new kinds of collectives. Instead of class we developed lifestyle groups, professional or special interest groups, or smaller ad hoc configurations. In the social sciences the concept of 'identity' (whose origins can be traced to the rise of the nation state in the mid-nineteenth century) has been critiqued for its failure to address contested and reflexive aspects. It was towards the second half of the twentieth century that globalization and postmodern deconstruction exposed the cracks in the edifice that makes up these imaginary communities, as Benedict Anderson (1983) calls them. As a result, the *national* narrative has increasingly evolved to a *multicultural* one in order to accommodate contingent, ambivalent and hybrid voices. Thus, conceptions of 'identity' have come to be seen more as a *process* of negotiated positions where members define their belonging – out of the cultural materials available to them – than as a process of reification of permanent properties.

In a paper entitled, 'Is identity a useful critical tool?' (2010) I argue that as identity is now more fiction than reality, we need to replace categorical with conversational thinking, and abandon the notion of identity in favour of the notion of *phatic community*. In this I take inspiration from Annette Jørgensen, who studied emotion markers in teenage language in several countries, and observed that teenage talk is first and foremost a phatic activity (Jørgensen 2010), i.e., it works to establish interpersonal connections. More than an instrument for transmission of particular content or 'story', it conveys emotion and connectedness: maintaining contact, communion and solidarity, creating a strong bonding effect and expressing affection. This is a good analogy for non-verbal behaviour that uses a visual medium to convey, both denotative (factual) information directly, and connotative (interpretative) meanings and associations indirectly.

The evidence is all around us that even at the level of objects, the meaning of stereotypes is in a state of flux. Fur once used to indicate luxury, now indicates cruelty. Tattoos were a mark of lower classes, and they now have gone upmarket; sportswear has gone from utility to designer; Burberry transitioned for a while from an iconic brand to a 'Chav' trademark; and veils have proved to be contested territory, ranging from liberation to oppression, with opinions divided even among its Indigenous clientele, to give just a few examples. Another example of the cracks that began to appear in the certainty of categories is 'occasion dressing' – another staple of the *stereotype approach* which tended to contrast ball gowns – the markers of formal event, where rules prescribed appearance – with jeans, the quintessential casual alternative. Jeans stood for anything and everything that was not prescribed. In recent years, however, jeans have become a high-fashion item. Indeed, notions of formality have proven particularly malleable historically. Wouters (2007) observed that formalizing manners and disciplining people had been dominant from the sixteenth up to the last quarter of the nineteenth century. From that point on, a process of informalization began, accompanied by greater demands on emotion management or self-control. We can see the equivalent in fashion with the rise of sports clothes to the status of ordinary or status clothes, with the normalization of tattoos, as well as with the recent phenomenon of 'normcore' – the rejection of labels in favour of non-branded style. Here, we see the ingredients of another process, one that represents a refuge from meaning, a *semiotic fatigue* (Tseëlon 2015).

Let me illustrate. In a series of studies with hundreds of respondents, and the use of a rich array of qualitative and statistical methods, I established that it was *not style* that explained women's sartorial choices and meanings. Rather, there were underlying *motivators* that influenced the wearing and interpreting of different kinds of clothing and adornment. The most persistent motivators throughout my programme of research were identified as:

> putting high or low effort into one's appearance, preferring to look individual or conventional, to blend in or stand out in a given context, needing the clothes to ward off anxiety, desiring to come across as stylish, sexy or high status.
>
> (Tseëlon 1989)

While the motivators were widely shared at the level of principles, their translation into specific clothing choices was far from uniform. This finding explains why cultural tendencies can reflect, at the same time, uniformity at the level of *motivational considerations* and diversity at the level of *style*. What gives different people confidence, what is considered as 'much effort' or what is considered sexy will vary across individuals. In fact, one dimension, which appeared most dominant, was visibility (see Figure 1). If you look at the distribution over the space you will discover that from one pole to another a dimension of *visibility* appears dominant (see also Tseëlon 2000). The implications of that factor are twofold. On the one hand, they reveal the deep connection between clothes and boundaries, as Watt (2013) argues, which are policed through a concern with confidence, social appropriateness and (dis)approval. On the other hand, the prominence of the *invisibility* at the opposite end of the *visibility* factor indicates that contrary to theories of fashion communication, people are not always looking to communicate anything, or to engage in an exchange of meaning. Rather, they desire to escape from visibility and the meanings that are associated with certain ways of dressing that are noted or marked. They express *semiotic fatigue*. Reaching a similar conclusion, Miller and Woodward (2012) found – on the basis of an international ethnographic study of blue jeans – that wearing jeans represents a space of ordinariness that they termed 'a post-semiotic space'.

It would have been tempting to reduce the (in)visibility dimension to the ubiquitous dichotomy into of invisibility=home and visibility=job interview. For some people, a job interview would be outside their comfort zone, for others it would be when they were in their element. Some people get nervous about exams, others do not care, but if they were to meet a celebrity or a new date – they would get extremely nervous. I want to use the (in)visibility dimension at its most heuristic. Invisibility has often been credited with 'authenticity' connotations, whereas visibility has been associated with staged behaviour. But equally, invisibility can simply mean away from normative pressures, as compared with visibility, where one feels observed, judged, evaluated and compelled to conform to

Figure 1: Part of my research was analysed using Multi-Dimensional Scaling (MDS), a method that uses qualitative data to represent statistical relationships between variables. A series of exploratory studies asked women to group situations according to their dressing considerations. MDS produced a multidimensional map that represented those relationships. A close examination reveals that the dominant dimension here is that of visibility/invisibility. The top left corner indicates a space of high visibility and anxiety, the bottom right corner reveals a relaxed space of low visibility. Source: Tseëlon 1989.

particular normative expectations. What triggers the feeling of invisibility or visibility will vary between individuals, as would the sartorial responses.

My studies confirmed that it is the main dimension of meaning that clothes occupy today, and actually the same dimension Goffman identified in his 'presentation of self' (Goffman 1959). Commonly, Goffman's metaphor is taken to refer to the manipulative-ness of 'on stage' performance as compared to the authenticity of 'off stage'. My reading of Goffman is that backstage is no more authentic than front stage: they are simply different kinds of stages (Tseëlon 1995). We are on a stage not just when we are 'making an appearance'. When people are on a stage where they feel invisible, it is still 'a stage' but one in which they will feel at ease, and in their clothing idiom there are certain clothing choices they are more likely to make. Such an approach shows that depth and authenticity are ideological categories. The presupposition is that authenticity lies at an inaccessible level far below the surface of social life, in folk culture or deep within oneself. Often, authenticity encodes the expectation of truthful representation hidden in the 'backstage'. In their own ways, Goffman (with his notion of backstage being just another stage, not a more authentic one) and Baudrillard (with his notion of postmodern signification which is a play of signifiers with no signifieds) both reject this presupposition of authenticity (Tseëlon 2015). My own empirical research, based on accounts from several hundred women also rejects the story of authenticity, which appears to be so fundamental to the study of fashion, and to notions of identity and meaning.

Another set of studies that I carried out was designed to empirically examine the notion of communication through clothing. Using visual questionnaires and also field experiments (1989, 1992) I compared women's interpretation of other people's clothes in a condition of no prior knowledge about those people's 'normal' dressing style, and where they had that knowledge. The results illustrated why it is impossible to reduce the complex web of visuals and meanings into a standardized matrix – because everyone has a different clothing vocabulary. What is one person's dressing-up gear when most conspicuous is another person's baseline when they are least conspicuous. And there is almost no agreed conversion of *meanings* to a specific choice of *garment* (see Figure 2).

A real-life experiment which confronted previously unacquainted women and compared their 'clothing intentions' with their 'clothing interpretations' of all other members of the group found that in terms of accuracy (match between what one intended to say, and what others perceived) the ability to decode was not much greater than chance, with some exception for highly coded individuals, or particularly insightful readers. But, even participants who were dressed in clichéd way were misread.

The results of my studies did not exhibit the neat regularities of fashion meanings that both theorists and journalists like to proclaim. Further, intentions and interpretations did not necessarily conform to those stereotypes that pass as clichéd interpretations. This indicates that people use fashion as a language in a different way. Within the broad parameters that define the spirit of the day, they select different visual signs and use them to convey a personal meaning, not necessarily in any kind of conventional way. And although I used relatively small samples to investigate these ideas, their value is heuristic. It functions like a counter-example to challenge a trend, much like the way mathematicians would use counter-examples to prove that something cannot be done. As Popper might have said, however, the many white swans that you encounter you cannot conclude that all swans are white, but one black swan is enough to falsify this assertion ([1935] 2002).

Figure 2: Analysis of my studies showed two dimensions (duty/pleasure and visible/invisible) that account for women's dressing considerations. Those two dimensions created four groups: Duty Invisible (Cluster 1); Duty Visible (Cluster 2); Pleasure Invisible (Cluster 3); Pleasure Visible (Cluster 4). This figure shows examples of how the respondents represented, through dressing a silhouette (A), the way that they would dress at home. This is shown in A8 and A9 in Cluster 1; A13 and A14 in Cluster 2; A4 and A12 in Cluster 3; A2 and A7 in Cluster 4. The other part of each pair (B) showed how they would modify the baseline home outfit to fit various types of situations. It highlights the importance of interpreting each woman's appearance in the context of her own visual idiom. What the women from Cluster 2, A13 or Cluster 4, A2 wear at home, for example, would be going-out clothes for other women. Thus, to regard the 'clothes themselves' as having inherent meaning would be distorting. Source: Tseëlon 1989.

From Stereotypes to Ideologies

Interestingly, out of the three levels of stories I identified at the start – the tales, popular culture discourses and theoretical frameworks – it is popular culture that reproduces most effectively the stereotyped approach with manuals, advice columns, ratings of best and worst dressers, and even news features that follow certain scripts such as stories about female politicians or first ladies' appearance, or about children expelled from school for deviations from the school uniform dress code. The media features celebrities who are admonished for spending too much money and time on fashion; it castigates others for being too thrifty to buy a new outfit for every outing; or reports on people who steal to fund their love of branded fashion luxuries. Women who lose their 'baby weight' as soon as they give birth are celebrated, as are troubled teens who overcome adversities to transform, like the ugly duckling, into a swan or into a fashion model. These are just some examples of the stock-in-trade mediated fashion narratives.

As part of my approach to *Critical Fashion*, I looked at other iconic symbols within cultural discourse, with a view to unearthing whether they were used to reproduce ideologies. I looked at Hans Christian Andersen's, *The Little Mermaid*, the stiletto heel, and school uniform among other instances. Some fashion discourse treats clothes almost as having magical properties. We find magical thinking in fairy tales, and we all know that fairy tales are a world apart. We all know that the story of Cinderella going to the ball and her shabby clothes being transformed by a fairy into sumptuous attire is not real, or that a frog does not become a prince when we kiss him, or that Santa Claus does not really bring us what we desire. We think that in moving into adulthood we have outgrown our belief in the magical transformations that many fairy tales tell us about, but actually we have not. Because when you look at the role that fashion plays in everyday life, you will find multiple examples referring to the magical transformations that clothes or appearance bring about, not unlike the king in *The Emperor's New Clothes*, with his unquestioning willingness to believe in a fabric that would have all these magical properties. This belief is played out in before-and-after make-up advertisements that present the made-up face as the key to success and happiness. It also frames many popular culture narratives, such as reality TV makeover programmes that materialize happiness and confidence in smoother skin, a new hairstyle or glamorous clothes. We know that make-up or new clothes do not buy friends and bring happiness – but we suspend that disbelief with the mantra 'when you look good you feel good'. Make-up, hairstyle and new clothes are somehow endowed with magic mood-lifting capacities.

The school uniform is another example of this type of magical thinking. My research on uniform (2006) identified the cultural discourse about the uniform to be surprisingly about magical thinking and not evidence-based reasoning. People project their anxieties onto it. They expect that by wearing it children will be prevented from feeling socially different because everybody will look the same – but of course they are not prevented. People assume that the uniform will stop children from being bullied about their appearance. No, it does not. They hope it will make the children more disciplined and it will, as would many methods of discipline, punishment and control. They believe it will make children less focused on vanity and fashion, and more on their studies, which is a bit difficult when the school itself makes such a song and dance about it, and excludes you because your bag is smaller than the dress code, your trousers are tighter than the dress code, your skirt is shorter than the dress code, your hair is more red than the dress code, or bans the charity bracelet that you wear on non-uniformed day in support of a fellow student who has cancer. Thus, instead of signalling that clothes are not important and distracting, the school uniform policy actually sends the message that clothes are important, even magical.

According to Richard Dawkins (2006), fairy tales inculcate a belief in the supernatural that opens the road to a belief in God. While people move beyond Cinderella and Peter Pan, and stop believing in Santa Claus, children still grow to believe in God, a supernatural entity that cannot be explained by science or by any theory we have about the universe. If so, then we have let them down because we have led them into a kind of magic universe that then becomes part of their taken-for-granted-way of looking at the world. In fact, as historian Yuval Harari

(2014) eloquently argues, humans alone can regard concepts that do not exist except in our imaginations or minds, such as 'mermaids', 'unicorns', 'money', 'human rights' and 'nation', as if they were real. Indeed, it is the capacity to use language to talk about imaginary constructions that turned *homo sapiens*, via the cognitive revolution 70,000 years ago, into the most successful species, allowing it to plan, communicate and flexibly respond to changing situations.

What I am arguing here is that at the current stage of development of signification we are telling the wrong story if we believe that concrete clothes have a static meaning outside of their context. Thus, much of the literature on this theme is as adept at reifying fictitious categories and equally at telling us what is really there. Woodward (2009) illustrated this point in her research, which found a romanticized notion of 'grass roots street fashion', featuring a handful of colourful dressers. This point follows the same logic of focusing on the exotic instead of the mundane, by making it seem like it is typical.

The Story of Science

I am now coming to another aspect of our storytelling capacity, this time via physics. Here, I will remind the reader about that little extract from *The Emperor's New Clothes*. Because when I say that this is a crucial metaphor in my argument, I mean it in yet one more way.

When we see the tailors in the story sewing, folding, ironing and then dressing the Emperor, we think of them as mime artists who go through the motions, but nothing is there. And when the Emperor persuades himself that he is wearing beautiful clothes, we know that there is nothing there, apart from the power of his imaginative storytelling capacity. Yet, there is an interesting twist to that story. Physics would tell us that everything we see is actually as visible as the Emperor's make-believe clothes, because the material world does not really look like we think. Every object that we see, ourselves included, does not exist as we see it. Things are made of atoms, and the nuclei are connected to each other, but they are not close together: there is actually nothing in-between them but gaps. The fact that we experience the world of objects as solid is because of the electromagnetic forces that bind nuclei together. Not only that, the reason why we do not see everything as transparent is because of the way that light hits those electromagnetic forces, creating images in our retina. This is why we see tables, cars, people and clothes. So, in fact, the whole universe of images and colours that we are so immersed in, and that is so central to our existence, is as real – visually speaking – as the clothes of the king in *The Emperor's New Clothes*. Let us remember that we are all storytellers by design, that everything we are taking about, even the things that look solid – as solid as can be in the physical world – are in fact all fiction.

Epilogue

At the start, I proposed to challenge the notion of fixed entities that are being transmitted and represent something in the form of clothes by saying there is evidence of magical thinking in the way that we attribute meaning and power to clothes. But actually, even something as supposedly well defined as a uniform, is not as simple as it looks at first glance. Much of the rhetoric of teachers and politicians in connection with school uniform (that it creates discipline, order, and focuses the mind on study, all by itself), for example, is indistinguishable from talk about the transformative power of magic clothes in fairy tales. So, the stories that fashion tells us relate to all aspects of its cultural existence: as artefact, as a concept, as a prop in the social theatre of life or in the research paradigm that organizes the way we interpret and understand reality. In that sense, all fashion is fiction.

References

Anderson, B. (1983), *Imagined Communities: Reflections on the Origin and Spread of Nationalism*, London: Verso.

Andersen, H. C. ([1837] 1949), *The Emperor's New Clothes: The Complete Andersen*, Odense: University of Southern Denmark, The Hans Christian Andersen Centre, http://www.andersen.sdu.dk/vaerk/hersholt/TheEmperorsNewClothes_e.html. Accessed 28 March 2016.

Dawkins, R. (2006), *The God Delusion*, New York: Bantam.

Goffman, E. (1955), 'On face-work: An analysis of ritual elements of social interaction', *Psychiatry: Journal for the Study of Interpersonal Processes*, 18:3, pp. 213–31. Rpt. in Goffman, E. (1967), *Interaction Ritual*, New York: Anchor Books.

——— (1959), *The Presentation of Self in Everyday Life*, New York: Anchor Books.

——— (1961), 'Role distance', *Encounters: Two Studies in the Sociology of Interaction*, Indianapolis: Bobbs-Merrill.

——— (1968), *Stigma: Notes on the Management of Spoiled Identity*, Harmondsworth: Penguin.

——— (1972), *Relations in Public: Microstudies of the Public Order*, Harmondsworth: Penguin.

——— (1983), 'The interaction order', *American Sociological Review*, 48, pp. 1–17.

Harari, Y. N. (2015), *Sapiens: A Brief History of Humankind*, New York: HarperCollins.

Jørgensen, A. M. (2010), 'Vocatives and phatic communion in Spanish teenage talk', in J. J. Normann (ed.), *Love Ya Hate Ya – The Sociolinguistic Study of Youth Language and Youth Identities*, Cambridge: Cambridge Scholars Publishing.

Lurie, A. (1981), *The Language of Clothes*, London: Heinemann.

Miller, D. and Woodward, S. (2012), *Blue Jeans: The Art of the Ordinary*, Berkeley: University of California Press.

Ovadia, R. (2013), 'Really seeing', talk delivered at Tovana: Israel's Insight Organization, Sangha House, Tel Aviv, 23 July.

Popper, K. ([1935] 2002), *The Logic of Scientific Discovery*, 2nd ed., London: Routledge.

Propp, V. ([1928] 1968), *Morphology of the Folk Tale*, 2nd ed., Austin: University of Texas Press.

Tseëlon, E. (1989), 'Communicating via clothing', D.Phil thesis, Oxford: University of Oxford.

——— (1992), 'Self-presentation through appearance: A manipulative vs. a dramaturgical approach', *Symbolic Interaction*, 15, pp. 501–14.

——— (2000), 'Ontological, epistemological and methodological clarifications in fashion research: From critique to empirical suggestions', in A. Guy, E. Green and M. Banim (eds), *Through the Wardrobe: Women's Relationships with Their Clothes*, Oxford: Berg, pp. 237–54.

—— (2006), 'Not just a historical relic: Contemporary debate on school uniform in Europe and the US', in E. Hackspiel-Mikosch and S. Haas (eds), *Civilian Uniforms as Symbolic Communication*, Stuttgart: Steiner Verlag, pp. 227–41.

—— (2010), 'Is identity a useful critical tool?', *Critical Studies in Fashion & Beauty*, 1, pp. 151–59.

—— (2012), 'How successful is communication via clothing? Thoughts and evidence for an unexamined paradigm', in A. M. Gonzalez and L. Bovone (eds), *Identities through Fashion: A Multidisciplinary Approach*, Oxford: Berg.

—— (2015), 'Jean Baudrillard: Postmodern fashion as the end of meaning', in A. Rocamora and A. Smelik (eds), *Thinking through Fashion: A Guide to Key Theorists*, London: Tauris.

Watt, G. (2013), *Dress, Law and Naked Truth: A Cultural Study of Fashion and Form*, London: Bloomsbury Academic.

Woodall, T. and Constantine, S. (2005), *What Your Clothes Say about You: How to Look Different, Act Different and Feel Different*, London: Weidenfeld & Nicolson.

Woodward, S. (2009), 'The myth of street style', *Fashion Theory*, 13:1, pp. 83–102.

Wouters, C. (2007), *Informalization: Manners and Emotions Since 1890*, London: Sage.

Chapter 8

From Tradition to Fantasy: National Costume for Puerto Rican Miss Universe Contestants

José Blanco F. and Raúl J. Vázquez-López

This chapter discusses the nature of national costumes worn by Puerto Rican Miss Universe contestants in the past two decades. As part of a global trend, costumes worn in the Parade of Nations have evolved from ensembles more commonly reflecting a national or folkloric dress to fantasy, and often 'over-the-top theatrical' costumes that loosely relate to the country's national identity or to symbols and images associated with the nation. Puerto Rican contestants have worn dresses inspired by subjects as varied as the national flower, cockfighting, boxing, sugar cane and local festivals. The notion of the country as defined by one singular national dress has been replaced by a postmodern collage of ever-changing signifiers for the concept of nation as it is branded and presented in terms of global consumption on the Miss Universe stage.

Background to the Parade of Nations Costumes

In the last two decades, the global trend for pieces worn in the Miss Universe pageant's Parade of Nations has been to present fantasy and often 'over-the-top theatrical' costumes that loosely relate to the country's national identity or to symbols and images associated with the nation. In 2013, for instance, Miss USA was dressed as a Transformer, Miss Canada as a Mountie, while Miss Sweden was dressed as a Viking with a metallic bustier and short skirt. Puerto Rican contestants have also worn fantasy pieces to the pageant inspired by imagined national themes such as the maga flower, sugar cane and boxing. In the past, however, dresses closely resembled the commonly accepted national costume of the country being represented.

The Miss Universe Pageant can be traced back to a 1952 'bathing beauty' competition organized by Catalina Swimwear in Long Beach, California. The contest is currently organized by the Miss Universe Organization, which also manages the Miss USA and Miss Teen USA pageants. The 1972 pageant was the first to be held outside of the contiguous United States. Staged in Dorado, Puerto Rico, the 1972 contest inaugurated the tradition of annual televised Miss Universe pageants held around the world. Puerto Rico, a commonwealth of the United States, also hosted the competition in 2001 and 2002. The televised shows highlight the cultural and tourism aspects of the host country.

Puerto Ricans, in general, are enthusiastic about the Miss Universe pageant and show great support for the island's delegate. Five Puerto Ricans have earned the Miss Universe title (Marisol Malaret in 1970, Deborah Carthy Deu in 1985, Dayanara Torres in 1993, Denise

Quiñones in 2001 and Zuleyka Rivera in 2006). Puerto Ricans engage in formal and informal discussions before, during and after the contest, analysing every aspect of the competition from the contestants selected to their make-up, hairstyling and wardrobe choices. Among the most discussed aspects is the choice of attire for the contestant's participation in the Parade of Nations.

The Parade of Nations' costumes are an important segment during the televised Miss Universe competition as it allows contestants to walk the stage wearing a costume that represents a salient aspect of their country. In the early years of the pageant, most of the contestants chose to wear an outfit that was either an exact example or a close variation of their official or unofficial national or 'traditional' costume. However, in the last few decades, the global trend in pieces worn for the Parade of Nations has been to present fantasy and often over-the-top theatrical costumes that only reference selected aspects of the country's national identity or the symbols and images associated with their nation.

Contested Presentation of Beauty

The Miss Universe pageant, as with other global beauty pageants, has been widely criticized in the academic and popular press for promoting a narrow and standardized view of beauty. Cohen et al. insist that 'one of the ways they [the pageants] do this is by promoting the illusion that there is, in fact, a beauty standard, that beauty can be measured objectively, and that beauty has a concrete existence apart from the individual' (1996: 7). During the Parade of Nations, however, attention shifts from the body of the woman as a signifier of beauty to that of the woman as a signifier of the nation; an embodiment of the cultural qualities assigned not just to her, but also to the country that she represents. Susan Kaiser (2012) supports this idea by suggesting that women's bodies often serve the purpose of representing the nation. Our analysis, therefore, sets aside issues related to gender construction and beauty standards in beauty pageants, to concentrate on the representation of the national as embodied by Miss Universe contestants during the Parade of Nations. Whatever is considered to constitute the 'national' in this setting is clearly subjective. This subjectivity in the representation of the national in the Miss Universe beauty pageant leads to the use of a variety of costumes for the parade that merely suggest the national and very often present a segmented and fictionalized account of the represented country. Puerto Rican contestants, for example, have often worn fantasy pieces to the pageant inspired by perceived national themes.

Tricia Langa (2011), Director of Domestic Licensing for Miss Universe, describes her favourite moment in the Parade of Nations segment: 'Nothing compares to the wings on the national costume of Denise Quiñones at the 2001 Miss Universe Pageant. It was stunning!' Cultural references are prominent in costumes worn by Puerto Rican contestants to Miss Universe as in 1993 when Dayanara Torres wore a costume inspired by cockfights with a headpiece displaying two fighting roosters. A similar theme was repeated in 2001 which was the year when Denise Quiñones was crowned Miss Universe.

The use of cultural elements in costumes is not exclusive to participants on the international stage. Carmen Graciela Díaz, cultural reporter for the Puerto Rican newspaper *El Nuevo Día*, told us that these elements also appeared in local beauty pageants. She explains:

This year, the contestants to represent Puerto Rico to Miss Universe 2014 wore a variety of costumes where the designs were inspired by local legends, the Puerto Rican flag, historic figures, popular songs as well as local flora and fauna. One of the contestants wore a dress inspired by the Arecibo Observatory. Another one wore pants as a tribute to feminist and syndicalist leader Luisa Capetillo. Others used dresses that did not reference anything related to the cultural life or any other national symbols such as the case of a contestant who wore a costume inspired by the rain and the song 'Yo me tomo el ron' (I drank the rum) by Chuíto el de Bayamón.

(Díaz 28 December 2013 interview)

These examples of recent costumes for local beauty pageants referenced in the paragraph above, and those costumes used to represent Puerto Rico in the Parade of Nations at the Miss Universe Pageant in Table 1, tell a fictionalized account of the country. The costumes highlight elements considered to be representative of aspects significant to Puerto Rico; however, the selection of a singular aspect to represent Puerto Rico as a nation can be questioned. Those invested in their country are often zealous about the items selected as national symbols. In the case of Puerto Rico – a former Spanish colony and current American colony – the defence of a national identity is crucial. To this end, the Puerto Rican government enacted Law No. 21 in 1983, defining parameters for dress representative of Puerto Rico. The law provides guidelines for materials, silhouette, construction, colour, embellishments and accessories of female dress. There are no penalties from the government or any of its institutions for not constructing a garment accurately, except that it shall not be considered representative.

The idea of having a national costume to represent the country became a common practice in the nineteenth century. Rebecca Earle suggests that 'In Europe, national dress, and "national culture" more broadly, often derived from a romanticized vision of a folk culture rooted in the land and exemplified by the peasantry' (2007: 64). According to Earle (2007), during the nineteenth century national dress also played an important role in the process of nation-formation for Latin American countries. Spanish elites in Latin America, however, were not willing to incorporate Indigenous and mixed-race groups into the process of building a new national identity. Peasants, on the other hand, were regarded as acceptable and, as Earle (2007) argues, became the basis for national dress in part due to the connection to white European traditional attire. Puerto Rico remained a Spanish colony until late into the nineteenth century. During the nineteenth century, incorporating existing Spanish traditions into national dress, while also referencing local cultures and ethnicities,

Table 1: Costumes worn by Puerto Rican contestants in the Miss Universe contest during the Parade of Nations 2000–2014.

Year	Contestant	Parade of Nations Costume
2000	Zoribel Fonalledas	Costume referencing the maga flower; the national flower
2001	Denise Quiñones	Costume referencing cockfighting; still a pastime in the island
2002	Iris Casalduc	Costume inspired by peasant dress, incorporating the national flower in the print and accessories
2003	Carla Tricoli	Costume inspired by sugarcane; once a very important crop in Puerto Rico
2004	Alba Reyes	Costume representing the Tainos (native inhabitants of Puerto Rico) that once inhabited Puerto Rico and other Caribbean islands
2005	Cynthia Olavarria	Costume based on Puerto Rico's nickname 'The Pearl of the Caribbean'
2006	Zuleyka Rivera	Costume inspired by Taino goddess Atabey, incorporating a cape with other Taino imagery
2007	Uma Blasini	Costume representing the Puerto Rican pirate Roberto Cofresí
2008	Ingrid Rivera	Costume inspired by Taino deities
2009	Mayra Matos	Costume inspired by boxing that included the Puerto Rican flag and several details in red, white, and blue
2010	Mariana Paola Vicente	Costume representing the rain forest
2011	Viviana Ortiz	Costume inspired by the Vegigantes festival in the southern town of Ponce
2012	Bodine Keller	Costume inspired by Taino culture, incorporating hieroglyphics in the cape
2013	Monica Perez	Costume inspired by coral reefs
2014	Gabriela Berrios	Costume titled 'Dancing Puerto Rico', a white ruffled dress referencing *mundillo* (white lace)

shaped national identity. Building the 'national' required a story that could be told, not only as authentic, but also as somewhat distinguishable from Spain. As in many similar cases in Latin America, the Puerto Rican national costume was a romanticized version of peasant-style costume and a creolized variation of Spanish dress. The resulting national costume, therefore, was already a product of nineteenth-century Romantic nationalism; it established a fantasy that idealized peasant life, while ignoring actual dress traditions in Puerto Rico. Through time, however, this type of traditional dress was accepted, not only as authentic, but also as unchanging. Therefore, the idea of the 'bastardized' representation of the national by way of recent fantasy costumes worn for Miss Universe would be cringe-worthy to those who in the past aimed to use national dress as a solid and unchangeable version of the nation.

Susan Kaiser (2012) argues that a dimension of national representation in dress is the nostalgic relationship to rural, peasant, ethnic, attire. Kaiser agrees with Lou Taylor (2004) who argues against the perception that rural peasant attire was static, insisting that it was constantly shifting, albeit its ultimate status as 'fixed' dress. Therefore, to represent the nation, a sample of dress usually related to peasants was 'frozen' in time and classified as authentic and autochthonous. Discussing the term 'national costume' Baizerman et al. (1993: 25) postulate:

> The emergence of the term can be correlated with political and social developments of nineteenth- and twentieth-century Europe, a time of considerable upheaval precipitated by the Industrial Revolution. The establishment of national dress signified political and/or social autonomy of a people becoming embedded in the romanticism of the period. The term reflected attempts to preserve cultural traditions and social institutions threatened by increasing modernization. Sentiment and nostalgia surrounding national dress reinforced efforts to perpetuate national identity.

The dresses representing Puerto Rico and other countries in the early years of the Parade of Nations at Miss Universe were mostly examples of these national costumes rooted in nineteenth-century romanticism and nostalgia. If the dresses, as worn by the contestants in the past, were already a fictional account of the nation and one that, arguably, represented only a segment of the country, then, are the current fantasy creations any less representative of the mostly fictionalized tale of a country during Miss Universe's Parade of Nations? Kaiser insists: 'Just as a nation is not an essence but rather a context, essentialist notions of national dress limit opportunities for interpreting ironies, ambiguities, and contradictions, as well as intersectionalities among subject positions' (2012: 54). The Puerto Rican national costume contributed to the elaboration of a national myth that ignored not only the political and economic struggles of peasants in Puerto Rico, but also the cultural contributions of other groups. As we argued above, the national dress was always an arbitrary work of fiction that did not represent the ethnic and cultural complexities of the country. The most recent fantasy creations change every year and, therefore, have the ability to highlight different elements of the mosaic that composes a nation.

Even if they merely represent one aspect of Puerto Rico for every Miss Universe contest, a composite of all of them may actually reflect more of Puerto Rico as a nation than the officially sanctioned national costume. Some aspects highlighted in the past include Taino imagery, sugar cane production, cockfighting, the tropical rainforest, boxing and the Vegigantes festival. The panorama of the country offered by these costumes also paints a picture of the controversies and contradictions that compose the 'national' in Puerto Rico, where – as most of Latin America – the nation is an amalgam of pre-Columbian, colonial and contemporary cultures tied together under the notion of nation. Nestor García Canclini (1989) proposes that Latin American cultures became hybrid cultures when their societies transitioned from traditional to modern. The resulting culture in Latin America is, therefore, an amalgam of interrelated cultures and the products created at their intersections. In a globalized postmodern world, costumes representing the national are also influenced by popular and global culture further augmenting the hybridity of the attire. A costume that assumes boxing is a significant element of Puerto Rican culture and asserts its significance by creating the ensemble in colours associated with the country does not ignore that boxing is a global sport and entertainment culture. The costume appropriates the globally consumed image of boxing to represent a direct link with Puerto Rico. The fantasy costumes as elements of postmodern culture question precisely the perception of a monolithic image to define a nation and the grand narratives that were established with romantic enthusiasm in the nineteenth century to define Latin American nations including national costumes.

Banet-Weiser (1999) supports this notion, in her book, *The Most Beautiful Girl in the World: Beauty Pageants and National Identity*, when discussing representational politics as reflected in the body of a woman chosen to represent the nation. The Miss Universe contestant becomes an embodiment and perhaps a metaphor for the nation. Banet-Weiser (1999) points out that this construction of national identity must be observed as a statement of the *gendered* nation and the feminine body as nation. In other words, every time a contestant appears in a fantasy costume in the Parade of Nations, her entire body and not just the costume she wears, becomes a symbol of the country she represents. These fantasy costumes are often seen as a vehicle, not only to represent, but also to promote the country. The beauty of the contestant's body decorated with elements of the nation is supposed to draw attention – particularly from tourists and others outside the country – into the country. Miss Universe reaches a wide global audience in its televised format. Costumes used in the Parade of Nations are carefully crafted to be not just somewhat representative of the country, but also visually appealing – they are indeed a living poster or a utopian fantasy, promoting tourism to each country. The national is paraded as a commodity on the global stage in the body of a woman, thus offering both the nation and the 'woman as nation' for entertainment and consumption on the global market. This exposure is particularly important for Puerto Rico since there are very few instances in which the island can present itself to the world as a nation separated from the United States. The Miss Universe pageant offers a context in which Puerto Rico competes independently from the United States, as is also the case of some sports events, particularly the Olympics.

The fantasy costumes used to represent different countries in Miss Universe are part of a current global trend in fashion discourse that – following a postmodern spirit – allows for the fragmentation of identity through fashion. The fragmented national identities presented by Puerto Rico and other countries during the Miss Universe pageant allow for the relativization of national symbols and expand the discussion of what is perceived as acceptable in representing nationality and the essence of a country on a global stage such as the Miss Universe event. Therefore, Puerto Rican contestants embody different components of a national identity every year. A look at the Miss Universe pageant national costumes reveals the way that participants, fashion designers and event organizers have decided to brand the country and to brand the concept of the national as expressed through dress and fashion as a communication device. This narrative created through the costumes worn by Puerto Rican contestants for the Miss Universe pageant offers possibilities to identify different ways in which the national – albeit in a fragmented form – has been expressed.

Carole McGranahan (1996: 161) argues that '[b]eauty pageants can be read as attempts to circumscribe women's worlds within that of the nation'. As a Puerto Rican contestant walks down the Miss Universe stage, then, she is charged with representing every cultural and ethnic element that composes Puerto Rico as a country. The contestant and the national dress she wears become – even for a short moment – the 'nation'. McGranahan (1996) urges us to question the ease with which female bodies are constructed as representations of the nation and insists that however we feel about beauty pageants in general we must question the discourse of gender generated when women embody the national in beauty pageants. In the case of most Puerto Rican and other Latin American contestants, the construct of the nation as woman takes a particular shape, in the sense that often Latino contestants expose more of their bodies during the Parade of Nations than participants from other regions. Most of the pieces worn take standard carnival costumes as a departure point and then build images of the nation upon the half-naked body of the contestant. This constitutes, in part, an act of 'self-tropicalization' not only of the contestant, but also of the national costume. According to Chávez-Silverman (1997) tropicalized bodies are encoded as exotic and hyper-eroticized, precisely the sort of femininity displayed at the Miss Universe pageant in the choices of national costumes for many Latin American contestants – and often for the Puerto Rican representatives.

Susan Kaiser (2012: 74) argues that:

Whereas masculinity has become equated with modern cosmopolitan citizenship (through, most notably, the modern business suit), femininity – especially in developing nations – has become emblematic of traditional cultural imagery. Although the particulars vary according to cultural context, the idea of a national costume is one that may use to represent the nation as an exotic entity and often, although not always, this entity is feminised.

Carmen Graciela Díaz (interview 28 December 2013) describes the costume worn by Viviana Ortíz representing Puerto Rico at the Miss Universe pageant in 2011, as a 'sensual vegigante' designed by Jaer Cabán, who made the embellished leotard and Kenneth Meléndez Padilla, who crafted the headpiece. The ensemble, although inspired by the Vegigantes Festival in Ponce, was more revealing than any garment ever worn at the festival. From a gender construct point of view, the costume presents the Latina body in a narrow perspective by transforming an element of Puerto Rican visual culture into a costume that emphasizes the exotic and tropicalizes the body. There seems to be an effort on the part of Puerto Rican and other Latin American contestants, costume designers and organizers to reinforce the interpretation of Latin American – particularly Caribbean countries – as exotic by representing the national through the use of revealing and exuberant fantasy pieces. The nation or 'body politic' (Parkins 2002) is then, made feminine, curvaceous, exotic, tropical, carnivalesque, and perhaps even 'savage' by the choice of fantasy costumes. Banet-Weiser (1999) posits that respectability and sexuality work symbiotically together on the body of the contestant representing the nation. Thus, we believe, a Puerto Rican contestant can freely walk the Miss Universe stage on a revealing and sexually charged fantasy costume representing the country because she carries the concept of Puerto Rico as a nation. In other words, she has been granted special permission to parade her sexuality in the name of the nation because her body is covered in symbols of the country. As Banet-Weiser says, 'The female body domesticates nationalism and national difference, constructing a vision of sexuality that is successful on the beauty pageant stage despite its uneven histories in terms of constructing feminine identity in other parts of the world' (1999: 194).

Viewed as a form of visual cultural production, the fantasy costumes worn by Puerto Rican contestants to the Miss Universe pageant can illustrate the complexity of Puerto Rico as a nation. Puerto Rico is a Caribbean island, a Latin American country, a former Taino nation, a former European colony, a commonwealth of the United States of America, a nation with a vibrant contemporary culture. How can a single national costume like that sanctioned by the government represent the entire complexity of Puerto Rico? The fantasy costumes used may be arbitrary and often present a narrow view of the country. They are also at fault for overplaying exotic, tropical and sexual elements in the body of a woman being presented for global consumption and as representative of the nation. Beauty pageants are indeed a contested field where notions of gender and the idea of the female body as an exotic representation of the country must be questioned. However, as Cohen et al. (1996: 9) argue: 'struggles over beauty contests are also struggles over the power to control and contain the meanings mapped on the bodies of competitors'. The authors believe that the problem of sending a coherent message through the wearing of a beauty contest costume is embedded in the structure of the beauty contest itself whereby meaning is always being negotiated between the contest and their mass consumption audience. Nonetheless, these fantasy costumes, particularly when viewed as a constantly changing paradigm, offer a postmodern construct of complex national identities. The selection of a costume for the Parade of Nations is not a frivolous pursuit. It is a decision made carefully in order to present an idea of the nation represented by the contestant. The ultimate goal is to guarantee support for the country's delegate and enhance her likelihood of winning, while generating curiosity about the country from a global audience. The costumes are important as an example of how the construct of the nation in postmodern societies is complex, multi-layered, all-inclusive and yet always exclusive. The 2013 costume representing Puerto Rico triggered a controversy because the contestant wore a boxing outfit that combined the Puerto Rican and gay pride rainbow flags. The outfit was in homage to Puerto Rican Olympic boxer Orlando 'Fenómeno' Cruz, who came out as being gay in 2012. Such a dialogue about the appropriateness of what represents a country could only happen if contestants and designers are free to explore different aspects of the national every year in the costumes created for the pageant. Kaiser seems to agree with the notion that national costumes at Miss Universe can be described as postmodern constructs. She writes:

The restructuring of global capital that occurred in the 1980s is one factor contributing to a major rethinking of the concept of nation. Well into the first half of the twentieth century, a nation had been imagined as a homogenous community, framed by a shared history, language, culture, and economy.

(Kaiser 2012: 60)

Conclusion

Therefore, in the past, national costume, such as the official Puerto Rican national dress, was expected to encompass the whole concept of nation. These romanticized versions of the country are often emphasized in the case of Latin America as peasant traditions that are heavily influenced by European culture. In turn, they usually ignored other ethnic groups and contemporary urban cultures in the dominant discourses of national dress (see Craik in this volume). The fantasy costumes currently used for Miss Universe do not merely subvert the notion of Puerto Rico (or any other nation) as a homogeneous and unchanging entity. Rather, they consider the 'traditional', but also incorporate elements of other cultures, ethnic groups and social classes, which ultimately were always part of the nation as favoured in the past – albeit being ignored in official or institutional representations of the country.

References

Baizerman, S., Eicher, J. B. and Cerny, C. (2015), 'Eurocentrism in the study of ethnic dress', in J. B. Eicher and S. L. Evenson (eds), *The Visible Self: Global Perspectives on Dress, Culture, and Society*, New York: Fairchild, pp. 97–106.

Banet-Weiser, S. (1999), *The Most Beautiful Girl in the World: Beauty Pageants and National Identity*, Berkeley: University of California Press.

Blanco F., J. and Vázquez-López, R. J. (2012), 'Dressing the Jíbaros: Puerto Rican peasants' clothing through time and space', in K. A. Miller-Spillman, A. Reilly and P. Hunt-Hurst (eds), *The Meanings of Dress*, 3rd ed., New York: Fairchild, pp. 379–86.

Chávez-Silverman, S. (1997), 'Tropicolada: Inside the U.S. Latino/a gender b(l)ender', in F. R. Aparicio and S. Chávez-Silverman (eds), *Tropicalizations: Transcultural Representations of Latinidad*, Hanover: Dartmouth College Press, pp. 101–18.

Cohen, C. B., Wilk, R. R. and Stoeltje, B. (1996), *Beauty Queens on the Global Stage: Gender, Contests, and Power*, New York: Routledge.

Earle, R. (2007), 'Nationalism and national dress in Spanish America', in M. Roces and L. Edwards (eds), *The Politics of Dress in Asia and the Americas*, Brighton: Sussex Academic Press, pp. 63–81.

García Canclini, N. (1989), *Culturas híbridas: Estrategias para entrar y salir de la modernidad*, Mexico City: Grijalbo.

Kaiser, S. B. (2012), *Fashion and Cultural Studies*, London: Berg.

Langa, T. (2011), 'The best of MUO's national costume competition', http://www.missuniverse.com/national-costume-competition/. Accessed 9 February 2014.

McGranahan, C. (1996), 'Miss Tibet, or Tibet misrepresented? The trope of woman-as-nation in the struggle for Tibet', in C. B. Cohen, R. R. Wilk and B. Stoeltje (eds), *Beauty Queens on the Global Stage: Gender, Contests, and Power*, New York: Routledge, pp. 161–84.

Parkins, W. (2002), 'Introduction: (Ad)dressing citizens', in W. Parkins (ed.), *Fashioning the Body Politic*, Oxford: Berg, pp. 1–17.

Taylor, L. (2004), *Establishing Dress History*, Manchester: Manchester University Press.

Chapter 9

From Iconography to Inspiration: Australian Indigenous References in Contemporary Fashion

Jennifer Craik

The incorporation of Australian Indigenous motifs in contemporary fashion in Australia is a long-standing, but increasingly contested area. Some motifs such as stylized boomerangs and kangaroos are regarded as generic symbols that, until recently, were used by anyone. However, the incorporation of symbols used in Indigenous artworks (such as paintings, screen prints and rock art) into textile or fabric design has become increasingly controversial. Issues about ownership, copyright and cultural authenticity abound. Numerous media, public, intellectual property and legal challenges have raised the awareness of the issue but not definitively resolved it. Despite the introduction of Codes of Conduct and Certificates of Authenticity, the use of Indigenous motifs as inspiration remains contentious. This chapter explores the state of Australian Indigenous fashion design including collaborations between non-Indigenous and Indigenous artists and designers.

Introduction

Indigenous inspirations in fashion have been called 'an uneasy cultural exchange' in an article in the *New York Times* (Trebay 2012). In a critique of the prevalence of 'Navajo chic' in New York's Spring 2012 collections, the appropriation of ethnic and subcultural references was received with media and electronic controversy by fashion and cultural commentators with comments such as the following: 'Fashion is culture's Godzilla, devouring everything in its path. Half the time, the monster doesn't know what it ate' (Trebay 2012). Trebay went on to question the 'cliché references' including 'squash blossom necklaces, beadwork, feathers, turquoise jewellery, Minnetonka moccasins, Pendleton-blanket jackets, clunky silver, fringed anything' (2012). Even a cursory analysis of recent collections shows that Native American Indian inspirations have featured in the work of many high-profile designers including Proenza Schouler, Anna Sui, Matthew Williamson, Etro, Levi and Isabel Marant, but particular objection was taken to the Urban Outfitters' use of the Navajo trademark and name.

In 2011, Urban Outfitters produced a collection of Navajo fashion including Navajo hipster panties and Navajo liquor flask, which created controversy within the media. The Navajo Nation filed a lawsuit against Urban Outfitters under trademark law (the 1990 Indian Arts and Crafts Act which was designed to ensure the authenticity of Indian products made by native people) (Anon. 2012; Landry 2013). Urban Outfitters removed the name Navajo from these products but counter filed on the grounds that 'Navajo' was a generic design inspiration for fashion products that consumers did not confuse with Navajo handcrafts and therefore did not violate trademark law (Lupo and Samman 2013). Although Urban Outfitters removed the label, Navajo, it did not withdraw the products or send an apology to the Navajo Nation and the lawsuit continued (Randles 2013). After failed mediation between parties, the lawsuit remained unresolved at the time of writing.

This example was a continuation of recurrent controversies concerning the use of Indigenous, ethnic or 'native' imagery, icons and motifs in decorative art and especially in textiles and fashion. However, whereas North American Indian culture had a tradition of Indigenous dress prior to European settlement, Australian Indigenous peoples 'were minimally clothed' (Blacklock 2010: 35) in conventional garments. Instead, Aboriginals wore a variety of cloaks, furs, rugs, shell necklaces, bone and wood ornaments, as well as body ornamentation, rather than clothing (Jones 2010). Early settlers and explorers were dismayed by the lack of clothing and energetically sought to dress Indigenous people in European garments (Kleinert 2010a). Over time, Indigenous Australians adopted European style clothing and some became ultra-fashionable following the fads and fashions of mainstream Australia. Only in recent times has the idea of distinctively Australian Indigenous fashion been legitimated and popularized, most notably in the use of Indigenous art prints on T-shirts, knitwear and shoes (Maynard 2000, 2001; Craik 2009). This chapter traces that journey.

What Is Australian Indigenous Fashion?

The currency of Indigenous motifs in fashion comes from the desire for the exotic, the 'other' and the primitive (Dwyer and Jackson 2003; Tranberg Hansen 2004). It has also been a constant theme in aesthetic movements that have appropriated elements of other cultures systematically especially preferring motifs (such as the hibiscus for Hawaii/Polynesia, totemic masks for Canadian first peoples or 'X-ray' kangaroos/fish/turtles for Australian Aboriginals) that are universally recognized as symbols of indigeneity. As Peter Shand has observed this is not a new trend:

> Clearly there is the sort of non-specific geography that characterizes artistic appropriation of Indigenous cultural heritage, wherein the precise meanings are evaded in search for a more generalized and imagined locale. To an extent, this place is like an imagined land, perhaps a *nave nave fenua* (fragrant land). To utilize the term [artist Paul] Gaugin coined. In this respect, there is a shift from a specific (often contested) location that one could align with a sense of the real to the realm of the designer's creative inventiveness and *savoir-faire*.
>
> (2002: 73–74)

The appropriation of the exotica of imagined cultures is sometimes taken for granted when motifs are widely recognized as belonging to a universal visual symbolic language, but on other occasions they appear to attract controversy, especially when questions are raised about whether the appropriation is a legitimate borrowing (Ayres 2013; Dwyer and Jackson 2003). In the wake of the Navajo chic collection, another controversy greeted the Fall 2012 collection by New York's label Rodarte designed by Kate and Laura Mulleavy. This collection was inspired by 'the rugged outback' of Australia even though the designers had never actually been there:

> Patterns referenced Indigenous art; handprints were inspired by ancient cave paintings. And instead of putting models in daunting and fragile stilettos, the designers had them wear chunky shoes with heels that looked like cantilevered, mechanical sculptures, and boots that were embroidered with beads in the manner of an Indian medallion.
>
> (Givhan 2012)

Although praised by fashion commentator Robin Givhan, it was criticized as 'an insensitive appropriation' and 'offensive' by Australian Aboriginal lawyer, Megan Davis, of the UNSW Indigenous Law Centre who argued that:

> It is completely insensitive to Aboriginal art and spirituality and land and how they are inextricably linked [...]. We know that these expressions, the rock art and dot paintings, are part of a religious Aboriginal system of knowledge and that there are cultural responsibilities for the protection and use of those images as well as custodial obligations.
>
> (quoted by Phelan 2012)

Rodarte replied that they had paid for the licensed images through the Aboriginal Artists Agency Limited and that 'the artists will share in the proceeds of the pieces inspired by their work' (Gosford 2012). Nevertheless, Davis insisted that the use of Aboriginal motifs raised 'complex intellectual property' issues and 'legal and policy challenges that cultural convergence and collaboration bring' (Phelan 2012).

In defence of licensing the use of Aboriginal artworks as inspiration for textile and clothing design, Anthony Wallis, of the Aboriginal Artists Agency Limited, declared that the arrangement was 'the right of individual Indigenous artists to make a living from the original work' unlike cultures that have no intellectual property protections (Gosford 2012). In short, he defended the arrangement, arguing that the licensing 'created a new income stream for Central Australian artists direct from a family company in the US' (Gosford 2012).

The case of Rodarte gave international exposure to the potential of Australian Indigenous inspirations in fashion as well as the issues associated with that practice. It effectively catapulted debate into the mainstream international arena – perhaps for the first time. So, where has the idea of Australian Indigenous fashion come from and why has this mythic construction occurred?

The Development of Aboriginal Indigenous Fashion Design

Aboriginal motifs in decorative arts have a long history but are especially documented from the 1920s when two developments occurred. During this time, the missions that ran Aboriginal communities taught sewing and revived crafts so that Aboriginals could make products for sale – especially as souvenirs for tourists (Powerhouse Museum n.d.-d). This was similar to what was happening in Native Indian communities (see Luke 1997; Landry 2013). Landry cites the research by Erika Marie Bsumek who explored the growing popularity of Navajo cultural inspirations in tourist souvenirs such as Navajo blankets and silver and turquoise jewellery. These products symbolized a romanticized idea of a 'primitive' and 'vanishing' culture and counterpoint to the belief in 'modernity and civilisation to the whites who purchased them' (Bsumek quoted by Landry 2013).

At the same time, there was a new awareness of Australian identity and associated aesthetics in which artist Frances Derham advocated 'a growing awareness among non-Aboriginal Australian artists of the aesthetic value of Aboriginal material culture' during the 1920s and 30s (Parsons 1989: 41). Margaret Preston, however, is better remembered for promoting the place of Indigenous culture in the national aesthetic when she wrote in 1925:

> In wishing to rid myself of the mannerisms of a country other than my own I have gone to the art of a people who had never seen or known anything different from themselves and were accustomed to use the same symbols to express themselves. These are the Australian aboriginals and it is only from the art of such people in any land that a national art can spring.
>
> (quoted by Kee 2006: 231)

Preston was subsequently accused of paternalism because she assumed that Aboriginals were mono-cultural, whereas there had been numerous external cultural influences long before European settlement (including Macassans, Polynesians and Chinese). However, she recognized that European Australians were belatedly acknowledging the integrity of Aboriginal culture and incorporating Indigenous motifs in design. Increasingly, professional artists, as well as school children, were 'carrying out their original designs based on Aboriginal motifs' prompted by similarities with Modernist trends in art. For example, the artwork of Frances Derham adopted the 'geometric form in aboriginal art that appealed to the modern designer' in her aesthetic philosophy (Parsons 1989: 42). In other words, the 'appropriation of Aboriginal motifs followed modernist examples, in Europe and America, of appropriation of various non-Western artistic traditions' and arguably 'played a small part in helping white Australians to perceive Aboriginal material culture aesthetically as well as ethnographically' (Parsons 1989: 42). Reflecting this trend, in 1941, Aboriginal artworks were included in an international tour of Australian art to the United States and Canada (Parsons 1989: 42). These created more interest and critical acclaim than the conventional European-style exhibits.

By the 1950s, Indigenous motifs were popularized in other forms of material culture such as ashtrays, tea towels, postcards, figurines, scarves and embroidery patterns. A common decoration in suburban gardens was an Aboriginal 'hunter' standing one leg holding a spear even though few white Australians had ever encountered an Aboriginal in person. More bizarrely, Aboriginal motifs and depictions of Aboriginal people (naked and in some de-contextualized 'outback' scene) became central elements of tourist promotion in advertising campaigns, posters, souvenirs, scarves and guidebooks.

Perhaps ironically, as Margaret Maynard has argued, the uniqueness of Aboriginal motifs proved a distinct advantage to Australian aesthetics:

> Australia is in something of a unique position here, for international European designers do not plunder our designs in the way they might, say, African motifs, although clearly Japanese designers of the 1980s have sourced their own traditions as well as being an inspiration for the West. But since the 1920s, when Margaret Preston called on Australians to appreciate Aboriginal art and design, Australian designers have taken possession of their own local motifs, and Australians both black and white have consciously turned to their own national imagery and to traditional Indigenous motifs for inspiration.

> (2001: 162–63)

The recognition of Australian Indigenous art expanded in the 1960s with schemes offering government support for Indigenous production and sale of art and artefacts using Indigenous designs as opposed to the generic symbols of Aboriginality as before. The establishment of Indigenous art centres, especially in remote communities in the 1970s, and the introduction of new techniques of art making resulted in the blossoming of new genres of Aboriginal aesthetics (such as dot painting and X-ray art as 2-D canvases). By the 1980s international art markets had recognized the potential of Aboriginal art as shrewd investments and fashionable acquisitions, in other words, desirable examples of conspicuous consumption (Myers 1991; Johnson 1996; Rothwell 2013).

One of the first international exhibitions solely of Aboriginal art was at the 1988 show 'Dreamings: The Art of Aboriginal Australia' held at the Asia Society Galleries in New York. The exhibition drew record crowds and introduced Aboriginal art to Americans. Gallery director, Andrew Pekarik, reflected that:

> The real significance of the acrylic movement is its ability to be a point of cultural communication. There hasn't been a language in terms of which these two sides [i.e. White and Aboriginal] could communicate. They are so far apart they can't but help misunderstand each other. And in these misunderstandings, the Aboriginal side has had the worst of it. These paintings are the first occasion for cross-cultural communication. For Aborigines they represent a way of dealing with the majority world. For outsiders, they represent a way of trying to hear what the other side is saying, because it is in a language that is not threatening.

> (quoted by Myers 1991: 46)

Within Australia, the recognition of Indigenous art coincided with a mixture of cultural assertion and cultural politics. Perhaps the most effective form of political statement was the T-shirt whose slogans and designs were a blackboard of identity and protest because they overtly portrayed issues of cultural appropriation, repatriation and authenticity. The T-shirt became the accessible envelope of the re-invented tradition of Australian Indigenous culture and identity (Kleinert 2010b). The T-shirt is a ubiquitous garment in the wardrobes of Australians as a cheap, functional and multi-purpose item of clothing and Aboriginal inspirations in T-shirt designs could be found in all sections of the marketplace – from the cheapest supermarkets to tourist souvenir shops, fashion boutiques and designer collections.

There was a flurry of activity during the 1980s, including collaborations. A celebrated example was the case of Jimmy Pike, an Aboriginal prisoner who met a non-Indigenous art teacher, Stephen Culley, during a sponsored art programme for inmates. Impressed by his prodigious talent, Culley (and his backer David Wroth) developed the licensing of Pike's designs for their company, Desert Designs, for use in creating textiles and furnishings that have become hugely sought after (Alstin 2010; Lowe and Fitzpatrick 2009; Wells 2011; Powerhouse Museum n.d.-a, n.d.-h; McKnight 2012). Desert Designs is a household name as a legitimate sponsor of the use of Indigenous artworks for mainstream interior design products, and Jimmy Pike has become a significant artist of national stature.

Within the world of fashion, a similar trend occurred during the 1980s. While non-Indigenous designers focused on Australian landscape, fauna and flora plus some references to the continent's 'ancient' people and 'traditional' culture, the first Indigenous fashion designers and labels emerged during this time with the aesthetic of reworking Indigenous symbolism and cultural references in a contemporary design language.

One of the best known was Bronwyn Bancroft who established Designer Aboriginals in 1985 as the first Indigenous-owned design company (Powerhouse Museum n.d.-a, n.d.-h; Maynard 2001). She experienced significant success domestically as a fashion designer showing her collections that featured exuberant screen-printed textiles incorporating Aboriginal motifs and made into spectacular garments. International recognition came with an invitation to stage a catwalk parade of her collection at the iconic department store, Printemps, in Paris, in 1987 (Maynard 2001). Bancroft still has a thriving art practice and has been collected by numerous leading galleries and museums in Australia and overseas.

A major factor in the expression of nationalist sentiment and attention to Indigenous culture was the popularity of the textile designs and fashions of non-Indigenous designers Jenny Kee, Linda Jackson and Rebecca Paterson from the late 1970s (Williamson 2010; English and Pomazan 2010; Mackay 1984; Powerhouse Museum n.d.-e; Templeton 2013; Traill-Nash 2013a, 2013b). Kee and Jackson, in particular, developed a new aesthetic of Australian identity including Aboriginal inspirations, which was promoted in their atelier-style store, Flamingo Park in Sydney's Strand Arcade. Kee became a nationally renowned figure as a Chinese Australian who had embraced Australian popular culture with verve and pushed the boundaries of national identity to new levels. Embracing

Australiana, Aboriginal culture, migrant cultures and a myriad of exotic other cultures, Kee became famous for her quirky and accessible garments and fashion products, notably her Australiana-inspired knits. As well as selling garments knitted by a specialist team of home knitters, Kee published several knitting pattern books which became bestsellers and inspired a generation to make their own Kee-derived jumpers and the like. These pattern books are now collectors' items.

Kee and Jackson were also part of an energetic and wild avant-garde artistic subculture that transformed Australian culture especially popular youth culture (Yang 2013). Although they subsequently went their separate ways, each has remained a vibrant force in articulating a new aesthetic of Australian design based on a deep level of collaboration with Indigenous artists and communities and an intensive knowledge of Australian landscape, flora, fauna, palette and environment (Yang 2013). Their incorporation of Indigenous motifs has not been confined to Australian references with both designers travelling overseas extensively and drawing on diverse motifs, as epitomized by Kee's 1982 collection 'Mali Oz' – a melange of 'Afro-Abo-Oz' prints with New Guinean masks (Kee 2006: 230–32) and her 'universal tribal' look of 1984 (Kee 2006: 234). Despite the success of these collections, Kee was acutely conscious of opposition from Aboriginal rights activists and went to great lengths to ensure that she engaged in collaborations and had the support of Indigenous and non-European figureheads to achieve the 'cross-cultural synthesis' she was striving for (Kee 2006: 233).

The excitement surrounding Australia's bicentennial celebrations in 1988 and the 2000 Sydney Olympics kept their inspirations to the forefront with Kee designing costumes for the Olympics opening ceremony. The enthusiasm for Australiana that accompanied the lead-up to the Olympics infected many design ventures. Kee and Jackson produced exquisite silk textiles inspired by the stunning colours and patterns of Queensland opals, as well as complex and refined references to Indigenous symbols and designs in a series of collaborative projects (Jackson 1987; Maynard 1999, 2000; Grey 1999; Craik 2009). These creative explosions attracted international acclaim with Kee's Black Opal silk design being used by Karl Lagerfeld as a jacket lining for his first prêt-a-porter collection for Chanel in 1983. Jackson's more nuanced and adventurous designs attracted less popular acclaim though were arguably more innovative and layered as artworks (Jackson 1987; Grey 1999).

In the populist vein, and reflecting the nationalist sentiment that pervaded 2000, fashion designer Peter Morrissey produced textiles featuring generic boomerang designs, as well as using an artwork by Indigenous artist Jacinta Numina Waugh, as the basis of another textile. While the boomerang fabric was accepted as an Australiana indulgence, the Waugh print attracted controversy even though Morrissey specially commissioned it, with the artist receiving a percentage of the sale price of each garment (Craik 2009: 433). Morrissey also used this print for commissioned costumes for the Sydney Olympics (Powerhouse Museum n.d.-e). For the mass market, Morrissey designed affordable T-shirts that mixed Indigenous, Australiana and popular Aussie symbolism in order 'to make a statement that the cultures of Australia should come together and celebrate something unique to us' (Powerhouse Museum n.d.-e).

Other successful Indigenous design companies include Jumbana, incorporating Balarinji Designs established by a non-Indigenous and Indigenous couple, Ros and John Moriarty in 1983 (AGDA n.d.). Their design style was popularized by their painting of a Qantas jet in a distinctive Balarinji design called Wunala Dreaming in 1994 (Qantas 2013). Peter Morrissey used another Balarinji design, Wirriyarra, in the fabric for his Qantas uniforms in 2003 (Qantas 2003). For a period, this confirmed the currency of Indigenous aesthetics for everyday design inspiration (Craik 2009: 430–33). In 1992, the iconic footwear company Blundstone held a painted boot competition won with an entry by an (unnamed) Aboriginal 'dot' painter. The finalists' boots toured nationally and internationally creating enormous interest overseas. This led to the annual Blundstone boot art competition in Canada which tours nationally. In 1997, the annual Alice Springs Beanie Festival was established encouraging entries from Indigenous and non-Indigenous knitted beanie (a close-fitting hat) devotees culminating in a 2006 book celebrating 10 years and a very popular travelling exhibition (Hughes and Waller 2006). The Beanie Festival has since become a much-loved annual event attracting national and international participants (and sponsorship by the Northern Territory government).

After the glow of the Sydney Olympics dulled and the new millennium garnered other preoccupations, the enthusiasm for Australiana appeared to wane. Kee and Jackson's stars faded in the 2000s only to be revived in the 2010s with new commissions and collaborations. Retrospective interest in their respective work resulted in an exhibition of Jackson's *Bush Couture* collection at the National Gallery of Victoria in 2012 (Jocic 2012) and a retrospective of Kee's work at the 2013 L'Oréal Melbourne Fashion Festival in Melbourne. Kee has also designed scarves for the National Gallery of Australia and National Gallery of Victoria. In 2013, her long-lasting contribution to Australian fashion was recognized with the award of the Australian Fashion Laureate in 2013. Reflecting her ongoing zeitgeist of the national design culture she collaborated with up-and-coming avant-garde fashion label, Romance was Born. Both Kee and Jackson still have ongoing collaborations with Indigenous communities in Australia and elsewhere.

However, in the new millennium, the revival of interest in Australian and Indigenous design inspiration has taken on a more critical tone. More sophisticated responses to the use of Indigenous symbolism have underpinned recent creative practices. In 2002, the Blaks Palace exhibition of Indigenous art and fashion during the L'Oréal Melbourne Fashion Festival challenged representations of Aboriginality. This included Christian Thomson's jumper critique of Jenny Kee's knitwear, which is discussed later. In 2008, the possum skin exhibition at Sydney's Powerhouse Museum revived interest in the wearing of possum skins by eastern Aboriginals (Blacklock 2010, n.d.). It has been followed by exhibitions of traditional and contemporary possum cloaks in a number of museums and the development of numerous workshops teaching Indigenous and non-Indigenous participants how to make possum skin cloaks.

These workshops have been led by New Zealand artists who have brought the know-how and the possum skins 'across the ditch', since possums are a pest in New Zealand, yet protected in Australia. This is an example of the re-invention of tradition, leading to the re-creation of replicas of possum skin cloaks around Australia. Some of these were on show in the *Naghlingah Boorais: Beautiful Children* exhibition, at the Bunjilaka Aboriginal Cultural Centre in Melbourne in 2013 (Museum of Melbourne 2013a, 2013b). And in 2010, London fashion label, Antipodium, collaborated with Aboriginal artists for their Ab-Fab collection.

In 2012, Indian-born Roopa Pemmaraju started collaboration between with Desert Designs, Coo-ee Aboriginal Art Gallery and Warlukurlangu Artists Aboriginal Corporation. The aim was to create a high-end resort collection produced by Indian artisans on Indian fabrics. This collaboration has been received positively by the fashion industry overall with department stores, Myer and David Jones, stocking the label. Stephen Culley from Desert Designs has said, 'In our combined 50 years in the industry, we have never seen a more grounded, inspiring project. Roopa has created a wonderful opportunity for cultural and economic collaboration across the Indian Ocean' (quoted by Safe 2012a). Adrian Newstead, the director of the label, Co-ee, has described the venture as: 'ethical, innovative and culturally sensitive. We are confident that the range will have a global impact on contemporary fashion' (quoted by Safe 2012a). Aware of the furore surrounding the Navajo Urban Outfitters collection and Rodarte outback collection, Pemmaraju saw her challenge as creating designs that were 'respectful' and ethical:

> I wasn't allowed to crop into the designs and had to find ways to show the prints in full. So the shapes are very simple, with just a few tucks here and there. There's a simplicity to the shape that allows the artworks to really stand out.
>
> (Pemmaraju quoted by Woolnough 2012)

Other recent initiatives include: the *AKIN* collection that came out of a collaboration between the Queensland University of Technology fashion incubator and North Queensland Indigenous designers (Queensland University of Technology 2012a, 2012b); the 2011 Black Heat fashion workshop in Cairns; the 2013 UflaUpla National Indigenous Textile Forum in Cairns; the Selling Yarns conferences (2006, 2009 and 2013); and the Indigenous Runway Show at the 2013 L'Oréal Melbourne Fashion Festival. The inaugural Australian Indigenous Fashion Week (AIFW) was held in 2014 to considerable critical acclaim (AIFW 2012, 2013; Baxendale 2013; Deutsch 2012; Huntington 2012; Johnson 2013). These initiatives have been welcomed as signs that 'the time is ripe for Black Fashion in Australia' (Ayres 2013).

Signposts and Frameworks

Underlying the emergence of Indigenous fashion design, however, lie questions about the appropriate use of imagery and motifs as well as their translation into fashion items for the fashion consumer more generally. As Margaret Maynard has noted:

Inspiration is different from appropriation, and copyright issues and questions of inappropriate use are also central to any discussion of the place of Indigenous design.

(Maynard 2001: 163)

To clarify what is and is not appropriate, Kleinert has distinguished between 'cultural pieces' that use traditional techniques and are regarded as museum artefacts that can be interpreted as a cultural trace or value, and 'individual and expressive objects' that push the boundaries of the medium and thus are regarded as artworks which are interpreted in terms of contemporary aesthetic values (Kleinert 2010b: 11–12). There is a fine line between these two types and fashion often blurs the boundaries. A commentator of Western Australian Indigenous fashion design argued that:

Today's fast-paced fashion industry is enriched by the depth and timelessness of Aboriginal designs. Fashion and its accessories have become more than wearable items. Aboriginal artists employ them to tell their stories of life, culture and heritage.

(Keller 2011: 29)

For others, the issue is: 'who may authorize and to what end?' (Shand 2002: 76). This also changes over time. There is a cyclical pattern of interest in the use of Indigenous inspiration. The use of Indigenous themes is a common way of contrasting the civility of European Australian culture with the Otherness and exoticism of Indigenous culture and Australia's ancient geological history and that of its Indigenous people. Perhaps because of the relatively short history of European settlement, Australians turned to the land and the past, including its people, for creative inspiration.

Maynard (2001) also suggests that because Europeans did not copy Australian design for inspiration, Australians had to look at something that was distinctive and exotic within their own culture and place. Initially, this included other inspirations that were non-European drawn from Africa, Asia, Pacific and generic 'native' motifs but as debate about defining the idea of national identity (same-ness vs difference), cycles of Aboriginal inspirations in design have coincided with intense periods of debate about national identity in Australia. The cycle proceeds from fads to mainstream references but once over-popularized (worn at barbeques and sold at airport shops) goes out of fashion. Australiana references become regarded as 'crass' and create a sense of unease and controversy. Such motifs are abandoned except in jest, and other sources of inspiration flourish. After a period of time, however, a new cycle of national angst prompts a revival of interest in, and visibility of, Indigenous iconography in creative representations of Australian identity.

Despite this cyclical pattern, over time, Aboriginality has become an integral part of the contemporary sense of Australian national identity as being different from European culture and this has been reflected in, and driven by, tourism campaigns and promotion as well as trends in global trade. As a result, the concepts of 'The Aboriginal and the Outback are, increasingly, the source of Australia's self-marketing for the international tourist industry as the "difference" they have to offer' (Myers 1991: 51). Indigeneity has become central to the 'emerging formulations of Australia's national identity' and, in this process, Aboriginal Indigenous art has given 'Aboriginal representations of place a particular value' (Myers 1991: 51).

As the success of Aboriginal art has shown, the incorporation of Indigenous inspirations in Australian cultural identity has often been triggered by an overseas/international uptake or imprimatur. Indeed, it has acted as a trigger for local interest and acceptance of Indigenous culture at a wider level. The scaled up reproduction of the painting, *Dayiwul Lirlmim* (Scales of the Barramundi) by Lena Nyadbi on the roof of Paris's Musee de Quai Branly in June 2013 – which could only be seen from the Eiffel Tower – was another example of the greater acceptance and celebration of Aboriginal Indigenous culture outside Australia rather than inside (Miller 2013). Never has a similar reproduction occurred in Australia! Indicative of the greater recognition of the significance of Australian Indigenous art internationally is the fact that the Musée du quai Branly has the largest collection of Indigenous art outside Australia.

Another contentious issue is who can do Australian Aboriginal contemporary fashion? Does a designer have to be Indigenous? Can a designer be a European Australian? Is it more acceptable for a designer to be non-European and possibly non-White Australian, for example, Indian, Chinese or Maori? The reality is that there are different models of Aboriginal Indigenous fashion design. For example, an Indigenous person may create explicitly Indigenous fashion designs based on 'dreamings' or instead create designs that incorporate subtle references to Indigenous culture or symbolism ('refined inspiration'). There are also cases of Indigenous designers creating designs and fashions that are essentially indistinguishable from mainstream fashion design. In addition, non-Indigenous designers may create designs that are explicitly inspired by Indigenous symbolism, for example, boomerangs, kangaroos, turtles, waterholes or rock art, where these symbols have a character of being generic symbols of national identity and culture. Alternatively, non-Indigenous designers might use licensed Indigenous designs or symbols, such as Peter Morrissey and Rodarte. Finally, there are examples of non-Indigenous designers (discussed below) collaborating with other Indigenous or non-Indigenous designers.

Nicolas Rothwell has argued that the very essence of what counts as Australian Indigenous art has radically changed, noting that:

> the crucial change is in the nature of the output. The revamped system tends to generate a certain kind of art. The art centres and studios of past decades bore the stamp of traditional authority. Thus only senior cultural figures were authorized to carve or paint. The present era has seen the rise and promotion of younger artists, and a quest for new looks and styles and stars. Innovation, in style, technique and form, has become critical. This is the fateful journey Aboriginal art is on, away from its origins in ceremony and law, towards visual rhetoric and decorative appeal.
>
> (Rothwell 2013: 15)

Reflecting Rothwell's pessimism, the growing popularity of Aboriginal Indigenous design, not only in art, but also in fashion and interior design generally has produced hybrid aesthetic forms and multi-faceted collaborations that dilute the Indigenous component in the assertion of multi-cultural melange of national identity.

The Pros and Cons of Collaborations

Is collaborative work between Indigenous and non-Indigenous people 'more acceptable' to both the tastemakers and gatekeepers of art as well as mainstream Australians? Collaborations seem to be less controversial and more easily 'naturalized' and thus able to be accommodated into mainstream European perspectives. The collaborations of Jenny Kee and Linda Jackson have been discussed above along with Balarinji Designs who had considerable success in the 1990s with their graphic design manipulated Indigenous artworks, fashions and homewares. According to Kleinert, collaborative artworks such as these 'contribute to social and cultural sustainability by rebuilding communities, by intervening as a witness to history and by challenging representations of Aboriginality' (Kleinert 2010b: 25).

While generally well received, collaborations have also created controversies. Kee cites opposition to her collaborative work in her autobiography despite going to considerable lengths to ensure protocols of use and friendship with Indigenous collaborators such as Tracey Moffatt, Hettie Perkins and Banduk Marika (Kee 2006: 230–33). And despite her close creative collaborations with Indigenous groups in Far North Queensland, where Linda Jackson now lives, there have been ongoing tensions. In 2002, Indigenous artist, Christian Thompson, in his 2002 Blaks Palace exhibition during the L'Oréal Melbourne Fashion Festival, referred 'directly to stereotypes of Aboriginality' through a series of knitted jumpers (Kleinert 2010b: 25).

Thompson directly targets the work of 1970s and 1980s designers Jenny Kee and Linda Jackson who produced fashions, printed fabrics and knitwear for their boutique Flamingo Park in Sydney. Using images of the kangaroo and boomerang, Thompson addresses the way in which Aboriginal art and culture is marketed as a unique symbol of Australia. However, the design of the jumper with its strange colour combinations and impossibly long sleeves is both a literal as well as metaphorical straitjacket challenges existing ideas of Aboriginality (Kleinert 2010b: 25). As Keller points out, traditional Indigenous symbolism is more commonly used to inform contemporary images of cultural identity. This was especially so in the 1980s when:

> Australian fashion designers focused more on the Australian landscape and its ancient people. Indigenous designs became *en vogue*, and Aboriginal designers made their way into the fashion industry.
>
> (Keller 2011: 27)

Debates about Indigenous Contemporary Fashion

Three main issues have emerged. Firstly, there is the issue of cultural authenticity, that is, the approved use of Indigenous artworks, symbolism and motifs through recognized systems of licensing, trademarks, codes of authenticity, makers marks and so on. While protocols have been introduced, most operate either through a bureaucratic mechanism, or are essentially informal arrangements between individuals, groups or companies. While successful to some degree, there has been considerable disquiet in the art industry about the effectiveness of such systems. With Australian law generally unable to deal with offshore infringements, there have been many cases of works being used and copied offshore. Despite a number of high-profile legal cases, there has been little by way of imposed outcomes (e.g. fines imposed on companies who go into liquidation cannot be enforced) (Johnson 1996; Powerhouse Museum n.d.-h).

Secondly, related to this issue, intellectual property (IP and copyright issues) is associated with the use of specific Aboriginal symbols and imagery. The issue of intellectual property has more recently been addressed by protocols such as licensing and certificates of authenticity; however, grey areas remain where imagery may be used appropriately or not, as noted elsewhere in this chapter. This relates to the third issue, namely the idea of imagery as cultural property, that is, that certain symbols and designs are believed to belong to a particular person, clan or nation who has exclusive authority to use that imagery. This raises subsidiary questions such as can the imagery be used in non-traditional places such as textile design (or artworks), can it be reproduced, can it be bought and worn by others who are not part of that ownership group and does it lose its symbolic meaning once used in fashion or design?

Issues of Inter-Cultural Communication

At the heart of the debate are questions revolving around inter-cultural communication issues. In an earlier discussion of Aboriginal art and its uptake in western culture, Myers (1991: 49) argued that there are three ways in which Indigenous-inspired art and fashion are rejected. First, that Indigenous artwork does not conform to dominant contemporary standards of aesthetics; second, that contemporary Indigenous art is not authentic because it is contaminated by western forms; and third, that because Indigenous artforms constitute commodities, they are not genuinely Indigenous but corrupt goods. This communication loop is imposed by observers of Indigenous art rather than by practitioners. In other words:

> Aborigines are triangulated by a series of discourses – which might represent positive benevolence, political support, sympathy, or renewed racism – discourses in which Aborigines are central but usually absent […]. Are Aboriginal actors able to make their practices have just the meanings they claim?
>
> (Myers 1991: 49)

By contrast, other commentators have argued that contemporary Indigenous art should be seen in relation to mainstream contemporary culture and conditions where such expressions are an example of 'cultural revival', the 'explosion of creativity' and evidence of the 'hybridization of [expressive] techniques' (Jennifer Isaacs cited by Myers 1991: 38–39). Isaacs argues that we should forget the quest for cultural purity and see Indigenous art not as a loss of authenticity or cultural subordination, but rather as a hybridization of the use of materials and techniques in a cultural explosion and response to policies towards Aboriginal development and self-determination (Isaacs cited by Myers 1991: 38–39). In this view, the expression of Indigenous identity is a dynamic process that responds to contemporary conditions rather than remaining 'tradition bound' (Myers 1991: 39).

If this position is accepted, then Indigenous art has the potential to be interpreted as the transformation and negotiation between cultures stemming from the dialectical relationship that connects the outside (non-Indigenous culture) with the inside (Indigenous culture). Andrew Pekarik, former Director of the Asia Society Galleries, argued that the marketing of Indigenous art to international collectors should be seen as:

> a point of cultural communication. There hasn't been a language in terms of which these two sides [i.e., white and Aboriginal] could communicate. They are so far apart that they can't help but misunderstand each other. [...] These [acrylic] paintings are the first occasion for cross-cultural communication. For Aborigines they represent a way of trying to hear what the other side is saying, because it is in a language that is not threatening.
>
> (Pekarik quoted by Myers 1991: 46)

While this is arguable for Indigenous artwork, does the same apply for examples of Indigenous-inspired fashion, that is, can and should the latter be regarded as an example of genuine inter-cultural communication?

Surface Markings versus Sculptural Forms and Shapes: From 2D to 3D Design Inspiration

The examples referred to here have primarily – even overwhelmingly – been examples of surface markings, that is, another way of depicting stories of place, belonging and identity (rather similar to the role of fleeting sand drawings in traditional Aboriginal Indigenous culture). Textiles incorporating Indigenous motifs have been the most successful and least controversial form of Australian Indigenous contemporary fashion and design especially when used in rugs, carpets, home furnishings, towels and hats (including beanies) possibly because these are prosaic everyday possessions.

However, Indigenous art centres (such as Ernabella and the Tiwi Islands) found that fabric and batik lengths were hard to sell directly and turned to more saleable items such as T-shirts, scarves and wall hangings. Even more lucrative have been the sale of printed textiles and prints to wholesalers for use in home furnishings and commissioned pieces (Tuggeranong Arts Centre 2007: 7–8). At Ernabella, mark making ('walka') has been transformed from rug making to 'painting on [kanga]roo skin moccasins, on burlap, on silk, batiked onto fabric, printed, etched, made into "dot" paintings, knotted into woollen floor rugs and most recently, applied to ceramics' (Young 2007: 26).

These examples suggest that there are significant possibilities for extending the incorporation of Indigenous inspirations into the shape and form of contemporary fashion design beyond mere surface markings in printed textiles such as silk-screened fabric. The collections of Rodarte, Pemmaraju, AKIN and Kee/Romance was Born, play with the relationship between between surface and form in their graphic designs and manipulation of shapes and silhouettes.

Conclusion

As Jenny Kee argues in her autobiography, there is a balance between the 'question of artistic licence and the dividing line between inspiration and plagiarism' (Kee 2006: 230) that still remains unresolved. There are, however, some initiatives that suggest that a more adventurous use of Indigenous inspirations is emerging in design practice and especially in fashion. For example, the L'Oréal Melbourne Fashion Festival has incorporated the Unearth Indigenous runway (SBS 2013), and Indigenous designers are now shown in the Mercedes Benz Fashion Week in Sydney. Indigenous blogger, Yatu Widders Hunt, provides regular updates on eco-style and the Indigenous fashion designers in the Australian media and online.

In examples like these, 'the past becomes a reference for the present' while offering new possibilities for expression, cross-cultural communication and collaboration (Kleinert 2010b: 26). However, as anthropologist, Eric Michaels observed: 'traditionalism and authenticity are now completely false judgments to assign to contemporary Aboriginal painting practices' (quoted by Myers 1991: 41). While Australians accept Aboriginal art as surface markings, mainstream Australia does not recognize Aboriginal ownership and entanglement with the land in the past. Thus, there is a difficulty in seeing these creative practices as more than decorative patterns. As a form of communication about the past alongside the present and future it ignores:

> the contradiction of its production [which] [...] so cheats this work of its position in the modernist tradition as well as to misappropriate it and misunderstand its context.
>
> (Eric Michaels quoted by Myers 1991: 42)

In this regard, fashion may have the potential to play a decisive role as an aesthetic and wearable bridge between cultures and points-of-view. Controversies about fashion statements and the legitimacy of Indigenous inspirations in fashion design have the potential to push the terms of debate and promote inter-cultural communication (see Blanco F. and Vázquez-López in this volume). As Kleinert has argued:

> These wide-ranging critiques of dress and its role in the broader framework of race relations unsettle the carapace of colonization. Such twenty-first century initiatives are a sign that dress continues to evolve as diverse expression of identity and difference.
>
> (Kleinert 2010a: 34)

This is the promise of future developments for Indigenous inspirations in Australian fashion. In the lead-up to the first Australian Indigenous Fashion Week, Indigenous artist and designer, Caressa Sengstock, reflected on the mentoring programme to develop collections by 30 Indigenous designers:

> Right now it's a great time – we're so many voices coming together and making a difference and pushing that message. We're not just representing fashion as a bubble, but as a culture.
>
> (quoted by Evans 2013: 29)

However, although the event held in April 2014 received critical acclaim, the organization backing the event, All The Perks (under director Krystal Perkins – from a well-known rights activist family) went into liquidation owing creditors and participants AUD$400,000 (WWD 2014). One of the creditors, Marguerite Julian of Stellar PR – commissioned to promote the event – commented that Perkins 'should be exposed for her bad business dealings' (Halliwell 2014). Due to the fallout from the collapse of the company, subsequent fashion weeks are reluctant to schedule and sponsor special Indigenous fashion events although respected Indigenous fashion labels like Desert Designs and Kooey Swimwear will show at other fashion weeks, showcases and events (WWD 2014).

This is a sad end to the tale of Indigenous fashion and, while perhaps just a roadblock along the way, it shows that successful fashion requires more than just design inspiration but also needs business expertise, gold-plated financial backing and professional management.

References

AGDA (n.d.), 'Balarinji Studio recently celebrates 20 years at the forefront of Australian design', http://archive.agda.com.au/eventsnews/national/events/2005/Balari.html. No longer accessible.

Alice Springs Beanie Festival (2013), http://www.beaniefest.org. Accessed 6 July 2013.

Alstin, C. (2010), 'You like desert country', *Russh*, http://www.russh.com/. No longer available.

Anon. (2012), 'Navajo nation sues urban outfitters for trademark infringement', *The Guardian*, 2 March, https://www.theguardian.com/world/2012/mar/01/navajo-nation-sues-urban-outfitters. Accessed 1 October 2014.

Australian Indigenous Fashion Week (2012), 'Australian Indigenous Fashion Week launches in Sydney', *Media Release*, 19 September, http://www.alltheperks.com.au/Australian%20 Indigenous%20Fashion%20Week%20Media%20Release.pdf. Accessed 6 July 2013.

―――― (2013), 'AIWF overview', AIWF Partnership prospectus, AIWF website, http://www.aifw. com.au/wp-content/uploads/2012/11/AIFW-Partnership-Prospectus.pdf. Accessed 6 July 2013.

Ayres, R. (2013), 'Black fashion', *Arts Law Centre of Australia*, June 24, http://www.aifw.com.au/ wp-content/uploads/2012/11/AIFW-Partnership-Prospectus.pdf. Accessed 6 July 2013.

Baxendale, R. (2013), 'Indigenous search unearths a fashion first', *The Australian*, 20 March, p. 3.

Blacklock, F. (2010), 'SNAPSHOT: Aboriginal skin cloaks', in M. Maynard (ed.), *Berg Encyclopedia of World Dress and Fashion, Vol. 7. Australia, New Zealand, and the Pacific Islands*, Oxford and New York: Berg, pp. 35–36.

Blacklock, F. (n.d.), 'Aboriginal skin cloaks', *National Quilt Register*, http://www. collectionsaustralia.net/nqr/fabri.php. Accessed 3 March 2014.

Craik, J. (2009), 'Is Australian fashion distinctively Australian?', *Fashion Theory*, 13:4, pp. 409–42.

Deutsch, A. (2012), 'Australia's first Indigenous Fashion Week launches, Aboriginal model Samantha Harris gives us the deets', *Fashionista*, 3 September, http://fashionista.com/2012/09/ australias-first-indeginous-fashion-week-launches-aboriginal-model-samantha-harris-gives-us-the-deets/. Accessed 6 July 2013.

Dwyer, C. and Jackson, P. (2003), 'Commodifying difference: Selling EASTern fashion', *Environment and Planning D: Society and Space*, 21, pp. 269–91.

English, B. and Pomazan, L. (eds) (2010), *Australian Fashion Unstitched. The Last 60 Years*, Cambridge: Cambridge University Press.

Evans, M. (2013), 'Into the spotlight', *The Sunday Telegraph*, 21 July, pp. 28–29.

Givhan, R. (2012), 'Rodarte channels Australia in Fall show for New York Fashion Week', *The Daily Beast.Com*, 14 February, http://www.thedailybeast.com/articles/2012/02/14/rodarte-channels-australia-in-fall-show-for-new-york-fashion-week.html. Accessed 6 July 2013.

Gosford, B. (2012), 'Art, fashion and copyright: from Papunya to US catwalks', *Crikey*, 21 March, http://www.crikey.com.au/2012/03/21/art-fashion-and-copyright-not-out-of-nowhere-but-out-of-papunya/. Accessed 6 July 2013.

Grey, S. (1999), 'Celebrating hybridity', *Art & Australia*, 37:1, pp. 96–101.

Halliwell, E. (2014), 'Australian Indigenous Fashion Week in doubt after company goes bust', *The Daily Telegraph*, 22 November, http://www.dailytelegraph.com.au/entertainment/sydney-confidential/australian-indigenous-fashion-week-in-doubt-after-company-goes-bust/story-fni0cvc9-1227131302230. Accessed 6 July 2013.

Hughes, M. and Waller, L. (2006), *Colours of the Country: Celebrating Ten Years of the Beanie Festival*, Alice Springs: Alice Springs Beanie Festival.

Huntington, P. (2012), 'Australian Indigenous Fashion Week to launch in September', *WWD. com*, 2 July, http://www.wwd.com/fashion-news/fashion-scoops/new-fashion-week-6037360. Accessed 6 July 2013.

Jackson, L. (1987), *Linda Jackson: The Art of Fashion*, Sydney: Fontana.

Jocic, L. (2012), *Linda Jackson: Bush Couture*, Melbourne: NGV.

Johnson, B. (2013), 'World first for Indigenous fashion', *The South Sydney Herald*, 2 April, http://www.southsydneyherald.com.au/world-first-for-Indigenous-fashion/#.UbkmnOcjy4Q. Accessed 6 July 2013.

Johnson, V. (1996), *Copyrites: Aboriginal Art in the Age of Reproductive Technologies*, Sydney: National Indigenous Arts Advocacy Association.

Jones, P. (2010), 'Aboriginal dress in Australia: Evidence and resources', in M. Maynard (ed.), *Berg Encyclopedia of World Dress and Fashion, Vol. 7. Australia, New Zealand, and the Pacific Islands*, Oxford and New York: Berg, pp. 17–26.

Kee, J. (2006), *A Big Life: Jenny Kee*, Camberwell, Victoria: Lantern.

Keller, C. (2011), 'From practicality to spirituality: WA Indigenous fashion design', *Art Monthly*, 242, August, pp. 27–30.

Kleinert, S. (2010a), 'Aboriginal dress in Southeast Australia', in M. Maynard (ed.), *Berg Encyclopedia of World Dress and Fashion, Vol. 7. Australia, New Zealand, and the Pacific Islands*, Oxford and New York: Berg, pp. 27–34.

—— (2010b), 'Clothing the postcolonial body: Art, artefacts and action in south eastern Australia', *Craft + Design Enquiry*, 2, pp. 1–34, http://www.craftaustralia.org.au/cde/index.php/cde/article/view/16. Accessed 6 July 2013.

Landry, Alysa (2013), 'Deadline looms for settlement in urban outfitters case', *Navajo Times*, 30 May, http://www.navajotimes.com/news/2013/0513/053013urb.php#.VPesntetSiw. Accessed 6 July 2013.

Lowe, P. and Fitzpatrick, K. (2009), *Desert Psychedelic: Jimmy Pike*, Catalogue, Gallery Artisan, 8 April–30 May, Brisbane, http://www.vision6.com.au/download/files/15118/1055035/artisan_Jimmy%20Pike_Catalogue_lores.pdf. Accessed 6 July 2013.

Luke, T. (1997), 'Inventing the Southwest: The Fred Harvey Company and Native American art', http://www.cddc.vt.edu/tim/tims/Tim464.PDF. Accessed 6 July 2013.

Lupo, A. and Samman, L. (2013), 'Court denies urban outfitters' motion to dismiss Navajo Nation's trademark suit', 15 April, http://www.arentfox.com/newsroom/alerts/court-denies-urban-outfitters-motion-dismiss-navajo-nations-trademark-suit#.VPesR9etSiw. Accessed 6 July 2013.

Mackay, E. (1984), *The Great Aussie Fashion*, Sydney: Elina Mackay and the Australian Fashion Office.

Maynard, M. (1999), 'The Red Centre: The quest for "authenticity" in Australian dress', *Fashion Theory*, 3:2, pp. 175–96.

—— (2000), 'Grassroots style: Re-evaluating Australian fashion and Aboriginal art in the 1970s and 1980s', *Journal of Design History*, 13:2, pp. 137–50.

—— (2001), *Out of Line: Australian Women and Style*, Sydney: UNSW Press.

McKnight, L. (2012), 'Interview: Desert designs', *Pages Digital*, 30 October, http://www.pagesdigital.com/interview-desert-designs/. Accessed 6 July 2013.

Miller, N. (2013), 'Dreamtime art celebrated on rooftops of Paris', *The Age*, 5 June, http://www.theage.com.au/world/dreamtime-art-celebrated-on-rooftops-of-paris-20130607-2ntpf.html. Accessed 6 July 2013.

Museum of Melbourne (2013a), *Beautiful Children Wrapped in Culture*, 26 June, http://museumvictoria.com.au/about/media-centre/media-releases/beautiful-children-wrapped-in-culture/. Accessed 6 July 2013.

———— (2013b), *Naghlingah Boorais: Beautiful Children*, exhibition, http://museumvictoria. com.au/bunjilaka/whatson/current-exhibitions/naghlingah-boorais-beautiful-children/. Accessed 6 July 2013.

Myers, F. (1991), 'Representing culture: The production of discourse(s) for Aboriginal acrylic paintings', *Cultural Anthropology*, 6:1, pp. 26–62.

Parsons, J. (1989), 'Aboriginal motifs in design: Frances Derham and the Arts and Crafts Society of Victoria', *The La Trobe Journal*, 43, autumn, pp. 41–42, http://www.slv.vic.gov.au/ latrobejournal/issue/latrobe-43/t1-g-t17.html#n42. Accessed 6 July 2013.

Phelan, H. (2012), 'UN calls Rodarte's Fall 2012 Aboriginal-inspired prints "offensive" – but are they really?', *Fashionista*, 15 March, http://fashionista.com/2012/03/un-expert-calls-rodartes-fall-2012-aboriginal-inspired-prints-offensive/. Accessed 6 July 2013.

Powerhouse Museum (n.d.-a), 'Contemporary Aboriginal and Torres Strait Islander textiles', HSC Syllabus Outcomes, NSW Department of Education and Training and Powerhouse Museum, http://www.powerhousemuseum.com/hsc/paperbark/contemporary. htm. Accessed 6 July 2013.

———— (n.d.-b), 'Fabric decoration techniques used in Aboriginal and Torres Strait Islander textiles', HSC Syllabus Outcomes, NSW Department of Education and Training and Powerhouse Museum, http://www.powerhousemuseum.com/hsc/paperbark/fabric_ decoration.htm. Accessed 6 July 2013.

———— (n.d.-c), 'Glossary', HSC Syllabus Outcomes, NSW Department of Education and Training and Powerhouse Museum, http://www.powerhousemuseum.com/hsc/paperbark/ glossary.htm. Accessed 6 July 2013.

———— (n.d.-d), 'History of Aboriginal and Torres Strait Islander textiles', HSC Syllabus Outcomes, NSW Department of Education and Training and Powerhouse Museum, http:// www.powerhousemuseum.com/hsc/paperbark/history.htm. Accessed 6 July 2013.

———— (n.d.-e), 'Influence of Aboriginal and Torres Strait Islander textiles on non-Indigenous designers', HSC Syllabus Outcomes, NSW Department of Education and Training and Powerhouse Museum, http://www.powerhousemuseum.com/hsc/paperbark/influence.htm. Accessed 6 July 2013.

———— (n.d.-f), 'Lenore Dembski: Paperbark Woman', HSC Syllabus Outcomes, NSW Department of Education and Training and Powerhouse Museum, http://www.powerhousemuseum.com/ hsc/paperbark/lenore.htm. Accessed 6 July 2013.

———— (n.d.-g), 'Paperbark Woman: Aboriginal and Torres Strait Islander fashion design', HSC Syllabus Outcomes, NSW Department of Education and Training and Powerhouse Museum, http://www.powerhousemuseum.com/hsc/paperbark/.

———— (n.d.-h), 'Symbols, motifs and ownership: Marketing and copyright issues', HSC Syllabus Outcomes, NSW Department of Education and Training and Powerhouse Museum, http:// www.powerhousemuseum.com/hsc/paperbark/symbols.htm. Accessed 6 July 2013.

———— (n.d.-i), 'Take it further', HSC Syllabus Outcomes, NSW Department of Education and Training and Powerhouse Museum, http://www.powerhousemuseum.com/hsc/paperbark/ further.htm. Accessed 6 July 2013.

Qantas (2003), 'Qantas unveils new uniforms designed by Peter Morrissey', Qantas Archives, http://www.qantas.com.au/travel/airlines/media-releases/jun-2003/2929/global/en. Accessed 6 July 2013.

—— (2013), 'Flying art', Qantas Airways, http://www.qantas.com.au/travel/airlines/aircraft-designs/global/en. Accessed 6 July 2013.

Queensland University of Technology Creative Enterprise Australia (2012a), 'AKIN Collection launch', 13 March, http://2012.creativeenterprise.com.au/2013/03/13/akin-collection-launch-2/. Accessed 6 July 2013.

Queensland University of Technology Marketing (2012b), 'Indigenous artists take on high fashion', *Media Release*, 4 October, http://www.news.qut.edu.au/cgi-bin/WebObjects/News.woa/wa/goNewsPage?newsEventID=51935. Accessed 6 July 2013.

Randles, J. (2013), 'Urban outfitters unable to resolve Navajo trademark suit', 5 August, http://www.law360.com/articles/462454/urban-outfitters-unable-to-resolve-navajo-trademark-suit. Accessed 6 July 2013.

Rothwell, N. (2013), 'Fragile picture of future', *The Australian*, 9 August, p. 15, http://www.theaustralian.com.au/arts/fragile-picture-of-future/story-e6frg8n6-1226693768389. Accessed 6 July 2013.

Safe, G. (2012a), 'Cultural collaboration', *Daily Life*, 17 September, http://www.dailylife.com.au/dl-fashion/fashion-week/cultural-collaboration-20120430-1xu6m.html. Accessed 6 July 2013.

—— (2012b), 'Indigenous flair with feeling', *The Sydney Morning Herald*, 28 April, http://www.smh.com.au/lifestyle/fashion/Indigenous-flair-with-feeling-20120914-25w1a.html. Accessed 6 July 2013.

SBS (2013), 'Indigenous designers wow Melbourne Fashion Week', *SBS World News Australia*, 25 March, http://www.sbs.com.au/news/article/1750170/Indigenous-designers-wow-Melbourne-Fashion-Festiva. Accessed 6 July 2013.

Shand, P. (2002), 'Scenes from the colonial catwalk: Cultural appropriation, intellectual property rights, and fashion', *Cultural Analysis*, 3, pp. 47–88.

Templeton, S. (2013), 'Jenny Kee', *webwombat*, http://www.webwombat.com.au/lifestyle/fashion_beauty/jennykee.htm. Accessed 6 July 2013.

Traill-Nash, G. (2013a), 'At 66, fashion designer Jenny Kee's time has come again', *The Weekend Australian Magazine*, 15 June, http://www.theaustralian.com.au/news/features/at-66-fashion-designer-jenny-kees-time-has-come-again/story-e6frg8h6-1226663795988. Accessed 6 July 2013.

—— (2013b), 'Jenny gonged for taking Aussie design to the world', *The Australian*, 20 June, p.3, http://www.theaustralian.com.au/executive-living/fashion/jenny-kee-gonged-for-taking-aussie-design-to-the-world/story-e6frg8k6-1226666531907. Accessed 6 July 2013.

Tranberg Hansen, K. (2004), 'The world in dress: Anthropological perspectives on clothing, fashion and culture', *Annual Review of Anthropology*, 33, pp. 369–92.

Trebay, G. (2012), 'An uneasy cultural exchange', *The New York Times*, 14 March, http://www.nytimes.com/2012/03/15/fashion/an-uneasy-exchange-between-fashion-and-navajo-culture.html?pagewanted=all&_r=0. Accessed 6 July 2013.

Tuggeranong Arts Centre (2007), *Miri Kutjara Tjungu (Skin to Skin)*, souvenir catalogue, Canberra: Tuggeranong Arts Centre.

Wells, K. (2011), 'Jimmy Pike and desert designs in Ningbo', *Craft Australia*, 18 March, http://www.craftaustralia.org.au/library/review.php?id=jimmy_pike_desert_designs. Accessed 6 July 2013.

Williamson, L. (2010), 'Interlaced: Textiles for fashion', in B. English and L. Pomazan (eds), *Australian Fashion Unstitched. The Last 60 Years*, Cambridge: Cambridge University Press, pp. 103–25.

Woolnough, D. (2012), 'Roopa Pemmaraju's Continental drift', *The Australian*, 8 September, http://www.theaustralian.com.au/executive-living/fashion/roopa-pemmarajus-continental-drift/story-e6frg8k6-1226465908137. Accessed 6 July 2013.

WWD (2014), 'Australian Indigenous Fashion Week in liquidation', *WWD.com*, 28 November, http://wwd.com/fashion-news/fashion-scoops/australian-indigenous-fashion-week-in-liquidation-8049333/print-preview/. Accessed 6 July 2013.

Yang, W. (2013), 'William Yang: My generation', Australian Broadcasting Corporation, Sydney, http://www.abc.net.au/iview/#/program/39999. Accessed 6 July 2013.

Young, D. (2007), 'Being in the picture', in Tuggeranong Arts Centre *Miri Kutjara Tjungu* (*Skin to Skin*), souvenir catalogue, Canberra: Tuggeranong Arts Centre, pp. 26–27.

Chapter 10

In Your Face: Masculine Style Stories and the Fashionable Beard

Maria Mackinney-Valentin and Trine Brun Petersen

Over the past decade, the full beard has been described as major style phenomenon to the extent of being 'the definitive visual shorthand for the early twenty-first century' (Saner 2013). The beard has seen a massive fashion revival in Europe and North America particularly in urban settings. This chapter considers the trend to have taken off in 2005 within a mainly Western context (Montandon 2006), and are still considered to be dominant in 2014 at the time of the study, despite speculation that the trend is declining (Sykes 2013; Saner 2013; Mchangama 2014). The concern here is with the personal and local practices of the full beard as a global style trend. The focus is on young Danish men, a group in which the beard has seen an intense revival (Solgaard 2013). The cultural context of this group is interesting because Denmark is considered to be a highly developed country in terms of gender equality, while the beard is also an archetypical male gender flag. The aim is to chart themes of masculinity and status representation as performed through the display and management of the full beard in contemporary society through in-depth focus group interviews.

This chapter considers the particular conditions of the beard as 'both clothes and body, both intimate and highly visible' (Hollander 1994: 183). Hair as simultaneously a natural extension of the body and a craftable sign has historically served to mark as well as blur boundaries between nature and culture, man and woman, human and animal (Rosenthal 2004). The fact that human hair is able to grow continuously, has made hair a species marker and contributed to the potential of hair for endless stylistic innovation (Cheang and Biddle-Perry 2008). Hair is a site for signalling shifts in the 'understandings of social status and identity across time and across cultures' (Cheang and Biddle-Perry 2008: 244), which in turn has created culture of hair management as part of social and cultural identity performance similar to other forms of body adornment such as tattooing and dress (Wilson 1985). Hair is malleable which makes it ideal for self-expression including the construction and performance of gender.

Dene October explores the cultural regulation of men's facial hair in the twentieth century with attention to the negotiation of modern masculinity as seen through mainly popular advertising (2008). The beard is considered to have conveyed maturity, wisdom, social status and military power until the middle of the nineteenth century when the beard became a fashionable display in line with attire. This stylistic shift brought with it an industry in etiquette manuals and products for managing facial hair (October 2008: 68).

In contemporary Western culture, the beard, just as any other type of hair, offers a highly prominent site for negotiating shifting norms and values concerning masculinity and social status. As articulated by one informant in the focus groups: 'For me, beards are like hairstyles'

(Gustav, 25). The beard is not only subject to shifting cultural, religious, social and political meanings (Shirazi 2008; Pancer and Meindl 1978). It is also a fashion accessory (Sykes 2013) of a highly gender-specific and personal kind. Just as any other type of fashionable display from garments to attitudes, the beard is subject to fashion's affinity for change. It is within the fashion logic of shifting social and cultural taste that the beard is studied. This approach to the beard is reflected in the focus group finding whereby the beard is referred to as 'a fashion accessory' and 'homegrown make-up'.

While the full beard as a fashion statement does represent a materiality, it is not subject to product distribution in the way that fashion garments are. Once a beard is shaved off, its social and cultural role cannot be transferred to other wearers in the way that a discarded item of clothing can. In this sense, the beard is not for sale because it is a physiological part of the owner, which implies that it has a particular, highly individual distinctive potential when considered within the framework of fashion. The focal point in this study of the contemporary fashionable beard is located in the charting of masculine style stories and in analysing how they might be seen to redefine fashion, status and exclusivity in the context of male presentation of self. In this study, the beard is seen to redefine these aspects mainly on two levels, namely bearding potential or biological capital as well as the celebration of

Figure 1: 'The guys who want to talk about my beard and touch it are the ones who can't grow one themselves. It's like this beard ideal we are seeing these days' (Gustav, 25). Photograph by Frank Cerri.

laziness or fashion lethargy as a contemporary means of individual differentiation outside the business aspects of the fashion system.

The Beard as Gender Flag

Desmond Morris suggests that the primary function of the male beard was originally as a natural 'scarf' to protect and warm the lower face and neck. In modern times, it is most identifiable as a gender marker. As one focus group informant in this study stated, a beard says: 'Hello, I am masculine' (Max, 21). Charles Darwin suggested that the beard from an evolutionary perspective was advanced via female choice as a highly attractive masculine adornment (Dixson and Vasey 2012: 1). A considerable portion of the research on perceptions of the beard is concerned with women's reactions to the bearded man. In 1969, Freedman reported that female students rated a bearded male face as more masculine, mature, independent and sophisticated than a non-bearded face. This approach is echoed in other studies concluding that women find bearded men more virile (Roll and Verinis 1971; Dixson and Brooks 2013). The tendency to consider the bearded man more potent is also seen within a historical context, for instance, in the Renaissance when the beard was seen as a 'marker of procreative potential' (Fisher 2001: 174). This is also reflected in studies of the beard in more recent times suggesting that bearded men are rated more socially mature, strong, sincere, masculine, self-confident, sophisticated and courageous than clean-shaven faces (Roll and Verinis 1971; Kenny and Fletcher 1973; Pellegrini 1973; Pancer and Meindl 1978; Neave and Shields 2008; Dixson and Vasey 2012). Related studies are concerned with women's sexual selection preferences in relation to men's facial hair. In their study of Wyoming college students, Feinman and Gill (1977) found that female students rated male facial hair lower in their sexual selection than previous studies also with female students (Freedman 1969; Kenny and Fletcher 1973). While these discrepancies may be caused by methodological differences or demographic variations, the change in preferences in regard to facial hair may also reflect stylistic shifts confirming the beard's role as a fashion accessory. While previous focus has been on the perception of the beard in terms of, for instance, sexual attraction from the opposite sex, the present study is focused on the fashionable beard as a tool for engaging in the process of social distinction mainly among men themselves.

Historically, the beard has held shifting cultural, religious, social and political meanings (Shirazi 2008; Pancer and Meindl 1978). Specific events or actions could contribute to determining whether the male population at a given time was clean-shaven or bearded. This could be influenced by an individual's action, such as a king choosing to grow a beard to hide an ugly scar, or a political leader not able to grow a beard, which would create the standard for that period. Legislation has also been a factor. In Elizabethan times, a tax was imposed on bearded men restricting beards to the upper social classes making them into a 'financial status-display' (Morris 1985: 113). While the beard has traditionally been considered as 'signs of divinity, class, and distinction' (Peterkin 2001: 17), there was an increase in the variations in appearance and meaning of the beard from the middle of the nineteenth century onwards (October 2008: 68). Despite the radical social and cultural changes, certain themes from the literature on beards are reflected in the present study such as visual camouflage of age or flaws and social distinction, for instance, albeit with more focus on beard growth potential than class distinction.

While all men are not equally genetically disposed to grow a full beard, there are also ethnic variations regarding the phenomenon on a global scale. The full beard is considered to be a Western symbol of masculinity, strength and social order in what is described as 'facial-haired hegemony' because many Asian men are not genetically able to grow a full beard (Deleon 2013). An interesting observation from the literature is that distinctions are made between clean-shaven, stubble and full beards, yet no distinctions are made between various types of beards such as the managed beard versus the wild beard (Roll and Verinis 1971; Reed and Blunk 1990). This forms a striking contrast to data elicited from the focus groups conducted in this current research study. As one informant states, 'It's a man thing. But it also depends on how you *do* the beard' (Max, 21). Distinguishing between various types of beards as well as the finer details of aesthetic management of facial hair in the focus groups became central in the negotiation of the concepts of masculinity and status as displayed through appearance.

Figure 2: 'I grew my first beard this past summer. It was a bet to who could grow the best looking beard. I lost badly' (Martin, 22). Photograph by Frank Cerri.

Another observation is the prominence of research performed in the 1970s when full beards were seen as an essential part of the hippie look, but there is hardly any research performed in the 1980s when the clean yuppie look was prominent. The volume of research on beards tends to reflect the contemporary style preferences towards facial hair. The link between the 1970s and the current time frame, 2005–14, may be seen in the textual representation on a larger scale when considering the 1970s revival of, for instance, knitting (Melik 2013) or micro- or home-brewing (Brignall 2009) and more specifically in relation to the revival of the beard (Saner 2013; Solgaard 2013; Cowles 2013; Gander 2014). These craft activities align with the larger hipster lifestyle trend of which the beard has become a prominent bodily symbol.

The Return of the Fashionable Beard

The beard has been widely associated with the hipster phenomenon linked with the New York City neighbourhood Williamsburg in the borough of Brooklyn (Alford 2013) and London neighbourhood Shoreditch (Godwin 2015). A hipster is used here in its general meaning as an urban style tribe often characterized by sporting a 'beard, plaid flannel shirt, vintage work boots' (Godwin 2015). In the early twenty-first century, the term has caused a media stir and a range of books publications (Lanham 2003; Bot 2012). The hipster term is considered ambivalent because there is general disagreement about how to define it (Rayner 2010) and even the individuals who appear to be hipsters generally do not identify with the term (Ferrier 2014). This rejection of the term is not rooted in a lack of dedication to the lifestyle, but rather it reflects an elusive strategy to avoid 'wannabe' emulation of this style culture as will become clear in the further analysis of the data from the focus group studies.

The beard has also seen a revival within the fashion system. Some examples from runway shows are Yohji Yamamoto (S/S 2011), The Maison Martin Margiela (A/W 2011), Jean-Paul Gaultier (S/S 2011), Paul Smith (A/W 2012), Missoni (S/S 2014) and Etro (A/W 2014). Examples from high-end fashion campaigns are Lanvin (A/W 2012), Vivienne Westwood (A/W 2012), Gucci (A/W 2013) and Hermes (A/W 2013). The beards represented in these runway shows and fashion campaigns range from the shorter, neatly trimmed beard to the wilder, rugged beard. High fashion and street style always mutually influence each other. So when luxury fashion validates the beard it means that the style becomes more acceptable not only to the mainstream, but also to the political and cultural elite. Beards have become gradually more widespread within mainly a Western context moving beyond trendsetters and celebrities to include prominent members of the White House administration, Wall Street titans, and golden boys in professional sports (Alden 2013; Kæmsgaard 2010; Williams 2014). The beard phenomenon is still, however, considered to be mainly an urban phenomenon reflected in the term 'urban beardsmen' (Boncompagni 2013).

This trend can also be seen in the increased demand for transplants of chest hair to the face in, for instance, the United States and Denmark (Gander 2014; Hansen 2014). Some media have reported on the business consequences of the trend, for instance, in regard to a dip in men's razor sales in North America (O'Neil 2013). When comparing articles in UK- and US-based national newspapers on the social and cultural aspects of the increased popularity of beards among mainly young men since 2005, the findings are generally equal to the Danish newspaper articles in the same period. Much of the media coverage of the beard revival is described as a reaction to women's growing economic power, and a way of reasserting men's masculinity (Eshun 2012; Solgaard 2013; Karkov 2014). While taste preferences in fashion and appearance are in part negotiated through social mechanisms (Simmel 1971; Bourdieu 1989), they are also subject to global influences such as fashion mediation and popular culture whose impact reach beyond national or cultural boundaries. So, while the Anglo-American sources serve to document the beard trend on a Euro-American scale, the Danish material both confirms the local manifestation of the global trend while also highlighting particulars of the Danish beard phenomenon such as references to the Nordic Viking heritage and themes of gender equality in contemporary Danish society in relation to, for instance, paternity leave.

Case Study: Bearded Style Stories

This chapter is a study of bearded style stories understood both as globally available visual narratives and as locally negotiated aesthetic choices. The study is informed by discourse analysis (Foucault 1997) as an analytical approach and uses focus groups as a methodology to determine what underlies this trend within a given population. As an analytical approach, discourse analysis is characterized by seeing discourses as constitutive of reality (Foucault 1997) and by an interest in how regimes of knowledge and values are established. A special interest is taken in how social identities are constructed within the discourse (Jørgensen and Phillips 2002). Discourse analysis as a theory and method has been explored by fashion scholars such as Viveka Berggren Torell (2007) and Joanne Entwistle (1997) as being useful in highlighting the social dimensions of sartorial and aesthetic regimes.

Semi-structured, in-depth focus-group interviews conducted in early 2014 by the authors form the core of the empirical material. As a methodology for data collection, focus groups are especially relevant for producing knowledge of the interpretations, interactions and norms of social groups (Halkier 2010). In contrast to individual interviews, the collective interview of the focus group produces data in which the negotiations of norms and social values are the primary source of knowledge of the phenomenon in question. As such the outcome of the interview was not only the verbalized expressions of the participants, but in equal degree their interaction and bodily gestures of the participants. To include these kinetic aspects, the focus groups were recorded on video and the analysis was conducted focusing both on verbal expressions and bodily gestures in order to understand how the practice of growing, grooming and displaying a beard is discursively constructed and negotiated by the informants as well as bringing attention to the question of the significance of male beauty regimes.

The informants were all bearded men, but the character of their beards varied greatly in terms of length, girth and aesthetic management. All lived in the greater Copenhagen area and the age range was from 21 to 70 years old. The sixteen informants were all associated with The Royal Danish Academy of Fine Arts, School of Design in Copenhagen either as students, teachers, studio employees, administrators or researchers. All informants were Danish except two, one Swedish exchange student and one teacher born in Poland but living in Denmark since 1971. The age range of the younger group consisted of 21–27-year olds, and they were all students but located in different academic departments. The middle group of six informants ranged from the ages 31 to 46 and had different professional roles including administrative, technical, teaching and research. The older group ranged in age from 61 to 70 and all five informants were part of the same academic faculty.

The relatively narrow focus of informant selection was chosen to create suitable conditions for the discussion of norms and values ascribed to different beard practices to unfold as freely as possible, thereby allowing the complexities and subtleties to emerge in discussion. Because of the common interest in the subject and the practice of design, these informants were considered to share a common awareness of style and therefore also a sensibility towards visual expressions that would potentially provide strong data when exploring an aesthetic phenomenon such as the beard. The fact that the informants shared the same institution either for work or study provided a sense of familiarity among the informants. This created a relaxed atmosphere that could potentially enhance the level of intimacy in the personal sharing adding depth and intensity to the data. The choice of students and faculty from different departments as well as different occupations for the older groups was made to assure sufficient diversity in the groups to generate discussion. The groups were divided according to age due to the assumption that the participants' relationship to their 'bearded selves', as well as their personal ascribing of meaning to different beards would vary considerably with age.

During the focus group sessions, one researcher acted as moderator and the other as observer of interactions and group dynamics. The focus groups were planned as a combination of open questions in order to gain access to the groups understanding of the beard as a fashionable practice as well as more specific questions posed in order to explore theory-led issues distilled from the literature review. The progression of the focus groups was planned to facilitate as much interaction among the participants as possible. Afterwards, the interviews were transcribed in their full length. In accordance with the choice of discourse analyses as an analytical framework, special interest was devoted to how knowledge about beards as a current style phenomenon was constructed and negotiated among the participants as well as to the construction of specific subject positions through various ways of wearing, grooming and presenting the beard.

Does Size Matter? The Beard and Masculinity

In line with previous research, the informants associated the beard with notions of authority and maturity. For the majority of the informants, the process of growing their first full beard was seen as a rite of passage into manhood and a way of looking older. As described by one informant: '[I]f I shave it all off, I look really young. They'll say I look like a boy' (Gustav, 25). Several of them remember having grown a beard as a preparation for an important event in their lives for which they wanted to enhance their perceived age such as applying for an important job. While the older informants viewed their beard as an integral part of their identity, there was a tendency for younger informants to see their beard as a changeable accessory. There was a sense that they were still 'growing into their beard'. As one informant explained:

> I am sometimes still surprised when I look in the mirror. Is that how I look? It's not the mental image I have of myself. I guess I haven't had the beard long enough.
>
> (Loui, 27)

While the beard provides age camouflage, it was clearly also seen as flaunting a growth potential – or even *biological capital* – as a social status marker when considered within a fashion context. Exploring identity through the beard was particularly marked in the younger focus group aged 21–27. Consequently, this group forms the key focal point of the chapter while data from the older groups provides context and perspective.

Especially for the two younger groups, the seemingly wild, rugged and untamed beards were seen as the ideal. They tied this ideal to the prevalence of the lumberjack as a fashion ideal also referred to in popular culture as 'lumbersexual' (Baxter 2014). Gustav described the bearded lumberjack look as 'arch-manliness' associating it with 'manual labour' and 'smelling like a man':

> The lumberjack might not be rich but he is rigged – everything is big on him. He is a handyman. He can build a house. It's like the Nordic Viking – he is so incredibly manly.
>
> (Gustav, 25)

In this particular context, masculinity is established as connected to physical strength and ruggedness. Manliness is also established as a pre-modern ideal of the arch-typical provider and protector. As a biological constant within a social and cultural dynamic of change, the beard, at least in a Western context, is an interesting site for studying the negotiation of norms and standards for what might be considered masculine within a given social and historical context – what fashion historian Christopher Breward terms the 'social and sexual construction of "manliness"' (Breward 2001: 166). Previous research on beards and masculinity show that female students rated a bearded male face as more masculine, mature, strong, independent and sophisticated than a non-bearded face (Freedman 1969; Roll and

Verinis 1971). Kenny and Fletcher (1973) found students to rate a bearded face as more masculine, strong, and sincere. As a contribution to the body of research on beards, the present study is concerned with the male perception of self rather than female's perception of the beard as part of sexual selection.

Most of the participants in the present study linked bearding to the construction of a masculine identity and for all the focus groups the exploration and enhancement of masculinity was a key aspect of their decision to grow and maintain a beard. One informant directly states that his beard makes him feel more like a man, while most informants agreed that a beard is 'a man thing' done by men and for men. This view was further supported by the choice of words used to describe a desirable full beard, which was associated with potency, authority and above all size. The fuller beards in the focus groups were described as 'masculine', 'manly', 'huge', 'great texture', 'savage', 'solid', 'very thick', 'powerful' and 'wild'. The weaker beards were described as 'delicate' or more directly: 'Well, there isn't much of a beard' (Max, 21) while those with a weaker growth say how they 'hope it will get thicker' (Martin, 22). However, social context appears to be a theme in the personal perception of the beard. Martin, 22, had one of the weaker beards in the group but had the self-perception of having a strong beard because he was the only one of his friends who could grow one: 'So with them, I am the guy with the beard'.

The equation between bearding and masculinity was emphasized not only verbally but also through body language as the informants with larger beards handled them both when speaking and listening. It appeared that they were manually sculpting the beards to maintain the desired shape. When considering the themes of authority and 'manliness', these gestures also serve to bring social attention to the symbol of their power tool: the beard. This body language appears to support the sense of 'beard envy' (Kurutz 2012) associated with the equation of size and masculinity: 'My friend Michael has this great beard – it's thick like a mat. You can't even run your fingers through it. And it's huge. He is just so manly' (Gustav, 25).[1] These almost phallic associations were mainly addressed indirectly through potent descriptions of other men's beards while also linking back historically to the idea of the beard as a marker of procreative potential (Fisher 2001).

Over the course of the focus group interview, there was a development from an understanding of social equality among the group towards a more distinct sense of differentiation according to the nature and management of the beard. These strictly local negotiations of what should be considered an attractive beard both in terms of shape, colour, styling and growth potential were highlighted through the focus groups of which the younger informants were particularly opinionated.

In the two younger focus groups, there appeared to develop a social hierarchy through describing one's own beard and the beards of the others in the group. Statements such as: 'The one's of us who are lucky enough to grow a beard' (Thomas, 44) may be read as an assertion of high beard rank in the group. As one of the younger informants said: 'I know I can't grow a long beard so I sometimes think: So they can do something I can't' (Martin, 22). This beard hierarchy was echoed in some of the comments in the group: 'The worst is those boys who can't really grow a beard but try to anyway' (Max, 21). This emphasis on the girth

Figure 3: 'It needs to have great texture. Some guys have this fluffy beard when it gets longer. They shouldn't grow it that long' (Max, 21). Photograph by Frank Cerri.

of a beard as power is prominent in the youngest group: 'From man to man, you rise in an unarticulated hierarchy with a good beard' (Loui, 27).

This sense of a beard-pecking order indicates that men with beards are not communicating to other women as suggested by previous studies for instance in relation to mate preferences, attractiveness, masculinity and parenting abilities (Dixson and Brooks 2013; Feinman and Gill 1977). In contrast, the present study shows that men are signalling not only their strong masculinity but also their fashionability through their beard to other men. As one informant stated: 'I think men are communicating to men – not women' (Max, 21). This mirrors the assumption that women dress for other women as much as for men (Woodward 2007: 94; Clarke and Miller 2002).

The emphasis on grooming in the focus groups further supports that bearding is primarily directed between men rather than intended as signals to women concerning, for instance, sexual selection. There was a surprising urge among the informants to share grooming style stories that included trimming methods, suitable beard lines, desirable shapes and prescribed lengths. The informants even shared intimate grooming practices: 'I wash my beard, because I have beard dandruff' (Max, 21).

The beard was also associated with societal and political aspects in the focus groups that reflected gender norms and social values in contemporary Danish society. These were

Figure 4: 'A beard gives a certain authority' (Jacob, 37). Photograph by Frank Cerri.

particularly concerned with the relation between the return of the beard at a time with high social and economic equality between the sexes in Denmark. One example is how all fathers in Denmark have two weeks paid paternity leave from when the baby is born, and in addition 37 per cent of fathers share part of the remaining six to twelve months leave with the mother (Olsen 2015). As one informant argues:

> The gender roles are being redefined as the woman are moving into domains that have traditionally been dominated by men – but also the other way around. So, maybe there is a need to show that there is still a difference between a man and a woman and that is where the beard comes into the picture.
>
> (Thomas, 44)

This sentiment is also reflected in contemporary Danish media coverage of the beard trend. Here, the beard is described as men's domain and being symptomatic of the changes and negotiations concerning the male role in Danish society (Poulsen 2011; Ostrynski 2012). The association between the full beard and an archetypical masculinity is, however, questioned by the older informants, because the beard was a symbol of the so-called 'soft man' in the 1970s. In the same vein, the informants debated the degree to which a beard is an unambiguous gender marker: 'When I look at Jacob with his low-cut T-shirt and good-looking chest hair, his style feels very current but it is also masculine in sort of a feminine way' (Thomas, 44). This indicates that the beard should not automatically be considered an emblem of masculinity, but rather as part of constant play with different ways of performing gender (Butler 2006), which is especially marked in the group of younger informants. So while the beard is a gender flag displaying masculinity from a biological perspective, the individual performance of facial hair may infuse this male symbol with feminine aspects through the grooming and overall sartorial assemblage.

Though some of the informants saw the beard trend as a reaction to increased gender quality, they expressed no resentment or wish to change this political situation. Instead, there was a tendency to challenge this social order by symbolic means only – such as growing big and conspicuous beards in order to emphasize their masculinity. An example of this was the informants that were fathers all had taken at least three months paternity leave. In this sense, the beard may be seen to represent an ideal of traditional perceptions of masculinity, yet this notion of masculine identity is played with by the informants rather than established as an essential given.

Style Stories and Negotiations

The empirical material in this study draws attention to the significance of the beard as a part of overall sartorial assemblage strategies and negotiation of appearances in which the beard serves as a marker of status. The beard offers a means to play with traditional emblems of power, wisdom and authority and allows the participants to negotiate and meticulously tune their public appearance in a play between traditional elements of femininity and masculinity as well as elements of high and low maintenance regimes (see Tseëlon in this volume).

The attention to the social process of differentiation and equalization (Simmel 1971) was particularly marked among the younger members of the focus group informants. The younger group expressed a distinct awareness of how the beard was part of the aesthetic regulation involved in negotiating social identity. There was agreement among the young and middle aged groups that a beard can show status and demonstrate membership of a group or a 'club': 'Beards show status, definitely. I will get these super-straight guys coming over and gushing over my beard, feeling it' (Gustav, 25). Gustav described these 'beard friends' as generally having a weaker beard than his linking back to the theme of male beard envy. The negotiations of social status were closely linked to the theme of masculinity, where the perception of a strong masculinity was associated with high social status because it related to themes of potency, power and authority.

While there were differences in opinion often based on the varying beard growing capabilities, there was a tendency for one or two informants to take central stage as alpha-males of the group defining what was the 'right' aesthetic management of the beard. This was seen in comments such as 'goatees are the worst' or 'I think we all agree'. Normative expressions such as these were typical among the younger group members and point to the way in which the beard can be viewed as a battlefield between legitimate and non-legitimate aesthetic choices. The dynamic appeared to be rooted in the force of social equalization led by those in the group claiming individual differentiation. This friendly power struggle is integral to the negotiation of social status in fashion (Simmel 1971).

The beard is about combining growth potential and grooming, but it also works in a larger game of assemblage and self-presentation (Goffman 1959). For Max, this sense of assemblage is expressed as a desire for a particular, individual balance. He has a mental checklist he uses when leaving the house to make sure the balance is right:

> The pants I am wearing today are sort of weird so I paired them with a more ordinary shirt. My beard is a masculine check – so I am sure I always look like a man. Because I do wear skirts sometimes.
>
> (Max, 21)

This sense of the beard being part of an overall sartorial assemblage strikes a chord with the informants possessing the strongest beards: 'I find that if I have shaved my beard off, some

Figure 5: 'I can't be bothered to shave' (Loui, 27). Photograph by Frank Cerri.

of my clothes don't work anymore' (Gustav, 25). The balance is essentially a potential that allows for the individual to play with the codes available to create a particular version of masculinity: 'I like the combination of the beard as this arch-typical symbol of the stone-age man and the suit which is the symbol of the modern man' (Loui, 27). In this sense, the beard becomes less a manifestation of masculinity in the face, so to speak, of the 'feminization of society', a narrative presented in the press (Poulsen 2012), and more a negotiation of social identity through a masculine gender marker. In this sense, gender is not a normative category to either conform with or reject. Nor do the informants seem to be engaging in unisex fashion or 'cross-gender emulation' (Davis 1992: 33), which has been prominent in fashion of the period since 2005 (La Ferla 2009). In other words, the beard appears to function less as a hairy mask that disguises the wearer, and more like a prop in a 'pleasurable' masquerade (Tseëlon 2003: 2) that aims to play with and recontextualize masculinity.

Lazy Chic

Distinct for all groups was the meaning and value of having a beard but also the ability in itself to grow one. This formed a sense of *bearding potential* or *even biological capital*: 'It is also about what we have to work with' (Flemming, 46). The suggestion here is that the growth potential as such represents an opportunity for distinction because it cannot be bought. This involves renegotiating the concept of exclusivity, which is no longer understood as that which is economically out of reach. In the case of the beard, exclusivity might be seen as that which is biologically unattainable or socially unacceptable such as looking 'wild' or 'savage' as described in positive terms by the informants. As Max, 21, said: 'Money isn't a sex symbol, not in my circles anyway'.

This negotiation of status through both bearding potential and aesthetic management was characterized by a celebration of casualness among the young informants. Here laziness was displayed as part of a social positioning through what could be termed *lazy chic*. The majority of the informants in all groups mentioned laziness as part of the reason for growing a beard: 'I am pretty lazy', 'I don't really do anything to my beard. For me that's the point', 'I just let it go', 'I have tried to shave it, but it's just too much trouble', 'I was tired of shaving'. While this is undoubtedly the case, this display of laziness forms a contrast to the surprising eagerness among all the informants to talk about grooming. Here, the idea of the *right* balance as seen in the sartorial assemblage is also seen in the attitude to handling the beard. Lazy chic involves a locally defined standard of effort versus reckless abandon. While laziness in the sense of lack of grooming was celebrated, the informants also associated the untamed beard with a 'slovenly impression', 'being dirty' and not caring about your appearance. The informants engaged in social negotiations to define the ideal level of laziness suggesting a display of staged casualness, what one informant referred to as 'accidental chic' (Max, 21). The common emphasis among the focus group participants was that the beard and general sartorial assemblages should not be 'too perfect', 'too forced', 'too deliberate' or 'too obvious'. As one informant stated: 'He tries too hard. His beard is just too sculpted' (Gustav, 25). The foregrounding of laziness works as a smoke screen that serves to stall the inevitable process of style emulation. The consequences for not striking the right balance between effort and abandon points to the importance of taste-knowledge regimes and how this affects social status: 'You don't want to be a stereotype' (Loui, 27). Loui is quite explicit in this negotiation of casualness when he initially stated: 'My beard is just there. I haven't done anything to it' but later modified his statement when explaining that he waxed his moustache so he did not 'look like an idiot'. The impression is not that the informant is inconsistent in his statements, but rather than he is socially in tune with the ongoing adjustments in the group of what the fashionable level of laziness is within this particular context. As one of the older informants summed it up:

> There is some kind of contradiction with a beard. I think a lot of people think that when you have a beard, it's like you don't care and you just let it grow and be free. But it takes quite a lot of work to have a beard so really there is a lot of vanity involved.
>
> (Thomas, 44)

This display of casualness may be seen as symptomatic of new strategies in contemporary social status representation. Since the rise of fast fashion, blogging and e-retail, the adoption process in fashion has become more complicated in the reduction of the time lag historically created through seasonal cycles and conspicuous consumption. The increased pace of fashion production has spurred new means for social differentiation that are more subtle or ambiguous. The growth of a fashionable beard cannot be accelerated or forced, but relies on biological ability alone. What makes the beard fashionable is the aesthetic management, which is by definition subtle because only the trained eye and suitable social context can determine what is the *right* beard for the right context. This forms a contrast to fashion where brand value and social status historically were easier to identify and therefore also more open to emulation. These new social strategies are by their very nature more difficult to adopt both in terms of growth and management. A beard is organic material and is therefore constantly evolving as opposed to fixed garments. In addition, the video recordings of the focus groups showed a continuous manual handling of the beard. In addition to possible phallic associations mentioned earlier this auto-corporal interaction with the beard served to contribute to this constant adjustment of what constitutes the *right* beard. This mode of displaying may be viewed as a radical departure from fashion as conspicuous consumption towards a strategy of sartorial 'undercoding' (Briggs 2005). Undercoding is seen here as a subtle means of demonstrating status. This was seen in the ambiguity of lazy chic where the right balance in grooming was continuously negotiated and demanded a key understanding of the social codes in their reading. In this sense, undercoding provides a means of apparently escaping representation, while still engaging actively in social identity play through subtle aesthetic regulation. Undercoding is effective beyond bearding in ubiquitous phenomena such as wearing All Stars sneakers or Levi's jeans, where the very mass appeal holds a paradoxical potential for social individualization (Mackinney-Valentin 2014).

Concluding Remarks

The beard invariably joins physical ability with public identity by affecting the complex mechanisms of the cultural productions of masculinity (October 2008: 67). The study showed a gap between media discourses and the informants' discursive construction of their own bearded identities. Only when asked directly, the informants discussed the return of the beard in wider political or macro-economic contexts. For instance, when presented with images of various bearded men, including a prominent spokesman from the Muslim community in Denmark, the focus was on the grooming and style alone. When being presented with the identity of the man in the image, the response was: 'I hadn't even thought that it could have any religious meaning' (Gustav, 25).

For the individual informants the media style stories did not figure prominently in their understanding of their own beards. Instead other male family members, especially the beards of father figures and friends, played an important role. This highlighted the close connection of the beard to the informants' personal life stories and perceptions according to the different phases of their life. To a wider extent, it also suggests that fashion codes are locally based and negotiated, rather than disseminated through a fashion system dominated by global media (Woodward 2007: 86; Clarke and Miller 2002).

Themes of age, masculinity and status figured strongly in the focus group findings, demonstrating how the beard can be employed as a means of identity exploration and gender performance. The beard was considered a symbol of masculinity, maturity and authority by most of the informants, but the younger group notably used the beard as a fashion accessory to play with notions of masculinity.

The exact look and styling of the beard was given prime importance by the informants. The younger informants demonstrated highly sophisticated codes to determine whether a beard was considered to be in style or not. It is therefore clear from the research material that the ability to navigate in the locally defined taste-knowledge regimes by 'making the most of what you've got' forms an important way of displaying social status. In a fashion context, beards cannot be referred to as an overall phenomenon but must be considered with a sensibility towards the beard as a style phenomenon in its own right as well as within its social and historical context.

In the particular context of this study, recognition and status are obtained by donning a relaxed, seemingly uncaring attitude towards one's own appearance of which the untamed full beards seem to be the most important accessory. In this sense, 'lazy chic' may be considered a fashion strategy typical of the younger informants in which trying too hard is the ultimate fashion faux pas. The importance assigned to such minutiae of appearance management through carefully balanced assemblage strategies, as well as the quality, shape and styling of the beards point to the beard as part of highly sophisticated distinction game in which 'undercoding' is a prevalent strategy in the complex play between being fashionable, while seemingly negating any attempt to be so.

References

Alden, W. (2013), 'At Davos: Goldman's chief bears a new look', *The New York Times*, 25 January, http://dealbook.nytimes.com/2013/01/25/at-davos-goldmans-chief-sports-a-new-look/?_php=true&_type=blogs&_r=0. Accessed 7 July 2014.

Alford, H. (2013), 'How I became a hipster', *The New York Times*, 1 May, http://www.nytimes.com/2013/05/02/fashion/williamsburg.html?_r=0. Accessed 8 August 2015.

Baxter, H. (2014), 'Out of the woods: Here he comes: The lumbersexual', *The Guardian*, 14 November, http://www.theguardian.com/commentisfree/2014/nov/14/lumbersexual-beard-plaid-male-fashion. Accessed 8 August 2015.

Boncompagni, T. (2013), 'The taming the beard', *The New York Times*, 30 January, http://www.nytimes.com/2013/01/31/fashion/taming-of-the-beard.html?_r=0. Accessed 8 August 2015.

Bot, S. (2012), *The Hipster Effect: How the Rising Tide of Individuality Is Changing Everything We Know about Life, Work and the Pursuit of Happiness*, New York: Sophy Bot.

Bourdieu, P. (1989), *Distinction: A Social Critique of the Judgement of Taste*, London: Routledge.

Breward, C. (2001), 'Manliness, modernity and the shaping of male clothing', in J. Entwistle and E. Wilson (eds), *Body Dressing*, Oxford: Berg, pp. 165–81.

Briggs, A. (2005), 'Response', in C. Breward and C. Evans (eds), *Fashion and Modernity*, Oxford: Berg, pp. 79–81.

Brignall, M. (2009), 'Home-brew return cheers money savers', *The Guardian*, 6 November, http://www.theguardian.com/money/2009/nov/06/home-brew-return-money-saver. Accessed 7 July 2014.

Butler, J. (2006), *Gender Trouble: Feminism and the Subversion of Identity*, New York: Routledge.

Cheang, S. and Biddle-Perry, G. (2008), 'Hair and human identity', *Hair: Styling, Culture, and Fashion*, Oxford: Berg, pp. 243–54.

Clarke, A. and Miller, D. (2002), 'Fashion and anxiety', *Fashion Theory*, 6:2, pp. 191–214.

Cowles, C. (2013), 'The Sartorialist's Scott Schuman talks beard trends and men's style', *New York Magazine*, 29 October, http://nymag.com/thecut/2013/10/sartorialist-scott-schuman-its-hard-to-find-stylish-guys.html. Accessed 7 July 2014.

Davis, F. (1992), *Fashion Culture and Identity*, Chicago: The University of Chicago Press.

Deleon, J. (2013), 'Why Asians dread movember', *GQ Magazine*, 11 November, http://www.gq.com/style/blogs/the-gq-eye/2013/11/why-asians-dread-movember.html. Accessed 7 July 2014.

Dixson, B. J. and Brooks, R. C. (2013), 'The role of facial hair in women's perceptions of men's attractiveness, health, masculinity and parenting abilities', *Evolution and Human Behavior*, 34:3, pp. 236–41.

Dixson, B. J. and Vasey, P. L. (2012), 'Beards augment perceptions of men's age, social status, and aggressiveness, but not attractiveness', *Behavioral Ecology*, Oxford: Oxford University Press, pp. 1–10.

Entwistle, J. (1997), '"Power dressing" and the construction of the career woman', in M. Nava (ed.), *Buy This Book: Studies in Advertising and Consumption,* London: Routledge, pp. 311–23.

Eshun, E. (2012), 'Welcome to Beardlandia', *Esquire*, September, http://ekoweshun.com. Accessed 7 July 2014.

Feinman, S. and Gill, G. W. (1977), 'Females' response to males' beardedness', *Perceptual and Motor Skills*, 44, pp. 533–34.

Ferrier, M. (2014), 'The end of the hipster: How flat caps and beards stopped being so cool', *The Guardian*, 21 June, http://www.theguardian.com/fashion/2014/jun/22/end-of-the-hipster-flat-caps-and-beards. Accessed 7 August 2015.

Fisher, W. (2001), 'The Renaissance beard: Masculinity', *Early Modern England Renaissance Quarterly*, 54:1, pp. 155–87.

Foucault, M. (1997), *The Archaeology of Knowledge*, London: Routledge.

Freedman, D. G. (1969), 'Survival value of beard – There's status in it and sexual magnetism', *Psychology Today*, 3:5, pp. 36–39.

Gander, K. (2014), 'Hipster beard trend sees rise in $7,000 hair transplants', *The Independent*, 27 February, http://www.independent.co.uk/news/world/americas/hipster-beard-trend-sees-rise-in-7000-hair-transplants-9157858.html. Accessed 7 July 2014.

Godwin, R. (2015), 'Death of the hipster: Why London decided to move on from beards, beanies and fixie bikes', *London Evening Standard*, 16 April, http://www.standard.co.uk/lifestyle/death-of-the-hipster-why-london-decided-to-move-on-from-beards-beanies-and-fixie-bikes-10178615.html. Accessed 7 August 2015.

Goffman, E. (1959), *The Presentation of Self in Everyday Life*, New York: Anchor Books.

Halkier, B. (2010), 'Focus groups as social enactments: Integrating interaction and content in the analysis of focus group data', *Qualitative Research*, 10:1, pp. 71–89.

Hansen, C. (2014), 'Unge danske hipsters betaler 45.000 kroner for et fuldskæg', *Metroxpress*, 26 February, http://www.mx.dk/nyheder/danmark/story/26507506. Accessed 7 July 2014.

Hollander, A. (1994), *Sex and Suits*, New York: Knopf.

Jørgensen M. and Phillips L. (eds) (2002), *Discourse Analysis: As Theory and Method*, Thousand Oaks: Sage Publications Ltd.

Kæmsgaard, K. K. (2010), 'Skæggerier', *Berlingske Tidende*, 5 December, p. 32.

Karkov, R. (2014), 'Skæg for sig', *Jyllands-Posten*, 20 April, http://m.jyllands-posten.dk/premium/indblik/Indland/ECE6654187/skaeg-for-sig. Accessed 7 July 2014.

Kenny, C. and Fletcher, D. (1973), 'Effects of beardedness on person perception', *Perceptual and Motor Skills*, 37:2, pp. 413–14.

Kurutz, S. (2012), 'Oh, to be just another bearded face', *The New York Times*, 30 May, http://www.nytimes.com/2012/05/31/fashion/oh-to-be-just-another-bearded-face.html?pagewanted=print. Accessed 7 July 2014.

La Ferla, R. (2009), 'It's all a blur to them', *The New York Times*, 19 November, http://www.nytimes.com/2009/11/19/fashion/19ANDROGYNY.html?pagewanted=all&_r=0. Accessed 7 July 2014.

Lanham, R. (2003), *The Hipster Handbook*, New York: Three Rivers Press.

Mackinney-Valentin, M. (2014), 'Mass-individualism and the paradox of sartorial sameness', *Clothing Cultures*, 1:2, pp. 127–42.

Mchangama, M. (2014), 'Færdig med fuldskæg', Kforum, 1 April, http://www.kommunikationsforum.dk/artikler/skaeg-og-medloebermode. Accessed 7 July 2014.

Melik, J. (2013), 'Granny skills help revival of wool industry', BBC World Service, 15 February, http://www.bbc.com/news/business-21441298. Accessed 7 July 2014.

Montandon, M. (2006), 'The beard: Hip, but hot', *The New York Times*, 16 July, http://www.nytimes.com/2006/07/16/nyregion/thecity/16bear.html?_r=1&. Accessed 7 July 2014.

Morris, D. (1985), *Bodywatching – A Field Guide to the Human Species*, London: Jonathan Cape Ltd.

Neave, N. and Shields, K. (2008), 'The effect of facial hair manipulation on female perceptions of attractiveness, masculinity, and dominance in male faces', *Personality and Individual Differences*, 45, pp. 373–77.

October, D. (2008), 'The big shave: Modernity and fashions in men's facial Hair', *Hair: Styling, Culture, and Fashion*, Oxford: Berg, pp. 67–78.

Olsen, T. L. (2015), 'Nye tal: Fædre holder ikke mere barsel', Danmarks Radio, 26 March, https://www.dr.dk/nyheder/politik/nye-tal-faedre-holder-ikke-mere-barsel. Accessed 7 July 2015.

O'Neil, L. (2013), 'Hipster beards blamed for poor razor sales', CBC News, 6 August, http://www.cbc.ca/newsblogs/yourcommunity/2013/08/hipster-beards-blamed-for-poor-razor-sales.html. Accessed 7 July 2014.

Ostrynski, N. (2012), 'Rigtige mænd kan gro et godt skæg', *Berlingske Tidende*, 28 September, http://www.b.dk/kultur/rigtige-maend-kan-gro-et-godt-skaeg. Accessed 7 July 2014.

Pancer, M. and Meindl, J. (1978), 'Length of hair and beardedness as determinants of personality impressions', *Perceptual and Motor Skills*, 46:3, pp. 1328–30.

Pellegrini, R. (1973), 'Impressions of the male personality as a function of beardedness', *Psychology*, 10:1, pp. 29–33.

Peterkin, A. (2001), *One Thousand Beards*, Vancouver: Arsenal Pulp Press.

Poulsen, A. K. (2011), 'Skæg er ikke for sjov', *Børsen*, 23 September, http://pleasure.borsen.dk/portraet/artikel/1/215689/skaeg_er_ikke_for_sjov.html. Accessed 7 July 2014.

Poulsen, H. D. (2012), 'Den femininiserede heteromand', *Berlingske Tidende*, 15 July, http://www.b.dk/kronikker/den-feminiserede-heteromand. Accessed 7 July 2014.

Rayner, A. (2010), 'Why do people hate hipsters?', *The Guardian*, 14 October, http://www.theguardian.com/lifeandstyle/2010/oct/14/hate-hipsters-blogs. Accessed 7 July 2014.

Reed, A. and Blunk, E. M. (1990), 'The influence of facial hair on impression formation', *Social Behavior & Personality: An International Journal*, 18:1, pp. 169–75.

Roll, S. and Verinis, J. (1971), 'Stereotypes of scalp and facial hair as measured by the semantic differential', *Psychological Reports*, 28:3, pp. 975–80.

Rosenthal, A. (2004), 'Raising hair', *Eighteenth-Century Studies*, 38:1, pp. 1–6.

Saner, E. (2013), 'Have we reached peak beard?', *The Guardian*, 24 July, http://www.theguardian.com/fashion/2013/jul/24/have-we-reached-peak-beard/print. Accessed 7 July 2014.

Shirazi, F. (2008), 'Men's facial hair in Islam: A matter of interpretation', in G. Biddle-Perry and S. Cheang (eds), *Hair: Styling, Culture and Fashion*, Oxford: Berg, pp. 111–22.

Simmel, G. (1971), *On Individuality and Social Forms*, Chicago: University of Chicago Press.

Solgaard, M. (2013), *Børsen*, 30 August, pp. 12–13.

Sykes, T. (2013), 'Beard backlash: The clippers are out', *Telegraph*, 18 October, http://www.telegraph.co.uk/men/fashion-and-style/10388072/Beard-backlash-the-clippers-are-out.html. Accessed 7 July 2014.

Torell, V. B. (2007), *Folkhemmets barnkläder: Diskurser om det klädda barnet under 1920–1950-talen*, Göteborg: Etnologiska Föreningen i Västsverige.

Tseëlon, E. (2003), 'Introduction', in E. Tseëlon (ed.), *Masquerade and Identities: Essays on Gender, Sexuality and Marginality*, London: Routledge.

Williams, A. (2014), 'The Brooklyn beard goes mainstream', *The New York Times*, 8 January, http://www.nytimes.com/2014/01/09/fashion/the-brooklyn-beard-goes-mainstream.html?_r=3. Accessed 7 July 2014.

Wilson, E. (1985), *Adorned in Dreams: Fashion and Modernity*, London: Virago.

Woodward, S. (2007), *Why Women Wear What They Wear*, Oxford: Berg.

Note

1 Name and age of informant. Corresponds with mode of reference for other informants.

Chapter 11

Becoming Animal, Becoming Free: Re-Reading the Animalistic in Fashion Imagery

Louise Wallenberg

Introduction

The setting in this fashion shot is apparently the African Savannah, showing a golden brown terrain with no green vegetation slightly out of focus. The photograph is taken from the side, showing – in full clarity – a black model in full figure running next to a cheetah, apparently running as fast as the animal. The model, with a determined and concentrated look in her face, is clad in a skimpy yet tight cheetah bodice, showing most of her muscular legs, arms and buttock.

This fashion photograph is taken at what seems to be a Zoo set in Africa, and it is shot slightly from above so as to include a small part of what is probably a larger, but restricted, area. At the centre of the photograph, a black model covered in a zebra patterned coat and wearing a zebra printed hat on her head, with bare feet and probably naked underneath, is skipping with two monkeys. Her facial expression is one of complete happiness and joy: as she jumps, she smiles broadly, with her head thrown back. In frame, to the right, a white, male animal keeper is squatting, and keeping a supervising eye on the three playmates.

The above descriptions regard two photographs by Jean-Paul Goude that are part of a longer fashion spread entitled 'Wild things' published in *Harper's Bazaar* US in the September issue of 2009, where the under-title of this spread reads, 'Supermodel Naomi Campbell journeys to Africa in safari-inspired stunners'. While both photographs clearly and unabashedly allude to and perpetuates old sexist, misogynist and racist notions of black women as animalistic and as threatening (while positioning men, white men, in a dominant, voyeuristic and controlling position), they also offer an invitation to see these images as expressions of a certain freedom. In the first photograph, we are invited to admire (and possibly desire) the model's strength, fastness, beauty and amazing *animality*; and in the second photograph, we are invited to share the model's complete joy and happiness as she engages and plays with animals. Running with the leopard, using the body and its capacity in ways that are indeed 'unhuman', and playing with apes, the species said to be closest to our own species, the model can definitely be read as if she were freer than most of us.

This kind of portrayal of women and animals in contemporary fashion imagery is not new, nor is it unique: fashion representations (as in photographs and sketches), that represent women together with animals, or women as animals, have been around for more than a century. In tandem with other kinds of cultural representations and narratives, fashion imagery helps sustain notions and images of women as aligned with the animalistic, and as such, fashion is part of a larger cultural and historical obsession with animals.

The affluence in representations depicting or telling the animalistic is indeed one of perpetuation and endurance throughout the history of many various, different cultures, Western culture included. This is not surprising, taken that animals like human beings constitute living species, and as species we are put to share the globe. Western culture's relation to the animal is however specific, given that this culture has used the animal in order to constitute humanity's Other, meaning that the animal has been used to help define the very Human. As my two short introductory examples show, there is however a difference in how the animal is used, depicted and narrated in relation to the human in terms of sex and race: while the animalistic is used as a difference to define man as human norm, in the case of women, it is used to define their supposed difference from men (and hence their deviance from the Human norm), and hence, to point out their affiliation with the animalistic.

When looking closely at fashion imagery (e.g. fashion advertisement, fashion photography and entire fashion spreads) there is no doubt that female models are often portrayed as (or with) animals: in fact, animalistic women have constituted a constant trope in most fashion imagery, from the early twentieth century up until today. While relying on old notions that are clearly misogynist, and which serve to try and dehumanize women, these images can be said to express a certain volatile desire, a desire that swings between loving, longing and fear or the animal persona. Just think of the early fashion drawings depicting sleek women together with similarly sleek greyhounds from the 1920s and 1930s; or the leopard clad models in high-end fashion magazines in the 1950s; and the more recent images of Helmut Newton's iconic Amazon women shot in the 1980s and 1990s. While such representations are typically both misogynist and sexist, I will seek to re-read this apparent juxtaposition of women models and the animal in fashion imagery in this chapter by relying on Gilles Deleuze and Félix Guattari's notion of 'becoming-animal' (1996). Through their prism, I will be arguing that fashion imagery of 'animal' women can in fact be re-read as a powerful representation of female inclusion and freedom. Before engaging with fashion imagery, however, I will shortly provide a discussion of how the animalistic has been used as a constant, continual trope in both visual and textual representations and as a 'definer' in Western culture and history, with a specific focus on Western Humanism.

The Hum/Animal as Continual Trope

While some cultures, like Native American Indian cultures, have more nurtured relationships with animals that are based both on respect and intimacy, Western cultures have tended to adopt somewhat contested relationships with animals, relationships that are less respectful and more domineering and hierarchical.[1] Historically and culturally, different ways of relating to animals are most apparent when looking at the mythologies of different cultures, especially the creation myths, and narrative representations about the origin of human beings. In Native American myths, human beings and animals share and participate in their creation, as equal beings in this process. These stories often represent animals and human beings as interchangeable, transforming into one another, and changing back again to their original form. Although most mythologies involve 'tricksters' who may be human or animalistic, and who may or may not be evil, one 'trickster' seems worse than any other, and it is one that per definition is an animal: the evil snake of the Judeo-Christian Eden.

In Western cultures, the hum/animal relationship has largely been based on *differentiation*. Based on oppositional, hierarchical and ontological differences, this differential boundary between human beings and animals entails a clear separation of human from animal, a separation that posits the human as the ultimate creation and as the unquestioned ruler of nature and culture. In promoting this unequal anthropocentric relationship, pre- and early modern science and religion have walked hand in hand, strongly in agreement of Man's sovereignty: that is, in representing Man as the utter fulfilment of Nature's Evolution *and* of God's Creation. Whereas the separation between human beings and animals has been next to impermeable in both science and religion, pre-modern Western popular fiction and storytelling has both reinforced and subverted this truth by offering threatening, yet titillating, stories about dangerous and unhealthy women and men who have transgressed this boundary. These representations – of which women who run with wolfs and men who turn into werewolves can be mentioned as examples – have been used as frightening examples of abnormality and evil, and as such, they have been used to keep people in order. These stories have probably functioned as threatening examples and as such, they have been used on several levels: within the more private realm of the family (as frightening 'tools' for upbringing) and within the external and authoritarian surveillance structure, like the church and the law. At the same time, one may imagine that these representations have offered deviant alternatives, probably terrifying for most readers – while possibly attractive to others. Here, the already mentioned notion of women who are aligned with wolves constitutes an old, threatening yet exciting trope, serving to de-humanize women, while also ascribing a certain dangerous power to them.[2] In her highly personal and emotional *Women Who Run with the Wolves* from 1992, Clarissa Pinkola Estés describes how women and wolves are aligned, both by nature and by their extinction:

> Healthy wolves and healthy women share certain psychic characteristics: keen sensing, playful spirit, and a heightened capacity for devotion. Wolves and women are relational by nature, inquiring, possessed of great endurance and strength. They are deeply intuitive, intensely concerned with their young, their mates and *their pack* [my emphasis], [...] Yet both have been hounded, harassed, and falsely imputed to be devouring and devious, overly aggressive, of less value than those who are their detractors. They have been the targets of those who would clean up the wilds as well as the wildish environs of the psyche, extincting the instinctual, and leaving no trace of it behind. The predation of wolves and women by those who misunderstand them is strikingly similar.
>
> (1992: 2)

Man's complex and at times paradoxical relation to animals, then, is one marked by difference, but also, by closeness and distance, necessity and fear. In most narratives and representations, most of which have been written by men from Ancient Greek culture up until contemporary times, this hum/animal relation is formed by a pendulous desire moving between love and fear (and one might add, between desire and disgust). While wanting to become *like* an animal – due to an over-empowering love for them – is portrayed as romantic and intimate (as in Luc Besson's *Le Grand Bleu* [*The Big Blue*] from 1988), the fear *of* them – that is, being killed and eaten by them, or even more so, the fear of becoming them (as in Robert Louis Steven's *Strange Case of Dr Jekyll and Mr Hyde* from 1886 and Val Lewton's *The Bagheeta* from 1930, the latter which was filmed twice as *Cat People* [Jacques Tourneur 1942; Paul Schrader 1982]) forms the truly horrific in many narratives. In the first scenario, it is a matter of becoming one with the loved other, and in the second scenario, it is a panicking fear of becoming the 'Other', of losing one's humanity and control.

In Western society, the emphasis on the separation and vilification of animals as beasts, i.e. as Man's Other, together with the tempting vilification of women who run with animals, was only further reinforced in modern times with the entrance of (Western) Humanism and its medical, philosophical, juridical and religious discourses. With its two main characteristics of anthropocentrism and phallo(go)centrism, this humanism has been crucial in broadening out the separation between human beings and animals. Both of these centrisms have at their core an emphasis on the human as dominant, which rests on a dualist opposition created and used to categorize every kind, each species and their supposed differences. As Gilles Deleuze and Félix Guattari have pointed out, natural history (crucial to the structuralism advocated by Claude Lévi-Strauss (see Lévis-Strauss 1969, 1974) is primarily concerned with 'the sum and value of differences or resemblances as very separate things', that is, with organizing species in terms of 'progressions and regressions, continuities and major breaks' and within which evolution works and defines in terms of 'genealogy, kinship, descent, and filiation'. Hence, '[n]atural history can think only in terms of relationships [...], not in terms of production [...]' (Deleuze and Guattari 1996: 234). And relationship, within this humanism, is always oppositional.

This ontological differentiation between human beings (i.e. *Man*) and animals is intimately connected to the differentiation made between the sexes, between ethnicities and races, and between sexualities, all of which are being forcefully 'discovered' and implemented in the eighteenth and the nineteenth centuries.[3] The animalistic in Western humanist thought is understood to combine all 'other-nesses', at least when aligned with women and with womanhood. Hence, the animalistic woman is during the height of humanism also represented and portrayed as non-white, 'primitive', non-civilized, as well as being extreme in her sexual appetite or as alternative in her sexual orientation. Here, German painter Franz von Stuck's (1863–1928) work, Irish author Bram Stoker's *Dracula* (1897) and contemporary Russian painter Alexander Antonyuk's (b. 1963) paintings may serve as prime examples.

Overriding and embracing all of these oppositions is one single, major opposition: the one dividing body and mind. This opposition is based in a Cartesian understanding of the mind ('the mental') as separate from the body ('the material').[4] According to this categorization, the human (that is Man) is positioned within the realm of Mind, while the animal is located within the realm of Body. Structured by anthropocentrism and phallo(go)centrism, this view suggests that women, non-whites, homosexuals and the working class are differentiated from the white, middle-class, heterosexual Man: hence they are more aligned with the body and the animalistic. Western humanism, then, is one that only celebrates and acknowledges white men as full subjects. To this dualist and dialectic line of thought (a thought which is inherently hegemonic and which structures a phallocentric, Eurocentric culture of separation and differentiation), various kinds of representations are fundamental. Dominant, mainstream (or *malestream*) discourse is widely and efficiently implemented, deployed and spread via storytelling and visual representations that tell and give evidence of the world, and of life. The adventures of Robinson Crusoe or Phileas Fogg all tell the story of white, male sovereignty and subject-hood, while making all non-male and non-white characters, no matter how positively and helpfully depicted they may be, into differentially constituted *others*. According to Teresa de Lauretis (1987), these narratives follow a Foucauldian understanding, constituting *technologies* of gender (i.e. of the *male* gender), that present truths and instruct audiences on how to conceive of the world, of themselves, of others, that is, *of life* itself.

Of course, modern times representations of animals as being the opposite of human beings were however nothing new and they did not originate with Western humanism and the Enlightenment. Within Western history and culture, wild and domestic animals have for long populated different kinds of representations; and within these representations – whether visual, written or oral – they have played various functions. One such function can be found in ancient and modern physiognomies, through the judging of (mostly negative) character traits deduced from facial resemblances with particular animals. Here, the work of architect and painter Charles LeBrun (1619–90), carefully depicting animal traits in human beings in his many portraits, stands out as a good example. In Ancient Greek and other Western mythologies (ranging from approximately 1700 BCE and onwards), animals have also been depicted as the other of – or *in* – human beings, making the animalistic both a possible and paradoxical human trait. The possibility of animalistic traits in human beings – or even the threatening possibility of turning into an animal – still informs much of early modern, modern and even contemporary representations. We see this in the works of Medieval painter Hieronymus Bosch (1450–1516), via the paintings made by surrealist painter and illustrator Leonore Fini (1907–96), and the literary works of prominent writers such as Robert Louis Stevens, Guy Endore and Franz Kafka, to the more recent film examples like *Grizzly Man* (Werner Herzog, 2005) and *Black Swan* (Darren Aronofsky, 2010). In all of these examples, possible animalistic traits or the sheer possibility of becoming animal is depicted as both menacing and desirable, hence exemplifying the pendular movement in relation to the animal mentioned above.

But there are also a cascade of visual and literary representations that are steadily focusing on the danger of the animal, and on the very difference or boundary between human and animal. From medieval paintings to modern photography, wild animals have been used to indicate danger on the one hand, and human strength on the other, often demonstrating

Man's power over animal. Here, the rich production of nineteenth-century American painter Frederic Remington (1861–1909) offers an appropriate example: in Remington's work, the relation between beast and man is one formed by Man's sovereignty and power, whether it regards his (un-)domesticated horse or a wild buffalo or bear, as in *The Cowboy* (1902) and *The Last Stand* (c. 1890). Also, tamed animals have been used pragmatically to represent the uncomplicated and friendly working relations between Man and his Other with animals being used for hunting, for farming and for herding. Again, these representations depict and narrate Man's power over the animal as it is being tamed to serve Man in his endeavours and his work. Equally, animals have been the very *object* of Man's hunting games demonstrating Man's ultimate power over the animal. In Remington's work, all the various relations between human beings (i.e. men) and animals can be said to be represented: the animal as a life-saving necessary Other (offering nutrition and warmth); as a life-threatening Other (highly capable of killing); and as Man's best and most reliable 'colleague', vehicle or even friend.

In portraiture, animals – alive or dead (often presented in dismembered parts: a paw, a tale, the fur or the teeth) – have been used to indicate the socio-economic status and power of the upper classes, and at times, animals have been used as allegories communicating political and social meanings, as in Bronzino's (1503–72) painting *Portrait of Guidobaldo II della Rovere* (1532). Alive or dead, animals have also been used as allegories to indicate gender status: most commonly men's strength and women's innocence, as in German painter Matthias Grunewald's (1475–1528) painting *Heilige Agnes* (painted sometime between 1500 and 1505) depicting the holy Agnes holding a small, white lamb to indicate her purity. Women's supposed slyness has also been depicted with the help of the animalistic, as in the Dutch Renaissance painter Maerten van Heemskerck's (1498–1574) painting *An Allegory of Innocence and Guile* (c. 1520), showing a young red-haired woman in dark green velvet, with a white dove to her right, and a snake in her left hand.

Animals for women, partial or whole, have at times been used as pure objects of fashion to either convey an ideal femininity or an ideal feminine purity, or even a threatening feminine exoticism, eroticism and danger. Within this discourse, the exotic other is conceived of and constructed, not only as female, but also as oriental (see e.g. Battersby 2007). Connected to this feminine oriental other, is of course the *effeminate* 'oriental', that is, the non-European other who is clearly differentiated in all of his otherness – both in terms of ethnicity, gender and sexuality. An interesting example of a female exotic is the infamous Italian Marchesa Luisa Casati (1881–1957) who performed her femininity and presented herself as a living work of art with the help of the animalistic. Furs, feathers, dogs and snakes were part of her eccentric *mise-en-scène*, playfully personifying the deadly stereotype advocated by the nineteenth-century misogyny, and filling it with fashion, pleasure and life. Posthumously, she has inspired the work of some contemporary fashion designers. Hence, in 1998 and 2008 John Galliano based his Spring/Summer (S/S) collections for Dior on Casati; while in 2007 Alexander McQueen paid tribute to her in his S/S collection; and in 2010, Karl Lagerfeld used her as a source of inspiration for Chanel's resort collection. In addition, her dramatic black-and-white look continues to inspire fashion spreads in famous fashion magazines and high-profile fashion icons with Tilda Swinton, Carine Roitfeld and Georgina Chapman all being styled as Casati on different occasions.[5]

Since antiquity animals have occupied central positions in literary works. In fables (by e.g. Aesop's Ancient Greek fables [sixth century BCE] and Jean de la Fontaine's fables [1668–94]) and in children's stories (e.g. in the work of the Brothers Grimm, Hans Christian Andersen and Walt Disney, to mention a few), they have been present as anthropomorphized animals, taking on a human form or shape or behaving like human beings.[6] And as anthropomorphized creatures, quite often holding an allegorical significance, they have populated theatre plays, novels, fairy tales and – of course – (animated) films. As for animated films, the works of Walt Disney stand out, yet there are other examples that are worth mentioning, like *Flåklypa Grand Prix* (*Pinchcliffe Grand Prix*) (Ivo Caprino, 1975) or *Fantastic Mr. Fox* (Wes Anderson, 2009). Animals in literature have often been portrayed as threatening and dangerous, such as the wolf in *Little Red Riding Hood* by Charles Perrault (1697); the winged monkeys of L. Frank Baum's *Wizard of Oz* (1900), or Behemoth, the gun crazy cat of Mikhail Bulgakov's *Мастер и Маргарита* (*The Master and Margarita*) (1966); and sometimes as Man's best friend, such as Baloo the bear in Rudyard Kipling's *Jungle Book* from 1894.[7] Literary and visual representations and storytelling have hence been infused with the animalistic, and with the relation between the human and the animal, almost obsessively promoting Man as civilized, moral and intellectual and the animal as either uncivilized, wild and immoral, or as amiable, servile and inferior, thus giving prominence to the dominant notion of human supremacy. Rooted in political, social and philosophical thought, these male-centred representations, almost always systematically aligning woman and animal with one another as Man's other, have indirectly served to 'trap women in the phenomenal, leaving them incapable of the full moral personhood or civil personality that raise the ideal male above the merely animal and the merely human' (Battersby 2007: 63). Yet women are not the only group that has been denied full moral personhood: any group external to the white, male, Eurocentric subject has been (and still is) denied full personhood. This differentiation is at the very basis of nineteenth- and twentieth-century western xenophobia and racism, wherein certain ethnic groups and certain animal species are correlated. Let me give two discernible examples: in an attempt to de-humanize and vilify the Jewish population, Nazis in the 1930s and early 1940s systematically correlated Jews with rats (as is made painstakingly clear in the propaganda film *Jud Süss* (*Jew Süss*) by Veit Harlan from 1940), and in the nineteenth century, the Irish population were diligently compared to apes by both the English and the North Americans (see e.g. Rogin 1998: 57).

Fearing the Female Other – *and Becoming-Animal*

In fashion imagery, too, the animalistic has been a dominant trope. Here we see a clear connection between female sexuality and gender with the animal – expressing and visualizing an existing discourse on women not so much as the weaker sex, but as the inferior, less human sex. When women are depicted as animalistic, as I have shortly mentioned above, it is mostly in relation to notions and ideas about the primitive, the exotic and the erotic, and as such, they are presented as *body*. They are, as animal women, presented as untamed, as uncontrolled and as sexually threatening, yet they are so as alluring bodies, thus separating them from the intellectual and moral mind. In Western representation at large, this abundant misogyny is tied up with the animalistic: Woman as Other, i.e. other from Man, is visualized, represented and classified as an abject, rowdy, uncontrollable and infinite body. A case in point here is womanhood as depicted in the sinister drawings and paintings by already mentioned German painter von Stuck. In his chauvinist imagery, Woman – as animal – is represented as overly erotic, as beastly and deadly, and as threatening to all men. Stuck's paintings – 'Die Suende'/'Sin' from 1893 and 'Salome' from 1908 could be given as explicit examples – were not an isolated phenomenon, indeed, they were very much part of a larger misogynist and xenophobic discourse of which art was only one area. Here, Otto Weininger's (1880–1903) misogynist, racist and anti-Semitic oeuvre *Sex and Character* from 1903, applauded by overtly woman-hating Swedish author August Strindberg (1849– 1912), and later to be used as inspiration within the Nazi party in Germany, could be mentioned as an integral part or expression of this discourse.

This kind of misogynist representation – serving to install fear and disgust of Woman as Other, as animalistic and as overly sexual and revengeful, is however one that has a long history: the vengeful characters of Medusa or Arachne – the latter who was transformed into a spider by Athena due to her blasphemy – could be given as early examples. Yet, it is at the turn of the last century, in the very passage from the nineteenth century to the twentieth century – a period often referred to as the height of Modernity – that we see the flow of misogynist representations depicting Woman as coupled with the animalistic abound. Her forced connection with the animalistic positions her as out of control and as overly sexual and deadly, and it does so in an opposition to Man as a perfectly controlled human being. As the uncontrollable Other, she, within a strictly patriarchal social structure and culture, has to be controlled and constrained: first, by fathers and brothers, then by husbands and sons (or, as in the photograph by Jean-Paul Goude, by a male animal keeper). Yet, her closeness to the animal is one of strong titillation – and it is definitely one of provocation and of danger.

This late nineteenth-century obsession with, and fear of, women as the Other of Man has been discussed in length by Bram Dijkstra, who in his books has described how the blurring parables between women and animals reach some kind of popular peak during the late nineteenth century (Dijkstra 1986, 1996). This sexist and misogynist imagery of course continues into the next century, and does so through two main mediated channels, namely film and fashion photography. Rooted in Western humanist anthropocentrism and misogyny, and connected to earlier Classical mythological representations, fashion imagery carries ingrained notions of sex, gender, sexuality and race. As I have argued elsewhere (Wallenberg 2013), there is no question about the inherent sexism of this visual form. Nor is there any doubt about it being part of a dominant body of male-centred representations constituting a 'relentless parade of insults' (Dyer 1993: 1). There is, however, a possible opening for reading this imagery as a critique of both androcentrism and of anthropomorphism. By applying the Deleuzian-Guattarian concept of *devenir-animal*, 'becoming-animal' (Deleuze and Guattari 1996), to fashion imagery, there are possibilities for re-reading fashionable representations of animal-women. Such a re-reading can posit a powerful understanding of how animalistic women in fashion represent and trigger becoming-animal as movement and as transgression, i.e. transgressing the inferior position ascribed to women to grant a new kind of freedom. The (neo)feminist practice of re-reading, a practice used much in the 1970s and the 1980s, can still provide derogatory and inherently sexist images with new meanings and a powerful vengeance.[8] Fuelling this practice with the notion of 'becoming-animal' may turn fashion representations portraying animalistic women into examples of feminist endeavour.

But what exactly does 'becoming-animal' entail? As a philosophical concept and as a political and ontological possibility, it is one that is the most interesting of the various concepts introduced by Deleuze and Guattari because of the 'unusual way it addresses one of the regulating questions of recent European thinking' – the question regarding 'what comes after the subject?' (Bruns 2007: 703). Subsequently, 'becoming-animal' should not be confused with the increasing love for domesticated animals most clearly expressed maybe in an expanding pet culture (a culture that involves both 'ordinary' pets such as cats, dogs and hamsters, and wild animals such as snakes, tigers and giraffes).[9] Nor should it be confused with subcultural erotic groups like the furry-culture or the so-called 'furverts', an erotic sub-group that seems to be increasing (at least within parts of Western culture). Nor should it be confused with the certain aesthetic transformations, like plastic surgery, that some people go through in order to look like their (inner) animal. Known popular examples would be Cat-man and Leopard-man, both highly visible and out with their becoming-animal-longing.[10]

With 'becoming-animal', Deleuze and Guattari mean a movement in which the subject no longer inhabits a safe realm of stability, but instead is folded into a nomadic mode of existence. In Bruns' words: it is a 'movement from major (the constant) to minor (the variable); it is a de-terriorialization in which a subject no longer occupies a realm of stability and identity but is instead folded imperceptibly into a movement [...] whose mode of existence is nomadic' (Bruns 2007: 703). Applied to the 'beastly' characteristic of much fashion imagery, and here my two opening examples may serve as two explicit samples, this notion helps re-read the persistent equation between woman and animal so that a new meaning or understanding can be detected: the blurring of woman and animal in fashion imagery may be interpreted as manifestations of liberation and empowerment. The process or the movement of becoming animal is not so much an animal metamorphosis as it is an achievement of non-identity, which for Deleuze and Guattari – as well as for some feminist theorists such as Rosi Braidotti – is the very condition of freedom, which for them is a central tenet.

Losing one's humanity is losing one's controlled identity, and in this loss, one may win a new freedom, that is, a kind of freedom that is not circumscribed by rules and morals, by societal and cultural norms and expectations, nor by political rigid systems. Becoming animal, then, is a movement that involves a breaking out of the restricted identity that is formed by the political and the social – which in Western culture is structured by a strong phallo(go)centrism 'Becoming' is about movement and process, yet it is also is about repetition. Moreover, becoming is about memories of the non-dominant kind: it is, as Rosi Braidotti argues, 'about affinities and the capacity both to sustain and generate inter-connectedness' (Braidotti 2002: 8). Such interconnectedness can only exist via de-individuated subjectivities – and here, the animal relationship between the human being and the animal may be seen as one way to reach this de-individuated state. This relationship is characterized by a kind of hum/animality, that is, it is one characterized by proximity, by symbiosis and by a sense of shared territory (or space) of indeterminacy between animal and human. Following Derek Ryan, Deleuze and Guattari's relationship to animals should not be characterized by a lack of curiosity so much as by *fascination*, (in-) formed by a more intense, ontological and perhaps ethical encounter with animal life and with animals as *pack*.[11] Theirs is a fascination with 'an animal reality, and the reality of the becoming-animal of the human-being' (Deleuze and Guattari 1996: 242).[12]

Becoming-animal, as an expression of nomadism, of de-territorialization and of the rhizomatic – all of which are crucial theoretical concepts *and* practical possibilities within Deleuzian thinking (and part of his nomadology) – is closely connected also to the Deleuzian notion of 'becoming-woman'. This notion, it should be mentioned, has been subject to fierce critique by certain feminists (see e.g. Jardin 1985 and Braidotti 1998) because, like most philosophy, it takes on a most male-centred position, excluding women subjects all together. To some extent it is difficult not to agree with this criticism: the concept applies more to men than it does to women (who are already women and who are in the becoming, and for whom this kind of becoming may not prove liberating). For men, on the other hand, 'becoming-woman' offers a way to break free (if only temporarily) from dominant restraints, and to try out the position of the 'other'. For women then, 'becoming-men' would be more interesting and more accurate – but that would not lead to nomadism, nor to de-territorialization, and it would not make possible any freedom rather the opposite. But whereas becoming-woman is a process or a movement that departs from a male standpoint and position, becoming-animal is construed in *gender-neutral* terms, although it most certainly must have different implications for men and women in their social roles (with women having more to gain from becoming-animal given their secondary status in patriarchal societies).

Yet, my own reading of Deleuze and Guattari lingers towards a more generous view on 'becoming-woman': following more recent feminist work (see e.g. Grosz 1994; Gatens 1996; Braidotti 2002, 2003; Lorraine 1999, 2011; Colebrook 2002), I do not believe that it is a possibility open to men alone. Rather, it is a possibility open to anyone who wishes to break loose from the conformist frames of socialized and subjected being. Hence, it is not yet another category that (straight, white) men can try on or try out, but a conscious (and painful) possibility to break with convention and the many constraints of (hetero) normativity in order to explore the possibility of living a life more fully. This painful openness makes it a gender-neutral possibility, a possibility of breaking out of, or of breaking free from, normative male-centred subjecthood. As such, it may, possibly, offer a way out of sexual dualism.

Not surprisingly, it is through the notion of 'becoming-woman' that Deleuze and Guattari have inscribed themselves in what has been referred to as *sexual difference theory*. Belgium philosopher and psychoanalyst, Luce Irigaray, in whose productive body of work this theory runs like a red thread, has perhaps, advocated this theory most loudly. But, whereas Irigaray's philosophy is one that is decidedly feminist, Deleuze and Guattari's philosophy is only implicitly so. Here, Italian philosopher Rosi Braidotti has proved crucial in unpacking the feminism inherent in Deleuze and Guattari. In her work, she has brought the two male thinkers together with Irigaray, pointing out their similarities and their joint, yet disparate, aim in what she claims is an overall feminist project that seeks to question and criticize phallo(go)centrism and dualisms: 'the two [that is, Irigarayan sexual difference theory and Deleuzian theory of becoming] can reinforce one another and strike a productive alliance' (Braidotti 2002: 5). Theirs, she argues, is a project that deals with the making possible a different kind of 'subject' (see e.g. Braidotti 2002, 2003), a subject that is not one (and hence, recalling 'that sex which is not one' [Irigaray 1977]).[13] Rather, their subject is one which is multiple and multi-layered, interactive and complex, and hence, it is *trans-individual*. It is nomadic and it is one that has differences within itself – it consists of many differences, functioning in a net of interconnections, and in this way it is *rhizomatic* – and it is indeed fleshy, it is embodied.[14] The difference brought forward by Irigaray and Deleuze and Guattari is not to be confused with Difference as hierarchical and exclusionary, which structures Western thought.[15] Indeed, one of the aims of sexual difference theory is to upset and overthrow the pejorative, oppressive connotations that are built not only into the notion of difference, but also into the dialectics of Self and Other. It wants to make difference an inclusive term, and to make differences equal – and to deconstruct the confines within which Woman is captured as otherness to Man's sameness. Braidotti writes about this new, possible subject that: '[s]he, in fact, may no longer be a she, but a subject of quite another story: a subject-in-process; a mutant; the other of the Other; a post-Woman embodied subject cast in female morphology who has already undergone an essential metamorphosis' (Braidotti 2003: 45).[16] Bearing this possibility of a new (female) subject-in-process in mind let me now turn to discussing a few emblematic fashion representations depicting woman-as-animal, using 'becoming-animal' as the critical lens through which I re-read their meaning.

Becoming-Animal in Fashion Imagery

Old fantasies of animalistic, uncontrollable and monstrous women, as represented in mythologies and visual art, have their most visible modern equivalent in fashion imagery – in fashion ads, fashion photography, fashion editorials, as well as in more recent fashion films. It is in this kind of cultural and commercial representation that we today most clearly can distinguish and detect the pendulous, swinging desire and fear expressed in relation to animals, i.e. find proof of how the long-lived desire/fear of the animal is indeed one of preservation. As I have indicated above, this kind of animalistic fashion imagery comes in two main categories or types: either it portrays women models together with animals as women who have chosen animals before men (recalling the male fear of women who 'run with animals'); or they are portrayed as animalistic, that is, as having transgressed the binary between human and animal, or as being in the act of becoming-animal. (Interestingly, in most fashion photography depicting women and animals, or women-as-animals, there are no men. Men are usually excluded from this scenario, and at focus is the supposed intimacy and proximity between woman and animal.) There is yet a third category, but this is less common: women about to be eaten by enormous, wild animals – visualizing the old fear of animal as killer machines, here combined with a misogynist and sadist desire to see women dead. Here, Helmut Newton's iconic photograph of a nude woman being 'eaten' by a large crocodile and the more recent spread in *Harper's Bazaar* (March 2015) depicting the singer Rihanna in a low cut swimsuit and high heels between the jaws of an enormous shark, commemorating the 40th anniversary of the film *Jaws* (Steven Spielberg, 1975), may serve as examples.

The first dominant type of fashion imagery, with women who seem to have chosen animals before men, and who are not yet transformed or transforming into animals, is often found in editorials in up-scale fashion magazines such as *Vogue* and *Harper's Bazaar* (see e.g. the fashion spread 'Beauty and the beast' shot by Annie Leibovitz for the April issue 2005 of *Vogue*, depicting actress Drew Barrymore dressed in ball gowns together with a huge lion by her side, or the spread 'An awfully big adventure' in *British Vogue*, December 2011, shot by Tim Walker and depicting model Kirsi Pyrhönen together with birds of prey, buffalos and deer). Here, the model is dressed and made up to look like the animals, hence sharing not only the space with them, but sharing their visual characteristics – indicating their proximity. This kind of imagery came into vogue already during the late 1920s and early 1930s, most commonly in the format of fashion drawings, and depicted women with domesticated dogs and/or wild animals. In the 1920s and 1930s, fashion drawings depicting sleek, white women together with white greyhounds were a common feature, and was used both in fashion ads and in other kinds of fashionable ads (e.g. for cigarettes and cars). Here, the woman was most often portrayed as at one with her animal. The 1950s saw a flow of fashion photography that continued to depict model women as being one with animals, no matter their size and wildness: be they sweet innocent puppies (as in Norman Parkinson's photo for *Vogue* in 1958 with model Nena von Schlebrugge surrounded by small dogs), or huge elephants or tigers (as in Richard Avedon's iconic photo of supermodel Dovima [Dorothy Juba] posing between two giant elephants from 1955).

The second form or type of fashion imagery, depicting women who are about to transgress, or have already, transgressed the boundary between human and animal, the women models are often dressed in fur or in tight animal patterns and prints. Further, they are often posing as animals, frequently on their four 'legs', as if in a hunting pose, i.e. as if ready to attack, or as if ready to be mounted. An infamous example of this kind of animalistic posing would be David LaChapelle's photograph 'Cat House' from 1999 showing model Naomi Campbell on her four legs positioned below a large tiger (who is painted on the wall). Alternatively, the latter type of imagery is most commonly found in fashion ads for specific high-end fashion brands such as Roberto Cavalli, Moschino and Versace, or in specific, single 'arty' fashion shots like the one by LaChapelle. Examples of this category of images would most commonly include a black model, visually correlating the wild and the truly animalistic with blackness, and hence, perpetuating the notion of black women as primitive and dangerous in this *animality*.

In Goude's editorial 'Wild things' in *Harper's Bazaar*, as we have seen, the two categories or types of animalistic fashion imagery seem to coalesce, and the focus is on the black female: in one of the shots, the model (Campbell), dressed in minimal, tightfitting leopard attire, runs next to a real cheetah, 'running with' the cheetah – while affectively transforming into one. Campbell, since her break-through into fashion as a young model in the late 1980s, has been depicted as animalistic and primitive uncountable times: as a black model in an industry dominated by whiteness, her difference is constantly emphasized and she is often aligned with the animal kingdom and with the 'non-civilized' (as constituted by the idea of 'Africa'). The few black models that have made it into the fashion world have all at one point been portrayed as animalistic, as wild and as primitive – and always in connection to 'Africa' (or some other wild setting): a black model dressed in leopard in an ad for Moschino's 'Cheap n' Chic' campaign in the late 1990s; and most recently, Chanel Iman as Mimi Mouse riding an elephant in a fashion spread made for *Vogue Germany* in December 2009, and Rihanna as wild animal – dressed in fur and appearing together with wolves – in a fashion spread entitled 'Bad girl: The world's wildest style icon' in the September issue of *W Magazine* in 2014.

White models, on the other hand, are portrayed as less primitive (and less explosive) in their relation with animals: whereas black models are teamed up with wild animals that are associated with the primitive, dangerous African jungle, white models are often teamed up with dogs, cats and horses, animals that emphasize these women's domesticity, but also, their whiteness. A prime example would be Edward Steichen's photograph 'White' from 1935, depicting three white women dressed in white creations standing next to a white horse, possibly an albino, against a white backdrop. Another example would be the more recent advertising campaign for Lanvin by Steven Meisel from 2009, depicting a hyper-white Kirsten McNemany on her back surrounded by black cats. McNemany's exaggerated whiteness, and her posing on her back, makes her look dead, hence recalling the disturbing association of white people with death (Dyer 1997: 207–42). Goude's 'exotic' fashion spread, it should be mentioned, has many fore-runners as well as many successors: for example, the *Harper's Bazaar* May issue of 1999, contained a fashion spread that was also entitled 'Wild things', this time shot by photographer Wayne Maser. Like Goude's spread, this was also shot somewhere in Africa but this time with a white model (Aurelie Claudel). Compared to Goude's series of images shot exactly 10 years later, Maser's series depicts the white woman engaging with wild animals, but she is definitely presented far less wild, and hence, as far less animalistic. Campbell is thus being made into an animal, whereas Claudel is only being aligned with them. In a twelve-page long fashion editorial for the September issue of *Vogue* in 2014, white model Sara Stone appeared with wolves, hence visualizing the old notion of 'women who run with wolves' and being part of their pack. In one shot, dressed in a shiny red, knee-length dress, she is clearly made to evoke the *Little Red Riding Hood*: but whereas the wolf is a threatening killer machine in Perrault's original fairy tale from 1697, here, the model woman is completely in compliance with her wild animals.

And while all of the above mentioned images (and I could add thousands of others) are both racist and sexist – relying on a male-dominant gaze informed by a male and heteronormative erotics – they can simultaneously be read as expressions of a certain 'freedom' through their representation of alliances between women and animals. In these images, the (female) spectator is invited to admire, desire and identify with the models in their closeness with animals, and in their possible metamorphosis, but also, with their strength, fastness and their apparent *animality*. If 'becoming-animal' entails a possible de-territorialization, i.e. a break from (or even termination of) heteronormative, patriarchal conventions, as well as a possible de-subjectivization, then these examples of fashion imagery, through their constant focus on the close relation between animal and woman, serve to visualize this possibility. In addition, they may serve to install a desire and a belief in the spectator: a belief in the very possibility to change the status quo, and to experience a freedom and a kind of inclusive subjecthood that is not restricted by phallo(go)centrism nor by anthropocentrism. And while such a freedom and such an inclusive and open subjecthood may seem as an impossibility (for how is one to exist outside of territorialization?), and as wishful thinking, it is important to remember that to wish and dream the utopian is not to dream the impossible. For, as once wrote Jacques Derrida, there must be something that precedes the dream, something that nurtures its existence: 'But where would the "dream" of the innumerable come from, if it is indeed a dream? Does the dream itself not prove that what is dreamt of must be there in order for it to provide the dream?' (Derrida 1995: 108). The 'innumerable' here refers to the possibility of breaking with dualist, hierarchical and binary sexual difference, and to instead understand humanity (and in close conjunction to humans, animals) in terms of a bigger plurality of sexes and genders. Such innumerability would dismantle the unequal and asymmetrical power structures between men and women, and between human and animal.

Through the lens of 'becoming-animal', the model women and the animal can in fact be read as absolutely fearless, having transgressed the boundary between human and the animalistic through their mutual engagement. These images demonstrate how the hum/animal, through a solidarity of metamorphosis, together engage in a proliferation of differences that do not obey hierarchical rules, but instead affirm heterogeneous assemblages that include both human and animal. In addition, these images can be read as forceful expressions of female (and animal) vengeance, upsetting and destructing male dominance and the male status quo. What these fashion photographs provide the (female) spectator with is the representation of an intense, ontological and possibly also ethical encounter with animal life and with animals. In these images, women and animals together make up a unified, yet diverse, *pack*.

However, it is not only in fashion representation, such as these, that a certain female (and animal) encounter and vengeance can be detected: there are also a few fashion designers who have used the animalistic as a recurrent theme or presence in their collections. Alexander McQueen, as an artist of fashion and costume whose collections were devoted to exploring the relationship between the human and the animal and blurring their boundaries, must have been aware of, and indeed inspired by, the notion of 'becoming-animal'. His Spring/ Summer 2010 collection, inspired by Charles Darwin's *The Origin of the Species* (1859), is notable in this regard, in addition to his S/S 2009 collection, which saw the stage filled with stuffed (real) animals, with the designer himself appearing dressed in a furry bunny suit at the end of the show. Apart from these specific collections, specific fashion pieces also come to mind as examples of investigations or explorations of 'becoming-animal'. McQueen's various creations (and head-pieces) that take on birdlike appearances, ornamented with thousands of real bird feathers, are perhaps the most obvious. These creations transform or metamorphosize women into bird-women, ready to spread their wings to break away from the laws of gravity that weigh them down, as if ready to transform. Looking back at his rich, and at times, uncanny productions (hence visualizing the already mentioned pendular movement between desire and fear), it becomes clear that his unique pieces were artworks through which the female body and the animal body were 'transformed' through their becoming-one, or rather, through their becoming-multiple – becoming a multiplicity of forms and meanings. The transformation made possible through his creations, although only imaginary, is one characterized not so much by filiation (as in kinship), as by *alliance* (Deleuze and Guattari 1996: 238). This alliance – which I believe can be detected in most animalistic fashion imagery – is one that welcomes a critical deconstruction of the 'erotic', supposedly upheld via the heteronormative contract and male-dominated eye that informs and shapes most fashion photography. Through the lens of 'becoming-animal', fashion imagery depicting women as animalistic, as in the process of becoming-animal, that is, woman as 'a subject-in-process; a mutant' undergoing an 'essential metamorphosis' (Braidotti 2003: 45), may be divested from the domineering male gaze, and hence, from the heterosexist imperative. This is not to say that bestiality becomes the erotic norm instead: but rather, that through the process of metamorphosis and in the alliance between other and other, non-normative and multiple erotics are made possible.

Conclusion

By applying Deleuzian and Guattarian notions of 'becoming-animal' as a prism, supported by feminist theory and politics as advocated by Braidotti, for example, this chapter tries to re-read fashion imagery depicting women and animals and to demonstrate how these images can be said to entail and express both feminist and anti-anthropocentric meanings. In addition to this, I have, although less astutely, described how these fashion images might work to criticize, upset and deconstruct the strong binary that produces notions of sex and gender whereby 'becoming-animal' as a political and ontological possibility – may serve to undermine the sexual dualism. The nomadic horizon visualized through and within these images, is a subjectivity that is 'beyond gender' in that it is dispersed and inclusive, never binary. Further, it is multiple, not dualistic; it is interconnected, not dialectical; and it is in a constant flux, never fixed.

Hence, an understanding of 'becoming-animal' that involves a disruption of an essentialist sexual difference and of a movement that is inclusive, inviting and striving for proximity is useful when considering the imagery of the animalistic woman as portrayed in fashion. And by bringing this concept to other kinds of imagery and fictions (i.e. art, literature, theatre, advertising, photography and film), the long-standing misogynist trope – as advocated by (male) artists and thinkers – can be interpreted and understood as representing an ethical stance that is about the solidarity existing between human and animal, and specifically, between woman and animal. While 'becoming-animal' can be a useful concept and a viable project for feminist enquiry, tightly connected as it is to both the political and the ontological, it is also an *ethical* project. Here, it is not so much about the ethics of distant compassion, as in pity, but rather an ethics through which one becomes worthy of the zone of proximity, an ethics of solidarity and of shared-ness between human and animal.

Acknowledgements

I would like to thank Adam Geczy for bringing to my attention the connection made between the animalistic and the oriental within modern Western discourse. I am also grateful to the Bergman Foundation on Fårö for housing me while finishing this chapter.

References

Anderson, W. (2009), *Fantastic Mr. Fox*, USA: Twentieth Century Fox et al.

Aronofsky, D. (2010), *Black Swan*, USA: Cross Creek Pictures, Phoenix Pictures, Protozoa Pictures, and Dune Entertainment.

Battersby, C. (2007), *The Sublime, Terror and Human Difference*, London and New York: Routledge.

Besson, L. (1988), *Le Grand Bleu* (*The Big Blue*), France and USA: Weintraub Entertainment Group.

Braidotti, R. (1994), *Nomadic Subjects: Embodiment and Sexual Difference in Contemporary Feminist Theory*, New York: Columbia University Press.

——— (2002), *Metamorphoses: Towards a Materialist Theory of Becoming*, Cambridge: Polity Press.

——— (2003), 'Be-coming woman: Or sexual difference revisisted', *Theory, Culture & Society*, 20:3, pp. 43–64.

Bruns, G. (2007), 'Becoming-animal: Some simple ways', *New Literary History*, 38:4, pp. 703–20.

Caprino, I. (1975), *Flåklypa Grand Prix* (*Pinchcliffe Grand Prix*), Norway: Caprino Filmcenter AS.

Colebrook, C. (2002), *Gilles Deleuze*, London and New York: Routledge.

Collignon, S. (2008), 'They walk! They talk!: A study of the anthropomorphisation of non human characters in animated films', *Animatrix: A Journal of the UCLA Animation Workshop*, issue 16, http://www.academia.edu/373293/They_Walk_They_Talk_. Accessed 30 October 2015.

Darwin, C. (1859), *The Origin of the Species*, London: John Murray.

Deleuze, G. (2003), *Francis Bacon: The Logic of Sensation* (orig. *Francis Bacon: logique de la sensation*, 1981), Minneapolis: Minnesota University Press.

Deleuze, G. and Guattari, F. (1996), *A Thousand Plateaus: Capitalism and Schizophrenia,* 3rd ed., London: Athlone Press.

Derrida, J. (1995), *Points… Interviews, 1974–1994* (orig. *Points de suspension. Entretiens*, 1992), in E. Weber (ed.), Palo Alto: Stanford University Press.

Dijkstra, B. (1986), *Idols of Perversity: Fantasies of Feminine Evil in Fin-de-siècle Culture*, New York and Oxford: Oxford University Press.

——— (1996), *Evil Sisters: The Threat of Female Sexuality and the Cult of Manhood*, New York: Knopf.

Dyer, R. (1993), *The Matter of Images: Essays on Representations*, London: Routledge.

——— (1997), *White*, London: Routledge.

Gatens, M. (1996), *Imaginary Bodies: Ethics, Power and Corporeality*, Hove: Psychology Press.

Grosz, E. (1994), *Volatile Bodies: Towards a Corporeal Feminism*, Crows Nest: Allen & Unwin.

Harlan, V. (1940), *Jud Süss,* Germany: Terra Film.

Herzog, W. (2005), *Grizzly Man*, Germany and USA: Discovery Docs and Lions Gate Films.

Irigaray, L. (1977), *Ce Sexe qui n'en est pas un*, Paris: Editions de minuit.

Jardin, A. (1985), *Gynesis: Configurations of Woman and Modernity*, Ithaca: Cornell University Press.

de Lauretis, T. (1987), *Technologies of Gender*, Bloomington: Indiana University Press.

Laqueur, T. (1993), *Making Sex: Body and Gender from the Greeks to Freud*, New Haven: Harvard University Press.

Lévis-Strauss, C. (1969), *Elementary Structures of Kinship* (orig. *Les structures élémentaires de la parenté*, 1949), Boston: Beacon Press.

——— (1974), *Structural Anthropology* (orig. *Anthropologie Structurale*, 1958), New York: Basic Books.

Lorraine, T. (1999), *Irigaray and Deleuze: Experiments in Visceral Philosophy*, Ithaca: Cornell University Press.

——— (2011), *Deleuze and Guattari's Immanent Ethics: Theory, Subjectivity and Duration*, New York: SUNY Press.

Pinkola Estés, C. (1992), *Women Who Run with the Wolves: Myths and Stories of the Wild Woman Archetype*, New York: Ballantine Books.

Rogin, M. (1998), *Blackface, White Noise: Jewish Immigrants in the Hollywood Melting Pot*, Oakland: University of California Press.

Ryan, D. (2013), 'The reality of becoming: Deleuze, woolf and the territory of cows', *Deleuze Studies*, 7:4, pp. 537–61.

Schrader, P. (1982), *Cat People*, USA: RKO Pictures and Universal Pictures.

Spielberg, S. (1975), *Jaws*, USA: Zanuck/Brown Productions.

Torneur, J. (1942), *Cat People*, USA: RKO Radio Pictures Inc.

Wallenberg, L. (2013), 'Fashion photography, phallocentrism and feminist critique', in J. Hancock, T. Johnson-Woods and V. Karaminas (eds), *Fashion in Popular Culture: Literature, Media and Contemporary Studies*, Bristol: Intellect, pp. 135–53.

Notes

1   This intimate relationship is perhaps most clearly represented in Native American cultures in the naming of men and women as animals, hence via the naming upheaving the border between human being and animal. There are animal names in Western cultures as well, but these are fewer. Examples within a Scandinavian context would be Björn (Swedish for Bear), Falk (Swedish for Falcon) and Varg (Norwegian for Wolf).

2   For descriptions of this trope in fairy tales, see Clarissa Pinkola Estés, (1992), *Women Who Run with the Wolves: Myths and Stories of the Wild Woman Archetype*.

3   It is during this epoch that the civilised, intellectual, rational and modern male subject gets positioned as if closer to God than the other categories – whom are being deemed closer to nature, and hence, to the animal kingdom (animalistic). It is now, during the late eighteen century, that the two-sex model is being introduced, following the timely 'discovery' of the female sex as entirely different from the male sex, which is positioned as norm. This dualist sexual difference – within which Woman is positioned as sex, and Man as human – soon becomes truth, and women are being classified as if they belong(-ed) to another species, different in every way from men in terms of physical and mental capacities. This discovery served to strengthen phallo(go)centric discourses, and left women as different, as *the* difference, from men. For a description of how sexual difference, that is the idea of two completely different and dualist sexes, is discovered and made into a single 'truth', see Thomas Laqueur (1993), *Making Sex: Body and Gender from the Greeks to Freud*.

4   According to Rene Descartes, the mental does not have extension in space, and the material cannot think.

5   See Swinton as the Marchesa for *ACNE Paper* in 2009 in a photo shoot by Paolo Roversi; Roitfeld photographed as the Marchesa by Karl Lagerfeld for *The New Yorker* in 2003; and Chapman as the Marchesa shoot by Peter Lindbergh for *Harper's Bazaar* in 2009.

6   Anthropomorphism has ancient roots as a literary device in storytelling (as fables), but also in art, and refers to animals acting like humans, or to humans having animal traits. See for example, *Aesop's Fables* from the sixth century BCE, and the Indian *Jataka Tales*, which employ anthropomorphized animals to illustrate principles of human life. See also the more recent anthropomorphic fairy tales by the Grimm Brothers; Rudyard Kipling's *The Jungle Book*; or Lewis Carroll's *Alice in Wonderland*.

7   For an overview of anthropomorphized animals in animated film from the early twentieth century and on, see Stéphane Collignon (2008), 'They walk! They talk! A study of the

anthropomorphisation of non-human characters in animated films', *Animatrix: A Journal of the UCLA Animation Workshop*, issue 16.

8   By reading apparently misogynistic images through this Deleuzian prism, I wish – in the long run – to also turn the female other towards the male self, hopefully opening up for a possible realm of *sexual indifference* – or what Deleuze would label polysexuality (and what I believe Derrida once labelled *asexuality*).

9   This relatively new fad in pet culture has been covered by several documentaries made for television. See for example, *The Elephant in the Living Room* (Michael Webber, 2010) and *Animal Odd Couples* (BBC1, 2013). Keeping wild animals as pets, is however nothing new: certain celebrities have kept wild animals as part of their self-presentations, the already mentioned Marchesa Luisa Casati and the entertainer Josephine Baker were known also for their infatuation with wild animals.

10 Having said that, I still think that there is an interesting connection between 'becoming animal' and the latter two examples here given: both of these two phenomena express a longing for breaking out of, or away from, the constraints of normative humanity and the social, sexual, gendered and cultural pressure that proper humanity requires.

11 Derek Ryan writes: 'To dismiss Deleuze and Guattari as "the enemy" of animal studies is to fail to recognize how rare an example they provide in Western philosophy of an animal theory that accounts for both anthropomorphic and anthropocentric uses of animals at the same time as providing a line of flight from such anthropomorphic conceptualisations and anthropocentric arrangements' (Ryan 2013: 339–340).

12 As an example, Deleuze gives the work made by British painter Francis Bacon (1909–1992), who he claims is a painter, or portrayer, of heads, not of faces. Discussing Bacon's painted deformations, or dismantling technique (which is a technique of 'rubbing and brushing'), Deleuze writes 'In place of formal correspondence, what Bacon's painting constitutes is a *zone of indiscernibility or undecidability* between man and animal' (Deleuze 2003: 20). He continues: 'This objective zone of indiscernibility is the entire body, but the body insofar as it is flesh or meat. [...] Meat is the common zone of man and the beast, their zone of indiscernibility; it is a 'fact', a state where the painter identifies with the objects of his horror and his compassion' (Deleuze 2003: 20–21). It has rightly been argued that Lucien Freud's images have a 'becoming animal'-quality to them: indeed, Freud was very inspired by Bacon, but his paintings – and this is my own personal impression – are not covering the indiscernibility or the undecidability between human being and animal as much as they are ample, yet aesthetic, investigations of human flesh(-iness) and the human body in its most naked condition. Whereas Bacon's paintings seam to *roar* – more than they seem to scream, Freud's paintings are indeed quiet, if you can hear anything, then it would the slow breathing of the models (and the painter himself, partly hidden behind the canvas).

13 Irigaray, especially in her earlier work, offers a poststructuralist philosophy on sexual difference – a sexual difference theory – and positions herself as a philosopher 'whose starting premise is the non-unitary vision of the subject' (Braidotti 2003: 43).

14 It is also a body and it is embodied. And Braidotti, following Irigaray, argues that 'the body, or the embodiment of the subject, is a key term in the feminist struggle for the redefinition of

subjectivity' (Braidotti 2003: 44). The body as interface, as 'a threshold, a field of intersecting material and symbolic forces, it is a surface where multiple codes (race, sex, class, age, etc.) are inscribed: it's a cultural construction that capitalizes on the energies of a heterogeneous, discontinuous and unconscious nature' (Braidotti 2003: 44).

15 'The fact that the notion of "difference" as pejorative goes to the heart of the European history of philosophy and of the "metaphysical cannibalism" of European thought makes it a foundational concept' (Braidotti 2003: 45). 'One of the aims of feminist practice therefore is to overthrow the pejorative, oppressive connotations that are built not only into the notion of difference, but also into the dialectics of Self and Other' (Braidotti: 2003: 45).

16 Here, Braidotti suggests that to get out from, out of the phallo(go)centric definitions of Woman, made up by patriarchy and by its emphasis on difference, we need to work through the images and representations that positions and help create Woman and the feminine as Other. She here relies on Irigaray's strategy of mimesis: women must speak the feminine, they must think it, write it and represent it in their own terms.

Chapter 12

Fragile Fashion: The Paper Dress as Art and Visual Consumption

Viveka Kjellmer

A period gown from the 1800s, made of hand-wrinkled floral paper, a candy wrapper corset and a dress made from black streamers – what can objects like these tell us about identity and fashion consumption? This chapter discusses fashion as art in relation to its role as a cultural statement and means of expressing identity and contemporary issues such as responsible consumption and sustainability, by studying the work of three Scandinavian designers: Bea Szenfeld from Sweden, Annette Meyer from Denmark and Virpi Vesanen-Laukkanen from Finland. Their garments, created as works of art in perishable or discarded materials, explore fashion as visual expression in relation to concepts such as functionality and wearability. Paper dresses raise questions about consumption, durability and the ephemeral aspects of fashion. Based on a theoretical discussion of clothing as cultural artefacts, a number of artworks made from controversial materials are analysed in terms of what I call *visual couture* – fashion as visual communication – further strengthened by the staging of the collections as museum exhibitions in the public domain (see also Kjellmer 2012).

Three Scandinavian Designers

To examine the paper dress as artistic expression in a contemporary context, I discuss three Scandinavian artists and fashion designers. All three works based on paper collections from different perspectives and their collections illustrate aspects of identity and consumption.

Annette Meyer's *Icon Dressed:* The Iconography of Fashion

Annette Meyer (b. 1966) works with paper to create something seemingly different. In her work, paper becomes a bearer of form as she explores the iconography of fashion through her collection *Icon Dressed*. Using thick, hand-wrinkled paper with floral print, she designs garments, each one typical of a historical era.

    Icon Dressed consists of fourteen mannequins with dresses characteristic of the eras they represent in fashion history, from 1800 to 1990. The mannequins have period hairstyles and make-up but no jewellery, shoes or bags. It is the form of the garments that is in focus (Meyer 2011a). The material is heavyweight paper of a type commonly used for packaging. It is wrinkled and processed by hand to get a soft, textile quality. The floral print comes from Flora Danica, a collection of botanical posters produced between 1761 and 1883. The illustrations are the result of a scientific survey and depict the entire Danish flora (Dahl 2007: 71–73). Flora Danica represents the Enlightenment fascination with science and knowledge but can also be seen as a sign of timeless beauty and good taste. It was from Flora Danica that the tableware of the same name, produced for the Danish royal court, took its well-known patterns. The print patterns in *Icon Dressed* are a direct reference to the tableware, down to the golden edging of the porcelain. The choice of paper instead of fabric is central to the work. As Meyer says:

> That's when they become objects. Like sculptures – and you see them with new eyes. Had I chosen fabric, they would have been clothing and the whole point would be lost.
>
> (Lindén Ivarsson 2008: 64)

Music that was specially composed adds an auditory dimension to the exhibition. The exhibition also includes displays, the so-called lenticular images, where the dresses are depicted from six different angles, photographed when worn by real women. All the facets of the dresses can be glimpsed at the same time, and the focus of the image changes when the observer moves sideways creating an illusion of movement (Jacobi 2007: 69). The

Figure 1: *Icon Dressed* by Annette Meyer at the Röhsska Design Museum. Photograph by Mikael Lammgård.

exhibition is an overall experience with static visuals playing a prominent role, but is also complemented by the music and the movement of the lenticular screens. The painstakingly kneaded paper surfaces contribute a tactile impression of materiality, even though visitors may not touch the artworks.

Icon Dressed premiered in 2007 consisting of mannequins arranged in two rows, face-to-face, thus constituting an avenue through which visitors passed. [1] Behind the mannequins on the walls the lenticular screens were hung, like large mirrors, on which the dresses were reproduced from different angles. The screens added depth to the room, and balanced the high cathedral ceilings in the church-like venue. Because the mannequins were not mounted on podiums but stood directly on the floor, face to face with the audience, an interaction was created between exhibition and visitors. The mannequins mingled with the audience as at an imaginary reception, and the optical illusions of the lenticulars strengthened the impression that the dresses on display were also moving in the room.

Although Annette Meyer's *Icon Dressed* seems to be about creating historical dresses in paper, this aim is not an accurate depiction. Meyer seeks not to recreate actual costumes, but to use the forms of historical fashion as part of an artistic exploration of body and identity in relation to time. Creating all the garments from the same kind of paper shifts the focus from their material to their form. Using a timeless print that also bears its own meanings of science, beauty and cultural sophistication ties the collection together, making the garments all part of a recognizable whole. Meyer's dresses become prototypes, form icons for a fashion story in which the garments are lifted out of their historical contexts and re-created in a new one. The garments become objects, artefacts that can be considered individually, which also take on new meanings when viewed together as a statement about clothing, women's bodies and appearance and fashion as a marker of identity as well as time. Through Meyer's work we are forced to reflect over how much of our identity resides in the garments we wear and how our perception of form and style changes over time. Equally, through her form icons, Meyer explores the concepts of timeless and time-bound, while also highlighting the aspect of recycling. The forms of fashion are constantly recycled – cuts, skirt lengths and other details are cited and referenced in everlasting cycles. Essentially, Meyer's iconic dresses direct attention to the whole versus the details provoking further questions such as, what links a garment to a particular era? Or, what is time-bound and what is timeless?

Meyer has long been interested in issues relating to global consumer society. Since 1998 she has been working with BODYWRAPPInc. clothing collections made of mass-produced packaging materials collected from around the world (Meyer 2011b). By making garments from potato crisp bags, for example, she indicates the similarities between fashion and product packaging. The function is basically the same: the crisp bag should say something about the product it contains, just as clothes should communicate something about the wearer's personality.

Icon Dressed can be seen as an extension of BODYWRAPPInc. In 2012 both collections were exhibited together at Trapholt Museum, Denmark (Trapholt Museum 2014). *Icon Dressed* is also about the body, and clothing as packaging, although the dresses are not literally made of discarded packaging. Instead, the body is wrapped in dresses of packaging paper, decorated with a pattern that signifies science, cultural heritage and refinement. The forms come from western fashion history and speak of how women's bodies have been shaped by fashion during the past 200 years. The exhibition problematizes the female body as an object, elegantly wrapped in floral wrapping paper. Ultimately, the exhibition is about identity. As a viewer, I am forced to think of myself as partly shaped by the clothes that I wear, and to ask what parts of my identity that reside in the packaging, and can be removed and thrown away as easily as wrapping paper.

Virpi Vesanen-Laukkanen's *Candy Wrapper Corsets:* Consumption and Recycling

Virpi Vesanen-Laukkanen (b. 1957) creates glamorous garments out of discarded and rejected materials. In the collection, *Candy Wrapper Corsets,* she transforms wastepaper into delicious corsets worked in shiny tinfoil. *Carla* is an example of such a corset. It is a life-sized garment that could be worn by a woman of average height. At first glance, the

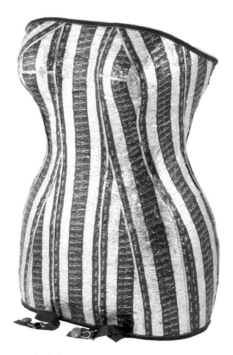

Figure 2: *Carla* by Virpi Vesanen-Laukkanen from the collection *Candy Wrapper Corsets.* Photograph by Mikael Lammgård.

rigid corset appears to be covered with a metallic shimmering textile in blue and gold, but on closer inspection the material turns out actually to be chocolate wrappers from Fazer Confectionery. The bodice is entirely covered with hundreds of candy wrappers, forming a longitudinal stripe pattern. The wrappers create a slightly wrinkled shiny metallic surface. Narrow, decorative gold textile ribbon covers the seams. Along the bottom edge of the corset are four black elastic suspenders with gold buckles. The top and bottom edges of the corset are covered with deep blue silk ribbons that lend a smooth finish to the shiny, hard corset surface. The inside of the garment is lined with the same type of candy wrappers and on the back there is a lacing of narrow gold-coloured silk ribbon strung crosswise through golden loops. The lacing is purely decorative; the corset will not open, and is not a wearable garment.

The rigid form of the corset can be read as having an ambiguous symbology. It encloses the body and forces it into a given shape. The corset shapes the woman after a perfect curvy template, forcing her to display a socially and culturally acceptable figure. At the same time, the hard shell is a cover that can be seen as defending against hostile glances from the outside world. No one knows what really hides behind the shiny surface of the corset. It can also be interpreted as a mask for those to wear who do not live up to the fixed standards of womanhood. Vesanen-Laukkanen's works focuses on a female world circumscribed by expectations and cultural conventions. Taking chocolate as a powerful metaphor for the most forbidden – an irresistible craving for candy – the artist provokes questions about what things a woman may treat herself to, and what expectations govern how she should look. The chocolate wrapper corset is both saviour and destroyer at the same time – the same forbidden chocolates that tempt us with their sweetness serve as a means for us to conceal our gluttony.

Carla is part of *Candy Wrapper Corsets* (2006), a collection of corsets made from candy wrappers sewn and glued to a paper backing. Some corsets have a single ribbon at the bottom; others end with a small frill. All the corsets are fitted with stocking suspenders complete with buckles. *Marianne* consists of red-and-white striped wrappers from the mint chocolate candy of the same name. The red-and-white striped corset is decorated with blue-and-white chequered ribbon, folded into a small frill at corset's bottom edge. *Angelica* is a silver corset with a green and golden brown pattern, lined with a double frill both at the bottom and along the neckline and straps. *Josephine* is coloured spectacular gold with black trim. Sugary sweet *Amanda* is a bit longer, more of a mini-dress than a corset, and ends at mid-thigh, lined with a wide frill. The colours are a symphony in pink and purple, the ruffles are light green with a pattern of daisies, and the light-green silk shoulder straps are decorated with a fabric rose in pastel pink (Vesanen-Laukkanen 2011).

When these corsets are exhibited as a collection, they make an almost supernatural impression, floating in the air, hanging from invisible threads (Vesanen-Laukkanen 2011). Together, they become a group of invisible women populating the room. Viewing the pictures from the exhibition, I see the group as a fairy-tale reference to Finnish writer Tove Jansson's story, *The Invisible Child* (1962). In the story, the invisible girl Ninni becomes visible when she encounters love and respect, when she is treated like a person. Only when she dares to show her anger, does her face become visible. The anger is the force that makes Ninni visible as an individual. With the help of this fairy tale, the corsets become an image of all invisible women who have to display their anger to be seen. They also become a metaphor for silence as a straitjacket, for a cultural view of women as ornamental and unheard. Meanwhile, women's roles are problematized through the chocolate wrappers, representing the conflict between the desire for the forbidden and the need to be unwavering. The choice presented here is yield or resist. The shape of the corset and its associations with a prison, protection or a mask – but also to sexuality and woman as temptation – gives the installation significance with many layers. The beautiful shiny corsets can be regarded as a powerful expression whose meaning is far from what the fragile, glittering surface initially suggests.

Virpi Vesanen-Laukkanen explores a complex world of demands and wishes, guilt and longing. The requirement to present a perfect, shiny exterior seems to conflict with the desire for the forbidden, the shameful pleasure of enjoying something for one's own sake. She points to the perception of women as decorative objects and shows how personality and anger are required if one is to be seen and claim space. The taboo chocolates are resurrected in the form of a corset, as a tool to shape the female body. The consumed sweets become a dress of shiny tinfoil, a beautiful gift box for the female body, which also turns into a magnificent and tempting treat.

Bea Szenfeld's *Paper Dolls:* Fashion as Installation

The paper dress as art is demonstrated spectacularly by Bea Szenfeld (b. 1972) in her collection *Paper Dolls,* which is all about unwearable garments and clothing as art in several senses. *Paper Dolls* from 2006 is Szenfeld's first collection of paper dresses. The entire collection consists of six dresses, with pins attached directly to black torsos resembling tailor's dummies. The material is paper of different qualities, colours and textures. *Miss Garland* is made from colourful garlands in white, red and orange tissue paper, *Mademoiselle Odette* is made of white paper bags and *Miss Gâteau* is built up of white lace-patterned cake-paper circles. The material of *Miss Wanda* is hand-wrinkled crème-coloured tissue paper, and *Lady Manual* is created from a history book and a magazine. *Madame Noire* is a dress made of black streamers (Szenfeld 2011a).

The black *Madame Noire* has a restrained character, despite the curly untidiness of the streamers in the dress skirt. The dress is made up of 213 metres of black streamers, 183 pins and 63 coffee filters. The bodice is tailored with a surface that gives the impression of pleats, where the narrow streamer strips are mounted close together. The dress is figure hugging, high-necked and sleeveless. The skirt fits tightly around the hips and widens into a wavy mass of streamers. The high collar is made of large industrial coffee filters, their recycled brown colour contrasting with the glossy jet-black finish of the streamers. The wavy hourglass shape of the collar makes the neck the obvious focus of the garment. Within the

Figure 3: *Madame Noire* by Bea Szenfeldt, from the collection *Paper Dolls*. Photograph by Ann-Katrin Blomqvist.

tight form of the black dress a conversation about form and structure takes place between the parallel strips of the streamers and the unruly curls of the skirt.

Bea Szenfeld's work has a lot to do with experimenting and showcasing the expressive possibilities of paper as material (Szenfeld 2011a). By letting the material bear these variations, she frees herself to focus on the form-related aspects of her work and creates relations between the individual garments and the collection as a whole. The collection covers a full range of colours and forms, from black to white and bright red, from tight and angular to organic, swelling forms. The dresses have a strong vintage feel in their shapes, if not in the material. While not actual period replicas, it is easy to imagine them in stiff silk taffeta or airy chiffon. Szenfeld chooses fashion as an expressive medium and pushes the boundary between clothing and art. *Paper Dolls* is art and fashion at the same time, or rather, the image of fashion in the form of paper dresses, a hand-cut feast for the eyes on a doll's body. Indeed, Szenfeld has continued working in paper in several collections after *Paper Dolls*. In *Whatever Forever*, from 2008, she further examines paper's material properties, creating imaginative garments out of layer after layer of shredded and sliced paper. The sculptural garments get a distinctive tactile quality from the paper's unexpected structures.

Neptune's Daughter is a playful swimsuit collection, with swimmer and movie star Esther Williams inspiring Szenfeld. The aquatic theme returns in *Sur la Plage,* a poetic study of possible and impossible manifestations of paper. *Sur la Plage* is inspired by the ocean and life below the surface. Szenfeld calls the collection 'haute papier' and emphasizes its visual and tactile qualities (Szenfeld 2011a). Outfits with fish scale-like sequins, giant necklaces of paper beads, lace collars and a jacket with a surface like a coral reef compose an evocative collection of garments and accessories.

Bea Szenfeld comments on the transience of fashion in her own way. When she works in paper, a non-durable material, the impermanence is tied to material rather than form. Szenfeld does not work with seasonal collections but designs garments that are beyond fashion trends. Her objects are artworks that are intended to be viewed for a long time in a museum context – highlighting sustainable development, despite the material's impermanence. She creates fashion that is not fashion, art that borrows its means of expression from the fashion world.

The Meanings of the Paper Dress and Identity Construction

To find answers to my initial questions, I examine clothes as bearers of identity and meaning, and fashion as art and visual consumption. I link my discussion to fashion in a museum context and anchor it in my analyses of the artworks studied.

How can we understand the image of fashion and, by extension, the role of the paper dress from the perspective of identity formation? In a study of image consumption and popular culture, Joanne Finkelstein discusses the concepts of identity and staging. She claims that popular culture is often based on the idea of illusion and that we accept this basic requirement in our daily consumption of images, film, advertising and other forms of visual expression. In the movie, the nerdy journalist is actually a superhero; in the book, the mistreated orphan boy gets revenge as a magician. In advertising, the overweight housewife becomes as glamorous as a movie star with plastic surgery. Illusion is a constant feature of everyday life. Accustomed to the idea that there are several layers of meaning, and that no one is what they appear to be, we also accept the idea that identity is negotiable. Although a core of our true selves remains somewhere, the surface and the mediated identity are always changing (Finkelstein 2007: 1–3). Finkelstein shows how we, through media and visual culture, get used to regarding appearance as synonymous with identity. She writes: 'Spectatorship cultivated through cinema, art, theatre and fashion has conventionalized the visual representation of identity. This emphasis on appearances provides a ready means for fabricating and popularizing certain aspects of identity' (Finkelstein 2007: 129). Finkelstein elaborates on the seductive power of the visual in a reflection on the unreliability of the **image:** Each day involves a series of visual performances where I can, as I wish, mask an identity or produce an identity with the use of a mask (Finkelstein 2010: 166).

Through this constant consumption of visual representations, appearance becomes so closely linked to identity that they merge. This obviously also means that identity can be replaced through a change in appearance as an unwanted identity can literally be cut away with the plastic surgeon's scalpel.

Consuming images becomes equal to testing new, possible expressions of identity. Fashion and fashion images are important players in this game of identity formation. Finkelstein calls fashion a classification system in which status, identity and social position can be read and constructed (Finkelstein 2007: 213–15). Applying Finkelstein's discussion of the concepts of identity and visual culture, the consumption of images can be understood as identity formation. Fashion images or reflections on fashion are as important in the construction of identity as the physical garment. This causes the garment's wearability or durability to be of less interest; a fashion installation made of paper serves the same function as, say, a fashion photograph or sketch. Paper dresses on display in a museum context can thus be understood as expressing both fashion and identity. Staging identity on imaginary bodies, they provide visual inspiration and add another piece to the ongoing construction of identity.

The Paper Dress as Visual Consumption

Nicholas Mirzoeff, who has long been interested in the field of 'visual culture', states that it is not very important what form the visual message takes; what matters is the communicative process between the viewer and the viewed. This he calls a 'visual event' (Mirzoeff 1999: 13). Mirzoeff shifts the focus from the medium itself to the visual event, the exchange between the viewer and the work. He thus paves the way for a broader definition of 'image', one that can include anything from traditional examples like drawings and paintings to digital images transmitted via television, film or the Internet, or other forms of visual expression, which can include such spatial experiences as a theatre performance, a museum visit or even a fashion show. Further, he points out that visual culture is a discipline where the focus lies on studying the experience from the consumer's rather than the producer's point of view (Mirzoeff 1999: 3). Put differently, visual culture can be understood as the study of visual consumption.

In a later edition of the book, Mirzoeff states that the discipline of visual culture is now so well established that he no longer needs to defend it. Instead, he highlights what he believes to be the distinguishing feature of the study of visual culture: the ability to abandon an object-based approach and instead compare media of different types and natures. Mirzoeff writes: 'It compares the means by which cultures visualize themselves in forms ranging from the imagination to the encounters between people and visualized media' (2009: 1). Instead of splitting the visual arts into different disciplines or fields depending on the medium used, we can get an overall picture in which new patterns emerge.

Jonathan Schroeder defines consumption as 'the allocation of time to activities – activities in which the consumer's lifestyle and identity is constructed, largely via images' (Schroeder 2002: 40). Schroeder's definition of consumption is interesting because it concerns time rather than objects. Consumption is understood more broadly as including choice and identity formation. It is not only about the selection of objects, but also about our choice of what to spend time on. Consumption can be described in terms of consuming time, rather than merely the products we buy. With a concept of consumption that includes time, there is no difference between window-shopping and 'real' shopping – both are equally valid expressions of consumption. This also means that cultural consumption – such as visiting museums – is equivalent to the consumption of goods, with the focus in that case shifted from physical purchasing to visual consumption.

Compare this to Mirzoeff's definition of a visual event, which is about the communication process between the viewer and the viewed. From the consumer's perspective, a visual event is identical with the visual consumption of images and experiences. Schroeder also shows that we live through images and how visual consumption can replace real consumption of both objects and experiences. Showing and discussing travel photographs is a way to establish a personality as a traveller or adventurer, and the images contribute to this identity formation (Schroeder 2002: 172). But, the viewer is also involved in the creation of identity: I do not need to make the trips myself; looking at my friends' pictures and discussing their trips is enough to establish myself as a person interested in travelling. Identity formation through visual consumption functions similarly in other fields: I do not have to wear the garment myself; reading fashion magazines or watching fashion shows on the Internet is enough to establish myself as a fashion-conscious person who can join the fashion discourse in a meaningful way.

'Visual consumption characterizes life in the information age' says Schroeder, claiming that images are a prerequisite for our modern consumer society (Schroeder 2002: 172). His point is that since visual consumption is such an important part of our identity formation, images and image analysis are effective tools for understanding our consumer culture. I would add that one could take this a step further and say not only that images provide a key for understanding the world, but the image, in the broadest sense, constructs the world as we know it. There is no longer a clear distinction between 'image' and 'reality'; image is a part of reality, and we handle images as easily as physical objects or experiences in creating our lives.

Mirzoeff shows that the concept of the image can be broadened to include all types of visual events. In addition to traditional two-dimensional images, visual experiences and the viewing of events, extended in both time and space, can be understood as images. What matters is the exchange between the viewer and the viewed. Thus, an exhibition serves as an excellent example of a visual event, and visiting a museum is a form of visual consumption.

A paper dress can be consumed visually on equal terms with a garment intended to be worn on the body. I stress this point by calling the objects of this visual consumption 'visual couture'. The medium is not important; the key is the communication involved in the viewing process. An artistic fashion installation, just like any fashion image, can contribute to an intellectual exchange with the viewer. Identity is created through visual consumption of impressions as well as consumption of physical goods. The fragile transience of the paper dress rather reinforces its status as a visual consumption object, i.e. visual couture.

The Paper Dress in a Museum Context

A common view is that garments should not necessarily be studied as objects in fashion research. The garment itself is usually not considered fashion because fashion is a phenomenon characterized by the interplay between body, movement and clothing (Dahl 2007: 71). Fashion at a museum would therefore, by definition, no longer be fashion. What is it then? Is it 'object', 'artefact' or still 'fashion' even though it is displayed in a museum? I would argue that it really does not matter: perhaps the question is not whether the object can still be seen as fashion, but whether it can *say something about fashion*. To the latter question, the answer is definitely yes. Through visual consumption, an object, as an image, can say something about fashion. It does not have to be wearable: it does not need to interact with the body – it can just as well interact with the viewer's mind. The garment is not worn, but it still awakens something in the viewer. The viewer appropriates the viewed; identity formation occurs through visual consumption.

Discussing the museum's role as a venue for fashion, Fiona Anderson claims that in the museum context there need not be any contradiction between the perception of fashion as 'object' and 'image'. She writes: 'The use of representations and a focus on garments as objects need not be contradictory, but can in fact be highly complementary and even revelatory' (Anderson 2000: 376). Anderson takes advertising as an example, observing that the particular garment, as an object in a museum, may well be supplemented by images from an advertising campaign, and that this can provide a broader, more complex picture of the collection or the designer's work as a whole. She finds that there has been a shift away from the view that the museum is a neutral zone where the garment is lifted from its context and exhibited as an artefact (Anderson 2000: 376–79).

Marie Riegels Melchior shows how the perception of fashion exhibitions has changed over time. She introduces the concepts of 'dress museology' and 'fashion museology', the former representing the older view, where fashion collections mainly focused on fashion history, materials and techniques. Fashion museology, on the other hand, refers to the contemporary view of fashion exhibitions that has become especially prominent since the late 1990s, with the emergence of specialized fashion museums and exhibitions staged as spectacular events conveying moods and conceptual experiences rather than substantive facts about individual garments. When fashion museology takes hold, a fashion museum's main interest shifts from backstage activities such as collecting and preserving to front-stage public events focusing on visual experience and mediated emotions (Riegels Melchior 2014: 6–14).

In summary, an exhibition makes just as biased a statement as any fashion show or advertising campaign. Instead of primarily collecting and preserving, the fashion museum's task is to participate in the fashion discourse and make critical statements in the form of exhibitions and events. Fashion museology creates a forum for visual consumption of fashion that gives museums an opportunity to participate in the fashion debate on equal terms as other fashion-related media.

Conclusion: Visual Couture

This chapter shows that identity is perceived as negotiable and as strongly tied to appearance, with fashion playing an important role. Visual consumption can be a way to try out new expressions of identity; hence looking at fashion in various forms can be understood as an essential part of identity construction.

Fashion can be viewed as a means to create identity through consumption, though not necessarily only by purchasing the garments. If consumption is defined in terms of time rather than just objects, visual consumption is as valid as physical consumption. Fashion may just as well be consumed when staged on another's body – the model on the catwalk or the imaginary body in an art installation.

By applying Nicholas Mirzoeff's definition of a visual event as the communication process between the viewer and the viewed, consumption of visual experiences or pictures can be regarded as visual consumption. Mirzoeff's concept of the visual makes it possible to expand the idea of the 'image' to include all types of visual events. I conclude that a fashion installation is a visual event and that seeing the exhibition in a museum is a form of visual consumption.

I have shown that visual consumption of fashion is about the act of viewing and the seeking of information; that it is not necessarily about owning things but about owning knowledge – or, in other words, connoisseurship. Through seeing exhibitions and visually consuming artistic works that highlight new aspects of fashion, this knowledge is extended even further.

Anderson's view that an exhibition is just as biased a statement as a fashion show or an advertising campaign gives the museum a new role. It becomes yet another arena where fashion is questioned and important discussions can take place. Applying Riegels Melchior's concept of fashion museology, according to which fashion shows are more about communicating conceptual experiences than detailed facts, further strengthens this view. With this approach the meaning of the garments is shifted from 'dress' to 'fashion', and as a phenomenon fashion can be visually conveyed in a museum context. In light of these perspectives, the paper-dress collections studied can be understood in a broader sense than merely as cultural artefacts or art installations in a museum. They question our perceptions of fashion and consumption by focusing on three important themes: body, time and identity.

Annette Meyer's *Icon Dressed* focuses on clothing as body packaging. Within the framework of Western fashion history, she highlights how women's bodies have been shaped over time along with changes in fashion. The body as object is problematized in this collection of floral paper dresses, presented as gift packages. *Icon Dressed* questions the intersection between identity and fashion. Can our identity be removed like a garment and be replaced with a new, more fashionable one? How much of our inner self is connected to the exterior, the body's packaging?

Virpi Vesanen-Laukkanen's *Candy Wrapper Corsets* is about women's lives, where external demands for perfection oppose the desire to claim space and allow pleasure for oneself. Chocolate is a powerful symbol of guilt and enjoyment. In this work the chocolate wrapper represents the packaging of both the forbidden pleasure and the woman's body.

Questions about women's consumption and delight are pitted against adaptation to society's expectations. What role does fashion play for the woman's body as a decorative item? How should we relate to fashion consumption, viewed in light of Vesanen-Laukkanen's guilt/pleasure dichotomy? How much of what we consume is an expression of our own identity and how much is an adaptation to prevailing conditions and trends?

Bea Szenfeld's *Paper Dolls* is a comment on the transiency of fashion expressed by means of material rather than form. Szenfeld uses the language of paper to challenge our perception of fashion and the everyday objects that surround us. Where do you draw the line between fashion and art, between usable everyday objects and decoration? In Bea Szenfeld's world, nothing is what it seems, and this challenges us to reconsider our view of what fashion can and should be.

Together, the three collections represent one aspect of what fashion in a museum context may be: visual couture for visual consumption, a critical statement within the discussion about fashion and identity formation. The purpose of this study was to explore, in the work of three Scandinavian artists, how paper dresses can be understood as art and as expressions of identity, and to discuss what this might say about fashion as visual consumption. To return to the introductory questions, I have shown that fashion can indeed be an effective means of artistic expression even if the garments cannot be worn. Consumption need not be physical, but can consist of viewing (see Wallenberg in this volume). The wearability of the garment is not decisive; in this context the important thing is the identity formation that occurs through visual consumption (see Tseëlon in this volume).

Furthermore, I find that the transformation a garment undergoes in a museum context is not about losing significance, but about gaining a new, expanded meaning. When the garment becomes an artistic object and can no longer be worn, it may no longer be usable in the physical sense, but remains so symbolically. As visual couture, the garment continues to communicate with the viewer, whether it was originally designed as wearable clothing or specifically created for an exhibition context where wearability is of secondary or no concern.

The paper dress is visual couture in its most extreme form. As a work of art, a paper dress clearly shows fashion's role in identity construction through visual consumption. Being exhibited in a museum enhances fashion's visual and unattainable aspects. Precisely because it is visual couture, an artefact and not a wearable garment, its statement is even more apparent. The paper dress interacts with the viewer beyond the physical domain, and is able to raise critical rhetorical questions about body, identity and fashion consumption.

References

Anderson, F. (2000), 'Museums as fashion media', *Fashion Cultures: Theories, Explorations and Analysis*, in S. Bruzzi and P. Church Gibson (eds), London and New York: Routledge, pp. 371–89.

Dahl, C. L. (2007), 'Icon dressed', in A. Meyer (ed.), *Icon Dressed*, Frederiksberg: S.I. Annette Meyer, pp. 71–77.

Finkelstein, J. (2007), *The Art of Self Invention: Image and Identity in Popular Visual Culture*, London and New York: I.B. Tauris.

—— (2010), 'Fashioned identity and the unreliable image', *Critical Studies in Fashion and Beauty*, 1:2, pp. 161–71.

Icon Dressed (2007), in A. Meyer (ed.), Frederiksberg: S.I. Annette Meyer.

Jacobi, F. (2007), 'The shape of things to come', in A. Meyer (ed.), *Icon Dressed*, Frederiksberg: S.I. Annette Meyer, p. 69.

Jansson, T. (1962), *Det osynliga barnet och andra berättelser* (*The Invisible Child and Other Stories*), Stockholm: Gebers.

Kjellmer, V. (2012), 'Visuell Couture. Om pappersklänningar och betraktandets konsumtion' ('Visual couture. On paper dresses and visual consumption'), in B. Mankell and P. Dahlström (eds), *Modets bildvärldar. Studier i Röhsska museets modesamling (Images of Fashion. Studying the Fashion Collection at the Röhsska Design Museum)*, Göteborg: Röhsska museet, pp. 14–41, 196–99.

Lindén Ivarsson, A.-S. (2008), 'Mode i pappersskrud' ('Paper fashion'), *Röhsska 07, Röhsska museet för mode, design och konstslöjd. Årsbok 2007* (*Röhsska 07. The Röhsska Design Museum Yearbook 2007*), Göteborg: Röhsska museet, pp. 62–65.

Meyer, A. (2011a), *Icon Dressed*, http://www.annettemeyer.com/fashion_art_concepts/icon_dressed.html. Accessed 24 July 2011.

—— (2011b), *BODYWRAPPInc.*, http://annettemeyer.com/fashion_art_concepts/bodywrappinc.htm. Accessed 9 October 2011.

Mirzoeff, N. (1999), *An Introduction to Visual Culture*, London and New York: Routledge.

—— (2009), *An Introduction to Visual Culture*, 2nd ed., London and New York: Routledge.

Riegels Melchior, M. (2014), 'Introduction: Understanding fashion and dress museology', In M. R. Melchior and B. Svensson (eds), *Fashion and Museums: Theory and Practice*, London, New Delhi, New York and Sydney: Bloomsbury, pp. 1–18.

Schroeder, J. E. (2002), *Visual Consumption*, London and New York: Routledge.

Szenfeld, B. (2011a), 'Haute papier', http://www.szenfeld.com/category/art-fashion/. Accessed 28 July 2011.

—— (2011b), 'News', http://www.szenfeld.com/category/news/. Accessed 28 July 2011.

Trapholt Museum (2014), *Icon Dressed/BODYWRAPPInc.*, http://www.trapholt.dk/udstillinger/udstillingsarkiv/2012/icon-dressedbody-wrappinc/. Accessed 5 July 2014.

Vesanen-Laukkanen, V. (2011), http://www.harakka.fi/virpi/index.html. Accessed 8 May 2011.

Note

1 Exhibited at the Röhsska Design Museum, Gothenburg, Sweden, 2 June–9 September 2007.

Chapter 13

'O Brave New World That Hath Such Costumes in It': An Examination of Cosplay as Fantastical Performance

Anne Peirson-Smith

This chapter examines the creative and role-playing aspects of cosplay, or costume costume play (Japanese: *kosupure*), the emerging transglobal trend for young adults to periodically dress up in themed costumes assuming the persona of characters from contemporary Japanese comic books (manga), animated cartoons (anime), video, online games and popular bands. While some academic attention has been paid to the phenomenon of role-playing in the online game community (McGonigal 2005; Moore 2011), cosplay has remained largely under-researched from a performance studies and creativity perspective as a means of explaining its rationale.

Firstly, the chapter defines cosplay as role-play-based performance and analyses its creative expression through play, while also examining the role that creativity plays in facilitating this fantasy-based process. Subsequently, it addresses how members of the cosplay community creatively enact their costumed identities and transform their everyday selves by drawing on the combined resources of role-play-based interpretation, collaboration and multimodal expression in a cultural performance (Singer 1972; Bauman and Briggs 1990) of a spectacular self as a quasi-liminal or liminoid phenomena (Turner 1969).

Embodied creativity on display in the practice of cosplay operates as the ultimate expression of agency, identity and transgression in the context of remediated 'fantasyscapes' (Napier 2007: 137) built on the fluidity of global media cultures that they derive from, and their impact on global mediascapes (Appadurai 1996). The central argument presented here suggests that in this geographic location cosplay is an illustration of transcultural creative performance in action. While this trend is a rapidly growing global phenomenon, I also argue that certain aspects of the performance are universal – preparation, sourcing, dressing up, authenticity and communicating in real and virtual spaces. Yet, other ways in which the performance are 'keyed' (Goffman 1974) are culturally grounded, drawing to some extent on local performance traditions, while at the same time connecting with a globalized fantasy universe beyond considerations of ethnicity, sex, gender and nationality.

Performance as Creativity

Creativity can be defined as the ability to articulate a message through the bringing together of previously unrelated ideas, and to combine them in unique, but relevant ways. It can also be used to break set, challenge the status quo and find expression in hybrid, adapted, fantastical cultural forms. This aligns with Victor Turner's notion of the ability of the creative

Figure 1: Cosplayers at Hong Kong Cosplay and Anime Society Event. Photograph by Anne Peirson-Smith.

Figure 2: Cosplayer Mizuki at Hong Kong University Cosplay Event. Photograph by Anne Peirson-Smith.

situational performance to unlock 'clues to the very nature of the human process itself' wherein creativity 'emerges from the freedom of the performance situation' (Turner 1987: 7).

In essence, cosplay is far more than a routine dressing-up act, merely satisfying a passing fetish to enrobe the body in spectacular accessories for individual gratification, although that embodied practice can also be a subset of the affective fan-based experience. Principally, this is a social act enabling the player to gain self-knowledge and gratification through individual or collective role-play and exploration of identity in 'the fantastical presentation of self' (Peirson-Smith 2012: 77). This practice also resonates with Turner's notions about the transactional and reflexive nature of human perfomance, through which an actor gains self-knowledge by watching and participating in the performances of others (Turner 1982, 1987). Typical of any creative performance and expressive act, cosplay is also a collaborative exercise involving playful group work, requiring the presence of, and interaction with, a validating audience who add a broader communicative dimension to this identity-forming activity by sharing photos or commenting on costumes, either in real-time or via social networking sites.

The tenor of the practice is carnivalesque, occurring as an urban festival within specified time and spatial frames, temporarily disrupting and inverting everyday life through sanctioned, playful activity (Bakhtin 1968). By radically changing their appearance and behaviour through masquerading (Tseëlon 2001) in the public domain and by creatively appropriating Japanese and North American superhero culture in embodied material form, these players exercise control over their reworked and multiple identities. In this way, they are representing themselves creatively through a variety of personas based on affective connections. At the same time, the players are finding a sense of 'belonging' to a recognizable youth tribe or neo-tribe style (Mafessoli 1996) in an entertaining and playful way, premised on collaborative creative practices that actively involve both players and spectators.

The material for this chapter comes from an ethnographic study featuring in-depth interviews and participant observation of players in Hong Kong, Macau and Beijing. The sample comprised a mixture of over 40 participants, often professionally located in the creative and communication industries. The ethnographic, qualitative research approach adopted here is intended to represent the subjective realities of the players themselves in their own words (Willis 1980: 91).

Cosplay as Performance

A performance can be defined as an activity or event whereby an individual or group enact a situation for an audience in a given context, often using costumes and props to transform self and setting in the interests of representing a dramatic narrative. As Henry Bial explains:

> The term 'performance' most commonly refers to a tangible, bounded event that involves the presentation of rehearsed artistic actions [...]. We can extend this idea of a performance to other events that involve a performer (someone doing something) and a spectator (someone observing something).

> (Bial 2004: 57)

Every human action can be considered as a ubiquitous performance in itself (Burke 1945), because in the social interactionist frame, all life is a performance in the presentation of self (Goffman 1959). Yet, an exact understanding of what constitutes performance has proved to be both elusive, ambiguous and wide ranging, involving both performer and spectator (Schechner 1988).

The same difficulties apply in attempting to draw a distinction between the individual performances of everyday life and individual/collective theatrical performances on stage or between social and cultural performances in terms of process, function and intention. Equally, there are still shades of grey when we examine cosplay, as it appears to be occupying a liminal place between stage performance and the multiple presentations of self. The player assumes an embodied identity of a chosen fictional character that they identify with based on character affinity or appearance, occupying a transitional space and place in a fantasy land similar to online game players, live action role-players or re-enactment communities. As Daniel

Mackay noted of fantasy role-playing gamers: 'A new kind of performance space requires a new kind of performance and it follows a new kind of performer' (Mackay 2001: 3). But in terms of character embodiment the performance can be differentiated from other forms of character identification, through online game avatars, for example (Fron et al. 2007). Rather, cosplayers appear to be more physically and behaviourally aligned with their assumed costumed identities beyond the virtual manipulation of character through keyboard and screen.

Cosplayers, as cartoon or fan tribute characters, enact their assumed personas like actors, impersonators or drag artists (Butler 1990), making their creative endeavours publicly visible with 'life and theatre intermingled' (Thacker 2002: 1). In this sense, cosplay is a specific type of cultural role-based performance as the players individually and in teams transform their everyday appearance by donning the extraordinary garb of a chosen comic book character and enacting this persona in public settings. As with other genres of dramatic enactment, the scope and form of the performance varies across and within cultures. In other words, the performance frame and display will be 'keyed' (Goffman 1974) in different communicative ways according to the particular cultural location in which it occurs, reflecting a grounded, subjective understanding of the activity. The role performance aspect of cosplay also manifests itself on a sliding scale of dramatic presentation from the informal to the formal and institutionally sanctioned. This ranges from individuals and groups posing for photographs at public events in convention centre hallways (Lamerichs 2011) in the classic manner of a tableau vivant (Chapman 1992), to individuals and groups ambulating around conventions 'in character' (Andersen 2015). It also includes teams competitively performing Japanese pop song and dance routines and enacting traditional myths or manga and anime plot-lines on stage in front of a live audience and panel of judges, like a veritable 'Cosplayers Have Talent'.

The tendency for dramatic and social presentation to overlap or collide results in a transitory space where participants can tap into recognized systems of cultural meaning – in the form of popular archetypes – characters, themes and events. Here they can experiment with, and transform their identity in the affective, cognitive and conative process of sense-making on an individual and collective level. Hence, the imitative or mimetic human capacity (Tausig 1993) as a means of learning, surviving, comprehending, escaping, experimenting, engaging with or controlling the lived experience also underpins this cultural performance.

Cosplay as Creative Role-Play

As the central feature of cosplay is to physically mimic a chosen character in a set timeframe, the cultural performance is perhaps most accurately characterized as a form of role-play. All social interaction can be regarded as role-play in projecting varying identities for the approbation of others (Goffman 1959) both in the frame of fantasy and reality (Bateson 1955, 1972). As Jonathan Thacker (2002: 8) observes, 'individuals identify with and act like dramatic characters they have witnessed on stage [...] they learn roles and role play'.

Cosplayers usually perform the multiple identities of various fictional characters by transforming the self and actively playing out their subjective identities in public city spaces. Here they appear to replicate normative, imitative and playful human behaviour. It also has a make-believe focus (Caillois 1958), stemming from childhood's adventure play patterns through various stages of child development (Piaget 1951) as a way of sense-making, socializing or mastering control, or as a means of evading reality (Winnicott 1971). In addition to imparting key learning experiences, play itself can enable alternative and innovative fantasies, giving rise to, and inspiring new and creative cultural forms (Sutton-Smith 1997; Goldman 1998). Play as a form of mimicry or mimesis (Huizinga 1955) is also regarded as an essentially creative act, enabling the player to invent an alternative identity and existence.

Fundamentally, play can also be all about having fun and finding self-gratification through the act of playing. Certainly, from close observations of many players across various events, there is a party atmosphere, the air is full of laughter and high excitement and all of the players appear to be enjoying the carnivalesque experience to the full. As one informant explained, 'We all love dressing up in characters that we love and sharing that with each other […] it is like going to a big party – it's fun' (Syn, female cosplayer, Beijing, age 20, June 2009).

This opportunity to playfully and creatively transform and control the remediated self by assuming the persona of a fictional character within a shared demographic group may explain why cosplay is increasingly becoming popular in transglobal youth cultures, with the proviso that it manifests itself in localized and individualized interpretations.

Figure 3: Cosplayers perform on stage at 'Cosplay of the World' competitive event in Macau, 2014. Photograph by Anne Peirson-Smith.

Yet, cosplay is also a more complex activity than a surface analysis would suggest. Mikhail Bahktin noted the significance of play in the spectacle of the medieval carnival as 'the people's second life [...] on the basis of laughter' (1968: 198). There also lurks a more complex interpretation of play and role-play as 'inherently deceptive, built on pretence' (Thacker 2002: 4). It is also a means of occupying a liminoid leisure zone where the player can traverse accepted ways of being and behaving within prevailing social structures (Turner 1979). Cosplay as role-play offers scope for playing with socially constructed and performed roles of gender and propriety outside the restricting frames of masculinist domination and everyday appearance using accessories and costumes to masquerade 'a sort of visual performance through artefacts: a vehicle for constructing and deconstructing identities' (Turner 1982: 103). In a performative sense (Butler 1990), players are also 'cross-playing'. Hence, females often role-play male characters and vice versa, from simple articulations of fandom to public expressions of transgendered states. This represents challenges to socially prescribed ways of being, evoking hostility from social institutions in the form of moral panic in the media where cross-playing is often framed as deviant behaviour. Equally, the Asian cosplay community can often appear uncomfortable with open expressions of the gendered other. Performers across time, place and space have often been distrusted and maginalized, as Zygmunt Bauman (1977) observed, because of their potential for subversion, which in some senses also validates their marginal or neo-tribal role. Historically, masquerading has operated as a critical subversive strategy that at the same time conceals, reveals, challenges and protects the wearer. This creates spaces where participants can play out their fears and desires by assuming a masked disguise and transgressing rules, regulations and controls normally constraining the body (Tseëlon 2001).

Cosplay and the Transformed Creative Self

The conversion of self to represent embodied other is critical to the notion of role-play-based performance. It is argued here that the transformation process embedded in the cosplay act is implicitly creative because it involves the construction of an alternative persona by the player based on the appropriation and re-mixing of material objects to create costumes and props, followed by a public presentation set against incongruous urban liminal spaces (Turner 1974). This cultural and material appropriation and re-appropriation has parity with youth trends in other cultural locations across the late twentieth century. Hence, neo-style tribes (Mafessoli 1996) such as Goths, Punks, Emos and Skaters have creatively used clothing and body modification (Hebdige 1979; Williamson 2001; Hills 2002; Hodkinson 2002) to signal generational and aspirational difference (Polhemus 1994) by radically and overtly transforming their appearance, often consciously or unconsciously challenging the status quo and celebrating their marginalization. As with the Lolita style tribe, which is not a form of cosplay but is rather a fashion/lifestyle-oriented presentation of self, it can be argued that this extraordinary dressing up activity is not a mere replication of character from existing narrative sources (see Hardy Bernal in this volume). The recreated identity is perhaps more of a subversive parody with flexible and multi-layered meaning.

From personal observation of detailed outfits at events and conventions in Hong Kong and elsewhere, there is nothing 'rough and ready' or crude about the construction of the costumes. These are usually of a high professional standard in terms of the fabric used and the workmanship applied to create them, suggesting that the transformation from ordinary to spectacular self is all-encompassing. Take the case of Mitsuki, age 21, a Hong Kong female fashion student who likes to dress up as classical princess characters, such as Marie Antoinette from the shoujo manga, *Rose of Versailles*. For the purposes of the research project she was invited to dress up in her favourite cosplay character in a studio setting, enabling the author to observe this radical transformation process more closely. Mitsuki arrived at the studio, dressed casually in a white t-shirt and dark jeans, like any other normal young woman enjoying some downtime on a Saturday afternoon in the city. With her mid-length dark hair falling loosely on her shoulders held back from her petite face by a pair of black sunglasses, she looked strangely normal. This was a surprise as the author had always seen her in high princess guise at the previous events. Once inside the studio she unpacked her costume, wig and make-up bag from a small red suitcase. Sitting in front of the dressing room mirror she chatted in a relaxed way about her life and her passion for all things princess-like. Explaining how she loved more than anything to dress up at every opportunity, she proceeded to tie up her mid-length dark hair efficiently into a topknot, which she then shrouded in a black hair net. Next, she lifted the long, curly blond wig with back-combed top bun bedecked with pearls from its black velvet stand, and placed it carefully on her head with a swift front-to-back flourish of hand. Then she secured it tightly all around the crown with long hairpins. The visual transformation had started. After careful application of stylized baby doll make-up, complete with sky blue eyeshadow, black eyeliner, red rouge and shell-pink lipstick, she stepped into the wide skirt hoop. She pulled on an off-the-shoulder, long, pale blue silk brocade eighteenth-century style crinoline dress, with lace-trimmed bodice and white silk bell sleeves, complete with a diamante necklace and matching chandelier earrings. Finally, she fitted a pair of high white platform shoes on her white stockinged feet and slowly but silently walked into the studio. The transformation from a normal twenty-something girl to a commanding, regal historic figure was complete. This fantasy character would have looked just as much at home in the palace of Versailles as in the pages of the stylized manga from which the original source of inspiration came. But the metamorphosis was more than just a physical or material construct, as her whole demeanour and behaviour changed along with the costume. Mitsuki now moved with a regal slowness, and her face bore no trace of emotion – gone was the broad smile or any trace of humour that had greeted the author and pervaded the dressing room chat. Now she looked remote, poised and confident.

She had transformed into a princess and was fully performing this role on all sensory levels – cognitive, affective and conative. She was also now ready to play. As she twirled around before bobbing down on the floor with expansive skirt billowing around her corseted frame, she uttered the command, 'Now you can take my photo!'

Creative Performance in Action

Creativity studies in general have tended to overlook the role of performance as a creative process, preferring to focus either on creative products (Sternberg and Lubart 1999) or on personality types and traits associated with creativity (Plucker and Renzulli 1999). One reason for this is that much performance, based as it is on the collective efforts of multiple parties (actors and other performers, directors, set and costume designers), challenges the 'myth' of the individual creative genius (Boorstin 1993; Bohm 1996; Csikszentmihalyi 1996). Sawyer's investigation into the notion of performance creativity exemplified by jazz music, stand-up comedy and acting are a refreshing acknowledgement in creativity studies that, 'performance is central to our explanation of creativity' (Sawyer 2006: 7). 'When you add performance to the mix', writes Sawyer 'you have to explain three important new things, improvisation, collaboration and communication'. These aspects of social and theatrical performance – interpretation, collaboration and expression – provide a useful preliminary analytical framework. Each of these three performance elements will next be re-addressed as a way of analysing the creative aspects of cosplay and how it opens up opportunities for spectacular self-expression of identity outside of, and transgressing, the prevailing normative societal and cultural constraints in a given context.

Interpretation

Cosplay is the perfect example of interpretation via role-play as it involves the expressive ability of the performer to spontaneously interpret and reinterpret or remediate a fictional text in an embodied capacity in real time. This process of interpretation, as we saw in Mitsuki's case above, begins with the 'Do It Yourself' (DIY) practice of choosing a character and assembling the composite outfit from shoes and swords, to wigs and coloured contact lenses. Yet, it is also about how the players behave and feel in costumes, and not only what the costumes in themselves bring to the performance. These are the props that facilitate the bodily transformation and are a prerequisite for the performer to actively appropriate the character as part of the creative endeavour.

Despite the fact that players are performing and citing within the constraints of established fictional characters and scripted storylines, there is often nothing set about these performances outside of the organized competitions. The players gather at commercial animation conventions and randomly pose for photographs for onlookers; they transform and adapt the familiar characters and storylines in varied contexts and for different kinds of audiences. This is particularly evident in the photo-taking rituals in which they

262

all continuously engage, comprising unpredictable interactions and responses within the highly ritualized framework of posing for improvised photo-shoots when the player is momentarily 'in character' as a form of theatrical denouement. Some scholars have noted the tendency for players in North America to execute a holistic character performance – remaining in character when playing a more inclusive cast of Japanese and Hollywood inspired superheroes (Duchesne 2005; Napier 2007; Winge 2006). In contrast, their Japanese and Taiwanese counterparts appear to take a less organic approach to the performance, and only replicate character affect when vogue-ing for photos, executing a presentation that is more akin to puppetry by layering the body with separate artefacts (Silvio 2006). From observations among cosplayers in the Pearl River Delta region, while few remained in character throughout the entire convention, as they perambulated through the events their role-play performances appeared intense and sustained. Equally, character choices were based on both Japanese and North American media sources, suggesting a broader cultural engagement than hitherto recorded and with some evidence of the complex global flows (Iwabuchi 2002) and cultural appropriations behind various competing forms of soft power (see Kimura in this volume).

In China, where the cosplay practice appears to be more controlled and is mainly organized around competitive, regionally based, local government-run events such as the 'China Joy' national and regional competitions, devising is apparent in the more traditional theatrical sense. Typically, teams of players enact their favourite anime plot or traditional Chinese legends (preferred by the local authorities over Japanese cultural texts such as *The Monkey King*) as would a Peking Opera theatre troupe. But, while they appear to use familiar characters and storylines, inspired by the *Final Fantasy* anime, for example, the scripts and soundtrack are composed by the group and evolve over months of rehearsals, right up to the point of competitive staged performance in front of a seated audience and judging panel.

Both the Japanese players on the streets of Tokyo, the Hong Kong players at the university-run days, and the Beijing cosplayers are perhaps continuing oral dramaturgical traditions within their own cultures, such as Peking Opera and Japanese Kabuki street theatre, which predated scripted theatrical performances (Barthes 1982). Andrew Gerstle considers 'kabuki a subculture of play, fantasy and creativity within the society' (2003: 364), which is also true of cosplay as it can be seen as loosely extending the tradition of an Asian popular performance in a modernist frame. This suggests that there is a deep human need across time, space and place to implement a culture of creative play for pleasure and escapism through performance for both player and audience.

Authenticity of character in terms of visual costume display, in addition to acting in character to the point of raising or lowering voice register, are paramount requirements of this performance. As one informant explained:

You have to let the people who are watching you know exactly which character you are acting. That is very important. For example, if a male character says, 'Oh my God!' then we have to say, 'Oh my God!' You have to talk like the character as well as look like them, and move like them so everyone knows who you are being.

(Sun, female cosplayer, Hong Kong, age 26, 2011)

Individual players have a competitive urge to look like and perform their chosen character in the best possible way, often resulting in negative feedback from members of the community if that improvisation is deemed to be inauthentic.

Such slavish replication or citation may indicate a lack of interpretative creativity, yet each player is also assembling and presenting their own costume resulting in a range of interpretations of a popular character at each event. This point is exemplified by the role-play act itself as two players can be dressed as the same character, but will interpret this in an individual way. At a recent convention in Hong Kong, two versions of Darth Vadar appeared in near identical outfits, complete with red flashing lightsabre. One character stood at a commanding six feet tall, with broad shoulders and looked every bit the part. The other had a smaller frame and at first glance was less convincing. As the onlookers and photographers crowded round each Darth Vader, forming two separate circles of interest, the diminutive version of this *Star Wars* anti-hero stole the show as his gestures and sweeping command of his sabre drew gasps of admiration from the crowd, compared with the taller version who looked the part, but was relatively inanimate.

Also, there is a sense in which every player is constantly interpreting and improvising unscripted performances on the spot. The improvisation of gender roles is a good example of this as the narrative content of some manga and anime texts seem to openly legitimize the androgeny and homosexual romantic tendencies of the central characters. In response, many female players dress up as male characters, while some male players also dress as females highlighting the gender fluidity and performative aspects of this dress-up practice where identity is the performance (Butler 1990). Perhaps as a reflection of China and Hong Kong's deep-rooted conservatism or anxiety, ambivalence and pleasure towards issues of gender, sex and sexuality in post-colonial Hong Kong, these players were often adamant that cross-dressing players were not expressing an alternative sexuality. Yet, this undoubtedly enables them to explore and objectify their sexuality in a safe collective, as one female player said:

I love the male character in the anime Naruto, and will dress as him even though he is a boy and I'm a girl. This isn't the point. We're not interested in what sex they are because I'm more interested in being him and his world as the best I can be.

(Rain, female cosplayer, Hong Kong, age 23, 2012)

Cosplayers in their stylized presentation of fictional selves also appear to re-interpret and re-appropriate the normal usage of public city spaces and material spatial practices as zones of representation (Lefebvre 1991) in which they regularly appear in character costumes. This leads us onto considerations of setting and context as essential criteria to facilitate the creative performance. The interpretive dimensions of this staged form of creativity also rely on appearing in the right setting of the city to facilitate the 'magic circle' as a shifting 'theatre, a series of stages upon which individuals could work their own distinctive magic while performing a multiplicity of roles' (Harvey 1989: 4–5).

One group of Beijing cosplayers who were tracked during research fieldwork in May 2010 regularly chose historic locations in the city such as the 798 Art District. This disused 1950s East German designed electronics factory zone on the edge of the city, complete with warehouses and a disused old steam train, was used as the improvised setting in which to conduct photo shoots. The players observed during this photo shoot seemed to relish recording the visually incongruous juxtaposition of the formalist architectural backdrop with their postmodern cartoon costumes. This underlines the importance of actively re-appropriating spatial settings both within the architecture of the modern Asian city, and in manipulating and aligning its surface meaning as a space for creative expression.

There is also a transparency accorded to the preparation of the performance with a blurring of the backstage and front stage effort. Cosplayers in Hong Kong and China usually limit their appearances to the official zones of conventions, transporting their costumes to the performance site in suitcases, unlike their counterparts in Tokyo. On arrival at the location they proceed to dress up and apply make-up in full public view, in the manner that Barthes observed of Bunraku puppetry which openly displays the art and the at the same time (Barthes 1971), inhabiting a space between reality and fiction.

Collaboration

The human creative process is basically social and collaborative. It involves teamwork or groups of people located at both back and front of stage, involved in performing or interacting with the performers as an audience. But what does collaboration add to the creative performance; and what form does collaboration take? The answer may be that it lies at the heart of the creative endeavour requiring complex teamwork to construct, enact, witness and record the creative performance.

From the initial stages of creation, the player is borrowing their inspiration from a mediated anime, manga or online game source that has already been collaboratively constructed in another commercial frame. In the context of this creative performance collaboration is essentially intertextual (Kristeva 1980) as the individual player borrows inspiration from, re-appropriates and re-presents a text from another mediated source in both material and physical form. Yet, the production and consumption cycle of a cosplay performance involves a range of people cooperating at different points and in diverse ways, with varying levels of agency throughout this lifecycle.

Cosplayers claim that the main benefits of their hobby embrace not only the thespian skills required in role-playing characters, but also the project management and teamwork needed to plan and execute a group performance in costume, in addition to acquiring the technical ability to craft their outfits, and deliver an entertaining public performance in the process. This collaborative process also operates on many levels beyond the individual textual reinterpretation because players share their creative performances with each other and with audiences in an ongoing interchange cycle.

The social environment changes both the behavioural and affective states of the individual players, their relationship with each other and the wider social relationships that they experience in their everyday life. And creativity resides in the interaction between players and their facilitators. One informant explained how it had changed her whole approach to life, connecting her to a community of like-minded players creating a 'cosplay family' offering unconditional support and filling the affective gap in Asian cities where the traditional nuclear family is increasingly fragmenting under the demands of post-industrial lifestyles:

I always was shy at school and didn't think that I was good at anything. I had no real friends actually. Then I started to cosplay [...] five years ago when a classmate invited me along. At first I didn't think of going [...] I was a bit scared [...] then I borrowed an outfit [...] like a Japanese school uniform. I was part of a group doing the same story. When we got to the place we all started to help each other get ready – putting on make-up and combing out wigs. It was friendly and about caring for each other.

(Tine, female cosplayer, Hong Kong, age 25, 2011)

Figure 4: Cosplayer prepares 'backstage' with help from a friend for Gamescom at Hong Kong Convention Centre, 2014. Photograph by Anne Peirson-Smith.

Collaboration between players and spectators is a key part of the creative process underlying the performance. It adds to the individual and group performance working on many levels, involving different group dynamics. It occurs between the players themselves, among their friends and family members, with the photographers and with a wider online community of players and fans. All of the involved parties contribute to facilitating the moment by utilizing their time, skills and effort to transform players into making the creative performance a reality. As in other performance domains, the division of labour between the team backstage creates the individual performance front of stage so that it is always founded on collaborative effort. In cosplaying, all the collaborators are often on visible display during this overtly theatrical event.

In a similar way to other performance-oriented practices, the duality of the individual and the collective coexists because dressing up in costume provides an opportunity both for self-expression and group identity formation. Individuals joining together in ad hoc groups at well-attended events also play in teams. As a point of cultural specificity the players in China appeared to work more cohesively as a group from production to performance as a reflection of collectivist tendencies. These relationships are founded on a collective collusion to believe in the recreated self, and in a fantasy world that is built on, and validated by mutual trust, common interest and collective interaction. For one heroic cosplayer it was a true family affair, with his wife playing the female *Star Wars* roles and his 5-year-old son who, playing Yoda, 'became a big hit with our local chapter being one of the few cosplay kids' (Joe, male cosplayer, Hong Kong, age 29, 2010).

Some players lamented the lack of interest, or the outright opposition of parents to their hobby, or disliked the conditions imposed on them of attaining good school grades, often forcing them to play in secret, many also had the support of siblings, parents or boyfriends in constructing costumes and photographing performances. Aside from the patent collaborative aspect of this encounter, the issue of creative control is also evident here as many of the collaborators consciously frame themselves as active agents of the creative transformation process facilitating the performance whether as stylist or photographer. Essentially, the helper role is as significant to the creative process and to Asian theatrical traditions as there is a general awareness of the critical importance of playing this part among the players as in any dramatic troupe.

Expression

Cosplay is clearly a distinctive form of creative performance enabling identities to be expressed through role-play. In terms of cosplay's communicative function questions emerge as to what are the players trying to say, how are they saying it, by what means and who are they saying it to (Burke 1945). Players consistently explain that the activity is all about expressing a deep devotion to a chosen character who represents their core self and inner feelings through presentation of self in character costume where dressing up is dressing into an ideoculture (Fine 2002). While this is an identity performance delivered in the subjunctive mood (Schechner 1985: 43) it is essentially a knowledge-based performance. In this way the players are signalling a personal fan based devotion to a fantasy-driven universe where manga, anime or superheroes reside, and at the same time expressing their affective connection with specific characters, signalling their bond with a like-minded fan cohort (Hills 2002; Napier 2007). These connections are played out amid an audience who recognize and actively decode these performances in the light of their interpretative frameworks based on shared memberships of 'webs of significance' (Geertz 1973: 5) and as knowledge communities enacting identities grounded in cultural products that are simultaneously culturally specific and globally recognized.

This practice certainly requires audience recognition, engagement and interaction from a varied audience to validate the existence of the players and to recognize, encode and activate this creative communicative act. It is a form of creative activity reliant on interpersonal discourse among the players themselves, and with the photographers, fans, onlookers, professional media and friends who regularly comprise their audience in replicated kinship terms. When informants were asked how they would feel if only players turned up at an event, one of them replied:

> No, it just wouldn't be the same. Sure, we would take photographs of each other and do the poses but it would feel strange and hollow like a rehearsal or something.
>
> (Dion, female cosplayer, Beijing, age 20, 2011)

Personal observations at Hong Kong, Beijing and Macau events, the presence of significant numbers of hobby photographers (almost as many as the players themselves) and friends or other players taking photos of the players seemed to validate the players' role as they enact static poses and frozen scenes from their heroic character-based narratives. From behind the camera lens the feeling of spectatorship at this moment, as opposed to casual onlooker, is heightened. At this point, one becomes conscious of actively playing the part of photographer/recorder of the moment and in adding to the performance in real time. This supporting role is also extended after the event, with photographer as both experiential consumer (Sontag 1977: 177) and archivist of the photographic data by subsequently downloading and sharing it in the public domain.

The reflected appraisals of others also seemed to matter greatly to all of the informants in a transactional way. Most noted having to deal with both negative and positive feedback from these sources in the public domain, suggesting that cosplay is still a socially contested and marginalized phenomenon. New ways of doing things or behaving and appearing, particularly by members of a younger generation in a given culture, are often met with institutional resistance, moral panic or negativity based on generational power relations. This has been the case in Hong Kong's media response to the activity over several years, for example, which often labels it as a pastime for socially challenged school failures or as a form of non-productive work. As one informant explained:

> The news reports or TV shots I have seen here in Hong Kong talk about cosplay in a bad way they think it is a naïve interest, and that we are abnormal or are outsiders isolated from the real world, who don't do well at school which is not true.
>
> (Krystal, female cosplayer, Hong Kong, age 23, 2012)

Hong Kong society seems to be increasingly more accepting of the trend, or is at least more ambivalent about it, to the extent that media commentary alongside their viewers and readers are less critical of the practice and casual observers did not tend to ridicule, stare or comment adversely. Some respondents believed that this was partly because the concept had entered the wider public entertainment domain and media agenda, having been appropriated by Hong Kong Cantopop celebrities, who sometimes dress up in cosplay-style outfits as part of their stage routine, or by shopping malls who sometimes hire actors dressed as players for promotional events. Celebrity endorsement seemingly legitimizes the practice, making the strange appear familiar.

This remediation of performance in real time is also extended into a virtual domain through online discourse. Here, creativity is located in the supporting activities of assistants and spectators and their tendency to record the encounter and re-appropriate cosplay images on social networking sites and other mediated channels. Thus, online communication channels via the 'internet playground' (Seiter 2005) are also fully utilized by the players to sustain these real-time relationships and also to connect with new audiences with a wider geographic and cultural reach. This collective identity was manifested in a virtual translocal domain, as many of the research informants regularly shared an affective and knowledge-based identity with peers in other geographical places and spaces in online discussion groups. Personal websites, blogs, social networks, Facebook, YouTube Cosplay.com, cosplayfu.com and renren.com in China, for example, are equally important sites for virtual 'cosing' from sharing photographs; information-seeking about costume construction; or chatting about past and future events. These virtual exchanges continue the embodied performance in the virtual sphere as 'a text-based virtual world might be an extension of the corporeal, as well as the physical, a reconfiguration or perhaps rather an incarnation of the textual' (Sundén 2003: 109) because 'the virtual does not automatically equate disembodiment' (Sundén 2003: 5).

Online communication is an extension of the creative performance. Players are actively re-appropriating and sharing recorded images of their transformed selves with a wider, often unseen, large, anonymous audience through social media channels. By engaging in this activity they are again seeking a valorization of their transformed self, but this time by opening up transglobal channels for verbal interaction and responsive commentaries on the images and the counter-posting of images. All players have their own websites, Instagram and Facebook sites where they regularly upload images of their latest costumes after each event. The pressure to display high quality post-event photos often motivates players to hire a studio and commission professional photographs for this purpose. By also engaging with these sites, the players, as with all social networkers, are shaping communication technologies to suit their social needs, and in turn are shaped by them, as photo sharing is a required practice.

When questioned about the rationale for sharing their images either on personal websites or by linking into social networking sites, one respondent said:

It's exciting because you wanna see what others say about you. You make friends that way too – with other cosplayers or people interested in doing it […] I sometimes go on cosplay forums and talk with Chinese overseas who want to do it and like my images or ask questions about how to make my costume or a sword as I do it all myself. It makes me feel good that people notice me from far away […] yes I made many friends that way too.

(Ran, female cosplayer, Hong Kong, age 22, 2016)

The online sites, in particular, appear to be more informal and interactive than face-to-face interaction, as if the wearing of a costume sets them apart from their audience, physically distancing them as they appropriate and embody the persona of their chosen character. Online chat between players and fans is animated, conversational, good-humoured and informational – something that the players at real-time events only usually reserve for close friends or assistants.

There is also a darker or contested side to this collaborative interface between the many players, from 'cosers', as they sometimes refer to themselves, to photographers and their interpretation of cosplay's cultural capital. Some respondents shared tales of photographers re-digitizing photographs and re-appropriating them on pornographic websites, while others were highly concerned about the tendency for players to be hyper-critical of each other's performance on forums. As a cross-cultural reflection, they lamented the fact that players in other cultural locations such as North America were less concerned about the alignment between the real body and the form of the character. As one respondent observed:

These days cosplayers are so much more critical of each other. They complain your costume does not look like the original character or your wig is too long, or short or is the wrong shade of blue […] Or they say you look too fat or too thin or that your teeth

Figure 5: Cosplayers at Hong Kong Cosplay and Anime Society Event. Photograph by Anne Peirson-Smith.

are bad [...] oh this pulls me down. And the new thing they say is that younger cosplayers don't understand their character and are not really into it for the right reasons. Some say young, pretty girls only want to be discovered as models and be very famous which gives it a bad name.

(Krystal, female cosplayer, Hong Kong, age 23, 2014)

Discursive conflict scenarios such as these reveal the latent power struggles that exist among the highly competitive players and an evaluative taste-based system in operation for good and bad play and performance. Yet, rather than being a destructive force, this critical feedback can actually generate creativity, as with all public performances, by provoking new perspectives on a practice or creating new approaches and responses. While some players admitted that they found this negative feedback to be increasingly stressful, others pointed out that when faced with harsh criticism from other players or anonymous commentators their friendships actually became closer, as they would often be verbally defended by their peers at an event or online, creating a stronger sense of attachment and commitment to play between the team members.

Conclusion

To summarize, creativity is found in the active process of transforming things from one form to another to convey ideas about the self and others in a unique way. Cosplay as an emerging and evolving example of contemporary creative performance draws on the combined resources of interpretation, collaborative input and multimodal expression to play with and project identity. Here, the player actualizes a narrative by re-envisioning the self in fictional form. The transformative dimension of this performance lies at the heart of its grounded uniqueness and its reliance on re-appropriation of fictional text, a re-enactment of material culture and recorded image. While the transglobal sources of inspiration for this performance are based on universally recognized Japanese and North American cultural products, they are remediated in localized versions of fantasyscapes in performances that reflect the sociocultural frames and performance traditions in which the practice occurs within the context of a global participatory fan-based culture (Jenkins 1992).

This complex creative process is expressed dynamically through various stages from preparation of costume and character research, to playful public performance, frenetic photo-taking and post-performance sharing of event photographs based on the interaction between players, their backstage assistants, friends and family, photographers, onlookers, passers-by and social networkers. These backstage and front of stage roles are not fixed and are constantly shifting, as player becomes photographer or onlooker and vice versa in the constructed cosplay 'family'. Of course, it is not all sweetness and light in their universe. In addition to the playful fun and friendship celebrated in this creative process, the darker side of human nature is manifested in the negative media coverage or critical comments received on the street from onlookers and on the net from other players. But these shifting power relations also generate creative interaction through the exchange of ideas as an ultimate expression of cultural hybridity and liquid late modernity (Bauman 2000). This practice emerges from the aspirations of a youth demographic that in Hong Kong emerges from an East-West cultural inheritance and China's increasing consumer base and enlightened socialism. In addition, it is enhanced in a virtual sense by an empowered social media generation that has transglobalized access to relatively uncontained social networks and mediated sources, and play with new empowered identities as outlets for life's pressures.

In the world of cosplay, the creative fantastical performance is located in the actions and re-actions of every member of the various backstage and front of stage cast members throughout the lifecycle of this role based performance. The playful, social, escapist act generates a string of complex and constantly shifting creative moments and identities in real and virtual fantasy places and spaces that are celebrated and contested in the urban cosplay carnival performance.

Acknowledgements

This research project was made possible by funding from a Hong Kong Government Research Fund Grant (GRF: 147608) 2008–11, Cosplay and the Dressing Up Box: An Examination of the Cosplay Phenomenon in Hong Kong.

References

Andersen, K. (2015), 'Becoming Batman: Cosplay performance, and ludic transformation at Comic-Con', in M. Omasta and D. Chappell (eds), *Play Performance and Identity: How Institutions Structure Ludic Spaces*, Routledge Advances in Theatre Studies, New York: Routledge, pp. 105–16.

Appadurai, A. (1996), *Modernity at Large*, Minneapolis: Minnesota Press.

Bakhtin, M. M. (1968), *Rabelais and His World*, 2nd ed., Bloomington: Indiana University Press.

Barthes, R. (1971), 'On Bunraku' (trans. S. MacDonald), *The Drama Review*, 15:3, spring, pp. 76–82.

—— (1982), *The Empire of Signs* (trans. R. Howard), New York: Hill and Wang.

Bateson, G. (1955), 'A theory of play and fantasy', *Psychiatric Research Reports*, 2, December, pp. 39–51.

—— (1972), *Steps to an Ecology of Mind*, New York: Ballantine.

Bauman, R. (1977), *Verbal Art as Performance*, Prospect Heights: Waveland Press.

Bauman, R. and Briggs, C. L. (1990), 'Poetics and performance as critical perspectives on language and social life', *Annual Review of Anthropology*, 19, pp. 59–88.

Bauman, Z. (2000), *Liquid Modernity*, Cambridge: Polity Press.

Bial, H. (2004), 'What is performance?', in H. Bial (ed.), *The Performance Studies Reader*, New York: Routledge, pp. 57–59.

Bohm, D. (1996), *On Creativity*, London and New York: Routledge.

Boorstin, D. J. (1993), *The Creators: A History of Heroes of the Imagination*, New York: Vintage Books.

Burke, K. (1945), *A Grammar of Motives*, New York: Prentice Hall.

Butler, J. (1990), *Gender Trouble: Feminism and the Subversion of Identity*, London: Routledge.

Caillois, R. (1958), *Man, Play and Games*, Urbana and Chicago: University of Illinois Press.

Chapman, M. M. (1992), *Living Pictures: Women and Tableaux Vivants in Nineteenth Century American Fiction and Culture*, New York: Cornell University Press.

Csikszentmihalyi, M. (1996), *Creativity: Flow and the Psychology of Discovery and Invention*, New York: Harper Collins.

Duchesne, S. (2005), 'Little reckonings in great rooms: The performance of cosplay', *Canadian Theatre Review*, 121, pp. 17–26.

Fine, G. A. (2002), *Shared Fantasies: Role-Playing Games as Social Worlds*, Chicago: University of Chicago Press.

Fron, J., Fullerton, T., Ford Morie, J. and Pearce, C. (2007), 'Playing dress-up costumes, roleplay and imagination', *Conference Proceedings, Philosophy of Computer Games Conference*, University of Modena Reggio and Emilia, 24–27 January, pp. 1–23.

Geertz, C. (1973), *The Interpretation of Cultures*, New York: Basic Books.

Gerstle, A. C. (2003), 'The culture of play: Kabuki and the production of texts', *Bulletin of the School of Oriental and African Studies*, 66, pp. 358–79.

Goffman, E. (1959), *The Presentation of Self in Everyday Life*, New York: Doubleday, Anchor Books.

—— (1974), *Frame Analysis: An Essay on the Organization of Experience*, London: Harper and Row.

Goldman, L. R. (1998), *Child's Play: Myth, Mimesis and Make-Believe*, London: Berg.

Harvey, D. (1989), *The Condition of Postmodernity: An Enquiry into the Origins of Cultural Change*, Oxford: Blackwell.

Hebdige, D. (1979), *Subculture: The Meaning of Style*, London: Methuen.

Hills, M. (2002), *Fan Cultures*, London: Routledge.

Hodkinson, P. (2002), *Goth: Identity, Style, Subculture*, Oxford: Berg.

Huizinga, J. (1955), *Homo Ludens: A Study of Play Elements in Culture*, Boston: Beacon Press.

Iwabuchi, K. (2002), *Recentering Globalization: Popular Culture and Japanese Transnationalism*, Durham: Duke University Press.

Jenkins, H. (1992), *Textual Poachers: Television Gangs and Participatory Culture*, New York: Routledge.

Kristeva, J. (1980), *Desire in Language: A Semiotic Approach to Literature and Art*, New York: Columbia University Press.

Lamerichs, N. (2011), 'Stranger than fiction: Fan identity in cosplay', *Transformative Works and Cultures*, 7, http://journal.transformativeworks.org/index.php/twc/article/view/246. Accessed 22 September 2017.

Lefebvre, H. (1991), *The Production of Space* (trans. D. Nicolson-Smith), Oxford: Basil Blackwell.

MacKay, D. (2001), *The Fantasy Role-Playing Game: A New Performing Art*, Jefferson, NC: McFarland & Co. Inc.

Maffesoli, M. (1996), *The Time of the Tribe: The Decline of Individualism in Mass Society*, London: Sage.

McGonigal, J. (2005), 'Super gaming: Ubiquitous play and performance for massively scaled community', *Modern Drama*, 48:3, fall, pp. 471–91.

Moore, C. (2011), 'The magic circle and the mobility of play', *Convergence: The International Journal of Research into New Media Technologies*, 17, pp. 373–87.

Napier, S. J. (2007), *From Impressionism to Anime: Japan Fantasy and Fan Cult in the Mind of the West*, New York: Palgrave Macmillan.

Opie, I. and Opie, P. (1951), *The Oxford Dictionary of Nursery Rhymes*, Oxford: Oxford University Press, pp. 99–100.

Peirson-Smith, A. (2013), 'Fashioning the fantastical self: An examination of the Cosplay dress-up phenomenon in South East Asia', *Fashion Theory: The Journal of Body, Dress and Culture*, 17:1, February, pp. 77–112.

Piaget, J. (1951), *Play, Dreams and Imitation in Childhood*, New York: Norton Press.

Plucker, J. A. and Renzulli, J. S. (1999), 'Psychometric approaches to the study of human creativity', in R. J. Sternberg (ed.), *Handbook of Creativity*, Cambridge: Cambridge University Press.

Polhemus, T. (1994), *Streetstyle: From Sidewalk to Catwalk*, London: Thames & Hudson.

Sawyer, K. R. (2006), *Explaining Creativity: The Science of Human Innovation*, Oxford and New York: Oxford University Press.

Schechner, R. (1985), *Between Theater and Anthropology*, Philadelphia: University of Pennsylvania Press.

—— (1988), *Performance Theory*, London: Routledge.

Seiter, E. (2005), *The Internet Playground: Children's Access, Entertainment, and Mis-Education*, New York: Peter Lang Publishing Inc.

Silvio, T. (2006), 'The body in Taiwanese digital-video puppetry and Cosplay', in F. Martin and L. Henrich (eds), *Embodied Modernities, Corporeality, Representation and Chinese Cultures*, Honolulu: University of Honolulu Press, pp. 289–326.

Singer, M. B. (1972), *When a Great Tradition Modernizes an Anthropological Approach to Indian Civilization*, New York: Praeger.

Sontag, S. (1977), *On Photography*, New York: Farrar, Strauss and Giroux.

Sternberg, R. J. and Lubart, T. L (1999), 'The concept of creativity: Prospects and paradigms', in R. J. Sternberg (ed.), *Handbook of Creativity*, Cambridge: Cambridge University Press, pp. 3–15.

Sundén, J. (2003), *Material Virtualities: Approaching Online Textual Embodiment*, New York: Peter Lang.

Sutton-Smith, B. (1997), *The Ambiguity of Play*, Cambridge, MA: Harvard University Press.

Tausig, M. (1993), *Mimesis and Alterity: A Particular History of the Senses*, New York: Routledge.

Thacker, J. (2002), *Role-Play and the World as Stage in the Comedia*, Liverpool: Liverpool University Press.

Tseëlon, E. (2001), *Masquerade and Identities: Essays on Gender, Sexuality and Marginality*, London: Routledge.

Turner, V. W. (1969), *The Ritual Process: Structure and Anti-Structure*, New York: Aldine.

———— (1974), *Dramas, Fields and Metaphors: Symbolic Action in Human Society*, Ithaca and London: Cornell University Press.

———— (1979), *Process, Performance and Pilgrimage: A Study in Comparative Symbology*, New Delhi: Concept.

———— (1982), *From Ritual to Theatre: The Human Seriousness of Play*, New York: Performing Arts Journal Publications.

———— (1987), *The Anthropology of Performance*, New York: PAJ Publications.

Williamson, M. (2001), 'Vampires and goths: Fandom, gender and cult dress', in W. J. F. Keenan (ed.), *Dressed to Impress: Looking the Part*, Oxford: Berg, pp. 141–57.

Willis, P. (1980), 'Notes on method', in S. Hall, D. Hobson, A. Lowe and P. Willis (eds), *Culture, Media, Language*, London: Hutchinson, pp. 88–95.

Winge, T. (2006), 'Costuming the imagination: Origins of anime and manga cosplay', *Mechademia*, 1, pp. 66–76.

Winnicott, D. W. (1971), *Playing and Reality*, London: Tavistock Publications.

Section 3

Brand Storytelling: Commodified Fashion Tales

Introduction

The branding of fashion by has been valorized for its creativity and also demonized for its manipulation of the masses, yet both stances acknowledge that it has become a ubiquitous part of the way that fashion is promoted in the interests of profit margins and consumer choice. Negative critiques of fashion branding perhaps overlook the fact that the process behind the branding relationship involves active engagement by the customer, who assists the producer in co-creating the brand and its narrative message thereby aligning it with their lifestyle aspirations – imagined or otherwise – to construct their own fashion story (see Hancock in this section). In this collaborative process, fashion producers execute brand identity through strategic brand storytelling using carefully crafted words and images and experiential in store and online brand consumer engagement, while the consumer actively co-creates and sustains the brand image.

The urban environment is the location for most fashion brands in its incarnation as the habitus of modernity and urban living. The retail presence of high end and high street offerings maps out the line of the cityscape (Lefebvre 2003), celebrating the visual story of the cultural economy of fashion in its market spaces, retail outlets and flagship stores at point of sale (see Kolakis in this section). Also, as an extension of this transglobal cultural branding effort major cities globally now vie for recognition as creative hubs and as world fashion capitals (Gilbert 2000; Breward and Gilbert 2006), thus constituting a form of soft power (see Kimura in this section). Whilst the fashion city status attracts support from the presence of iconic global fashion brands, there is a danger for emerging fashion centres in Asia to appropriate the established narratives of other fashion centres and rely on a saturated, well-worn discourse with limited resonance (see Berry in this section), rather than focusing on the unique selling points of inspirational local heritage brand stories (see Radclyffe-Thomas in this section). This section highlights the fact that fashion brands are able through storytelling both to circulate freely and assert a visual and verbal presence without boundaries in the printed pages of magazines and on digital sites and blogs. At the same time, fashion brands can position themselves across dynamic global fashion centres symbiotically borrowing associative interest and reinventing themselves along the way in an attempt to develop a transactional and experiential relationship with the fickle fashion and lifestyle consumer.

References

Breward, C. and Gilbert, D. (eds) (2006), *Fashion's World Cities*, Oxford: Berg.

Gilbert D. (2000), 'Urban outfitting: The city and the spaces of fashion culture', in S. Bruzzi and P. Church Gibson (eds), *Fashion Cultures: Theories, Explorations and Analysis*, pp. 7–24.

Lefebvre, H. (2003), *The Urban Revolution* (trans. Roberto Bonnono), Minneapolis: The University of Minnesota Press.

Chapter 14

'Paris of the East'? Collapsing Fashion Capitals through Fashion Photography of Shanghai and Hong Kong

Jess Berry

The global geography of fashion is expanding. While Paris, London, New York and Milan still hold prime positions as the world's fashion capitals, peripheral cities as diverse as Moscow, Sao Paolo, Mumbai and Dubai have emerged as prominent style sites at various points in time. As Christopher Breward (2006), David Gilbert (2013) and Lise Skov (2011) all suggest, the fashion city itself is subject to the fashion cycle.

Recently, China has become the prime industrial producer of fashion internationally, and is one of the main consumers of fashion in the twenty-first century. Further, it would appear that Tokyo's position as a fashion capital, as established in the 1990s, has been surpassed by both Shanghai and Hong Kong as the most prominent of the East Asian fashion capitals. This is particularly evidenced by fashion 'buzzword' analysis of Internet and print media undertaken by the Global Language Monitor, which ranked Shanghai above Tokyo in 2013, and Hong Kong above Tokyo in 2014 as 'Top Global Fashion Capitals'. While Gilbert is tentative in claiming that either of these cities might be able to break through the consecrating power of Western-dominated fashion, as Armida de la Garza and Peng Ding (2013: 56) argue of Shanghai, there is significant potential for this city to cement its position as a future fashion global capital; given its connection between fashion and architecture, and its 'traditional role as site of encounters between East and West'. These same arguments could equally be applied to Hong Kong.

New Fashion Capitals – Shanghai and Hong Kong

As Gilbert and Skov have outlined, the formation of fashion city identity is a complex set of systems that involves production industries, international acknowledgement of local design prowess, government policy, the presence of associated cultural industries and institutions, street culture, sites of consumption and media dissemination. While Shanghai's and Hong Kong's fashion city status is dependent on the ability to negotiate the production and consumption of fashion within a changing geopolitical context, it is also important to consider how these cities harness and promote their own symbolic economy of fashion through representation.

Advertising, magazines, the fashion press, blogospheres, fashion week and the media at large are powerful determinants in creating a symbolic economy for fashion. Mainstream fashion media sources are located both within their own culture as well as in the broader context of globalized media networks, which influence the aesthetics, representation and consumption of fashion. As Gilbert (2013: 11) argues, while there might be 21 national editions of *Vogue*, they all fit a consistent pattern, where local fashion designers and information is 'mixed with constant reference back to the established centres of fashion's world order'. While such a system continues to assert Western fashion dominance, as well as prevailing Orientalist discourses, as de la Garza and Deng argue, 'the broadening of the boundaries between fashion as art, industry and cultural product [is now] a truly global […] endeavour', as new fashion cities emerge, 'they require an engagement with the earlier capitals in order to thrive' (2013: 61).

This chapter further develops my continuing inquiry regarding how fashion photography has used the city to accessorise fashion (Berry 2011, 2012a, 2012b). In 'Modes of the metropolis: The city as photography's fashion icon' (2011), I establish that 1940s and 1950s photographers, including Louise Dahl-Wolfe, Willy Maywald, Georges Dambier and Norman Parkinson, collectively modelled the city as a fashion object and established ongoing fashion narratives and characters for fashion capitals that continue to be represented in contemporary fashion photography. Thus, fashion photography, along with film and street style blogs, can be seen to play a central role in creating a discourse of style around particular fashion capitals.

Fashion photography, like touristic photography, frequently poses the city in such a way as to recall previous representations, referencing conventional iconographies. As Annette Pritchard and Nigel Morgan argue:

> Fashion shoots are texts about previous texts of place, just as are travellers' texts. If tourists select for their personal photographs images already seen in art, travel broachers, postcards […] [that] they are already familiar with, then so too do fashion photographers.
> (2005: 285)

Their view has resonance with Gilbert's characterization of such images where he suggests that with both postcards and fashion photographs, 'there is value in those symbols that are unambiguous identifiers of a particular city' (2000: 21).

Fashion photography thus presents a way of seeing the city that is influential in shaping how the public conceives that city to be in the collective imagination. The ongoing narrative of the world's fashion capitals played out in fashion photography and advertising since the 1940s and 1950s suggests that Paris is composed and elegantly chic, New York is dynamic and modern and London both traditional and transgressive. As such, this paper will argue that the emergent fashion cities Shanghai and Hong Kong appear to be increasingly adopting similar rhetorical devices in shaping the city as style site, where prominent architecture and recognizable street scenes are represented in the fashion media as exciting and romantic modern metropolises.

In analysing recent magazine and advertising photography this chapter will interrogate the language and mythology of fashion city rhetoric. Specifically, I contend that Shanghai and Hong Kong have been posed in such a way as to collapse the distinctive identities of the traditional fashion capitals with each other. That is, the emblematic devices that Paris, New York and London have continually exploited as unique and iconic to accessorize their individual fashion city personas are being co-opted through direct reference and allusion by their Asian fashion city counterpart so as to participate in the symbolic economy attributed to the renowned global fashion capitals. Further, this chapter questions if in making these allegorical comparisons fashion photography continues to create problematic narratives of Orientalism for Asian fashion capitals or, alternately, if such images are a means to indicate China's ability to generate an image for the fashion city comparable to its Western counterparts.

A Tale of Two Cities: Shanghai and Hong Kong as Global Cities

In order to consider how current fashion photography might attempt to present Shanghai and Hong Kong as fashion cities, it is firstly important to overview the historical positioning of these two cities as style sites in relation to the Western dominated fashion system. Cultural scholarship in the fields of literature and film studies have often posited Shanghai and Hong Kong as 'a tale of two cities', they are seen as mirrors of each other, twins, whose history and future is tacit in the other's development. According to cultural studies theorist Ackbar Abbas (2000), Shanghai and Hong Kong have always had a special relationship to each other in the way that these cities interface with the rest of the world. Historically, both cities were created by Western colonialism after the Opium Wars and developed a form of cosmopolitanism under colonial conditions. This has been punctuated by the decline and resurgence of each other through China's communist past and capitalist future. As Tsung-yi Michelle Huang (2005: 73) concurs, the narrative of these global city regions is that 'Hong Kong and Shanghai are cities "linked at birth" being 'metropolises that have been imagined as "the Pearl of the Orient" vs. "the Paris of the East"', where both are sites of encounters between East and West. Further, as Abbas and Huang concur, Chinese films and books that depict these cities underline that Shanghai and Hong Kong are interrelated in establishing their image as global cities of the future, and this has grown from their shared histories of constructing selfhood by observing the other. Huang makes the case for this interlinking of both cities' imagery stating that, '[o]nce the birth of Old Shanghai can be miraculously traced in the urban spectacle of Hong Kong, the linearity of history implies that the future Shanghai will resemble that "splendor on the sea"' (Huang 2005: 77).

Shanghai of the 1920s and 1930s generated a set of images about itself that contributed to its glamour and mystique. Old Shanghai, as Abbas argues (2000: 771), was 'a dream image of Europe more glamorous even than Europe itself at the time'. The city's built space was made up of an eclectic mix of European architecture on the Bund, along with Shanghainese lane houses. New spaces of cosmopolitanism, including department stores, coffeehouses, cinemas and dance halls, also contributed to Shanghai's modernity and consumer culture. As a city, Shanghai of the 1930s could be understood 'as the appropriation by the local of "elements of foreign culture to enrich a new national culture'" (Lee quoted in Abbas 2000: 775). This image of glamour was directly related to fashion where Shanghai's women were renowned for paying exquisite attention to dress, and the Nanjing Road shopping district also epitomizes pleasure and luxury with its 'aura of rich variety, silver, silk, satins and furs' (Belk and Zhao 2012: 143). Advertising of the era visually captured and promoted sensuous and alluring images of modern women dressed in *qipao* and high-heels to sell everything from cigarettes to telephones. These calendar and poster art images (*yuefenpai*) often portrayed Chinese women conforming to Western stereotypes of beauty in front. The Huangpu River's glittering skyline at night, was a frequent backdrop to these advertisements, with captions such as 'Shanghai – a prosperous city that never sleeps' (Postrel 2013: 132) so reinforcing the city's cosmopolitan urban lifestyle and its link to modern fashionability.

These representations held resonance with the Hollywood version of Shanghai glamour, mythologized by Marlene Dietrich and Anna May Wong in Joseph Von Sternberg's *Shanghai Express* (1932). The movie, while largely set on a train, managed to create an image of the city as dangerous, mysterious and erotic through the characters of the two beautiful courtesans who were the main protagonists. The film epitomizes what Edward Said (1977: 1) describes as the long imagined 'Orient', 'a place of romance, exotic beings, haunting memories and landscapes, remarkable experiences'. *Shanghai Express* did much to embed Shanghai as the 'Paris of the East' in the collective cultural imagination, equating the exotic city and its desirable pleasures with the luxuries of its European counterpart. As Virginia Postrel (2013: 131) argues, 'Shanghai represented an intriguing zone between the familiar and the foreign [...] a golden city beyond the imagination'. This dream image was equally persistent to Chinese as well as Westerners, where Postrel claims, 'a Francophile Chinese intellectual could walk the streets of the French Concession and imagine himself in Paris' (Postrel 2013: 132).

Under the People's Republic of China, Shanghai became a 'lost civilization' to many people's eyes, and its dominance as an international metropolis was overtaken by Hong Kong in the 1950s and 1960s. Hong Kong's modernization was influenced not only by Britain's colonial presence, but also by the marshalling of cultural activities in the city; a process that Leo Ou-fan Lee describes as Shanghainization, where that city's flow of cultural arbiters in the fields of fashion, film and theatre moved to Hong Kong in 1949. As design historian Daniel Huppatz argues (2009: 21), 'the particular aesthetic that Shanghai migrants bought with them was both cosmopolitan and urban, mixing American and European Art Deco and modern styles with local references'. During this period Hong Kong presented an East meets West image where the continuity of Shanghai's commercial culture of glamour, mystery and exoticism was coupled with the colonial narrative of the city's modern development. As with Shanghai, Hollywood presented an Orientalist fantasy version of the city. Richard Quine's film *The World of Suzie Wong* (1960) provided a metaphor of Hong Kong through Nancy Kwan's prostitute character; representing the city as exotic, erotic and mysterious, however benefiting from the Western influence as epitomized by the film's American love interest.

While the city embraced both East and West aspects, fashion photography from the late 1950s and early 1960s as depicted in magazines, *British Vogue* and *Harper's Bazaar*, represented Orientalist and exoticizing images of the city. For example, Francesco Scavulo's photograph for *Harper's Bazaar* (1962) contrasts the fashion model as an elegant and isolated figure surrounded by a busy crowd of Hong Kong shoppers on the Duddell Street stairs. Here, the Western model is presented as cultured and sophisticated compared to the 'Otherness' of the numerous Chinese men that surround her. Alternately, Gleb Derujinski and Harry Clarke, for *Harper's Bazaar* (1958) and *British Vogue* (1960) respectively, present the typical touristic image of the fashion model sailing Victoria Harbour on a Junk. Such images confirm imperialist discourses of conquest, pleasure and the exotic. These Orientalist stereotypes continue to underpin many Western fashion images of Hong Kong. For example, a recent fashion editorial by Nick Scott for Australia's *Madison* magazine titled 'A day in Hong Kong', August (2011), contrasts the high fashion of the sophisticated and refined Western fashion model with the body of the Chinese worker who serves her. The fashion story presents longstanding postcard fantasies of Hong Kong's 'foreign' tourist locations from red-lacquer doorways to rickshaws and bird markets in order to reinforce the city's exotic image.

According to Lee, by the 1980s 'Hong Kong had not only supplanted Shanghai but surpassed it' (1999: 331). However, Shanghai's rebirth in the 1990s coincided with Hong Kong's handover and fears that the 'transnational status it had established would be submerged into the national' (Abbas 2000: 771). From the late 1990s, Shanghai as a 'City of the Future' would begin to match Hong Kong's cosmopolitanism and modernity through fashion, nightlife and café culture (Watterstrom 2003). As such, there appears to be a level of rivalry between the cities as to which holds the upper hand in the global city stakes, where each metropolis attempts to mobilize its image as a global city.

The Hong Kong and Shanghai tale of two cities is one that, as Lee argues, has grown from a mirror image of looking at each other, where he contends that 'the cultural texts of one city make those of the other more intelligible' (cited in Huang 2005: 74). In comparing current fashion photography depicting Shanghai and Hong Kong, I argue that beyond the Orientalist images that have developed from Western perspectives of these two cities rendering them as exotic, mysterious, dangerous and erotic, another discourse emerges that draws from the fashion city rhetoric of Paris, New York and London. Further, and paradoxically, I contend that while directly referencing the established fashion cities' imagery it homogenizes and collapses these cities together in a way that makes their authenticity and distinctiveness uncertain, while such images might also operate to distinguish Hong Kong and Shanghai from each other within the fashion city network.

Paris of the East: Shanghai

Since the redevelopment of the Pudong skyline in 1990, with its recognizable architecture including the Oriental Pearl Radio and TV Tower, Shanghai Tower and Jin Mao Tower, Shanghai has developed an image of fashionable futurism. As Steven Miles argues, 'Shanghai is a city of gleaming dream worlds', which makes a 'significant statement about the aspirational modernity inherent in a new China' (2010: 78). It is surprising then that the narrative accompanying Shanghai fashion stories often places less emphasis on this modern and futuristic interpretation of the city's fashion currency, and instead evokes a sense of looking to the past with regard to Shanghai's 'Paris of the East' reputation. For example, two recent fashion editorials, John Minh Nguyen's *Shanghai with Love* (Vogue China August 2012) and Choi Yong Bin's *Shanghai Calling* (Harper's Bazaar Korea December 2013) along with Li Qi's 'Valentino, My Name Is Red' (2014) advertising campaign are among many fashion images that pose the city in such a way as to recall iconic images of the French fashion capital.

Parisian fashion photography is idealized as romantic, elegant and timeless. Its monuments and streetscapes have become a central character in fashion's narrative with photography creating aesthetic and symbolic value for the city in the same way a dress or a shoe is rendered a protagonist in a fashion story. The ongoing narrative of Paris revolves around that of a modern and stylish woman on a quest for self-discovery and romantic liaison, where the city's architecture and streets are modelled as a central character in this fashion fantasy. The Eiffel Tower, as Agnes Rocamora (2009) has argued, is undoubtedly inextricably linked to Paris' representation as a fashion city, as are picturesque backdrops of the Seine, street-side cafés, cobbled streets and Beaux-arts architecture.

In surveying Shanghai fashion editorials it becomes clear that these supposedly Parisian signature sites, monuments and icons are being co-opted and alluded to by their Asian fashion city counterpart. Just as glimpses of the Eiffel Tower accessorize 1950s fashion photography by Louise Dahl-Wolfe, Georges Dambier, Henry Clarke and Willy Maywald, Shanghai's Oriental Pearl Radio and TV Tower is positioned as a monument of a glamorous and romantic destination. Equally, the Huangpu River is cast as the Seine, and European architecture and ambience is exploited to tell the story that Shanghai fashion is a continuation of the Parisian narrative. In both Nguyen's and Yong Bin's photographic fashion stories models take up wistful and romantic poses against the backdrops of window frames, iron-work balconies and hazy-focused street corners in the same manner as Bettina modelled for Willy Maywald or Suzi Parker posed for George Dambier in their iconic 1950s images. A similar aesthetic is adopted by photographer Todd Anthony Tyler in the editorial 'Stepping back in Shanghai' for *Destinasian* magazine (July 2009) (Figure 1), in which the model poses against the backdrop of cobbled alleyway. As such, images posed by contemporary fashion photographers draw on an established visual language of French ambience that is instantly recognizable to the fashion reader.

In adopting the visual rhetoric of Paris' fashion city status, Shanghai is seen as its equivalent. Further, such images also reinforce a distinct cultural policy of preservation and looking to the past. According to Abbas, while Shanghai's skyline has been 'Manhattanized' aspects of Shanghai's legendary past have been retained for the purposes of symbolic capital (see Radclyffe-Thomas in this volume). He argues that,

Figure 1: 'Stepping Back in Shanghai'. Photograph and creative direction by Todd Anthony Tyler for *Destinasian*; styling by Karina Smith, make-up and hair by Jessica Jean Myers, model Sun Fei.

'invoking a continuity with a legendary past [...] enhances the city's attractiveness, gives it historical cache [...] as a *soi-disant* "City of Culture"' (2000: 781). Thus, the Parisian mise-en-scène provided by the city's colonial buildings is exploited to suggest Shanghai's historical fashion status and enforce its traditional role as a site of encounters between East and West.

Arguably, these images present another form of Orientalism, while they do not appear to overtly exploit the perceived exoticism and eroticism of much fashion photography that is present in 'Paris of the Orient' stereotypes, instead we are presented with a Francophile vision of China. That is, colonization through the photographic lens. Here the Eurocentric view that fashion occurs in the West is reiterated by suggesting that the presence of France is a necessary component of Shanghai's fashionable status. As Simona Segre Reinach (2012: 62) argues, 'French luxury brands – Dior, Hermes and Chanel – have all drawn on colonial and postcolonial rhetoric [...] [to rework] classic Orientalist stereotypes'. For example Dior's short fashion film *Lady Blue Shanghai* directed by David Lynch (2010) and the accompanying print campaign photographed by Steven Klein adopts the narrative of the fashionable Western woman eroticized by the Eastern male gaze. In the film, old Shanghai is romanticized through its cobbled alleyways and arched doors with clichés of Eastern mysticism and danger played out through the storyline.

The Guardian journalist Jenny Zhang, in critiquing another of Dior's Orientalist fantasy campaigns, *Shanghai Dreamers* (2010) notes, 'The message couldn't be clearer – the Chinese are ignorant of their own history, desire to imitate the West and need a cultured European to educate them' (cited in Reinach 2012: 62). This claim could equally be made of Karl Lagerfeld's fashion film *Paris-Shanghai: A Fantasy* (2009) in which Coco Chanel visits China of the Cultural Revolution and dresses Maoist revolutionaries in her iconic suit. His view that Shanghai is a space of the exotic imagination is encapsulated by his claim that 'Shanghai for a European is an idea. It's the Shanghai of the future, it's the Shanghai of the past, and it's a mysterious city' (cited in Goh 2011: 96). Such readings are also relevant to the images presented in *Vogue* and *Harper's Bazaar* editorials, which not only reinforce colonial narratives, but also contribute to a market that has a distinct desire for European luxury brands.

It is interesting to note that many of these same luxury labels have produced items of apparel that imagine equally clichéd and stereotyped versions of Chinese fashion that are marketed specifically in Shanghai flagship stores. For example, Chanel's 2010 *Paris-Shanghai* collection, which featured dragon totem jewellery and Chinese take-away box handbags suggests a form of cultural appropriation that attempts to quote back to the Chinese market a bizarre interpretation of imaginary cultural artefacts.

The argument that Francophile images of Shanghai are playing out colonial fantasies of the East is relevant to their interpretation and confirms continued Western dominance in the fashion system. However, it is also worth considering that the image of Shanghai represented as Paris in relation to the narrative of the tale of two cities between Shanghai and Hong Kong; for while Shanghai is positioned as the equivalent to the romantic European fashion capital, Hong Kong replicates the exciting and dynamic characters attributed to London and New York.

London, New York: Hong Kong

Just as Paris has established an iconic fashion city image, London and New York have been similarly reduced to recognizable vistas in order to build a narrative of differentiation from other fashion capitals. New York is portrayed as dynamic and exciting, a place for the fashionable femme to stand out against a towering backdrop. London fashion has been similarly styled, though often accessorized with the backdrop of black cabs, pillar-boxes and double-decker buses. Here the modern woman is elegantly poised against the chaos of urban activity.

Due to Hong Kong's British colonial past, it is not surprising that iconic fashion images of London might provide a suitable set of cityscapes for Hong Kong fashion editorial to appropriate. For example, Baldovino Barani's 'The Final Frontier' photographs for *Prive Asia* (2010) of a couture clad model alighting a tram are reminiscent of Norman Parkinson's iconic *Traffic Queen* (1960) and Georges Dambier's *Angleterre* (1959), both of which feature the speeding double-decker bus as a dramatic counterpoint to the model's elegant silhouette. While there are sure signs in Barani's images that this is London through a looking-glass lens, this scene of modern urbanization is far from the image of Orientalist red lacquer and Harbour Junk that frequently conflates Hong Kong fashion and tourist imagery.

However, London is not the only urban identity that Hong Kong fashion city rhetoric borrows from. More predominantly, editorial published in both Asian and European fashion magazines makes the analogy between Hong Kong as New York. Towering skylines, neon lights and yellow cabs are all part of the fashion lexicon that has established New York as a fashion city of dynamic chic, yet despite these iconic associations they all feature prominently in Hong Kong's fashion city narrative. For example, Alan Chan's 'Giedre, Un Jour À Hong Kong' for *Factice Magazine* (2012), Jeffrey Chan's 'Hong Kong Pink' (2012) (Figure 2) and Gregori Ceveri's 'Vibrant Hong Kong' for *Spain Woman* (2013) all draw heavily on David Baily's recognizable images of Jean Shrimpton in New York (1962). Bailey's New York story actively posed Shrimpton surrounded by quintessential city street scenes; pedestrian crossings, graffiti covered walls, stop signs and roof top vistas. While these vantage points are common to all cities these elements have characterized New York fashion in such an iconic manner that they continue to be replicated in DKNY advertising campaigns, such as Mikael Jansson's photographs of Cara Delevingne for Spring/Summer 2014.

For example, in Jeffrey Chan's fashion photographs Hong Kong is styled and posed to resemble New York. In the same way a model is styled and posed to take on a character, the city is modelled to masquerade as another city. In these images Hong Kong recites New York's fashion objects, taxis, street signs and neon lights in a familiar narrative of a confident modern woman on a cosmopolitan urban adventure. That these images of Hong Kong make such clear allegorical comparisons to New York collapses together the distinctive objects that are that city's unambiguous identifiers.

This visual co-opting of another prominent fashion city thus reinforces the tale of two cities, that is Shanghai and

Figure 2: 'Hong Kong Pink', 2012. Photograph by Jeffrey Chan, jeffreychan.ca; styled by Viviens (Sydney); make-up and hair by Ryan Wing Li, model Eve Smith. Photographs courtesy of Jeffrey Chan.

Hong Kong. It suggests that both these cities look to each other as to how to develop an enduring identity and fashion city status while simultaneously looking to more dominant fashion centres. Like many other peripheral fashion cities, that is, Shanghai and Hong Kong draw upon a lexicon of style where cities masquerade as each other so as to participate in the fashion capital's symbolic value. Dior's 2010 campaign featuring Marion Cotillard posed against the backdrop of Paris, London, New York, Moscow and Shanghai is just one example where the distinctiveness of the fashion city is used to suggest consistency rather than differentiation. These images operate within an understanding that the world's fashion capitals, and their retail spaces are becoming increasingly uniform. As Gilbert (2013: 26) surmises, this 'geography of increasingly similar branded elite consumption spaces' is the new world city order.

The rhetoric of Shanghai as Paris, or Hong Kong as London or New York is aspirational. It is an attempt to build a narrative for these Asian fashion cities within the Western dominated fashion system, and in many instances can be read as a revisiting and reinvention of Orientalist stereotypes, particularly in relation to East meets West encounters. These images are not conducive to making an authentic and distinguishable image for Shanghai or Hong Kong as fashion cities. Instead, they merely offer a homogenized view of globalized fashion that copies Paris, London and New York. While this approach might undermine the necessary distinctive place-making approach that underpins the fashion city image, I contend that this approach might help Hong Kong and Shanghai to differentiate from each other within a discourse that often conflates the two.

In constructing and consolidating an image for Chinese fashion culture, Shanghai as Paris draws from its legendary past to construct an ongoing image of fashion built from the city's cosmopolitan history. Equally, Hong Kong's nod to the similarities between that city and London and New York is an assurance of its continued relevance within the global city network. Huang (2005: 87) has noted that as global cities, Shanghai and Hong Kong are not necessarily rivals, while both are important to China's economic development, 'they have different roles and characteristics'. The narrative of Shanghai as Paris and Hong Kong as New York highlights these different roles, though ultimately demonstrates how Western aesthetics and cultural articulations of fashion have influenced 'Chinese' fashions modes of representation, dissemination and consumption.

Gilbert, Skov and de la Garza and Ding similarly conclude that emergent fashion capitals not only need to engage with the dominant capitals in order to evolve, but also create new and divergent fashion cultures. Perhaps, in the case of Hong Kong and Shanghai's tale of two cities, looking towards each other can represent the new cultures. The 2012 *Harpers Bazaar Hong Kong* editorial, 'Shanghai! Shanghai!' by Steven Cheung, offers a different view of Shanghai as a fashion city. While there are echoes of the Francophile and Orientalist images of Shanghai here, the everyday urbanism of the city's back streets contrasted with the model's couture outfits is a different mode of imaginary geography. Here, fashion provides the pleasure, fantasy and escapism from the real. The Chinese model Jia Jing becomes an object of exoticism among people going about their daily lives, shopping, travelling on scooters and bicycles. The city is not iconically recognizable, but maybe with a retelling of similar narratives it could be.

References

Abbas, A. (2000), 'Cosmopolitan de-scriptions: Shanghai and Hong Kong', *Public Culture*, 12:3, pp. 769–86.

Barani, B. (2010), 'The final frontier', *Prive Asia*, February, http://antm411.com/tag/elyse-sewell-for-prive-asia-magazine/. Accessed 28 August 2014.

Belk, R. and Zhao, X. (2012), 'Advertising and consumer culture in old Shanghai', in S. Okazaki (ed.), *Handbook of Research on International Advertising*, Cheltenham: Edward Elgar.

Berry, J. (2011), 'Modes of the metropolis: The city as photography's fashion icon', *Third Global Fashion Conference*, http://www.inter-disciplinary.net/critical-issues/ethos/fashion/project-archives/3r/session-11b-fashion-cities/. Accessed 14 August 2014.

―――― (2012a), 'Street-style: Fashion photography weblogs and the urban image', in J. Berry (ed), *Fashion Capital: Style Economies, Sites and Cultures*, Oxford: Inter-disciplinary Press.

―――― (2012b), 'The metropolis in Masquerade: Melbourne through the looking-glass lens of fashion photography', *Streetnotes*, 20:1, pp. 31–48, http://escholarship.org/uc/item/7xm2q42g. Accessed 14 August 2014.

Breward, C. and Gilbert, D. (eds) (2006), *Fashion's World Cities*, Oxford: Berg.

Chan, A. (2012), 'Giedre, Un Jour À Hong Kong', *Factice Magazine*, http://alanchanstudio.com/shoot/giedre-un-jour-a-hong-kong-for-factice-magazine/ Accessed 28 August 2014.

Chan, J. (2012), 'Hong Kong pink', http://bentrova.to/classic/photography/hong-kong-pink-by-jeffrey-chan/. Accessed 28 August 2014.

Cheung, S. (2012), 'Shanghai! Shanghai!', *Harper's Bazaar Hong Kong*, September, http://visualoptimism.blogspot.com.au/2012/09/shanghai-shanghai-jia-jing-by-steven.html. Accessed 28 August 2014.

Civera, G. (2011), 'Vibrante Hong Kong', *Spain Woman*, December, http://www.vintagesnoise.thechildlikeempress.com/2011/12/alexa-corlett-by-gregori-civera-for-woman-spain/. Accessed 28 August 2014.

Derujinsky, G. (1958), 'Hong Kong harbour', *Harper's Bazaar*, January, http://derujinsky.tumblr.com/page/5. Accessed 28 August 2014.

de la Garza, A. and Ding, P. (2013), 'A new fashion capital: Shanghai', in S. Bruzzi and P. Church Gibson (eds), *Fashion Cultures Revisited*, Oxford: Routledge.

Gilbert, D. (2000), 'Urban outfitting: The city and the spaces of fashion culture', in S. Bruzzi and P. Church Gibson (eds), *Fashion Cultures: Theories, Explorations and Analysis*, Oxford: Routledge.

―――― (2013), 'A new world order?: Fashion and its capitals in the twenty-first century', in S. Bruzzi and P. Church Gibson (eds), *Fashion Cultures Revisited*, Oxford: Routledge.

Goh, K. (2011), 'The power of C', *Harper's Bazaar Singapore*, June, pp. 92–99.

Global Language Monitor 2014 (2014), 'Top fashion capitals', http://www.languagemonitor.com/fashion/sorry-kate-new-york-edges-paris-and-london-in-top-global-fashion-capital-10thannual-survey/#more-8227. Accessed 14 August 2014.

Huppatz, D. J. (2009), 'Designer nostalgia in Hong Kong', *Design Issues*, 25:2, pp. 14–28.

Largerfeld, K. (2009), *Paris-Shanghai: A Fantasy, The Trip That Coco Chanel Only Made in Her Dreams*, http://chanel-news.chanel.com/en/home/2009/12/paris-shanghai-a-fantasy-the-trip-that-cocochanel-only-made-in-her-dreams-a-short-movie-by-karllagerfeld.html. Accessed 29 August 2014.

Lee, L. Ou-Fan (1999), 'Shanghai modern: Reflection on urban culture in China in the 1930s', *Public Culture*, 11, p. 104.

Lynch, D. (2010), *Lady Blue Shanghai*, Paris: Christian Dior Production.

Minh Nguyen, J. (2012), 'Shanghai with love', *Vogue China*, August, http://visualoptimism. blogspot.com.au/2012/07/shanghai-with-love-monika-jagaciak-by.html. Accessed 28 August 2014.

Miles, S. (2010), *Spaces for Consumption*, London: Sage.

Postrel, V. (2013), *The Power of Glamour*, New York: Simon & Schuster.

Pritchard, A. and Morgan, N. (2005), 'On location: Re (viewing) bodies of fashion and places of desire', *Tourist Studies*, 5:3, pp. 283–302.

Qi, L. (2014), 'Valentino, my name is Red', *Vogue China Collections February Extra*, https:// astairwaytofashion.com/2014/01/28/valentino-my-name-is-red-vogue-china-collections-february-extra-2014-issue/ Accessed 28 August 2014.

Quine, Richard (dir.) (1960), *The World of Suzie Wong*, USA: World Enterprises.

Rocamora, A. (2009), *Fashioning the City: Paris, Fashion and the Media*, London: I.B. Tauris.

Said, E. (1977), *Orientalism*, London: Penguin.

Scavulo, F. (1962), 'Antonia in a dress by Dynasty', *Harper's Bazaar*, June, http://mudwerks. tumblr.com/post/14660804110/via-antonia-in-a-dress-by-dynasty-photographed. Accessed 28 August 2014.

Segre Reinach, S. (2012), 'The identity of fashion in contemporary China and new relationships with the west', *Fashion Theory*, 4:1, pp. 57–70.

Skov, L. (2011), 'Dreams of small nations in a polycentric fashion world', *Fashion Theory*, 15:2, pp. 137–56.

Tsung-yi Michelle Huang (2005), 'Mutual gazing and self-writing: Revisiting the tale of Hong Kong and Shanghai as global city-regions', *Concentric: Literary and Cultural Studies*, 31:1, pp. 71–93.

Von Sternberg, J. (1932), *Shanghai Express*, USA: Paramount Pictures.

Watterstrom, J. N. (2003), 'The second coming of global Shanghai', *World Policy Journal*, 2:20, pp. 51–60.

Yong Bin, C. (2013), 'Shanghai calling', *Harper's Bazaar Korea*, December, http://wearesodroee. com/2013/12/05/shanghai-calling/. Accessed 28 August 2014.

Chapter 15

Weaving Fashion Stories in Shanghai: Heritage, Retro and Vintage Fashion in Modern Shanghai

Natascha Radclyffe-Thomas

The most powerful successful brands have stories attached to them.

(Lindstrom 2010: 134)

Opening with an old-time newsreel countdown, the promotional fashion film for the relaunched Chinese beauty brand Shanghai VIVE transports viewers back to Shanghai's golden era. Two *qipao*-clad beauties wander through sets populated with sepia images of 1930s Shanghai while the voiceover reminds us of Shanghai's cosmopolitan history and the iconic 'Shanghai *Xiaojie*' (Shanghai Miss) who populated the city and set the Shanghai style that is still so familiar to international fashionistas today. In emphasizing the provenance of the brand and its association with one of the most iconic fashion cities in Asia, Shanghai VIVE is complicit in the practice of city branding, as evident in fashion marketing in the historic fashion capitals of Europe: Paris and London.

Shanghai's identity as a fashion city is inexorably linked to its past, both real and imagined. The growth of international trade due to its geographic position and the resulting confluence of cultures put Shanghai at the forefront of China's development in the early twentieth century and the city became a fascinating destination for international travellers. Its iconic architecture, particularly the Bund, featured in images seen around the world and the city, spawned its own modern it-girl identity (Dong 2008) in the form of the Shanghai *Xiaojie* or Chinese flapper, whose likeness continues to be referenced in fashion shoots today. Writing in *Fashion's World Cities* (Breward and Gilbert 2006) David Gilbert asks whether its twenty-first century renaissance might see Shanghai develop an alternative fashion city identity to those established in the West, yet contemporary evidence is to the contrary. This chapter is based on fieldtrips to Shanghai to investigate the fashion retail market, observations and interviews with retailers, focusing especially on how heritage, retro and vintage are evidenced in product and promotions, and puts the evidence collected in the context of recent literature on Shanghai's fashion identity.

A brand's history is key to its claims for authenticity and credibility 'which is one of the reasons why a brand's background and the stories swirling around it are so important' (Lindstrom 2010: 133). Heritage has been seen as a key driver for differentiation of international fashion brands, especially in the luxury segment (Okonkwo 2007) and has been a popular strategy for Western brands' entry into the Chinese market (Lu 2008). The domestic Chinese fashion market is also adopting this marketing approach with the re-launch of heritage brands, or *laozihao* (time-honoured) brands. Brands such as Shanghai VIVE have relaunched themselves with a brand identity firmly situated in pre-1949

Shanghai. Brands such as Shanghai Tang, although founded in Hong Kong, bases its entire brand identity on the celebration of Shanghai's opulent era, designing product, interiors and brand marketing communications that exploit customers' interest in *fugu* (retro) (Radclyffe-Thomas 2015). Many Western luxury brands have used retro-Shanghai as a backdrop to their fashion shows and marketing campaigns, e.g. the fashion film that accompanied Dior's handbag launch: *Lady Blue Shanghai* (Lynch, 2010). Similarly, Shanghai Tang has recently held its catwalk shows in Shanghai, affirming the authenticity of the brand identity. The city of Shanghai itself has emerged as the driver of China's retro brand renaissance, including both brands that celebrate the early modern period but also those that reference Mao-era aesthetics, such as fashion brand Ospop whose classic *jie fang jie* (liberation) shoes are 'proudly Made in China'.

Fashion consumers make positive associations with brands that mediate the brand experience through storytelling (Hancock 2009; Lindstrom 2010) and while the interest in heritage and retro brands and their associated fashion stories appears common to both Western and Chinese fashion consumers, it has been commonly stated that for Chinese fashion consumers vintage was a stylish step too far; Confucian cultural beliefs associating pre-owned clothes with death and economic austerity (Palmer and Clark 2005) precluded a market for vintage fashion. Yet, Shanghai now boasts a burgeoning vintage fashion scene with clothing and accessories sourced overseas and sold in boutiques like Lolo Love Vintage, vintage fairs, luxury vintage consignment stores as well as snapped by Shanghai Streetstyle bloggers.

Heritage Fashion in Shanghai

The curtain of the golden era of Shanghai has never fallen.

(Shanghai VIVE fashion film)

It is a feature of the contemporary fashion industry that fashion brands leverage the provenance of their brand story and heritage in order to differentiate themselves (Kapferer and Bastien 2012). Many historic brands have opened their archives and the development of digital marketing has enabled fashion houses to share their fashion histories online. Many of the prestige fashion marques of Europe have enjoyed unprecedented success entering China and storytelling based on their heritage has been central to their marketing. Along with excellent quality, high prices, uniqueness, superfluity, aesthetic and emotional content, a brand's heritage is cited as one of the six attributes necessary for success in the Chinese luxury market, and consumers have been particularly interested in histories of the luxury firms (Lu 2008). This interest has enabled international brands to introduce consumers to the founders of fashion houses, to the stories of their brand's developments, to foster brand loyalty and thus to promote new products and services. Due to the fact that China was closed to Western fashion for several decades and brands could not rely on established brand recognition and customer loyalty, several European houses have moved beyond traditional marketing campaigns and used exhibitions to educate and engage consumers about the history of their brands. *Esprit Dior,* held in late 2013 at Shanghai's Museum of Contemporary Art was representative of recent collaborations between luxury brands and cultural institutions in showcasing historical garments, fashion photographs and archival materials in exhibitions designed to educate and inspire visitors who can then more fully appreciate shopping the brand. These fashion exhibitions are also coming out of museum and art gallery spaces and into the fashion retail environment. During my fieldtrip to Shanghai the atrium of Shanghai's Plaza 66 was hosting the Berluti *Heritage Exhibition* – an interactive exhibition previewing a new store and showcasing the French custom shoemaker's brand history and artisanship. Digital screens and a history wall traced the development of Berluti since its founding in Paris in 1895, accompanied by display cases showing artefacts such as design sketches and samples of the 'emblematic Berluti knot' and a display of rainbow shoes: the classic Alessandro in a range of fabulous colours and finished with the 'art of patina'.

Another aspect of heritage is that the fashion system has established a hierarchy of fashion cities (Breward and Gilbert 2006) and place marketing leverages the power of particular geographic locations to imbue certain cities with the cachet of chicness or innovation with respect to those brands founded or operating within them. A significant part of Shanghai's aesthetic appeal is in its architecture and many of its neo-classical and art deco buildings have been repurposed for office or retail space. Construction and modernization are evident all over Shanghai, and the Shanghai Municipal government has enacted building preservation measures since the 1990s that cover more than 2000 buildings with varying levels of classification to restrict alterations. Bi-lingual Chinese-English Heritage Architecture plaques adorn many of the buildings I pass; heritage buildings appeal to developers as they are likely to be well-situated 'near the heart of the city and offer interesting spaces and architectural details, and have more soul than newer places' (Warr in Sin 2008: 29). Brands like Dunhill have very much embraced the use of Shanghai's heritage architecture with their Dunhill Home situated in a renovated 1920s neoclassical-style villa on Huaihai Road in the former French concession. Mixed office and retail space at the Shanghai Central Plaza occupies the 1909 former Municipal Council Building of the French Concession also in the Luwan District on Huaihai Middle Road. Just South of Huaihai Road and also within the former French concession is one of Shanghai's most successful and well-known heritage complexes: the commercial restorations that are Xintiandi (new heaven and Earth). A 30,000 square metre site of renovated and reconstructed Shanghainese *Shikumen* houses arranged over two blocks (North and South) of retail, restaurants and apartments, symbols of Shanghai's consumer culture that sandwich the First Congress Hall of the Chinese Communist Party.

Authenticity is a valuable asset for fashion brands in their drive for customer engagement and it is relatively straightforward for Western fashion brands to revisit their archives, to revive former design classics, to host physical or virtual exhibitions that ground their current products and promotions in the vestiges of their past. This is a much more complex position for Chinese fashion brands to take. China has a disjointed fashion history and in Lu's words: 'The last vestiges of the old-wealth heritage of lifestyle and thinking were removed by the Cultural Revolution (1966-76)' (Lu 2008: 11). Fashion marketers seek to reinvent the past through claims on Shanghai's past; for example Tian Zi Fang, which is a newer development than Xintiandi, trades on the evident nostalgia for Shanghai's golden era. Another *Shikumen* redevelopment, the 'Culture Industry Park' throngs with tourists who are greeted by a history of the area complete with diorama, images of *Yuefenpai* (Shanghai calendar girls) at every turn, as are multiple stores selling *qipao* with names that reference Shanghai's past but are in fact recent ventures, e.g. Shanghai Lady and Shanghai 1936 (founded in the 1990s).

The *qipao* remains the most iconic of Chinese garments; the fashion embodiment of golden-era Shanghai and escaping the tourist trap of Tian Zi Fang it is the *qipao* tailors of Changle Lu (or Cheongsam Street) who in fact continue the traditions of the 1920s Shanghai tailors, craftsmen who became world-renowned through their amalgamation of Chinese aesthetics with Western cutting. Tailor-made *qipao* can still be commissioned in multiple glass-fronted stores that use their windows to display their credentials through fine work, press cuttings and images of famous clients. Each with their own speciality, brands like Dun Lin, Han Yi Garments, Hangzhou Zhujun and Li Gu Long claim a genuine fashion heritage and, much as in London's Savile Row, it is the skill and experience of their tailors that give authenticity to the brand stories. It was Han Yi Garments' *sifu* Chu Hongsheng, then in his eighties, who made one of the most recognizable film costumes: Maggie Cheung's series of *qipao* for Wong Kar Wai's 2000 film, *In the Mood for Love*.

Walking on Changle Lu, in the footsteps of novelist Eileen Chang, it is easy to romanticize the golden era of the Shanghai tailor yet coming under the shadow of the many modern retail developments springing up around Shanghai, one wonders to what extent Chinese fashion brands are able to capitalize on their traditional heritage brands. Certainly in the era of fast fashion and made-in-China, European brands have felt confident in the superiority of their artisanship and mocked the idea of China having fashion craft traditions that could rival their own. UNESCO recognizes craft knowledge and skills in its global system of listing 'Intangible Cultural Heritage' traditions, and the Shanghai Municipal Government has designated *qipao* tailoring as among Shanghai's Conservation List of Intangible Cultural Heritage traditions. Several Chinese heritage fashion brands have been accorded this title along with the Ministry of Commerce's endorsement of *laozihao*. Close to Changle Lu, Shaanxi Bei Lu is identified by a brass plaque designating it 'China Time-Honored Brand Shanghai No.1 Street'. Stores endorsed by central and local government for their brand heritage display bilingual Chinese-English plaques and itemize their many heritage and craft recognitions.

Perusing the plaques adorning the storefronts along Shaanxi Bei Lu, I uncover several heritage brands. Established in 1936 the Shanghai Ka Department Store Co Ltd, known for its shirts and woollen sweaters, was one of the earliest to be designated as a *laozihao*. The Shanghai Xinda Meihua Shoes Co Ltd, established in 1940 specializes in women's embroidered shoes. The Shanghai Baromon Suit Company, established in 1928 claims over 40 honours issued by the Municipal and District Governments. The Shanghai Wings Garment Co Ltd established in 1917 is endorsed as a China Time-honoured Brand, and its women's tailoring ('Wings Lady-style Garment Craft') have been added to the Shanghai Conservation List of Intangible Cultural Heritage – as have the skills of the *qipao* makers of the Long Feng Chinese style Garment Company Ltd, established in 1936 and one of the earliest brands to be listed (in 1993), which has had to relocate its flagship store from Nanjing Road due to increasing retail rents.

However, despite government recognition and media interest in the stories of these Chinese heritage brands, it is estimated that only 1500 of the 15,000 traditional Chinese brands (across all industries) are still in business and only ten are doing well (Lin 2012). With Shanghai's rapid expansion, and in common with other major fashion capitals, there is enormous pressure on retail space and Nanjing Road East, which in its heyday boasted more than 60 time-honoured brands is now home to only twenty, retail spaces being dominated by Western multinational fashion brands. According to Shao Yuling Secretary (general of the Shanghai Time-Honored Brands Association): 'There used to be a lot of time-honoured brands along Nanjing Road and they were the symbols of the street. But now, when you look around it's all foreign brands. The old days now exist only in memory' (Liu 2012).

A few of the Chinese *laozihao* heritage brands are adopting new brand strategies and attempting to establish themselves in the international market. A Chinese brand formerly located on Nanjing Road, and using its heritage as a marketing strategy, is Humsuit, the tailoring firm established in 1929, whose tailoring techniques have been placed on the Shanghai municipal government designated Shanghai Intangible Cultural Heritage List of 157 traditions. Apparel brands such as Heng Yuan Xiang, a luxury woollens producer established in 1927, has rebranded itself, raised brand awareness and aims to establish itself as a key international player in luxury branded goods (Bevolo et al. 2011).

One of the most high-profile relaunches of a *laozihao*, with a marketing strategy by the French company Cent Degres, is beauty brand Shanghai VIVE, a brand whose name combines one of fashion's fantasy cities with an allusion to the golden era of Shanghai's French concession. Relaunched in 2010 with a branch in Tian Zi Fang nestled among the nostalgia retailers, the brand's flagship store is consciously situated within one of Shanghai's key heritage buildings, the Peace Hotel (formerly Sassoon House) just off Shanghai's famous Bund. Its styling and promotional materials very much associate Shanghai VIVE with recollections of 1930s Shanghai. A section of the building's exterior windows feature Shanghai VIVE promotions and reinforce its associations with the city through photographs of the product against a backdrop of Shanghai architecture and with actual product displayed among installations of Shanghai's architecture reproduced in paper sculptures. The store itself is styled in slick black and pink with an art deco sensibility. The beauty line has been extended with art deco bags and silk scarves illustrated with stylized 1930s modern women; product is displayed in glass-topped counters and visual references to the Shanghai calendar girls are presented along with the modern but retro-styled beauty images – the two girls of the original marketing rebranded for the twenty-first century, and attention drawn to the brand's long history which the saleswomen are happy to recount.

According to the brand's promotional materials, *Shuang Mei* (two sisters) perfume and beauty products was founded in Hong Kong in 1898 by the Feng family, and had its first retail store on Nanjing Road. It launched its iconic Radiance Restorative Cream in 1915 and this product raised the brand's international profile, being awarded a gold medal at the Panama-California Exposition in San Francisco. At the Tian Zi Fang branch a fashion film runs on an in-store screen setting its appeal with a throwback to 1930s glamour and establishing its pedigree by taking consumers through the brand's history, telling the Shanghai VIVE story. The film shows how the brand became associated with the modern Shanghai of the 1930s and its celebrity culture, and how its international reputation and accolades from the Parisian beauty industry led to its nickname Shanghai VIVE. The film underlines Shanghai VIVE's association with the city, which is described as 'the most open, dynamic and glamorous city in China', showing sepia-tinted images of its art deco architecture followed by a snapshot representation of Shanghai's it-girls' lifestyle: residing in the chic art deco apartments of Eddington House (Shanghai storyteller Eileen Chang's former residence on Hart Road [now Changde Road]), shopping on Xiaofei Road (now Huaihai Road), and dancing at the ultra-moderne Paramount dance hall. The film establishes historical brand ambassadors by featuring legendary and accomplished socialite beauties of the 1930s: Tang Ying (fashion designer), Lu Xiaoman (artist), Zhang Ailing (Eileen Chang) and Zhou Shuping (translator). Shanghai's identity is firmly linked to the image of these modern women and we look over the shoulders of two representative retro-styled beauties at a clock face with hands whizzing, fading out to show the modern Pudong skyline before a change in soundtrack and shots of red carpets and ribbon-cutting announce Shuang Mei's 2010 rebirth as Shanghai VIVE: 'the legendary beauty story of Shanghai aristocratic ladies'.

Retro Fashion in Shanghai

The objects we consume can be seen as a live information system, through which cultural messages are conveyed and contested.

(Gabriel and Lang 2006: 44)

The fashion system constantly reinvents the past and an abiding trend in Western fashion has been the reviving of recent fashion history through retro. The relatively recent past is trawled through by trend agencies and fashion magazines and presented for fashion consumers through increasingly visual fashion media communicated through print, digital and social media. This practice is amplified by multiple nostalgia-driven trends e.g. *down aging* (faithpopcorn.com) and fuels the current upsurge in retro. Shanghai has been the inspiration for and site of several Chinese retro brands; designers in Shanghai, both natives

Figure 1: The Shanghai VIVE boutique in Shanghai's Peace Hotel. Photograph by Natascha Radclyffe-Thomas.

Figure 2: Shanghai Tang's Cathay Mansion flagship store, Shanghai. Photograph by Natascha Radclyffe-Thomas.

and newcomers plunder personal memories and/or imagined histories of the city creating new fashion lines for consumers with an appetite for Shanghai stories.

As stated earlier, brands such as Shanghai Tang have built a brand identity based on consumers' obsession with retro, in their case basing product, in-store environment and marketing on the glamour of 1930s Shanghai. Launched in 1994 in Hong Kong by Sir David Tang aimed at an expat and tourist market, the brand has celebrated its landmark twentieth twentieth anniversary, targeting international expansion, attempting to maintain associations with Shanghai's golden era glamour but avoiding *cheongsam* clichés. The rebrand is evident in its Shanghai flagship store located in the renovated Cathay Mansion at the junction of Huaihai Middle Road and Maoming South Road; the world's largest Shanghai Tang fashion flagship is housed in a 1932 art deco heritage-listed building it shares with Shanghai's second oldest cinema. The mansion offers several different zones that encompass the womenswear, menswear, childrenswear, accessories and lifestyle ranges. Located in an area renowned for tailoring, the importance of Shanghai tailoring to brand identity is shown in the Imperial Tailoring boutique, which displays antique sewing machines, bolts of fabric and Chinese knot fastenings in a 1930s Shanghai salon atmosphere, where I sit and enjoy Chinese tea. The tea is served in delicate turquoise teacups decorated with the brightest orange goldfish on saucers decorated with stylized Chinese cloud patterns and I briefly remind myself how much I regret not having bought this particular crockery while it was still in production, as the marketing team start to talk me through recent brand developments.

While the Shanghai Tang *cheongsam* remains a core product in honour of Sir David Tang, the brand is expanding its fashion lines and increasing its product offer capitalizing on increased domestic interest in Chinese history and products. The accessories and women's fashion lines have been extended, as has the menswear. While the womenswear still references Chinese design aesthetics, if not so much in silhouette but clearly in the print designs, the menswear references the leisure wardrobes of the Western expats who inhabited

Shanghai in the 1920s and 1930s. The polo shirt has been a core product for Shanghai Tang, who have recently collaborated with the Shanghai Rugby Union Football Club and issued a series of rugby polo shirts featuring the logos and in the colours of the pre-war interport clubs: the Hankow 1921 Historical Collection.

Retro is not just about style and reliving history; it can be about reviving past craft skills. Founded in 1998 by Shanghai native Denise Huang Mengqi, Suzhou Cobblers is situated just off the Bund; its core products are hand-sewn embroidered Chinese slippers with designs featuring classic Chinese motifs, e.g. cherry blossom, birds and fish in a rainbow of colours in '100% Chinese silk, the kind that long made Shanghai tailors the envy of the world' (suzhoucobblers.com). There is also a small collection of high heels and reticule-style embroidered silk bags and a selection of 1930s Shanghai fashion illustrations on display. Suzhou was and remains a centre of embroidery and Suzhou Cobblers employs quality and artisanship as a differentiator for the brand, one that obviously appeals to the international luxury shopper (the brand is featured in the *Shanghai Luxe* shopping guide). The brand's website gives an insight into the design strategy of Suzhou Cobbler, linking the style back to its founder's idea of what her 'style-conscious grandmother' would have worn and revealing that the 'colors and patterns reflect Shanghai's grandest era, when my hometown was a fashion capital' (Huang 2014).

Figure 3: Retro store 1691, Shanghai. Photograph by Natascha Radclyffe-Thomas.

A bilingual Chinese-English display in the window of Shanghai Trio's Xintiandi store explains the philosophy behind the brand and their design inspiration: 'Breathing in and experiencing the smells of the marketplace that permeates the streets and lanes of Shanghai'. Shanghai Trio is another retro brand whose design ethos is based on an appreciation of Shanghai's past, but counter to much of the Shanghai-inspired fashion brands, the past they are reviving is not the exclusive after-dark one of dance-halls and *qipao*, but the commonplace one of workers, bicycles and markets: 'our ideas transpire from personal memories and wandering around China' (Notes on Design 2014). Their website front-page proclaims: 'Details have a story' and Virginie Fournier founded Shanghai Trio in 1998 to create fashion products that celebrate the traditional arts and crafts of China, and promote the luxury of hand-made products inspired by the traditional artefacts of Chinese daily life (http://www.shanghaitrio.com). A key product is their Post Office bag: elevating the everyday to the designer, it is made from the original fabric used by the Chinese Post Office but produced in revamped colours. Electrician's bags and vintage 'Shanghai street' bags are also inspirations for accessories as well as rice-measures, which are reimagined as a series of vanity cases. Customers are increasingly interested in the story of how their products are made and Shanghai Trio is keen to promote its socially responsible production. Although mainly known for its accessories, Shanghai Trio also produces high-quality garments based on the simple shapes of Chinese scholar robes.

Another retro brand born from a fascination with Chinese workwear is the online retailer Ospop (One Small Piece of Pride) whose key product is the canvas *jie fang xie* (liberation shoe) that harks back to the footwear of the Mao era. Ospop's founder Ben Walters has taken this classic shoe, adorns each pair with the Chinese character *gong* (labour) and, referencing the Shanghai construction workers who were the brand's inspiration, produces them in a rugged colour palette of cement, slate and brick. Ospop has leveraged the world's interest in China and produced memorable marketing campaigns like its 'Proudly Made in China' series to take the brand global before trying to develop in the domestic market (*Jing Daily* 2011). Ospop uses its website to spread the brand story and uses its ethical domestic production – the shoes are made in Henan – to proclaim that they are proudly made in China.

Although one feels that Shanghai's past is very much alive in the modern city, not all the retro stories told in Shanghai are Chinese ones. Behind its commune grey exterior adorned with a large communist red star, the company 1691 on Changle Road is very much a celebration of US retro. The stock of denims, flight jackets, khaki flying suits and rucksacks are displayed against a rugged interior of exposed brick and wood panelled walls and stripped floorboards reminiscent of a hunting lodge. With references to Western pop culture throughout the store, including the Route 66 Hi-Way café, this store could be anywhere.

Vintage Fashion in Shanghai

Secondhand used to mean less value.

(Julia, founder of Annata Vintage)

The appeal of dressing-up in someone else's history has been popular in Western fashion since at least the 1960s. But more recently what traditionally had an underground appeal has been established as a key fashion trend with specialist second-hand clothing stores like Beyond Retro expanding from its base in London's hipster favourite Shoreditch to several retail stores and a website claiming to feature more than 25,000 vintage pieces. Vintage has moved from an underground to a mainstream trend in the West, yet fashion commentators have repeated the commonly held belief that Chinese consumers eschew vintage fashion due to its associations with poverty and cultural superstitions around wearing a dead person's clothing. However, there is also a Chinese saying: 'There is nothing the Cantonese

Figure 4: Lolo Love Vintage, Shanghai. Photograph by Natascha Radclyffe-Thomas.

will refuse to eat and nothing the Shanghainese will refuse to wear' and there has been a lot of press about vintage stores opening in China. The final act of this story sees me wandering up *longtangs* (alleys) and stairwells and peeping behind hidden doorways to explore vintage fashion in Shanghai and discover the stories of their collections.

One of the features common to Shanghai's vintage stores is that they rarely seem to stay in one place. Lolo Love Vintage is one of Shanghai's highest profile vintage stores, founded in 2010 and already in its third location, close to the former French concession in Xuihui district. A sign illustrated with a line drawing of a stylized vintage beauty with blue eyes, rose-bud lips and a hairdo that features a prominent strawberry hangs above the blue door which marks the store's location: it is notable that the sign is only in English. The blue door, itself also decorated with a 1920s fashion illustration, opens onto a garden courtyard featuring real palms, fake cacti, indoor furniture outdoors, a vintage pram and life-size animal sculptures – a giant rabbit welcomes you at the entrance to the store. In common with current practice in many designer retail spaces, the store is not designed for purely transactional purposes, but rather as somewhere to spend time; the previous incarnation of Lolo Love Vintage had a coffee shop and although this store does not, it has a relaxed salon atmosphere and the garden encourages customers to hang out. The whimsy of the courtyard is continued in-store with an interior featuring antique furniture, crystal chandeliers and satin evening shoes displayed in a birdcage. It is quite a large store with several rooms over one floor, every surface of which is covered in garments, accessories, vintage illustrations and photographs. As testament to the growing interest in vintage, a flier for an upcoming Shanghai vintage fair is on the counter next to a vintage till.

Fashion stylist Lolo founded Lolo Love Vintage in 2009 and the stock covers the 1920s to 1980s. The garments are overwhelmingly womenswear although there are collections of childrenswear and a selection of men's ties, all sourced from France, Germany, the United Kingdom

Figure 5: Annata Vintage founder Julia, Shanghai. Photograph by Natascha Radclyffe-Thomas.

and Los Angeles. The store reminds me of any fabulous vintage emporium anywhere with day dresses and separates, lingerie, and evening and wedding dresses, handbags, shoes and costume jewellery, silk scarves, hat boxes and sunglasses. The majority of clothing is Western, but there are a few Chinese fashion items including a 1960s beaded *qipao*. Shanghai is destination shopping and as the popularity of vintage spreads tourists come from all over China to buy vintage at Lolo and, according to the shop assistant, range from high school students to fifty-year-olds. Additionally, stylists and fashion magazines raid the cornucopia of fashion finds for use in fashion shoots.

A more recent addition to the vintage retail scene and also located in Xuihui is Annata Vintage. Peering doubtfully down a *longtang* I spy a hand-painted sign that informs me the store is to be found 89 steps from the entrance of Lane 316 – and it is, behind a green door that leads into a small courtyard, across which is the entrance to the store. The founder, Julia, tells me that Annata is Italian for 'years' and invites me to sit and enjoy tea while she tells me her vintage story. The small one-room store has an antique hospital bed at its centre; the deco bedside table beside it has a pair of antique cups and saucers on it and a novel with a pair of vintage spectacles placed casually on it. The bed is made up and has a sleeveless vintage top and full skirt laid out on it along with a handbag and a couple of vintage magazines, giving the impression that a fashionable 1950s young woman is about to re-enter and dress for the day. Surrounding the bed are racks of vintage pieces, and above those shelves of vintage handbags, magazines and ephemera, which also spill out from vintage suitcases on the floor.

I am served flower tea in another exquisite porcelain teacup, but this time it is a vintage one, one of Julia's first collectibles, a souvenir brought back from a trip to Europe. The concept behind the Annata Vintage store is one of collating memories: 'old things have a story and memory'. Julia talks enthusiastically about the stories behind the vintage pieces on display, notably an unworn silk blouse with embroidered panels, made in China but sourced in Japan. Julia studied marketing and then fashion and her appreciation of construction informs her choices for the store as she focuses on workmanship, materials and has a keen eye for zips, buttons and stitches. Although she herself sports a 1920s gamine bob and bee-stung red lips, she says that as women's bodies have changed, pre 1940s clothes look gorgeous but do not fit, and furthermore her customers are modern women who appreciate vintage clothes but do not want to 'look vintage'.

The majority of the clothing and accessories in the store are Western fashion – I spot a Schiaparelli hat and a Liberty print day dress on the racks. They were initially sourced from Japan but sourcing has expanded to Korea, the United Kingdom, Holland, Italy, Ireland and the United States – taking advantage of friends' and relatives' travels. According to Julia vintage is a very new but upcoming trend in Shanghai, the majority of local fashion consumers are not interested in vintage, second-hand was deemed of less value and locals would rather shop at H&M and Zara. Annata was only founded in 2013 but has already become a destination shop – Julia proudly tells me about a group of fashion students from Northern China who made Annata the first stop on a three-day cultural trip to Shanghai. *China Vogue* also keeps an eye on the store's inventory in order to borrow pieces for fashion editorials – notably 1970s pieces, and last year a lot of evening styles to complement a *Great Gatsby* story. Although considerably smaller than Lolo Love Vintage, Annata is also intended as a salon store and a few regulars pop by and partake of tea and conversation during my visit. Customers are Western and *haigui* (Chinese who have studied abroad), who are familiar with vintage fashion from their overseas' experiences and whose mini Polaroid photos decorate the walls of the changing room.

While these vintage stores are reminiscent of vintage stores in the United Kingdom and the United States, Old Lyric, found down a *longtang* and up the staircase of a period building in the Luwan district, is a different type of vintage fashion store altogether. In contrast to the other Shanghai vintage stores, the environment at Old Lyric is reminiscent of an upmarket boutique. Brushed concrete walls, an antique dressmakers' dummy and sparse merchandise, the atmosphere is also notably cooler (in both senses). The vintage pieces – both womenswear and menswear – are curated luxury from key international avant-garde fashion designers, pieces selected to represent the highpoints of the careers of sixteen designers including Ann Demeulemeester, Comme des Garcons, Dries Van Noten, Yohji Yamamoto and Jean Paul Gaultier. Another recent addition to Shanghai's vintage retail scene, Old Lyric – its logo is a bass clef – was only founded in 2013 by Zephyrance Lou but has already received a lot of fashion media attention, especially for the way it uses social media to educate consumers about the designers and products it features (*Jing Daily* 2013).

US writer and *New Yorker* columnist Emily Hahn lived in Shanghai in the late 1930s and her observation that 'Shanghai is always changing' is quoted in many pieces on modern Shanghai. Fashion marketers have discovered the power of storytelling and these vintage stores are the newest chapter in Shanghai's fashion story. Lindstrom argues that consumers are 'entranced by stories (particularly ones they can complete with their own imaginary endings, or meanings)' (2010: 134), and it is interesting to imagine, as David Gilbert did, what the future of Shanghai's fashion will be (see Berry in this volume). Will there be more brand relaunches as is happening with European fashion houses? Will time-honoured brands be able to capitalize on their heritage? Will retro brands be able to develop wide product-bases? Will their customers allow them to move beyond their imitative styles? How are the cultural associations of vintage changing, and will the Chinese fashion tourist continue to want to dress up in somebody else's fashion story? But that's another story.

References

Bevolo, M., Gofman, A. and Moskowitz, H. R. (2011), *Premium by Design: How to Understand, Design and Market High End Products*, Farnham: Gower Publishing, Ltd.

Breward, C. and Gilbert, D. (eds) (2006), *Fashion's World Cities*, Oxford and New York: Berg.

Dong, M. Y. (2008), 'Who is afraid of the Chinese modern girl?', in A. E. Weinbaum, L. M. Thomas, P. Ramamurthy, U. G. Poiger, M. Y. Dong and T. E. Barlow (eds), *The Modern Girl around the World*, Durham and London: Duke University Press, pp. 194–219.

Faithpopcorn (2014), *17 Trends*, http://www.faithpopcorn.com/trendbank/. Accessed 3 August 2014.

Gabriel, Y. and Lang, T. (2006), *The Unmanageable Consumer*, London: Sage.

Hancock, J. (2009), *Brand Story*, New York: Fairchild Books.

Huang, D. (2014), *My Chinese Slippers*, http://www.suzhou-cobblers.com/about_us. Accessed 1 May 2014.

Jing Daily (2011), 'A conversation with Ben Walters of Chinese sneaker brand Ospop', 18 January, http://jingdaily.com/a-conversation-with-ben-walters-of-chinese-sneaker-brand-ospop/. Accessed 1 May 2014.

——— (2013), 'Old lyric: A Shanghai pioneer of "timeless" vintage', 2 December, http://jingdaily.com/old-lyric-a-shanghai-pioneer-of-timeless-vintage/. Accessed 1 May 2014.

Kapferer, J.-N. and Bastien, V. (2012), *The Luxury Strategy: Break the Rules of Marketing to Build Luxury Brands*, London: Kogan Page.

Lin, L. (2012), 'Top 10 time-honored Chinese brands', 8 November, http://www.china.org.cn/top10/2012-11/08/content_27046348_3.htm. Accessed 1 May 2014.

Lindstrom, M. (2010), *Brand Sense*, New York: Free Press.

Lu, P. X. (2008), *Elite China: Luxury Consumer Behavior in China*, Singapore: Wiley.

Lynch, D. (2010), *Lady Blue Shanghai*, France: Christian Dior S.A.

Notes on Design (2014), 'Virginie Fournier: Founder of Shanghai Trio', http://www.sessions.edu/notes-on-design/virginie-fournier-founder-of-shanghai-trio. Accessed 1 May 2014.

Okonkwo, U. (2007), *Luxury Fashion Branding*, Basingstoke: Palgrave Macmillan.

Palmer, A. and Clark, H. (eds) (2005), *Old Clothes New Looks: Second-Hand Fashion*, Oxford and New York: Berg.

Radclyffe-Thomas, N. (2015), 'Stitching across time: Heritage and history in contemporary Hong Kong fashion', *Clothing Cultures*, 2:3, pp. 241–55.

Sin, L. H. (2008), 'Preserving the past', *Insight*, March, pp. 27–30, http://www.amcham-shanghai.org/amchamportal/InfoVault_Library/2008/Preserving_the_Past.pdf. Accessed 1 May 2014.

Suzhou Cobblers official website (2014), 'About us', http://www.suzhou-cobblers.com/about. Accessed 1 May 2014.

Chapter 16

X Marks the Spot: The Phenomena of Visuality and Brandscaping as Material Culture

Demetra Kolakis

This chapter will explore the phenomena of visuality and brandscaping by conducting a research case study-based enquiry into the representational conventions of environment, image, time and space and by questioning the paradox of vision and attention; merging aesthetics and cultural commentary in ways that initially mask underlying meanings of spectator/shopper; consumerism and hyper-consumption. The aim of this chapter is to investigate the use of spatial communication of brandscaping as material culture by exploring this through aesthetics, form and function to better understand the role of the fashion environment as spatial communication. Firstly, this analysis will identify the reasons why fashion brands are using this approach to branding, and secondly it will examine how brands in general are using it. The findings will offer additional insights into the multi-sensory experience of the brandscaping concept. This study explores the meaning and use of branded spaces and atmospheric strategies in addition to those who experience the fashion environment. According to John Potvin, 'the encounters with fashion happen within a space at a given place and do not simply function as backdrops but are pivotal to the meaning and vitality that the experiences of fashion trace' (Potvin 2009). Space is a vital component of the communication matrix developing the individual and daily experiences of fashion, from blogs to Facebook, and in the general presentation of fashion. Hence, this research provides opportunities to identify emotional and psychological connections in differentiating and distinguishing a brand as an image. This reinvestigation of space will consider fashion's function as conceptual, literal and experiential, lived as a sensory stimuli. The sensory experience of branding is linked to the individual's striving for identity, as well as self-fulfillment and entertainment. This image building is linked to the consumption of brands and experiences giving individuals an opportunity to create their own unique identity and image.

Marc Augé's theory of the 'non-places in super modernity' (Augé 1995) is the basis of an exploration of the image as temporal and changing within space/non-space. To explore the creation of environmental, architectural and digitalized space, the image can be used to focus on the creation of a physical, emotional, narrative and performance space and its effect on the audience inhabiting that space, whether even momentarily. This introduces chance, spontaneity and time into visuality in a new way as the spectator chooses which one to preserve in their memory.

Instances of non-place as forms of transience, as highways, airports and supermarkets are places with no historical reference, which pervade our everyday experiences in an increasingly technological, and communication-based culture. Our visual language is based on our acceptance of a physically limited engagement of visuality as being reality through our own interests and visual pursuits. We often respond and remember these uninhabitable experiences in the non-place, as though we had physically been there, as Augé notes, 'Modernity in art preserves all the temporalities of place, the ones that are located in space and in words' (Augé 1995: 77).

This research project as a whole comprises a visual archive, and case study analyses. In this instance, the author to record experimentations as a reference and to create documentation to examine visual thinking using the methodology of observation and visual perception inside the non-space initiated the creation of a visual archive. Within the current context, the act of researching uncovered and enabled new combinations of imagery – 'spaces' that are characterized by a degree of uncertainty that make them more challenging. As such, in addition to the archive, a series of case studies were conducted to analyse and address the subject of brandscaping from a multisensory perspective.

Essentially, this project investigates the spatial communication of brandscaping as a cultural form of expression conveying the suggestive power between image and identity, innovation and tradition, consumerism and fashion. This research study considers the new visual relationship between static printed and physical space. In turn, this results in a questioning and redefining of the configuration of space and public through the experience of viewing.

Visuality and Brandscaping

Exploring visual communication regarding the fashion image and representation often challenges the discipline and critiques the role that fashion can play in reshaping cultural practices and society whereby, '[i]dentity is no longer crystallized in images: it is configured precisely as a fluid dimension, nomadic, in constant transformation, in constant migration' (Marchetti and Quinz 2007: 120). As new technologies are introduced into the field of fashion imagery, they change the possibilities of how things are rendered by creating new options for what forms the actual object in the world will take.

The image, as digital data, has become an infinite unit that can be reshaped to form sequences and transformations, creating a multitude of possibilities for images to cross over into other disciplines. The fashion image becomes a fluid form, ready to become a print, a frame on a web page or a frame in a film crossing all forms via visual communication, including performance, installation, public art, intervention or production and is one component connected to a larger visual field. The expanded form of the fashion image from print to a simultaneous presence in multiple locations, at any given time, becomes a new form of time-based visuality. The fashion image becomes an experience, through repetitive actions in an interactive environment leaving traces of the image behind. The visual concepts, languages and processes that shift through boundaries and disciplines provide a new approach to the fashion image, which has developed through expanded media creating a new visual dialogue. This is an examination of the relationship that digital technologies and new media have on existing media, as well as the new ways in which they function as new media in visual communication.

New technologies have allowed artists/designers to continually expand the limits of form and function in fashion through visuality and beyond. As a result, fashion is becoming intangible, and the event, spectacle and experience are as important as the quality of the fashion object. The garment is only one element and the representation of the fashion object as the intangible experience is the event. The 'artifying' of stores enables consumers to live an entire experience, to feel unexpected and polymorphous pleasures, such as the aesthetic delights of the store 'in short, the shopper feels improved by the experience' (Lipovetsky and Manlow 2007: 165). The 'artification' of retail spaces becoming part art gallery, cafe or boutique thereby blurring the boundaries between art, and fashion, and addressing fashion through a site-specific experience. A hybrid form of art and fashion places are created where architects, fashion designers and artists have collaborated resulting in representing the label or collection as a cultural experience, such as museum/gallery-based exhibitions, installation, film or performance.

Fashion communicates through images, signs and symbolic elements, such as social semiotics that are difficult to summarize on the basis of a single item. The attention has shifted from product to brand identity thus developing a need for visual consistency between the fashion image and the brand image. The one objective is to immediately communicate the name of the brand, establishing the store or the physical space, to become a part of the visual mass communication dialogue. It is through the spatial communication of the brand message that the spatial environment is established redefining visuality as being experience-oriented. Brandscaping transforms the brand itself into a location. Anthropologist John Sherry is credited with coining the term 'brandscaping' in 1986 (Upshaw 1995: 48), a term that can be defined as,

> Brandscaping: (BRAND.skayp) *n.* The brand landscape; the expanse of brands and brand-related items (logos, ads, and so on) within a culture.
>
> (Wordspy 2000)

One could argue that fashion and visuality are always in a state of flux, due to the rapid, ever evolving state of technology and, as a result of meditization visual media is today constantly infiltrating us. Brandscaping introduces moments of visual redefinition, when the institutionalized realms of power open up spaces of experimentation to retrace the path towards the future of fashion image, brand identity and fashion media through new platforms of the communicative dialogue.

Digital communication and the Internet are replacing traditional forms of communication and are becoming increasingly attractive to the young affluent consumer who will search globally and online for their favourite brands (Soloman et al. 2013). Consequently, the retail market has been redefined and retail spaces play an integral role in the communication between brand and consumer. This is evidenced by a multitude of emerging retail epicentre or flagship stores, where brand image and experience are the prevalent forms of communication and retail design. Brands are challenged in creating distinctive environments and are designed to create atmospheric experiences in order to provide for shopping's new dimension of entertainment. The brand image sells the product, and not vice versa. The brand image informs consumers of the functional capabilities while simultaneously communicating the symbolic values and meanings of the brand. Appropriately, the brand image is likely to be formed by the simultaneous absorption of fashion media/branded environment. The new retail spaces where consumer and product interact need to develop a brand fascination and a shopping experience, which cannot be replicated by ecommerce. As a result to the growth of ecommerce, brands must ensure that physical shopping environments are desirable places for consumers; otherwise there is no real reason to visit when there are so many alternatives to choose from.

Writing in a Prada manual Rem Koolhaas states, 'in a world where everything is shopping and shopping is everything [...] true LUXURY is NOT shopping' (2001: 43). This is key in understanding how fashion stores are incorporated into the larger conceptualization

Figure 1: Demetra Kolakis, *Untitled* (Visual Archive Series), C Print, 2011.

of shopping as culture, and articulated in the architecture and retail design of the brand. According to Koolhaas, retail space becomes a medium and a space where the multivalent expression of the *brand* may be consumed, exhibited and experienced. The fashion store no longer wants to be a reduced to having a role of simple retail functionality, instead it must be a source of aesthetics, cultural and sensory experiences, reflecting the changing values of society and culture where the act of purchasing is richly situated aesthetics and cultural emotions defining hyper-consumption. Prada, for example, has turned their store into a sort of theatre of culture, a place for intellectual refinement with the possibility of shopping being added on. These creations of new spaces of interaction turn the experience of shopping into an adventure for the consumer who will probably not necessarily buy anything aside from remembering the experience of being there. The world of new store spaces and those of cinemas are similar being imaginary visual tours through alternative worlds extending visual access to fashion and luxury. The shoppers' gaze and the movie spectators' viewpoint share the same cultural logic where the visual experience is an indirect form of possession, as the framed visuality becomes a commodity itself. Here, the verb 'to shop' implies choice in the relation between looking and having as a mode of visual speculation.

Research Case Studies: Multi-Sensory Fashion Brands

When shopping, therefore, I am immersed in culture as this activity stopped being primarily about purchasing things long ago. Whether or not the consumer ends up purchasing a product or service, the images themselves are being consumed. This case study based project research addresses the issue of aesthetics, in relation to the atmosphere of retail environments. Brands used to be distinguished by their name and visual logo; however, now the idea is that they should ideally be registered in as many senses as possible, based on the notion that the consumer is most likely to form, retain and revisit memory when all five senses are engaged.

Hence, this research explores the multisensory consumer experience in retail environments, examining the visual interactions with other elements (available tactile information) in order to examine the underlying interactive effects of consumer behaviour and reactions to sensorial stimuli. The scope of this research has the potential to provide direction to both retailers and consumers towards the creation and use of sensory stimuli in retail environments. By going beyond traditional communication, brands can establish a stronger connection with consumers given that this research suggests the key element in communicating the brand was the visuality of the space, the consumer identity and the shopping experience. This occurrence is similar to visiting an art gallery or museum, or sitting at a themed café, individuals immerse themselves in the fashion environment of the concept store. It becomes a walk-in lifestyle magazine where customers leave the

Figure 2: Demetra Kolakis, *Untitled* (Visual Archive Series), C Print, 2011.

environment essentially untouched. The aesthetics of every experience created within the individual is real, whether stimuli are natural or stimulated (Pine and Gilmore 1999: 35).

According to Kant in *Anthropology from a Pragmatic Point of View* (1974), the only senses capable of aesthetic reasoning are sight and sound because they include factors capable of objective reasoning due to perception/perceptive. The power of aesthetics is the ability to give one a sense of personal identity in producing a world of what is thought to be important. However, experience is usually modelled on pre-fabricated images. For example, film and media have presented the public with an idea of what love and being in love is and looks like. For example, Tiffany's centre their brand image on the theme of 'true love'. In direct response to the rise of Instagram, Tiffany's incorporated an aesthetic-based approach by introducing Instagrammers to document images that represented true love in New York and Paris, then share these images through their account.

The visuality of an experience is produced from brand images in the visually influenced, consumption-oriented psyche. Therefore, it is completely correct to say that the public consumes or purchases both experiences and identity through media. Sociologist Gerhard Schulze in *The Experience Society* (2005) refers to the aesthetics of lifestyles.

Schulze identifies the goals of previous generations as being primarily material ones in terms of their own house or their own car – and today we define the meaning of our life in psychological and physical terms, in terms of what makes me feel good. Retail spaces are setting the stage, an arena for experience, becoming a mix of shopping and entertainment, and are seen as an offensive to its electronic competition. According to Pine and Gilmore (2011: 156–57), retail spaces are constructed as facades, similar to a theatre stage or movie set, as an area for the consumer experience. The transformation of product into consumer experience is fabricated in a fixed space, similar to a theatre set including props, displays and actors as consumers with happy endings when they reach for a credit card to make a purchase.

Brandscaping case studies were conducted on flagship stores/epicentres to subjectively examine the brand experience first-hand. One example of such a case study is Acne, both in London and Paris, where the store has the same visual genre and voice. The brand image, even though distinct and unique to each locale, has a foundation and elements true to brand representation. Putting forth a contemporary urban feel, Acne uses and reuses locations such as former garages, creating an industrial feel. Also, in this respect, the Acne environment is suggestive of a contemporary art gallery whereby the collection is housed and displayed with the garments presented as artistic objects, crafted and unique. The Acne experience/space evaluation is visually activating as one explores the spaces. By breaking out from the endless stream of couture boutiques, partially through the conversion of industrial spaces combined with a contemporary Scandinavian design aesthetic, the result is that of a conceptual space blurring art, experience and fashion.

Another case study example, Dover Street Market in London, is a destination where the boundaries between fashion and art also blur. This urban space generates the experience of being in an exhibition, where selected pieces of a collection are displayed and housed. Part gallery, part café, part shop, this is an environment which includes temporary exhibitions, book launches and presentations from invited artists culminating in the experience of a stimulating visual journey from floor to floor. Walking through this market from floor to floor, the visual experience is a journey, very much parallel with that of visiting an art gallery or museum. The encounters of escapist experiences at this concept shop involve the innovation of fusing fashion, arts, design, books, photography, music, food and technological marvels together in one space; creating a place worth escaping to, for spending time, browsing, relaxing, dining and socializing.

Flagship stores offer experiential moments than their counterparts. They are seen as the ideal of, or the source for the brand image and offer up more to the consumer. The flagship store is a showcase for the brand, providing something unique that enables the individual to interact with the brand on a multisensory level, thus generates an emotional response and attracts attention. The best flagships offers one the opportunity to be inspired, to have fun, to be entertained, to be awe-struck, to free their imaginations, to be pampered, to socialize or to relax. In short, they provide the best, most memorable shopping experience *ever*, therefore the pinnacle of success for any flagship is to become such a destination.

In the example of Miller Harris, the fragrance perfume shop located in Mayfair's Bruton Street, London, scent tests are offered with afternoon tea. As such, Miller Harris is not simply a perfume shop but an experiential destination. The customization of space for the brand image as communication is also clearly seen in the case study of Paul Smith's first flagship store, Westbourne House, at Notting Hill, London, where the shop is a converted townhouse, or better yet, a shop located in a townhouse. The brand philosophy of Paul Smith, seen as a modern classic offering where traditional and contemporary combine, is clearly communicated and visually experienced as one journeys through the store, from the bespoke tailoring atelier to the modern glass staircase with accents of modernity and one-off antiques all mixed together in aesthetic harmony.

As the case study analyses in this project progressed, the examination of the flagship store in other locales, such as airports, department stores and shopping malls, was explored. These case studies were essential in the exploration and understanding of brand identity. This was a study of brand identity as a visual fingerprint of the brand. 'Brandtelling', a term I coined, is where the brand has a narrative that is communicated regardless of the locale, the brand image is the constant factor.

In the case study of Prada, whether on Bond Street, Heathrow or Paris, all locales possess a visuality that communicates the brand identity metonymically through the geographic references. In this instance, fashion and style are core aspects of a project that surpass the production of clothes, footwear and handbags. The impression here is that of something beyond the physical limitations of boutiques and showrooms, interacting with diverse, seemingly distant worlds and introducing, very naturally, a new way of creating fashion. The distinctive visuals of the checkered marble floors and the pastel green fabric walls evoke the sense of an intimate, luxury atelier. This visual distinction is felt, both conceptually and viscerally, literally at the moment a consumer enters a Prada shop and stepping onto this marble floor.

The case study of Stella McCartney highlighted the fact that the brand is visually communicated, whether based in Harrods or at the flagship store in Mayfair, London, as all presentations of the collection have a minimal aesthetic, with sculptural rails crafted to display the artistic pieces of the collections. However, in this case study, in all locations, scents were introduced. The latest fragrance is a predominant factor and this distinction is made. This multisensory appeal directly affects our perception of the brand, as a sensory stimulus that arouses the olfactory sense and in turn leaves the individual with an emotional connection to the brand, Stella McCartney.

In the case of Marni, regardless of whether it is the flagship store at Sloane Square or in Selfridges, London, the contemporary architecture and design encourages full exploration of the brand, from collection to collection, and from room to room. Bright, contemporary architecture and design accented with music (techno and mod music) is a simple but very unique characteristic of the Marni space. The vibrant fashion environment is enhanced by a distinctive audible experience, reinforcing Marni as experience and perception.

As part of the case study analysis of visuality in spaces, time experiments were conducted in order to evaluate the spatial narratives and dialogues resulting from the notion of identity space in time (month or season) and to map the transformation that occurred. For example, the display windows at Selfridges were documented in June and July 2012. The earlier work reflected the post Jubilee moment with a British themed modern chic aesthetic while the July windows referred to the summer Olympics using themes of 'Britain Creates and Innovates', the fusion of technology, fashion and the best of Britain on display. Harvey Nichols and Harrods also had similar positions with regards to their window displays during the same time period reflecting the Jubilee celebrations, the sale season and the London 2012 Summer Olympics. Of particular interest here is the articulation of the aesthetic preferences in combination with acknowledging and referencing key moments in time as a chronological list of events.

Finally, case studies were conducted on the use of image as sole communication, where the window is a mural seen from across the road, as in the case of Burberry, the Knightsbridge Store in London. Here the photograph (the image) is the immediate factor, with classic black and white photographs (murals stretching from pavement to sky) instantly expressing the brand identity with the image largely selling and communicating the products.

Research Visual Archive

Initially, this research study was inspired with a revisiting of the iconic opening scene of the film, *Breakfast at Tiffany's* (directed by Blake Edwards, written by Truman Capote, 1961). In the early hours of the morning a young woman, Holly Golightly, with coffee and pastry in hand, is standing in front of and looking into the vitrine of Tiffany & Co. Her expression is at once of tranquillity and longing. There is an instance that the viewer is made aware of as she sees herself reflected onto the jewellery in the vitrine. Later in the film, it is revealed that this act of looking into the vitrine is the only thing that can cure her of the 'mean reds', a state of anxiety that is worse than fear. Overall, this scene presents a powerful portrayal of the individual's interaction with the vitrine:

> The glass and the mirror or the shop-window beckon the potential customer by arousing doubts and desires about his self image/self identity. It is as if looking at the product behind the glass showcase, the consumer is looking at an ideal image of himself (in the mirror).
>
> (Graham et al. 1979: 72)

Now more than ever, the visual language is based on the viewer's acceptance of a physically limited engagement of the fashion image as being reality through their interests and visual pursuits. The viewer responds and remembers these uninhabitable experiences in the non-place, as though they had physically been there. Some existing formats include television programmes, the Internet, historic recreations and store windows. The passageways are where visual imagery activity occurs, but the relationship between use and space remains unnamed and this is the premise for this photographic research. The intent of this research is based on the theory of the non-place, to explore various roles within the photographic/fashion medium. Essentially, it develops a practice of staging, recording, constructing and deconstructing fashion photographs, in order to explore these dimensions as they unfold, meaning that:

> The link between individuals and their surroundings in the space of non-place is established through the mediation of words, or even texts. We know, for a start, that there are words that make image – or rather, images.
>
> (Augé 1995: 94)

As such, the primary research in this project was the creation of an archive. This archive exists as a visual exploration through photography, established to record the experimentation as reference and documentation in order to examine visual thinking in the methodology of observation and visual perception within the non-space.

This photographic exploration was employed to examine the space of convergence between fashion, art and visuality. The resulting images are based on a series of photographs of iconic store windows in London. The storefronts, as non-spaces, are designed to introduce the grammar of photography, the relationship between form, material and content in terms of the connections between fashion as object and image. Here, the relationship between visual material/language, form and communication expands into areas where the idea of influence is investigated as visual sequence and, at the same time, investigating perceptual and visual skills, the perception of time, space and reality.

The photographs, through the use of light and reflection, explore the role and treatment of the fashion image in a non-place in historically, stylistically, spatial terms. The photographs document the ephemeral qualities of the fashion brand and its space, with both a past and a present, and as an inquiry into the representational conventions of environment, image,

Figure 3: Demetra Kolakis, *Untitled* (Visual Archive Series), C Print, 2012.

Figure 4: Demetra Kolakis, *Untitled* (Visual Archive Series), C Print, 2012.

time and space. This is a questioning of the traditional through a new consideration of the image within the framework of the current. Confronting what happens in relation to the image after it is created provides a new visual dialogue for the medium.

X Marks the Spot

Prompted by the importance of space and its relationship to fashion, identity and culture, this project is an analysis and exploration of the phenomena of perspective, infinite space and illusion, the fixed eye, the gaze and the relationship between vision and power. Inspiration was drawn by the fact that the viewer is constantly, on a daily basis, looking into these non-spaces or storefronts. This project began as a research enquiry into how one looks into the space, the store front, to the spot, like the mark for an actor on stage, where, the X marks the spot, for the next 'it' item. Specifically, this is an exploration of how non-spaces are designed to be passed through, and how there is little engagement between the

Figure 5: Demetra Kolakis, *X Marks The Spot*, photo installation, 2012.

non-place and viewer and particularly, how we are not considered as individuals, but rather as an object functioning as a consumer.

> The glass used for the showcase, displaying the products, isolates the consumer from the product at the same time as it superimposes the mirror-reflection of his own image onto the goods displayed. This alienation, paradoxically, helps arouse the desire to possess the commodity. The goods displayed are often part of a human mannequin – an idealized image of the consumer. Glass isolates (draws attention to the product's surface appeal, 'glamour', or superficial appearance alone (attributes of 'workmanship' which link craftsmen to a specific product being lost) while denying access to what is tangible or immediately useful. It idealizes the product.
>
> (Graham 1979: 72)

This ethnographic research is an inquiry into the representational conventions of environment, image, time and space question the paradox of vision and attention; merging aesthetics and cultural commentary in ways that initially mask underlying meanings of spectator/shopper; consumerism and hyper-consumption. As a result, self-reality is replaced by another reality, where the individual is considered as an object of fashion, as one questions and redefines the configuration of space and public through the experience:

> The customer's gaze is focused upon the cantered object's external form; focus creates value. The spectator's 'self', unseen, projected into the space is identified with the thing(s) represented. The spectator's gaze, his 'self'-projection, organizes meaning around the cantered object, meeting his cantered look.
>
> (Graham 1979: 72)

This study interrupts our expectations of space, by considering aspects of the environment and contemplating how fashion imagery mixes with memory, while affecting a sense of visual memory. Based on principles of visual perception, and the methodology of observation, this project explores aesthetic production in the totality of the non-space.

Conclusion

Fashion fluctuates constantly, not existing fully until seen, photographed or exhibited. This project investigates the spatial communication of brandscaping as a culture's form of expression mirroring to convey the suggestive power between image and identity, innovation and tradition, consumerism and fashion. Marshall McLuhan (1964: 13) said, 'the medium is the message' regarding the relationship between media and society and in establishing the role of the medium relevant within the context of contemporary society. As such, space is a highly visual medium and is an important part of brand building. The brand is the message and the space it appears in is viewed as a part of this communication. The physical retail space is used to primarily conduct retail business. Today, the flagship store is simply too visible as an asset to leave out of the brand-building equation/communication. Space is one of the variables employed in creating the customer's experience of a brand. Consumers bring certain expectations with them and what is seen and experienced will either validate or dismiss the brand image and identity. Because the space creates the physical experience of the brand, it generates results. This research provides opportunities to identify emotional and psychological connections in the differentiating and distinguishing of brand as image. Image building is linked to the consumption of brands and consumer experiences, which give individuals an opportunity to create their own unique identity and image. The sensory experience is linked to the individual's striving for identity and image, as well as self-fulfillment and entertainment.

In conclusion, the significance of brandscaping is that the brand image emerges when interactions occur through the consumer's sensory experiences. The experience becomes the image, which, in turn, produces the final outcome within a brand perspective. The image is then synonymous with the brand. The image is based on how consumers perceive and experience the brand where X marks the spot of engagement. The concept of brand identity is defined as a unique set of brand associations that are created and maintained (see Hancock in this volume). The contribution of this research provides an in-depth analysis of brandscaping in relation to the consumer experience of a brand as an image. This research suggests that it is essential to recognize the impact of the sense of sight as a powerful device in discovering and motivating changes and differences within the fashion-branding environment. This study also suggests that additional research on the multisensory interplay between visuality and brandscaping can provide development and a fuller use of the multisensory brand experience in which the brand may even become more individual and personal to the consumer.

References

Augé, M. (1995), *Non-Places: Introduction to an Anthropology of Supermodernity*, London: Verso.

Edwards, B. (1961), *Breakfast at Tiffany's*, USA: Paramount.

Graham, D., Asher, M. and Birnbaum, D. (1979), *Video, Architecture, Television: Writings on Video and Video Works 1970–1978*, Halifax: The Press of the Nova Scotia College of Art and Design.

Kant, I. (1974), *Anthropology from a Pragmatic Point of View*, The Hague: Nijhoff.

Koolhaas, R. (2001), *Projects for Prada. Part 1*, Milano: Fondazione Prada.

Lipovetsky, G. and Manlow, V. (2007), 'The artification in luxury stores', in J. Teunissen (ed.), *Fashion and Imagination*, Arnheim: ArtEZ Press.

Marchetti, L. and Quinz, E. (2007), 'Invisible fashion', in J. Teunissen (ed.), *Fashion and Imagination*, Arnheim: ArtEZ Press.

McLuhan, M. (1964), *Understanding Media: The Extensions of Man*, New York: McGraw-Hill.

Pine, J. B. and Gilmore, J. H. (2011), *The Experience Economy*, Boston: Harvard Business Review Press.

Potvin, J. (2009), *The Places and Spaces of Fashion, 1800–2007*, London: Routledge.

Schulze, G. (2005), *The Experience Society*, London: Sage.

Solomon, M. R., Russell-Bennett, R. and Previte, J. (2013), *Consumer Behaviour: Buying, Having, Being*, Frenchs Forest, NSW: Pearson.

Upshaw, L. B. (1995), *Building Brand Identity: A Strategy for Success in a Hostile Marketplace*, New York: John Wiley and Sons Ltd.

Wordspy (2000), 'Wordspy', http://www.wordspy.com/words/brandscape.asp. Accessed 20 February 2012.

Chapter 17

Cargo Pants: The Transnational Rise of the Garment that Started a Fashion War

Joseph H. Hancock II

The Summer War of 2016

On 1 August 2016, the *Wall Street Journal* printed a story discussing how Ashleigh Hanson, the wife of Dane Hanson, had been systematically throwing out her husband's collection of cargo shorts (Hong 2016). The article went on to discuss that relationships (mostly of a heterosexual nature) across the United States were being threatened by the inability of men to stop wearing these shorts. Transversely, many upscale golf courses have banned cargo shorts and do not allow them on their greens. In 2012, Michael Jordan was refused entry onto a course in Miami while wearing the said shorts (Hong 2016).

However, despite men being bullied by women to stop wearing these garments, the cargo industry (pants and shorts) still accounts for over USD700 million worth of revenue for retailers in the United States, according to market research firm NPD Group (*CBS This Morning* 2016). The industry database, Worth Global Style Network (WGSN), in 2015 reported that cargo shorts made up over 15 per cent of new short styles sold, up from 11 per cent in 2014 (Bhasin 2016). Additionally, there is an assumption that this garment has a much higher market share globally – being continually worn in countries such as Australia where they have over 24 different types of shorts (Lonnborn 9 October 2016 interview).

Because of this controversy, and as the scholar who wrote his dissertation on cargo pants (Hancock 2007), I recently became the centre of the cargo shorts debate and was featured on many radio and talk shows discussing the rise of cargo pants as a garment of twentieth-century fashion that has now become somewhat despised. But the media hype, or what I am calling *cargo-mania*, has risen without much discussion of the actual evolution of the actual garment and its origins.

I was elated when *CBS This Morning* was actually interested in an interview for their story. Off-camera, we discussed how after the barrage of media was over, perhaps I needed to reiterate the cargo pants/shorts story for the academy in a new publication. I agreed after being bullied myself by many female scholars from around the globe who found the fact I did my dissertation on cargo pants completely idiotic. One such email was from a professor of criminal justice who found the topic ridiculous, to which I simply replied, 'Have you noticed what some police officers wear for pants?' She did not reply.

I have not written about cargo pants since 2010 in the *Australasian Journal of Popular Culture* (Hancock and Augustyn 2010), but I feel it is time to tell the story again. Furthermore, with the new propaganda hype concerning this transglobal garment it was important that the misnomer be replaced with facts and that the actual fashion story of the pants be told. During the late 1930s or early 1940s, cargo pants were designed, manufactured and developed as a utility garment for use in the military. During the last century, these pants have gone from being a traditional military uniform to a popular casual pant worn by almost every segment in the global consumer market. Despite their rising popularity and a large market share of retail dollars, little has been written about these pants. While they are visually prevalent in popular culture, and at times, dominate fashion trends (especially menswear), much about cargo pants still remains a mystery.

Since the 1970s, when hippies wore army surplus vintage styles as a sign of protesting against the Vietnam War, until today, cargo pants have undergone a considerable transformation, changing both in fabrications and form. They are a part of the basic core of casual garments that has grown and developed over the last 40 years. With casual dress having secured its place in the workplace today, in addition to changes in consumers' active lifestyles, and a growing awareness and development of global brands and mass fashions, cargo pants no longer relate to their original use as just a functional utility work garment.

These pants have become part of styles that Eicher et al. refer to as 'world dress' (2008: 52). Like jeans, cargo pants have become a transnational style worn in both Western and Eastern cultures as everyday fashion and defined as a 'quickly shifting style of dress worn simultaneously in many worldwide locations' (Eicher et al. 2008: 54). They are sold globally, from retailers such as Abercrombie & Fitch in the United States, to Uniqlo in Japan. This chapter will present the origins, histories and myths surrounding the development of cargo pants as a military garment. It will also highlight the induction of cargo pants into mass culture through various popular culture intermediaries such as the military, subcultural style, film, media, retail and merchandising; demonstrating how this garment has become part of world dress and transnational mass fashion, as well as an icon found in many global popular culture narratives.

The History, Origins and Myths of Cargo Pants

Where did cargo pants come from? Was there a design genius that suddenly created the pants? Or did they evolve over time developing from other military garments? This investigation began with the intention of discovering where cargo pants originated and what division of the military developed these pants. However, cargo pants do not have a single history, but multiple histories, among various regimes of global military divisions that have incorporated various styles of these types of pants into their regimes. This creates a conflicting dialogue as to the exact originator of this particular garment and to whom the credit should be given. History and research reveals that cargo pants were inspired by other garments already in existence in the military and were most probably developed because of utilitarian necessity.

Cargo pants do not seem to have come from one specific country, although evidence does suggest that they evolved across the military regimes of the United Kingdom, Spain and the United States almost simultaneously. More than likely, various countries influenced each other's uniforms and dress in a similar fashion that today's designers are influenced by one another (Hanson 2006). Since the design process of military uniforms during this time required a lead time of about a year, it is also quite possible that various armed services discussed future designs with each other, or that the manufacturers of these uniforms were the same across these regimes, much like fashion companies today produce divisions of garments under one roof. This is the case with the American designer Ralph Lauren, who manufactures most of the garments for his men's divisions such as Polo Ralph Lauren, Ralph Lauren Black Label, Ralph Lauren Double RL, Rugby, Ralph Lauren Home, Ralph Lauren Outlet and the new Ralph Lauren Denim & Supply under the same manufacturers (Crawford 2010).

With one leader, Ralph Lauren, the structural format of information dissemination and design ideas, across various boundaries and divisions, is somewhat inevitable and signifies the global branding process. Although each division services a specific male consumer lifestyle market, and they represent a specific division of the company, it is most likely that each of these divisions influences one another, under the same trends, styles and aesthetics. This may explain why the various divisional lines may look similar or appear to mimic each other; for example, during the Spring 2011 season, Ralph Lauren Double RL featured a Grand Canyon Ripstop Cargo Pant for USD225.00, Polo Ralph Lauren featured a similar pant Authentic Army Parachute Pant for USD145.00, while Rugby their Patrol Cargo Pant for USD118.00. This divisional aesthetic of functional fashion is quite similar to the divisions of the Army, Navy, Air Force and Marines that are all housed under the purview of the US Government, each operating under different leadership, but having one Presidential Commander-in-Chief.

Military Beginnings and Original Cargo Pant Identities

In the United States, the word 'cargo pants' originated from the military battle dress pant known as *fatigues*. Sometimes they are referred to as two-pocket, six-pocket, seven-pocket, eight-pocket, etc. depending on the number of pockets on the garment. Like most military garments, each pant was assigned a numerical identity for instant recognition and for the assemblage of entire uniforms for soldiers. Ralph Lauren, Levis Dockers, Abercrombie & Fitch, as well as other designers have adopted these same numeric identifiers in order to give the garment a sense of authenticity. For example, the contemporary D-2 cargo pant is what most people associate as the standard cargo pant (Figures 1 and 2). D-2 cargo pants can also be referred to as an eight-pocket because it has two-cargo pockets on the side legs, two-front pockets off the waistband, and two-back pockets off the waistband. This type of pant is called a field pant, because of its use primarily as battle dress and not for formal and ceremonial military regime. Cargo pants are usually produced from fabric such as wool, cotton, polyester, silk and nylon and in fabrications and weaves such as plain, twill, herringbone and brushed flannel.

Figures 1 and 2: Abercrombie & Fitch-2003 D-2 Cargo Pants with a back and front view. The viewer will notice the two-side `cargo' pockets, two front pockets off the waistband, and the two back pockets off the waistband. This pant is sometimes referred to as a Six-Pocket Cargo Pant. Photograph by Joseph Hancock, all rights reserved.

Chris McNab writes in *Modern Military Uniforms* that the leg pocket on military uniforms was not present prior to the late 1930s and seems to have been designed during the Second World War (2000: 6–13). McNab credits the Air Force for developing leg pockets on the front of flight pants as the first sign of cargo-like styles. Since the cockpit of many fighter planes was so narrow, Air Force pilots required pockets on the front of their flight uniforms, allowing them access to supplies during flights. This allowed the pilots to feel more comfortable while being cramped in the plane's cockpit. McNab's theory is reinforced through such military uniforms as the Airman Bomber Command Royal Air Force England 1939 uniform (2000: 221), the US Marine Corps Bougainville 1943 uniform (2000: 263), and the Bomber Crewman 8th Army Air Force England 1945 uniform (2000: 275).

Luther Hanson, curator of the military museum in Fort Lee Virginia for the past 25 years and a national military uniforms expert, claims that global retailers and designers visit the large collection of military uniforms for inspiration in creating the latest military looks. According to Hanson, versions of American field cargo pants did not appear until 1942. The concept for fatigues came from the Paratrooper Jump Coat Model #1 during the Second World War. He suggests that the design for cargo pants would have come from a Quarter Master Sergeant. Also during the Second World War, the Quarter Master regime designed uniforms at a rapid pace sending orders to various manufacturers who worked as a team specifically tailoring uniforms to each of the battle units. During these world wars, military uniforms became a method for identifying specific units. There was a functional design and the mass production of uniforms for both world wars and many specifications required rapid production alterations when the original planned design did not work.

Specifically with regards to cargo pants, it was Major William P. Yarborough who helped design the pant for field soldiers in 1942 (Amazing Stories 2010: 72). Yarborough, also known as the 'Father of the Modern Green Berets', was given the military assignment to design

Figure 3: Green Herringbone M-43 Combat Pants, 1943. Photograph courtesy of Vintage Trends.

Figure 4: British battle dress circa 1940s. The reader will note that the pockets on these cargo pants are place on the front. One large pocket rests on the commando soldier's lower left leg, while a smaller pocket rest higher on his right upper thigh. These fatigues were being manufactured in both Britain and the United States. Photograph courtesy of Vintage Trends.

paratrooper's boots, uniforms and qualification badges (Bernstein 2005). At Fort Benning in Georgia, with the help of the quartermaster regime, Yarborough probably developed what would eventually be called the four-pocket cargo, which contained two deep side pockets that hung below the thigh and two back pockets (Figure 3).

Terry Sullivan credits the British for inventing cargo style pants (2003: 44). He suggests that British soldiers and paratroopers used these pants prior to the Americans. His article identifies that the major reason for cargo pockets was for soldiers to carry ammunition when they were climbing or hiding in high places. He believes the pockets cushioned and reduced noise where utility belts did not. Sullivan's theory reflects the uniforms worn by British soldiers during this time such as the uniforms worn during the Second World War by the No. 1 Commando Unit at St. Nazaire (McNab 2002: 232). An example so this uniform can be seen in Figure 4.

Ironically, during this time, many of the United States' military webbing for uniforms was being produced in the United Kingdom, while many of the British uniform garments were produced in American manufacturing facilities. This was due to the United States having more space and not being considered a major battle zone. Since the manufacturing of British battle dress began in January 1943 from specifications drawn up in autumn 1942, it would have been quite simple for the United States to borrow design elements from the British and vice versa suggesting that each country was influenced by the other military uniforms and therefore design of cargo pants (in conversation with Hanson).

The Spanish Generalissimo Francisco Franco has also been credited for the design and manufacturing of cargo pants, or what he called 'Franco Pants' (Ziegler and Ziegler 1986: 92–93). During the Spanish Civil War from 1930 to 1939, Franco would become enraged when he viewed his soldiers placing their hands in their front pant-pockets. To remedy this problem, the Fascist general had the pockets of the pants moved to below the upper thigh. His new pants were very similar to the two-pocket fatigue pants (Figure 1), with back pockets as well. Franco was also recognized for developing the reinforced bulls-eye patterned patch that appears on the seat between and surrounding the buttocks that you see, even today, on contemporary styles of cargo pants. Whether the invention of the Generalissimo Francisco Franco, Great Britain, Major William Yarborough, the Air Force, the Army, the Navy or even Marines, there is a general consensus that cargo pants did not appear in military uniforms until the late 1930s. It can be safe to assume that the origins of cargo pants definitely relate to military uniform traditions and their original use was based upon function and not fashion.

With the military continuing to reinvent cargo styles during the 1940s and into the 1950s, unique styles of cargo pants that were designed and manufactured include the wool khaki battledress pants of 1951, the F-1 sage nylon air force pants of 1955 and a green polyamide hot weather fire resistant cargo pant in 1979 (Hanson). Each of these styles represents the evolution of cargo pants during the early to mid-twentieth century.

While there were many styles of cargo pants developed by the military, as previously stated, most individuals associate the D-2 style as the true cargo style (Figure 1). This pant seems to have become the iconic style most commonly replicated not only by the military, but by the designers and retailers too (Hanson). Even today, cargo style pants have been, and continue to be, worn by military troops across almost all countries. The traditional forms of two-pocket, six-pocket and fatigue styles of cargo pants continue to be copied and reinvented in almost every country making cargo pants a true transnational garment and world dress (Eicher et al. 2008: 52).

Cargo Pants in Popular Culture

The connotation of cargo pants changes with each decade and is influenced by mainstream popular culture. During the 1950s and 1960s, cargo styles are still mainly associated with military themes. But, they were soon adopted by Hollywood, not only for movies related to war, but for movie themes exploring exotic travel and safari. Who can forget Red Buttons (1919–2006) as Pockets in the *Hitari!* (1961). In this film, John Wayne leads a group of highly qualified professional game hunters in the wilds of Africa. His group sets out to capture animals for zoos and circus attractions. Red Buttons plays his assistant Pockets, usually seen wearing green herringbone two-pocket cargo pants similar to those in Figure 1. Throughout the entire film, Pockets keeps valuable items needed for the safari in his cargo pockets. In the movie, Wayne and other characters refer to the distinction of cargo pant pockets differentiating them from regular, traditional pants pockets. This movie marks a direct reference to cargo pockets that still remains unique in film history.

Another major popular cultural event occurred in 1958 when Che Guevera (1928–67) was photographed wearing cargo pants while playing baseball (Amazing Stories 2010: 70).

During the 1960s and early 1970s, cargo pants took on a new connation while becoming incorporated into protests and the Hippie movement. In protests against Western consumer culture and the Vietnam War, much of the Hippie style clothing was self-made. Personalized and embroidered garments such as old military fatigues had become part of anti-fashion outfits worn during this time. By re-stylizing traditional military dress, the hippie movement illustrated its counterculture attitudes towards the assimilation and strict codes of soldier dress (Baldwin et al: 1999: 340–41).

In his book, *Don We Now Our Gay Apparel*, Shaun Cole identifies garments such as military fatigues and cargo pants as part of sub-cultural dress in the mid-to-late 1970s. Gay men who wanted to identify as extremely masculine and butch became obsessed with clothing that symbolized ruggedness (Cole 2000: 93–106). Cargo pants were one of these items since they had originally been associated with signifying the military and the combat soldier. Music bands such as the Village People reinforced these style notions. The group referenced hyper-masculine stereotypes such as Alex Briley, the army soldier (in addition to other looks such as the construction worker, the cowboy, the Indian and the leather daddy) giving him a 'homo-stylized' look for singing such songs as *In the Navy* and of course, *Macho Man*.

Since cargo pants are a part of military dress and represent an aspect of traditional American culture, it was not surprising that during the 1980s these pants became associated with the high social status of the *preppy look*. With designers such as Ralph Lauren, Izod, Liz Claiborne and Calvin Klein, and retailers such as L.L. Bean, Eddie Bauer, Lands' End, The Gap and Banana Republic leading the *preppy fashions* of the 1980s, cargo pants became a part of the conservative style (Birnach 1980).

With the media exposure of movies such as *Sixteen Candles* (1984), cargo pants were visually represented to both the teen and *preppy* markets. As a preppy teenager in high school, heartthrob Jake drives a Porsche, has very successful parents, lives in a mansion, has lots of money, is the most popular senior, and dresses in conservative, yet hip fashions. Jake appears on the cover of the current DVD and in the motion pictures main poster wearing a plaid woven shirt, cargo pants and deck shoes.

During the 1980s, and into the early 1990s, cargo pants were adopted by the new countercultures such as mainstream punk, new wavers, rappers, grunge and various other Music Television (MTV) generation icons. Inexpensive military surplus stores became the major suppliers of garments for music groups such as The Clash, Bananarama, The Belle Stars, Thompson Twins, Sex Pistols, Nirvana, Beastie Boys, Run DMC and The Fat Boys who influenced mass fashion by wearing garments such as cargo pants on stage in their music video clips (Amazing Stories 2010: 70). In response, teenagers flocked to similar military surplus stores hoping to find garments and styles worn by their favourite music videos performers.

In the United States, retailers such as The Gap, County Seat and manufacturers such as Bugle Boy gained popularity by copying MTV looks and selling their products in the teen market. During the 1991 Super Bowl, Bugle Boy debuted their television ad, featuring the iconic 1980s band The Go-Go's, to sell their cargo pants (Bugle Boy 1991). In the middle of *We Got the Beat*, band member Belinda Carlisle stops the music to ask a male audience member 'Excuse me…are those Bugle Boys you are wearing?' While Internet searches and bloggers suggest this ad is for jeans, it is actually for the line of cargo utility pants that the company was producing at the time as the company expansion into this apparel. By producing trendy fashionable styles of cargo pants, retailers such as The Limited and Express gained popularity with their cargo pant brands such as *Outback Red* and *Forenza* for women.

During 1998–99, Limited Brand's Structure (now Express) decided to investigate how many companies actually carried cargo pants in their assortment. The company wanted to decide if producing mass quantities of the pants would prove profitable. The American retailer discovered that cargo pants were being sold at almost every specialty store retailer in the nation. Specialty retailers, from high-end to low-end, had the pants well represented on their sales floors. The company also discovered that, not only did these retailers carry the pant, most had as many as five or six styles on their selling floors. Cargo pants had become a basic part of every mass fashion retailers' basic assortment. According to Leslie Wexner, C.E.O. of Limited Brands, the retailer Abercrombie & Fitch was leading the resurgence of cargo pants (Structure).

Abercrombie & Fitch had gained the attention of the public with their controversial advertising campaign that featured half-naked American college graduates (coeds), with photographer Bruce Weber as the creative genius behind the company's advertising campaign. Consequently, sales at Abercrombie & Fitch soared (see Figure 5).

Historically, Abercrombie & Fitch were known for upscale traditional outdoor, camping and safari clothing for men and women. After being bought by The Limited Corporation in 1988, the business was reinvented and the clothing was changed to target a younger

Figure 5: Abercrombie & Fitch (A&F) advertisement from the 1999 Back-to-School season. The reader will note the three models wearing three distinct styles of cargo pants. This allowed A&F to visually display the various styles that the stores carried in order for shoppers to purchase them. © Photograph by Bruce Weber, all rights reserved.

Figure 6: Cover of the Target Sunday Circular, 17 August 2003. © Photograph by Target, all rights reserved.

and more fashion-oriented consumer. The company continues to sell basic items such as khakis, T-shirts, sweaters, peacoats, baseball caps, active wear and of course cargo pants. But, what made this company extremely successful was their use of semi-nude models in their advertising campaigns (Figure 5). Their ability to re-contextualize, brand and merchandise cargo pants into new youthful settings allowed them to continue gain sales and grow, as well as popularize these pants with a new generation of mass consumers (Hancock 2009: 94–104).

Twenty-First Century 'Fashionable' Cargo Pants

Target, the second top big box retailing giant in the United States, featured cargo pants during their 'Get A Jump on School…Go Cargo', 17 August 2003 weekly newspaper circular (Figure 6), demonstrating the significant monetary market share that these pants have when it comes to consumer spending in their stores. At the same time, this advertisement reveals how cargo pants have reached market saturation in their popularity, or lack of it. The advertisement not only features cargo styles for men and women, but also gives evidence of how cargo pants have influenced contemporary fashion styles such as shorts and skirts in various consumer markets.

Target continued to merchandise and brand cargo pant styles through its new designer line, by British former singer and songwriter Keanan Duffty. Graduating from St. Martin's College, University of the Arts, London, he has displayed his designs on runways in Italy, London and the United States, becoming one of Britain's high-end designers, specializing in clothing that resembles garments from other fashion designers such as Vivienne Westwood. Duffty not only designs high-end runway garments, he also a produces and directs music videos, and his aim is to build a brand that is heavily influenced by both music and fashion.

For the 2006 Back-to-School season, Target debuted Duffty's special line of clothing which included a pair of ripstop khaki cargo pants that had a large patch of the Union Jack flag sewn onto the seat of the garment and adjustable waistband and leg openings (Figures 7). Target's description of the pants suggests that they are '80s rocker-chic inspired'. Other brand detailing of the pants includes a red patch above the right pocket stating, 'England's Dreaming of Keanan Duffty' with a coat of arms emblazoned with a large KD in the centre. Target attached a paper waistband tag above the left pocket that mimics the patch, with the front featuring a skull and crossbones and guitar on a background of the Union Jack Flag with the phrase, 'England's Dreaming of Keanan Duffty'. The backside of the tag also features a biography of Duffty with his photo and the price of the cargo pants.

Gentlemen's Quarterly recognized cargo pants as a successful and 'wonderful addition the mass fashion business' (Sullivan 2003: 44). Even the Cotton Incorporated's Lifestyle Monitor (2003: 2) section of the fashionwear industry's leading newspaper *Women's Wear Daily* noted what they called 'The New Cargo Pants' coming from such fashion houses as Prada and Jil Sander in luxury fabrics. Similarly, the British men's magazine *Fantastic Man* published the

Figure 7: Keanan Duffty for Target. Cotton ripstop cargo pants $29.99, Fall 2006. Note that the style of the cargo pants is that of the D-2. © Photograph by Joseph Hancock, all rights reserved.

Figure 8: Old Navy 2010 Back-to-School wall display for cargo pants at their Flagship Store on 34th Street in New York City. © Photograph by Joseph Hancock, all rights reserved.

article 'The fashion test cargo pants', which conducted an experiment to see which style of premium priced cargo pants were the best and incorporated garments from Thom Browne, G-Star, Dolce & Gabbana and Ralph Lauren Black Label (Jonkers 2010: 32–33).

The proliferation of cargo pants continues with fashion styles such as Uniqlo's (RE)cargo for USD39.90, J.Crew's Stanton urban slim fit cargo for USD79.50, Country Road Australia's Engineered cargo pant for AUD119.00, all the way up to Ralph Lauren's Double RL rugged versions ranging from USD225–USD328.00 – making it clear that these pants are a fashion icon in popular culture. In addition, the recent rise and focus of most retailers in the area of men's fashion have some male consumers infatuated with finding the perfect pair of cargo pants. Men's fashion blogger Luxury Obsessed documented how thrilled he is when he finds the 'perfect pair' of cargo pants. He writes:

> I pop into Uniqlo about every other week to check out what is new. I often leave empty handed, but this trip I was pleasantly surprised to see these dark camouflage 'Perfect Shape Cargo Pants', which absolutely live up to their name [...]. The touch of stretch is great if you want to wear them tight (like me), because you can look sleek and still comfortably sit down!
>
> (Luxury Obsessed 2 February 2011)

Style editor of the *New York Times Magazine*, Carrie Donavon (1928–2001), was featured in an advertisement for American fashion label Old Navy stating, 'I love these pants, they're so fab, and they have pockets!' Old Navy's 2010 Back-to-School in-store presentation of cargo pants reveals that even in the twenty-first century, it considers it to be a basic style, at USD29.50 (Figure 8). The retailer has pleated and plain-front pants. This large item-impact display signifies the importance of cargo pants in merchandise assortments (especially at a large volume, mass discount retailer like Old Navy) during this time period (Hancock and Augustyn 2011).

The mass merchandising and rebranding of cargo pant has shifted people's perception of this garment. Their high price points and fashionable silhouettes have changed the perception of some consumers who

Figure 9: The author wearing Fall 2016 Ralph Lauren Double RRL priced at USD390.00. Photograph by Dan McQuade.

now see these pants as quite stylish even when offered at expensive price points (Figure 9). In her *New York Times* column, Lily Burana (2006) suggests that consumers love the appeal and style of military fatigues and find them sexy. They have a quality that makes women (and men) feel like they are wearing a part of cultural heritage and style. There is something special about them that will never go away. And commentators who have issue with this garment need to reassess its cultural significance because they no longer represent the same thing as they did in past. Having been significantly reinvented, re-appropriated and restyled their transglobal heritage will endure.

References

Baldwin, E., Longhurst, B., McCracken, S., Ogborn, M. and Smith, G. (1999), *Introducing Cultural Studies*, New York: HarperCollins Publishers, Inc.

Bernstein, A. (2005), 'Lt. Gen. William Yarborough dies', *The Washington Post*, 8 December, http://www.washingtonpost.com/wp-dyn/content/article/2005/12/07/AR2005120702473.html. Accessed 9 July 2011.

Bhasin, K. (2016), 'They may be ugly, but cargo shorts are still king', Bloomberg.com, 16 September, http://www.bloomberg.com/news/articles/2016-09-16/they-may-be-ugly...ce=twitter&utm_medium=social&cmpid%3D=socialflow-twitter-business. Accessed 16 November 2016.

Birnach, L. (1980), *The Official Preppy Handbook*, New York: Workman Publishing Company, Inc.

Bugle Boy (1991), 'We got the beat – Bugle Boy', http://adland.tv/commercials/bugle-boys-go-gos-1991-030-usa. Accessed 7 November 2016.

Burana, L. (2006), 'Army's fashion fatigue', *New York Times*, 5 October, p. A29.

CBS This Morning (2016), 'Cargo shorts debate: To wear or not to wear?', *CBS This Morning*, 25 August, http://www.cbsnews.com/news/cargo-short-debate-to-wear-or-not-to-wear-fashion-faux-pas/. Accessed 7 November 2016.

Cole, S. (2000), *Don We Now Our Gay Apparel*, Oxford: Berg Publishers.

Cotton Incorporated (2003), 'Lifestyle Monitor: The new cargo pants', *Women's Wear Daily*, 27 February, p. 2.

Crawford, C. (2010), personal communication, New York, 7 July.

Eicher, J., Evenson, S. L. and Lutz, H. A. (2008), *The Visible Self*, New York: Fairchild Books.

Esquire (2010), 'Amazing stories: The intrepid history of three style icons', *Esquire the Big Black Book*, spring/summer, pp. 69–72.

Hancock, J. (2007), *These Aren't the Same Pants Your Grandfather Wore!: The Evolution of Branding Cargo Pants in 21st Century Mass Fashion*, Columbus: Ohio Link, https://etd.ohiolink. edu/ap/10?0::NO:10:P10_ACCESSION_NUM:osu1174323221, Accessed 7 November 2016.

———— (2009), 'Brand storytelling: Context and meaning for cargo pants', in P. McNeil, V. Karaminas and C. Cole (eds), *Fashion in Fiction*, Oxford: Berg Publishers, pp. 95–104.

Hancock, J. and Augustyn, E. (2010), '"Fashionable pockets": The transnational rise of cargo pants into popular culture', *Australasian Journal of Popular Culture*, 2:2, pp. 183–95.

———— (2011), 'Pants, trousers. Updates', in J. Eicher (ed.), *The Berg Encyclopedia of World Dress and Fashion,* London: Bloomsbury, http://www.bergfashionlibrary.com/. Accessed 7 November 2016.

Hanson, L. (2006), personal telephone communication, 5 October.

Hawks, H. (1961), *Hitari*, USA: Paramount Studios.

Hong, N. (2016), 'Nice cargo shorts! You're sleeping on the sofa', *The Wall Street Journal*, 1 August, http://www.wsj.com/articles/nice-cargo-shorts-youre-sleeping-on-the-sofa-1470082856. Accessed 7 November 2016.

Hughes, J. (1984), *Sixteen Candles*, USA: Universal Studios.

Jonkers, G. (2010), 'The fashion test: Cargo pants', *Fantastic Man*, spring/summer, pp. 32–33.

Lonnborn, H. (2016), personal telephone communication, 9 August.

Luxury Obsessed (2011), 'Uniqlo perfect shape cargo pants', 2 February, http://www. luxuryobsessed.com/search?q=Uniqlo+Cargo+Pant. Accessed 16 November 2016.

McNab, C. (2000), *Modern Military Uniforms*, New Jersey: Chartwell Books, Inc.

———— (2002), *20th Century Military Uniforms*, New York: Barnes & Noble.

Structure (2000), *Back-to-School Actual Report*, Columbus: The Limited Corporation Publication.

Sullivan, T. (2003), 'Cargo pants', *Gentlemen's Quarterly*, January, p. 44.

Ziegler, M. and Ziegler, P. (1986), *Banana Republic Guide to Travel and Safari Clothing*, New York: Ballantine Books.

Chapter 18

Cool Japan: Fashion as a Vehicle of Soft Power

Tets Kimura

Japanese society is known for offering limited flexibility to its people. Due to the restrictive social structure, combined with the dragged-out economic slowdown that has no end in sight, 'hope' is said to be waning in Japan. In this environment, contemporary Japanese fashion has developed as an aspect of social rebellion, as fashion is a unique place where freedom can exist. This empowers people from the 'street' to produce various styles as an aspect of unique self-expression. Elite Japanese fashion corporations and designers are not shy to adopt, adapt and improve the street ideas. The Japanese bottom-up fashion structure makes Japanese fashion 'cool' in a Western dominated world of fashion, as traditionally the West has top-down fashion flows. The term 'cool' has also been used as an adjective for Japanese fashion as part of Japan's governmental 'Cool Japan' policy. This newly promoted official initiative is associated with Nye's concept of soft power, which is the ability to achieve a political goal through attraction rather than coercion. Japan's main political objective for the last 25 years has been economic revitalization. To enable this, Japan today attempts to export aspects of its home-grown culture, including fashion, under the brand of Cool Japan. This chapter will critically examine the potential of Japanese soft power with specific reference to fashion in meeting the nation's political goals. An analysis of existing quantitative surveys of Cool Japan suggests that fashion is not the strongest vehicle of Japan's soft power. Contrasted with this, qualitative interviews conducted by the author with various specialists in Japanese culture, and with other respondents, including government officials and fashion producers, both in and outside of Japan, find that the soft power potential of Japanese fashion is high in comparison to other Cool Japan products such as anime, manga and pop music. Where the efficiency of Cool Japan branding as a whole appears to be largely pan-Asian rather than global, Japanese fashion is well-integrated and consumed throughout the world due to its wide acceptance. Thus, this chapter argues for the existence of an engaging storyline of Japan's soft power policy within the field of fashion.

The Country of No Hope

Japan's post-Second World War continuous economic growth came to a halt in the early 1990s when its economic bubble burst. After 20 years, Japan's minimum wage is now half of the minimum wage earned in Australia, another developed country in the Asia-Pacific region.[1] In the 7 years preceding 2014, the wages of Japanese casual factory labourers had only increased by ten yen, which is less than ten US cents (see *Asahi Shimbun* 2014). Due to the rapid growth in the economies of many Asian nations outside of Japan, it is predicted there will be huge repercussions for the Japanese economy in the lead up to 2050 (Komine and Kabe 2007). Furthermore, Japanese society offers inflexible employment options where workers are trapped as either over-worked full-time employees or are suffering from poverty in low-paid casual labour. More importantly, if newly graduated university students fail to find a full-time position before graduation, the chance of them securing a full-time position after graduation becomes improbable, not just in the short term, but for the rest of their lives. These dire employment prospects await current university students and allegedly 40 per cent of them have considered committing suicide (*Yomiuri Shimbun* 2012). In short, if they miss this job-hunting window, society will consider them to be both social and financial failures, leading to future mental health issues (Oshio and Inagaki 2014). Even if they are successful in getting a job, 'service *zangyo*' or unreported, unpaid overtime work is the usual work option (Kopp 2012). This unofficial employment practice is not tangible in international surveys because it is not accurately recorded, if it is recorded at all (Ogura 2007: 9). Furthermore, according to Ogura (2007: 6), the definition of long working hours is 60 hours per week in Japan, whereas this figure is usually 49 in other developed countries. Refusing to meet such expectations leads to financial and social exclusion; the Japanese social and employment systems are not designed to provide a second chance across all sectors without an individual proving that he or she has outstanding talent and ability.

Furthermore, the university students referred to above are all around the age of 20. Japanese companies often employ newly graduated students aged between 22 and 24 only. So, mature students have no realistic chance of full-time employment and are treated as black sheep by society. Social expectations drive the vast majority of the Japanese to remain at their desks until late into the night, giving rise to the phenomenon of *karoshi* (sudden death from overwork), a term that is now listed in English-language dictionaries. The extreme pressures of Japanese work and home life is well expressed in Ryu Murakami's (2012) famous novel *Kibo no Kuni Exodus* (*Exodus, The Nation of Hope*). At the climax of this story, a middle-school student in front of the National Diet makes the following speech, 'This country has everything. You can find whatever you want here. The only thing you can't find is hope'.

This speech is a reflection of the feelings of many Japanese people about today's Japan, and is not just a fictional story, nor an over-exaggerated view. It could be said that Japan is materially rich, but spiritually poor. Young people in particular feel stuck and unable to break through these barriers.

As I started writing this chapter, a well-known J-pop lyricist Yasushi Akimoto created a song entitled *Kimi no Na wa Kibo* (*Your Name Is Hope*) to reveal the lack of hope facing young Japanese students. The song was recorded by the J-pop girl group Nogizaka46, and reached the top of the charts in the first week of its release (Oricon Style 2013). The song could be regarded as social evidence of the need for youth to communicate frustrations in their life, as John Shepard (1994: 235) notes, 'music as a socially constructed symbolic medium speaks immediately [...] to the experiential worlds of different individuals'.[2] This social evidence was expressed comprehensively in the song by both the lyric, nostalgic melody and the singers' school uniform-like costumes. In addition to the younger Japanese generation, Shino Sakuragi (2013), a Naoki Prize[3] winner, expressed in her novel *Hotel Royal* that older Japanese people are also experiencing similar social pressures. In the novel, a middle-aged mother with a part-time job finds herself socially trapped due to her family's tight budget, except when the mother unexpectedly has 5000 yen (approximately USD45) and a couple of hours to spare. Then, she cajoles her husband into going to a 'love hotel'[4] to experience long forgotten pleasures. Many people in Japan are too busy surviving and have no joy in their life, just like this couple in Sakuragi's story. The absence of hope in Japan has also been observed in the West, for example, *The Washington Post* reported that young Japanese people could not feel positive about life in today's Japan (Harlan 2012).

The Meaning of Japanese Fashion

Fashion researchers have also monitored this social and cultural reality. For example, in Yuniya Kawamura's contribution to *The Fashion Reader* (2011) on the subject of Japanese street fashion, she has an explanatory title, 'The urge to be seen and to be heard'. Kawamura (2010: 212) on another occasion argues that as Japan has endured a recession since the early 1990s, the young Japanese find 'no hope' in their future thus 'see the assertion of individual identity as being more important and meaningful'. Consequently, in every season many different styles of fashion are created in Japan, if not every week or every day, as a form of rebellion against society and in the desire to express the self. People from the 'street', not necessarily professional and/or educated designers, typically produce these fashion items. Wearing Japanese street style is a way of telling society who you are, and as Dick Hebdige (1979) mentioned, it expresses the self within a subcultural system as a way of communicating identity. The strong street nature of Japanese fashion is very different from the traditional Western institutional structure theorized by classic fashion scholars. For example, Thorstein Veblen argued in his well-known book *The Theory of the Leisure Class* (1899) that fashion is essentially a class-conscious object and is used as an expression of social and economic advantage by those who are privileged in society. Furthermore, Georg Simmel acknowledged that upper class fashion is usually imitated by the lower class in the desire to better them. Fashion in the Western world traditionally has a top-down structure. Simmel (1904: 135) revealed it 'as soon as the lower classes begin to copy their style, thereby crossing the line of demarcation the upper classes have drawn, the upper classes turn away from this style and adopt a new one, which in its turn differentiates them from the masses; and thus the game goes merrily on'. In short, as one style is widely adopted throughout different social classes, a new style is introduced by the upper class to identify their class differentiation.

However, in Japan, fashion did not historically develop in line with that of the West, due to Japan's 'Far East' physical and historical isolation until the middle of the nineteenth century. Once Japan joined the global network, fashion was in many ways an expression of modernity rather than of a class system under the imperial Empire of Japan (from 1868 until the end of the Second World War) (see Slade 2009), and is now, as explained earlier, seen as an expression of the more liberated self within a highly constrained society.

At the *Japan Fashion Now* exhibition,[5] all sorts of Japanese styles were exhibited, including street and subcultural styles, such as the well-known Lolita look (see Figure 1), Gothic-Lolita styles (see Hardy Bernal in this volume), and a newly established *Mori* Girl style.[6] Less consumed styles such as cosplay costumes (see Figure 2, also see Peirson-Smith in this volume), *tokkofuku* (known as 'kamikaze suit' worn by the young Japanese motor gang members), and maid uniforms (usually seen at maid cafés inspired by *otaku* 'geek' culture) were also displayed at the exhibition. Japanese street fashion is iconic, and simultaneously consumers can be both serious and flippant in their choice of fashion. In Ted Polhemus' analysis (1994: 131), the 'Supermarket of Style' or a stylistic promiscuity emerged in Japan, and by this, the wearers are '"Punk" one day, "Hippies" the next [...they] fleetingly leap across decades and ideological divides'. Polhemus also compares Japanese fashion to opening up different kinds of soup cans and 'throwing a spoonful from each into one pot' (1994: 134). It is not just the variety on offer, but a notable characteristic of Japanese fashion lies in its ability to offer, 'an extremely fast-moving trend cycle' (Azuma 2002: 137) as the consumers of these street styles are urged to express the self in new and different ways as a way of beating social expectations and pressures.

According to fashion academics, such as Kawamura (2004, 2005) and Jennifer Craik (2009), who emphasise that fashion is predominantly a concept originating in the West, Japan, or at least its (fashion) capital Tokyo, produces a variety of fashion items, yet it does not offer a traditional institutional fashion environment. In essence, Tokyo as a fashion city lacks the structural strength and status that the West, particularly France, offers (Kawamura 2004: 98). Unlike the West, where fashion is associated with traditional institutional culture, in the non-Western world of Japan, fashion, whether as a concept or practice, is

Figure 1: Participants of a Lolita fashion event in Kobe, Japan, 29 April 2013. © 2013 The Mainichi Newspapers Co., Ltd. all rights reserved.

Figure 2: Cosplay performers at the World Cosplay Summit in Nagoya, Japan, 3 August 2013. © 2013 The Mainichi Newspapers Co., Ltd. all rights reserved.

detached from tradition. The lack of Western institutionalisation and a centralised fashion establishment in Japan enables the self-expression of the 'street' to develop freely. In Tokyo today, fashion is a method for groups to 'celebrate the superficiality of their posed identities without denying that that is all they are' as different styles of subcultures are 'enacted in a self-reflexive masquerade without regard for appearing natural or authentic' (Craik 2009: 159). Fashion is used as a symbolic cultural product to express the self – not necessarily in the form of social expectation or status, but in terms of who you are and what you want to be.

Unlike Kawamura and Craik, Toby Slade (2009) argues that a fashion system did develop in Japan in pre-modern Edo, nowadays Tokyo. Slade employs Shuzo Kuki's concept of *iki* – an aesthetic concept associated with simple beauty or coolness as an expression of simplicity and sophistication. Kuki ([1930] 1997) argues that since there is no equivalent word for *iki* in any other language, *iki* is a uniquely Japanese aesthetic concept. The essence of *iki* was a reflection of ethical ideology, and therefore, was used to express the self-identity of ordinary Edo people in their kimonos and hairstyles (Kuki [1930] 1997: 81). For example, the geishas in Edo's Fukagawa district had simple and less colourful costumes, used less cosmetics and their 'stage' names were less girly or sexy: these characteristics were seen as *iki* – all of which were quite opposite to those of the Kyoto geishas, who presented themselves in bright, colourful and even jazzy props and costumes. The description of *iki* is not limited to the entertainment world, but is also applied to the characteristics or the personalities of ordinary people. After all, Slade, like Kawamura and Craik, maintains that Japanese fashion is not based upon the traditional Western top-down model, but rather on bottom-up movements where anyone can potentially start up a new Japanese fashion trend.

In addition to the 'street' nature of Japanese fashion, it should also be noted that the adjective for contemporary Japanese fashion has largely been 'cool' in the West since the 'discovery' of the famous 'big three' designers, Issey Miyake, Yohji Yamamoto and Rei Kawakubo, around 1980 (Kimura 2015a). However, Japanese youth may not actually experience cool lives, but rather frustrating ones. Many of them accept the customary Japanese way of thinking, not realising that there are alternative lifestyles (Kimura 2007).[7] As a result, a social reconstruction of any sort is unlikely to occur, even if it could improve the Japanese people's overall happiness.

Rather than changing the social system itself, Japan's goal for the last 25 years has been economic revitalisation within the established structure. Economists and scholars, including Joseph Nye (2011), have acknowledged that the Japanese economy is no longer the world's second largest. As an alternative to selling manufactured products such as TVs and cars, Japan is aiming to increase its sale revenues by the exportation of creative products such as fashion as part of Cool Japan so that the Japanese economy will 'take off' once more (see Mihara 2013: 3, METI n.d., and Figure 3).[8] According to the Japanese government, 'we should promote a Cool Japan strategy to transform the appeal of Japanese culture [...] and create new growth industries, thereby preparing employment and opportunities for

SMEs [Small and Medium Enterprises] and young people' (METI 2012a). Throughout its Cool Japan initiatives, the Japanese government is attempting to 'acquire foreign demand amounting to 8 to 11 trillion yen' from the current 2.3 trillion yen (METI 2012a).[9]

The Cool Japan policy is supposedly widely supported by Japanese citizens. According to a Japanese government source, more than 80 per cent of the Japanese people believe that Japanese culture, including fashion, can be a driving force to save Japan from its economic difficulties (METI n.d.). This approval rate is lower according to another survey conducted by the Tokyo Polytechnic University (2010), yet the majority, notably 60 per cent of people in the survey, believe in the ability of Cool Japan to bring about an effective economic recovery.

What Is Cool Japan?

Cool Japan has been the official government policy since the Office of Cool Japan was created in 2010 within the Ministry of Economy, Trade and Industry to promote the brand of Cool Japan (see METI 2012b). Although the term Cool Japan has no clear definition (Kobayashi 2013), the idea that Japan has a distinct aesthetic quality that can be described as 'cool' has existed longer than the government office. Douglas McGray, a journalist from the United States, published an academic article titled 'Japan's gross national cool' (2002). McGray (2002: 53) developed the idea of 'national cool' based on Nye's concept of soft power, which is the ability to achieve a political goal through attraction rather than coercion. According to McGray, Japanese cultural commodities such as Sony PlayStation, Hello Kitty and Japanese fashion are Japan's national cool – 'fusing elements of other national cultures into one almost-coherent whole' (2002: 48). This idea links with the points raised by fashion scholars in relationship between Japanese fashion and other forms of Japanese culture. For example, Polhemus (1994) indicates that Japanese fashion benefits from the greater recognition of Japanese popular culture internationally. Steele (2010) finds that some Japanese fashion designs are linked to the contemporary anime and Kawamura (2004) thinks the linkage with traditional designs. In a manner, anyone with an interest in an genre of Japanese culture is a potential consumer of the whole Japanese culture under the national branding of Cool Japan.

Consequently, 'Japan looks more like a cultural superpower today' (McGray 2002: 44) than it did in the late 1970s and 1980s when the country was known as an economic superpower and recognized as the possible number one global economy (see Vogel 1979) until its economic bubble burst in the early 1990s. Japan produces popular culture, which has spread to the rest of the world (Kimura 2015b; Daliot-Bul 2009; Iwabuchi 2002a). Japan's demonstration of soft power may not be calculated by economic figures such as its Gross National Product (GNP), yet McGray (2002) believes that instead of merely calculating the relative economic power through GNP, countries should be measured by another index based on soft power such as their 'gross national cool'. In terms of this type of index, Japan is as large and as important as the United States. Despite the strong global cultural dominance of the United States in the global content market, with a share of 41 per cent, Japan is still the second largest producer despite its share being only 9.5 per cent (Otmazgin 2008: 79; see also METI 2005). Japanese coolness is constituted of various attractive contemporary cultural items such as fashion; this implies that Cool Japan branding is an important vehicle of Japan's soft power.

What Is Soft Power?

The concept of soft power was originally developed in the late 1980s when the American dominancy became questionable due to the growing presence of Japan and West Germany led by their strong economic performance (Nye 1990). Soft power is typically seen as being opposite to the more traditional and widely understood concept of hard power, which typically refers to military and economic hegemony that rest upon 'inducements and threats' (Nye 2008: 29). Nye argued that the use of coercive military and/or economic threats cannot be the only way to play a strong role in the global village, as opposed to the menace imposed by the 1980s American government officials and citizens as the country was getting weaker. Nye introduced the power of attraction, which he famously theorized in his book *Soft Power* (2004).

The primary resource of soft power is culture (Nye 2004: 11). Unfortunately, soft power is often misunderstood and trivialized as though it is merely the influence of cultural commodities and consumer goods such as Coca-Cola, Hollywood and blue jeans (Nye 2004: xi). Soft power is not about the consumption or diffusion of cultural items in foreign countries, but is rather about how successfully one country's political goals are accomplished in foreign countries through cultural influence. For example, Josef Joffe (2006: 103) mentions that the iconic logo of the New York Yankees is nothing more than a cool apparel item with 'a pleasing art nouveau logo' for non-Americans. In summary, popularity does not guarantee soft power (Nye 2004: 12; Joffe 2006: 103). However, the tendency for global wider cultural acceptance can still offer the greater potential to be a vehicle of soft power, as such the United States remains the number one soft power player due to its globally deployed 'universalistic culture' (Nye 2004: 11).

In today's world, apart from the United States, which is currently *the* alleged global superpower, there are five other notable major power players; the European Union, Japan, China, India and Russia. This idea is widely supported by the analysis of the major institutional organisations specialising in international relations, including the Centre for Strategic and International Studies (USA) (see CSIS 2009), the International Institute for Strategic Studies (UK) (Taylor 2010), the Stockholm International Peace Research Institute (see Anthony and Rotfeld 1999), the Centre for European Policy Studies (see CEPS 2008) and the Japan Institute of International Affairs (2011). Yet, Nye insists there are only three major soft power players, the United States, Europe and Japan (Nye 2004).[10] Rapidly emerging countries such as China and India have hard power assets, but their soft power assets are not as efficient because their cultures are less globally recognized (such as India's Bollywood since its cultural effectiveness is limited within the Indian subcontinent), thus they cannot practice soft power or 'smart power', which is an exercise of hard and soft powers combined that was developed from the notion of soft power (Nye 2008).[11] Furthermore, there are smaller, emerging countries such as South Korea and Sweden that are increasing their cultural presence, respectively via the diffusion of K-pop music and H&M/IKEA. However, powers obtained by these smaller countries are still insubstantial in comparison to those of the major players. Thus, soft power projected by less powerful countries cannot be as effective as that of powerful cultural resources of Coca-Cola, Hollywood and blue jeans for example.

Nye has taken into account the significance of Japanese soft power as expressed in cultural products such as fashion, music, food and art, where they 'have long found followers outside the country' (2004: 86). According to Leheny (2015), scepticism regarding this view seemed to vanish from Japan after the publication of McGray's 'Japan's gross national cool' (2002), because 'Japanese officials and pundits alike started to argue that the international popularity of anime and manga might enable Japan to earn "soft power"'. However, Groot rejected this idea in arguing that Japanese popular culture lacks universal values so that its soft power ability is limited (2006: 59). This view was even supported in Japan by a

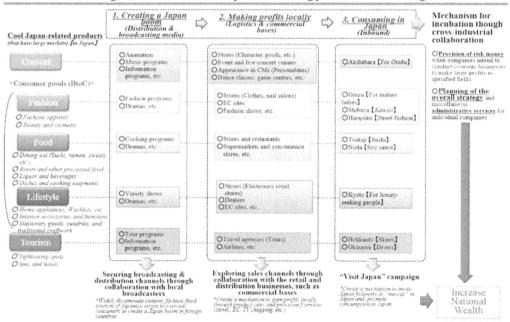

Figure 3: Overall Image of the Cool Japan Strategy to Make Large Profits (METI 2012: 6).

well-known animation director, Makoto Shinkai who admitted that non-Japanese people may not appreciate his film *Byosoku 5 Senchimetoru (Five Centimetres per Second)* (2007), as it was produced with the expectation that the audience understood the sentimental Japanese role of cherry blossom (Chikuma 2011).

Another limitation of Japan's soft power is that its culture remains 'inward-oriented' in comparison to that of the United States. This can be linked to the history of Japanese imperialism (colonialism) until the end of Second World War. Nye (2004: 88) argues that Japan now limits its ability to expand to avoid the pathway of its tragic history. The threat of cultural 'Japanisation' is still felt among many Asians, due to the legacy of Japan's previous imperial efforts (Iwabuchi 2002b: 74 and Lam 2007: 357). After all, anti-Japanese sentiment in China and Korea is still regularly reported more than 70 years following the end of Second World War. Having said that, Japan's popular culture can still be commodified into an effective means to transcend political and historical antagonism. Selling contemporary Japanese fashion, for example, is just pushing quality fashion, not Japanese imperial history. Despite the recent exacerbation of Japan-China/Korea tensions, Japanese cultural commodities are still popular with Asian consumers. In fact, contemporary Japanese culture in general is internationally acceptable, as it carries almost no religious and/or ethnic messages. It is a culture for everybody, regardless of age, nationality and heritage (Aoki and Barakan 2009). Elite culture is no longer at the centre of Japan's way of life. Instead, popular culture is at its centre, and in its neutrality has the potential to reach people all around the world.

The Potential of Japanese Fashion

Although no single item is officially prioritised under the Cool Japan operation, fashion is regarded as one of the core Cool Japan items by the Japanese government.[12] As listed in a government report, Cool Japan consists of 'fashion, food, animation, daily goods, [and] traditional craftwork of Japanese origin' (METI 2012a). Considering this, however, when the Japanese public was asked, 'what Japanese culture would you like to introduce as an item of Cool Japan?' in a survey conducted by Tokyo Polytechnic University (2010), great attention was given to anime, manga and food. Anime was the only item that was supported by the majority (56.9 per cent) followed by manga (49.9 per cent) and food (47 per cent) while fashion only came in thirteenth place (12.6 per cent).

Outside Japan in nearby Asian countries, the perception of Japanese fashion is given more or less equal status as it is in Japan. According to a survey by *Yomiuri Shimbun* newspaper (2006), anime and manga were the most attractive Japanese cultural items in Korea, Indonesia and Malaysia. Japanese cuisine was also understood to be more attractive than its fashion in all five countries that were included in the *Yomiuri* survey. Among the eight categories of cultural products measured in this survey, fashion ranked as high as third in Korea and as low as last in Indonesia (see Table 1 below).[13]

Table 1: Anime and Manga survey by *Yomiuri Shimbun* newspaper, 2006.

	South Korea	Indonesia	Malaysia	Thailand	Vietnam
Anime and Manga	25.6%	29.7%	31.5%	18.2%	12.0%
Japanese Cuisine	17.2	17.3	20.7	25.0	12.6
Movies	9.7	21.7	18.2	19.1	16.7
TV programs	8.5	20.0	24.6	16.6	13.0
Fashion	**14.6**	**7.3**	**13.1**	**17.0**	**8.4**
Pop music	5.8	7.8	12.4	9.1	9.2
Sumo and baseball	9.2	8.0	5.9	6.1	6.5
Traditional culture	2.4	8.3	7.9	10.1	9.8

From observation of these two quantitative surveys from both inside and outside Japan, it could be said that even though both Japanese and other Asian people find the Cool Japan strategy effective, fashion is not regarded as one of the most valuable items. However, these objective or mathematical analyses can be criticised; since what people experience in everyday life is a constructed reality, which is based on the subjective interpretation of each individual (Sarantakos 2013: 37–38). This could be interpreted broadly as there are as many realities as there are people. For example, even though Japanese fashion is found to be less important in Cool Japan from the findings of the quantitative studies cited above, this does not always mean that the value of Japanese fashion and its role in generating soft power should be ignored.

Qualitative interviews are rich sources of information, enabling researchers to identify the latent meaning from multiple viewpoints. To test the validity of the conclusions drawn from quantitative studies regarding fashion, I conducted interviews with Japanese cultural specialists from a number of professional fields, including government officials and designers.

Before the interviews, however, it needs to be remembered that today's large acceptance of Japanese fashion is due to the fact that it is framed by the 'Western hegemony' of fashion (Narumi 2000: 327). Today's major fashion countries, such as France, Italy, the United Kingdom and the United States, are all located in the West, except for Japan. Even though Japanese fashion is seen as unique due to its strong bottom-up influence and its egalitarianism, it is not excluded from the movement of fashion as a whole and is still well consumed globally (Steele et al. 2010). Additionally, the influence of the 'big three' designers is still particularly evident (see Ince and Nii 2010), because they directly challenged the discourse of Western fashion, 'by avoiding vivid colours, employing new synthetic materials such as polyester and applying traditional Japanese folding techniques seen in the kimono and origami to present modern two-dimensional designs' (Kimura 2015c: 130).

Equally, Gene Sherman in my interview points out that the influence of Japanese fashion is ubiquitous in today's fashion capitals. However, not every Cool Japan item has received wide global validity like Japanese fashion has. For example, the Japanese fashion designer Nozomi Kawasaki, who used to be a member of the charismatic J-pop music group AKB48, admits that unlike Japanese fashion, the mega success of AKB48 is limited to Asia due to the similarly shared social platforms (personal communication). The *kawaii* cute image created by the all-female performers offer fantasy to escape from the realities of Asian society where pressures to meet social expectations is high. Kawasaki's former group is selling their music like hotcakes, and due to its expanded popularity with its nearby Asian neighbours such as China and Indonesia, sister groups have also been created in these countries. Despite this, Kawasaki believes that AKB48 will never be a global success, only an inter-Asian one. Sayuri Tokuman of the Japan Foundation's Sydney office has a similar concern about Japanese animation (personal communication). Tokuman has observed that the majority of anime supporters are Asians (whether they are Asian Australians or Asians originally from Asia). Unlike the J-pop music and animation, both Kawasaki and Tokuman agree that Japanese fashion, however, has the ability to expand beyond Asian borders and that Japanese fashion is already present in the Western fashion world.[14]

Having said that, what the Japanese government can do to expand exportation of Japanese fashion under the current Cool Japan policy has limitations. Yoshimitsu Kaji, media adviser to the Japanese Prime Minister Shinzo Abe, is aware that Japanese fashion is largely street driven, thus official governmental involvement in Japanese fashion is limited (personal communication). He said that the government's strategy is to become a patron of Japanese fashion, rather than actively engaging in the creative processes. For example, under the 'Hello Shibuya Tokyo' project held in Singapore,[15] the government's role was to create a marketing platform where small fashion brands could promote themselves to Southeast Asian retailers and consumers. Similar fashion events were also held in Taiwan, China and Saudi Arabia; otherwise, these fashion brands would be too small to operate outside the Japanese market. It is certainly too early to assess the impact that these projects will have on the Japanese political goal of economic revitalization. According to a government source, these events have successfully promoted current Japanese fashion, attracting both business and consumer interest (see METI 2013). As long as Japanese fashion remains an attractive cultural item on a global scale, it will certainly provide the potential that Japan's soft power needs.

Conclusion

Within Japan's inflexible society, fashion is left as a sanctuary for freedom of self-expression. Japanese fashion today has its roots in its bottom-up flows, which developed in the pre-modern Edo era. This movement is opposite to the Western fashion establishment alleged by the classic Western fashion scholars such as Veblen. Within the Western domination of the fashion world, Japanese fashion delivers a unique offering through its strong street influences; this is attractive to fashion consumers globally. This wide acceptance is a key component of soft power – the ability to meet political goals by attraction to influence others' actions. Japan's political goal for the last 25 years has been economic revitalisation, by increasing the consumption of Cool Japan products outside Japan under the soft power initiative. Existing quantitative surveys indicate that anime and manga are the more preferred Japanese cultural items both in and outside Japan.

However, newly conducted qualitative interviews in this study show that the highly regarded Cool Japan items are generally limited to having an appeal within Asia; whereas Japanese fashion is globally enjoyed since around 1980 when the 'big three' designers debuted in Paris. As the launch of the Office of Cool Japan was only 2010, it is too early to fully assess whether Japanese cultural attractions can become a significant vehicle of Japan's soft power under its current operation – but Japanese fashion, based on its wide international attraction, certainly appears to have a realistic soft power potential.

References

Anthony, I. and Rotfeld, A. D. (eds) (1999), *A Future Arms Control Agenda: Proceedings of Nobel Symposium 118*, Solna: Stockholm International Peace Research Institute, http://books.sipri.org/files/books/SIPRI01AnRo/SIPRI01AnRo.pdf. Accessed 10 December 2014.

Aoki, T. and Barakan, P. (2009), 'Nihon Bunka wa "Mix Bunka"?' ('Is Japanese culture a "mixed culture"?'), *Wedge Infinity*, 8 October, http://wedge.ismedia.jp/articles/-/550?page=2. Accessed 2 May 2014.

Asahi Shimbun (2014), 'Jikyu, 7 Nen de 10 En Agatta dake: Hiseiki no Kojo Rodosha wa', 23 February, http://www.asahi.com/articles/ASG2Q5FJDG2QUTIL010.html?iref=comtop_6_01. Accessed 24 February 2014.

Azuma, N. (2002), 'Tokyo-style – Emergence of collection-free street fashion in Tokyo and the Seoul-Tokyo fashion connection', *International Journal of Retail & Distribution Management*, 30:3, pp. 137–44.

Cabinet Office (2013), 'Kokumin Seikatsu ni Kansuru Yoron Chosa' ('A survey regarding the lives of citizens'), 12 August, http://www8.cao.go.jp/survey/h25/h25-life/4.html. Accessed 5 September 2013.

Center for Strategic & International Studies (CSIS) (2009), 'Democracy in US security strategy: From promotion to support', http://csis.org/files/media/csis/pubs/090310_lennon_democracy_web.pdf. Accessed 10 December 2014.

Centre for European Policy Studies (CEPS) (2008), 'European Security Forum: What prospects for Normative Foreign Policy in a Multipolar World?', ESF working paper 29, http://aei.pitt.edu/11494/1/1682.pdf. Accessed 10 December 2014.

Chikuma, A. (2011), 'Shinkai Makoto Kantoku no Saishinsaku wa Anime ppoi Anime!? Gekijo Anime "Hoshi wo Ou Kodomo", 5 gatsu 7 ka Kokai' ('Director Makoto Shinkai's latest anime appears like an anime!? Cinema anime "Children who chase lost voices from deep below", released 7 May') *My Navi News*, 3 May, http://journal.mycom.co.jp/articles/2011/05/03/shinkai/index.html. Accessed 2 May 2014.

Craik, J. (2009), *Fashion: The Key Concepts*, Oxford: Berg.

Daliot-Bul, M. (2009), 'Japan brand strategy: The taming of "Cool Japan" and the challenges of cultural planning in a postmodern age', *Social Science Japan Journal*, 12:2, pp. 247–66.

Fair Work Ombudsman (2013), 'National minimum wage', 5 March, http://www.fairwork.gov.au/pay/national-minimum-wage/Pages/default.aspx. Accessed 20 May 2013.

Groot, G. (2006), 'Soft power in the Asia-Pacific post 9-11: The cases of China, Japan and India', in P. Jain, F. Patrikeeff and G. Groot (eds), *Japan and India. Asia-Pacific and a New International Order: Responses and Options*, New York: Nova Science Publishers, pp. 53–69.

Harlan, C. (2012), 'A declining Japan loses its once-hopeful champions', *The Washington Post*, 28 October, http://www.washingtonpost.com/world/asia_pacific/a-declining-japan-loses-its-once-hopeful-champions/2012/10/27/f2d90b2e-1cea-11e2-9cd5-b55c38388962_story.html. Accessed 2 May 2014.

Hebdige, D. (1979), *Subculture: The Meaning of Style*, London: Methuen & Co.

Ince, C. and Nii, R. (eds) (2010), *Future Beauty: 30 Years of Japanese Fashion*, London: Merrell Publishers.

Iwabuchi, K. (2002a), '"Soft" nationalism and narcissism: Japanese popular culture goes global', *Asian Studies Review*, 26:4, pp. 447–69.

——— (2002b), *Recentering Globalization: Popular Culture and Japanese Transnationalism*, Durham: Duke University Press.

Japan Institute of International Affairs (JIIA) (2011), 'Asia Taiheiyo Chiiki ni okeru Kakushu Sogo no Chokiteki na Tenbo to Nihon no Gaiko', http://www2.jiia.or.jp/pdf/resarch/h22_chiki_togo/all.pdf. Accessed 10 December 2014.

Joffe, J. (2006), *Überpower: The Imperial Temptation of America*, New York: W.W. Norton.

Kawamura, Y. (2004), *The Japanese Revolution in Paris Fashion*, Oxford: Berg.

——— (2005), *Fashion-ology: An Introduction to Fashion Studies*, Oxford: Berg.

——— (2010), 'Japanese fashion subcultures', in V. Steele, P. Mears, Y. Kawamura and H. Narumi (eds), *Japan Fashion Now*, New Haven: Yale University Press, pp. 210–26.

——— (2011), 'Japanese street fashion: The urge to be seen and to be heard', in L. Welters and A. Lillethun (eds), *The Fashion Reader*, 2nd ed., Oxford: Berg, pp. 467–69.

Kimura, T. (2007), 'Why Japan is deaf to whaling protests', *The New Zealand Herald*, 12 March, pp. A13.

——— (2015a), 'Fashioning Japanese fashion?', *Art Association of Australia and New Zealand 2015 Conference: Image Space Body*, Brisbane, 24 November.

——— (2015b), 'Roundtable panel: Exporting Japanese aesthetics and soft power: Processes, methods and reasons', *The 9th International Convention of Asia Scholars*, Adelaide, 8 July.

——— (2015c), 'A discourse of Japanese fashion "discovered"?', *Australian and New Zealand Journal of Art*, 15:1, pp. 130–32.

Kobayashi, K. (2013), 'Cool Japan Yushutsu ni "Kabe": Sorewo Norikoeru niwa' (The "wall" for exporting cool Japan: How to overcome it'), *Asahi Judiciary*, 7 August, http://judiciary.asahi.com/outlook/2013071800002.html. Accessed 2 May 2014.

Komine, T. and Kabe, S. (2007), 'Demographic change and the Asian economy: Long-term forecast of global economy and population 2006-2050', Japan Center for Economic Research, http://www.jcer.or.jp/eng/economic/long.html. Accessed 17 October 2015.

Kopp, R. (2012), 'Over worked and underpaid Japanese employees feel the burden of Sabisu Zangyo', *Japan Intercultural Consulting*, 4 September, http://www.japanintercultural.com/en/news/default.aspx?newsid=203. Accessed 2 May 2014.

Kuki, S. (1997), *Reflections on Japanese Taste: The Structure of Iki* (trans. J. Clark), Sydney: Power Publications.

Lam, P. E. (2007), 'Japan's quest for "soft power": Attraction and Limitation', *East Asia*, 24:4, pp. 349–63.

Leheny, D. (2015), 'Naruto's limits: What soft power can actually achieve', nippon.com, http://www.nippon.com/en/in-depth/a03902. Accessed 17 October 2015.

McGray, D. (2002), 'Japan's gross national cool', *Foreign Policy*, 130, May/June, pp. 44–54.

Mihara, R. (2013), 'Shiron: Cool Japan to Tsusho Seisaku' ('Hypothesis: Cool Japan and trade policy'), *RIETI Discussion Paper Series 13-J-051*, http://www.rieti.go.jp/jp/publications/dp/13j051.pdf. Accessed 22 May 2014.

Ministry of Economy, Trade and Industry (METI) (2005), *Digital Contents Hakusho*, Tokyo: Digital Contents Association Japan.

—— (2012a), 'Cool Japan Strategy (Modified version of the interim report submitted to the Cool Japan Advisory Council)', September, http://www.meti.go.jp/english/policy/mono_info_service/creative_industries/pdf/121016_01a.pdf. Accessed 17 August 2013.

—— (2012b), 'Dai 4 Sho: Soto tono Tsunagari ni yoru Nihon Keizai no Aratana Seicho ni Mukete', http://www.meti.go.jp/report/tsuhaku2012/2012honbun/html/i4220000.html. Accessed 17 October 2015.

—— (2013), 'Heisei 24 Nendo Cool Japan Senryaku Suishin Jigyo' ('The Cool Japan strategy for the financial year 2012'), 17 June, http://www.meti.go.jp/policy/mono_info_service/mono/creative/HPkaigai130617.pdf. Accessed 2 May 2014.

Ministry of Health, Labour and Welfare (MHLW) (2012), 'Chiikibetsu Saitei Chingin no Zenkoku Ichiran' ('The list of national minimum wages by areas'), 5 October, http://www.mhlw.go.jp/seisakunitsuite/bunya/koyou_roudou/roudoukijun/minimumichiran. Accessed 20 May 2013.

Murakami, R. (2012), 'Little eucalyptus leaves' (trans. R. F. McCarthy), in E. Luke and D. Karashima (eds), *March Was Made of Yarn*, London: Harvill Secker, pp. 189–98.

Narumi, H. (2000), 'Fashion orientalism and the limits of counter culture', *Postcolonial Studies*, 3:3, pp. 311–30.

Nogizaka46 (2013), *Kimi no Na wa Kibo* (*Your Name Is Hope*), Japan: Music Records.

Nye, J. S. Jr. (1990), *Bound to Lead: The Changing Nature of American Power*, New York: Basic Books.

—— (2002), *The Paradox of American Power: Why the World's Only Superpower Can't Go It Alone*, Oxford: Oxford University Press.

—— (2004), *Soft Power: The Means to Success in World Politics*, New York: Public Affairs.

—— (2008), *The Power to Lead*, Oxford: Oxford University Press.

—— (2011), *The Future of Power*, New York: Public Affairs.

Ogura, K. (2007), 'Tokushu Chojikan Rodo: Nihon no Chojikan Rodo — Kokusai Hikaku to Kenkyu Kadai', *The Japan Institute for Labour Policy and Training*, http://www.jil.go.jp/institute/zassi/backnumber/2008/06/pdf/004-016.pdf. Accessed 17 October 2015.

Oricon Style (2013), '2013nen 03gatsu 11nichi kara 2013nen 03gatsu 17nichi no CD Single Shukan Ranking (2013nen 03gatsu 25nichizuke)', ('The single CD weekly ranking for the week of 11 March 2013 [Announced 25 March 2013]'), 25 March, http://www.oricon.co.jp/rank/js/w/2013-03-25. Accessed 11 December 2013.

Oshio, T. and Inagaki, S. (2014), 'Does initial job status affect midlife outcomes and mental health? Evidence from a survey in Japan', *RIETI Discussion Paper Series 14-E-025*, http://www.rieti.go.jp/jp/publications/dp/14e025.pdf. Accessed 22 May 2014.

Otmazgin, N. K. (2008), 'Contesting soft power: Japanese popular culture in East and Southeast Asia', *International Relations of the Asia-Pacific*, 8:1, pp. 73–101.

Polhemus, T. (1994), *Streetstyle: From Sidewalk to Catwalk*, London: Thames and Hudson.

Sakuragi, S. (2013), *Hotel Royal*, Tokyo: Shueisha.

Sarantakos, S. (2013), *Social Research*, 4th ed., New York: Palgrave Macmillan.

Shepard, J. (1994), 'The analysis of popular music', in *The Polity Reader in Cultural Theory*, Cambridge: Polity Press, pp. 231–36.

Shinkai, M. (2007), *Byosoku 5 Senchimētoru* (*5 Centimetres per Second*), Japan: CoMix Wave.

Simmel, G. (1904), 'Fashion', *International Quarterly*, 10, pp. 130–55.

Slade, T. (2009), *Japanese Fashion: A Cultural History*, Oxford: Berg.

Steele, V. (2010), 'Is Japan still the future?', in V. Steele, P. Mears, Y. Kawamura and H. Narumi (eds), *Japan Fashion Now*, New Haven: Yale University Press, pp. 1–139.

Steele, V., Mears, P., Kawamura, Y. and Narumi, H. (eds) (2010), *Japan Fashion Now*, New Haven: Yale University Press.

Taylor, B. (2010), *Sanctions as Grand Strategy*, London: The International Institute for Strategic Studies.

Tokyo Polytechnic University (2010), 'Chosa Kekka News Release: Cool Japan ni Kansuru Chosa' ('A survey result, media release, regarding cool Japan'), 18 May, http://www.t-kougei.ac.jp/guide/images/100518.pdf. Accessed 27 September 2010.

Veblen, T. (1899), *The Theory of the Leisure Class: An Economic Study of Institutions*, New York: Macmillan.

Vogel, E. F. (1979), *Japan as Number One: Lessons for America*, Massachusetts: Harvard University Press.

Yomiuri Shimbun (2012), 'Daigakusei 4 wari "Jisatsu Kangaeta": Kangakudai Imamura san chosa', 15 November, http://www.yomiuri.co.jp/kyoiku/news/20121115-OYT8T00372.htm?from=yoltop. Accessed 7 March 2013.

Notes

1. For Australia's minimum wages, see the Fair Work Ombudsman (2013). For Japan's minimum wages, see MHLW (2012).
2. Although this is a reference to the US pop music, the idea is relevant to other types of pop music from other countries.
3. This is one of the most prestigious Japanese literary awards.
4. A short-stay hotel designed for couples to maintain privacy for sexual activities – common in Japan and its neighbouring countries.

5 The *Japan Fashion Now* exhibition was held at the Fashion Institute of Technology's Museum in New York between 17 September 2010 and 2 April 2011. I visited the exhibition on 21 and 22 January 2011.

6 The less fashion-conscious 'Forest Girl' style appears as if the wearer comes from a Scandinavian forest – this style originated from the chic but more laid back areas in western Tokyo such as Shimokitazawa and Koenji, where subcultures of the areas perhaps reflect the style.

7 Interestingly, despite Japan's extreme working conditions, more than 70 per cent of Japanese people feel some degree of satisfaction in their lives (Cabinet Office 2013).

8 This was also confirmed in June 2013 by interviewing two Japanese public servants – Mr Yoshimitsu Kaji, Director of Global Communications Strategy, Prime Minister's Office and Mr Mirai Odagiri, Assistant Manager of Cool Japan Promotion Office, Ministry of Economy, Trade and Industry. They denied that an expansion of Japan's international political presence, such as becoming a permanent member of the United Nations Security Council, is Japan's soft power aim or goal.

9 In the US dollar equivalent, this is an increase from $19 billion to $66–91 billion.

10 See Chapter 2 'Sources of American soft power' and Chapter 3 'Others' soft power'.

11 In Nye's 2008 book *The Power to Lead*, he further developed the soft power theory to smart power, in which a combination of hard and soft powers is necessary to be today's important international political power player.

12 Confirmed in June 2013 by interviewing Mr Yoshimitsu Kaji, Director of Global Communications Strategy, The Prime Minister's Office.

13 Lam (2007: 363). Source: Yomiuri Shimbun, 10 September 2006, multiple answers, respondents aged 18 and above.

14 Confirmed in July and August 2013 by interviewing Mr Andy Watson, the owner of Right Hand Distribution (fashion outlet in Adelaide's East End), Dr Maarten Rikken, fashion model, and Dr Gene Sherman, the Chair and Executive Director of the Sherman Contemporary Art Foundation.

15 The promotion of 30 individual Japanese fashion brands in Singapore, February 2013.

Notes on Contributors

Jess Berry is Senior Lecturer in Design History/Theory at Monash University, Australia. Her research is concerned with the fashion city, fashion new media and fashion's intersections with art, architecture and the interior. Recent articles have appeared in the *Journal of Design History*, *Craft + Design Inquiry* and *Critical Studies in Men's Fashion*. Her forthcoming book is *House of Fashion: Haute Couture and the Modern Interior* (Bloomsbury, 2018).

José Blanco F., Ph.D., is Associate Professor in the Department of Apparel Merchandising and Design at Dominican University in River Forest, Illinois. His research focuses on dress and popular culture in the second half of the twentieth century, with an emphasis on male fashion. He is also interested in fashion and visual culture in Latin America. José Blanco F. is the general editor of the recently published four-volume encyclopaedia *Clothing and Fashion: American Fashion from Head to Toe*. He has co-authored with Raúl J. Vázquez-López several articles and book chapters on Puerto Rican dress, costume and fashion.

Colin Cavendish-Jones, Ph.D., lives in Iraq and teaches at the American University of Kurdistan. His principal research interests are European Nihilism, the Victorian religious unsettlement, the Romantic, Aesthetic and Modernist movements, the reception of classical literature, and connections between literature and philosophy. He has written on a variety of nineteenth and early twentieth-century writers, including Pater, Wilde, Trollope, Chesterton and Proust. Dr Cavendish-Jones studied classics at Magdalen College, Oxford, and subsequently practiced as an international lawyer in London, Dubai and the United States. After working as a teacher, lecturer, journalist and theatre director in numerous countries throughout Europe, Asia and the Americas, he returned to academia and completed a Ph.D. at the University of St. Andrews on art as a counterforce to Nihilism in the works of Oscar Wilde.

Pamela Church Gibson is Reader in Cultural and Historical Studies at the London College of Fashion, University of the Arts London. She has published extensively on film, fashion, fandom, history and heritage; recent books include *Fashion Cultures Revisited: Theories, Explorations, Analysis* (with Stella Bruzzi, Routledge, 2013) and *Fashion and Celebrity Culture* (Bloomsbury, 2012). She is the Principal Editor of the journal, *Film, Fashion &*

Consumption, which she founded in 2012. In the same year she hosted the first conference of the European Popular Culture Association, and became its first President.

Jennifer Craik, Ph.D., is Professor and Head of Fashion at Queensland University of Technology in Brisbane, Australia. Her research interests include interdisciplinary approaches to the study of fashion and dress. She has also researched aspects of cultural studies, cultural policy and arts funding. Her publications include: *The Face of Fashion* (Routledge, 1993), *Uniforms Exposed: From Conformity to Transgression* (Berg Publishers, 2005) and *Fashion: The Key Concepts* (Berg Publishers, 2009).

Antonia Finnane, Ph.D., is Professor of History in the School of Historical and Philosophical Studies at the University of Melbourne. She studied at the University of Sydney, the Beijing Language Institute, Nanjing University and the Australian National University, graduating from the Department of Far Eastern History in 1985, with a Ph.D. in Chinese history. Her publications include *Speaking of Yangzhou: A Chinese City, 1550-1850* (Harvard East Asian Monographs, 2004), winner of the 2006 Levenson award for a work on pre-twentieth-century China; and *Changing Clothes in China: Fashion, Nation, History* (New York: Columbia University Press, 2008). Her current research focuses on the impact of Maoism on handicrafts in Beijing in the 1950s, with particular reference to tailoring.

Joseph H. Hancock II, Ph.D. is Professor at Drexel University. He comes from a 20-year retailing background having worked for Gap Inc., The Limited Brands, at Target Corporation. He is an international authority in the area of fashion branding as a form of storytelling. He just released *Cotton: Companies, Fashion and the Fabric of Our Lives* (Intellect, 2016) and the 2nd Edition of his book *Brand/Story: Explorations and Cases in Fashion Branding* (Bloomsbury, 2016). His works on branding and storytelling have appeared in publications such as *The Brand Challenge* by Kartikeya Kompella (Kogan Page, 2016) and *Strategic Design Thinking* by Natalie Nixon (Bloomsbury, 2015). Dr Hancock is the principal editor of the peer-reviewed and indexed journal *Fashion, Style and Popular Culture* (Intellect Publishers).

Kathryn A. Hardy Bernal is an art and design theorist and historian. She is currently teaching Critical and Contextual Studies at the College of Creative Arts, Massey University, Wellington, where she is a Ph.D. candidate in Visual and Material Culture, under the supervision of Vicki Karaminas. Previous roles include Fashion and Textiles Theory Coordinator and Senior Lecturer in Theoretical Studies (Art and Design) at Auckland University of Technology. Her main research focus is on the Japanese Lolita subculture, on which she publishes and presents widely. In 2007, she was Curator of *Loli-Pop* (Lolita + Popular Culture), an exhibition held at Auckland Museum.

Julia Hargassner, Ph.D., graduated from the Ural State University in Ekaterinburg (Russia) and the Paris Lodron University in Salzburg (Austria). She is Senior Lecturer at the Slavonic Department of the University of Salzburg. Julia Hargassner is co-editor (with Eva Hausbacher and Elena Huber) of the book *Fashion, Consumption and Everyday Culture in the Soviet Union between 1945 and 1985* (Verlag Otto Sagner, Munich 2014). Currently Julia Hargassner is engaged in publishing her Ph.D. thesis, 'The language of clothes in the artistic text: Soviet codes of clothes between 1954 and 1985'.

Tets Kimura is Australian Postgraduate Award Scholar at Flinders University, Adelaide, and is completing his doctoral research to reveal soft power influences of Japanese fashion in Australia. He has published refereed papers on Japanese history, politics, culture and media issues, and conveyed a panel called 'Exporting Japanese Aesthetics and Soft Power' at the 9th International Convention of Asia Scholars conference. He recently won the Paul Varley Award at 2016 Japan Studies Association conference. He is a council member of the Asian Studies Association of Australia, and on the editorial boards of the *Flinders Journal of History and Politics*.

Viveka Kjellmer, Ph.D., is Assistant Professor teaching art history and visual studies at the University of Gothenburg. Kjellmer also holds a university degree in economics and has previously worked in marketing. Her research concerns fashion, costume, body and identity, as well as the relations between olfaction, architecture and space. Kjellmer has published studies about the visual language of advertising, focusing on the image of scent, and has also written about fashion exhibitions and visual consumption.

Demetra Kolakis is Course Leader for the BA (Hons) Fashion Media Programme at the University of the Arts London. Her research interests include the interplay between consumption, production and experience in relation to contemporary fashion, modernism, visual culture and cultural processes. In addition, she has worked collaboratively and individually on a variety of interdisciplinary projects exploring fashion media within the wider field on the rise and the impact of new technologies on the mediation of fashion. Demetra Kolakis' work has been exhibited at pop ups, galleries and international shows including Ideal Berlin, Best Shop Berlin, Designers Against Aids and Premium Berlin.

Maria Mackinney-Valentin, Ph.D., is Associate Professor at The Royal Danish Academy of Fine Art, School of Design holding an MA in English literature from the University of Copenhagen and a Ph.D. in trend theory from The Royal Danish Academy of Fine Art, School of Design where she is currently an Associate Professor in the Department for Fashion Design. Her research has been published in journals such as *Design Issues, Luxury: Fashion, Lifestyle and Excess, Critical Studies in Fashion and Beauty* and *Journal of Fashion, Style and Popular Culture*. Her book *Fashioning Identity* was published by Bloomsbury in early 2017.

Royce Mahawatte, D.Phil., University of Oxford, is Lecturer in Cultural Studies at Central Saint Martins. He is the author of *George Eliot and the Gothic Novel* (University of Wales Press, 2013). Forthcoming publications are 'Horror in the nineteenth century 1820–1900' in *A Literary History of Horror* (British Library, 2016) and 'Fashion artifice and adornment' in *A Cultural History of Hair*, vol. 6, 1920–2000 (Bloomsbury, 2017). Royce Mahawatte's research interests are Victorian fiction, the Gothic and cultures of fashion and the body.

Anne Peirson-Smith, Ph.D., is Assistant Professor in the Department of English, City University of Hong Kong teaching and researching fashion communication and branding, creative industries, popular culture, public relations and advertising and has published numerous articles and book chapters on these subjects. She has co-authored *Public Relations in Asia Pacific: Communicating Beyond Cultures* (John Wiley, 2009) and *Global Fashion Brands: Style, Luxury & History* (Intellect, 2014). In addition, she is an associate editor of *The Journal of Fashion, Style and Popular Culture* (Intellect) and *The Journal of Global Fashion Marketing*. She is also on the advisory board of *The Journal of Global Business* and *The East Asian Journal of Popular Culture* (Intellect).

Trine Brun Petersen, Ph.D., is Assistant Professor at University of Southern Denmark, Department of Design and Communication. She holds a Ph.D. on the subject of design and behaviour from Design School Kolding and has done research in design in institutional contexts such as prisons, hospitals and museums. Her recent research interests include uniforms, work wear and fashion for children. Publications include 'Material matters – The social choreography of the state prison of Eastern Jutland' (in *Rask*, 39, October 2013), 'Katvig – børnemodel mellem Retro og reform' ('Katvig – Children's fashion between retro and reform') (in *Designkulturanalyser*, Syddansk Universitetsforlag, 2015) and 'Pockets, buttons and hangers. Designing a new uniform for health care professionals' (in *Design Issues*, 31:1, 2016).

Natascha Radclyffe-Thomas, Ph.D., is a University of the Arts London Teaching Scholar, Senior Fellow of the Higher Education Academy and Course Leader for BA (Hons) Fashion Marketing at the London College of Fashion. Natascha has extensive international experience having taught fashion in the United Kingdom, Asia and the United States. Natascha teaches fashion branding and marketing strategy at undergraduate and postgraduate level. Natascha's research looks at how issues such as culture, heritage, city-branding and social entrepreneurship manifest themselves in contemporary fashion marketing in Asia and the West, and she has presented at conferences internationally and published articles and book chapters on these subjects.

Efrat Tseëlon, Ph.D., is a multi-disciplinary social psychologist who specialized in cultural analysis of fashion and appearance. Since receiving her Ph.D. from Oxford University on Communicating via Clothing she developed the perspective of Critical Fashion, which interrogates the ideological claims of fashion as a cultural practice. Drawing on her rich industrial experience, she introduced qualitative consumer behaviour methods from marketing research into the academic study of fashion, and extended the research agenda from a focus on designers and artefacts to privileging everyday clothes and consumers' experience. Tseëlon pioneered Intellect books series of fashion studies, and is the editor-in-chief of *Critical Studies in Fashion & Beauty*. She is the author of numerous publications including *The Masque of Femininity*, *Masquerade and Identities* and *Fashion Ethics*.

Raúl J. Vázquez-López is an independent researcher. His research emphasis is in the production and consumption of Puerto Rican cultural symbols and literature. Along with José Blanco F., he recently guest-edited a special issue on Latin American Fashion for *Fashion, Style & Popular Culture*. In his free time, Vázquez-López tries to sit in front of his loom and weave. He was born and raised in Puerto Rico. He currently works for Pearson Higher Education as a World Languages Consultant.

Louise Wallenberg, Ph.D., graduated with a doctorate in Cinema Studies from Stockholm University (2002). She is Associate Professor of Fashion Studies and was the establishing Director of the Centre for Fashion Studies at Stockholm University between 2006 and 2013. Her research focuses on issues dealing with gender, sexuality, class and ethnicity in cinema and fashion, as well as in organization and management. She is currently writing a book on sexual difference theory and co-editing an anthology on fashion and film in the 1960s to be published by Indiana University Press in 2017.

Lightning Source UK Ltd.
Milton Keynes UK
UKHW030159170621
385633UK00002B/31